Struggles for Shalom

Studies in Peace and Scripture
Institute of Mennonite Studies

Titles in the series

Struggles for Shalom

Peace and Violence across the Testaments

Edited by

Laura L. Brenneman
and *Brad D. Schantz*

Foreword by *Ben C. Ollenburger*

PICKWICK *Publications* · Eugene, Oregon

STRUGGLES FOR SHALOM
Peace and Violence across the Testaments

Pickwick Publications
An Imprint of Wipf and Stock Publishers
199 W. 8th Ave., Suite 3
Eugene, OR 97401

www.wipfandstock.com

ISBN-13: 978-1-62032-622-0

Cataloguing-in-Publication data:

Struggles for shalom: peace and violence across the testaments / edited by Laura L. Brenneman and Brad D. Schantz ; foreword by Ben C. Ollenburger.

xxiv + 376 p. ; 23 cm. Includes bibliographic references and indexes.

ISBN-13: 978-1-62032-622-0

1. Bible—Criticism, interpretation, etc. 2. Peace—Biblical teaching. 3. Violence—Biblical teaching. 4. Christian ethics—Biblical teaching. I. Brenneman, Laura L., 1975–. II. Schantz, Brad D., 1969–. III. Ollenburger, Ben C. IV. Titles. V. Series.

BS680 P4 S101 2014

Manufactured in the U.S.A.   04/22/2014

Contents

PART 2: **Peace and Violence in the New Testament**

Illustrations

Series Preface

Visions of peace abound in the Bible, whose pages are also filled with the language of violence. In this respect, the Bible is thoroughly at home in the modern world, whether as a literary classic or as a unique sacred text. This is, perhaps, a part of the Bible's realism: bridging the distance between its world and our own is a history filled with visions of peace accompanying the reality of violence and war. That alone would justify study of peace and war in the Bible. However, for those communities in which the Bible is sacred Scripture, the matter is more urgent. For them, it is crucial to understand what the Bible says about peace—and about war. These issues have often divided Christians, and the way Christians have understood them has had terrible consequences for Jews and, indeed, for the world. A series of scholarly investigations cannot hope to resolve these issues, but it can hope, as this one does, to aid our understanding of them.

Over the past century a substantial body of literature has grown up around the topic of the Bible and war. Numerous studies have been devoted to historical questions about ancient Israel's conception and conduct of war and about the position of the early church on participation in the Roman Empire and its military. It is not surprising that many of these studies have been motivated by theological and ethical concerns, which may themselves be attributed to the Bible's own disjunctive preoccupation with peace and, at the same time, with war. If not within the Bible itself, then at least from Aqiba and Tertullian, the question has been raised whether—and if so, then on what basis—those who worship God may legitimately participate in war. With the Reformation, the church divided on this question. The division was unequal, with the majority of Christendom agreeing that, however regrettable war may be, Christians have biblical warrant for participating in it. A minority countered that, however necessary war may appear, Christians have a biblical mandate to avoid it. Modern historical studies have served to bolster one side of this division or the other.

Meanwhile, it has become clear that a narrow focus on participation in war is not the only way, and likely not the best way, to approach the Bible on the topic of peace. War and peace are not simply two sides of the same coin; each is broader than its contrast with the other. Since the twentieth century and refinement of weapons of mass destruction, the violence of war has been an increasingly urgent concern. Peace, on the other hand, is not just the absence of war, but the well-being of all people. In spite of this agreement, the number of studies devoted to the Bible and peace is still quite small, especially in English. Consequently, answers to the most basic questions remain to be settled. Among these questions is that of what the Bible means in speaking of *shalom* or *eirēnē*, the Hebrew and the Greek terms usually translated into English as "peace." By the same token, what the Bible has to say about peace is not limited to its use of these two terms. Questions remain about the relation of peace to considerations of justice, integrity, and—in the broadest sense—salvation. And of course there still remains the question of the relation between peace and war. In fact, what the Bible says about peace is often framed in the language of war. The Bible often uses martial imagery to portray God's own action, whether it be in creation, in judgment against or in defense of Israel, or in the cross and resurrection of Jesus Christ—actions aimed at achieving peace.

This close association of peace and war presents serious problems for the contemporary appropriation of the Bible. Are human freedom, justice, and liberation—and the liberation of creation—furthered or hindered by the martial, frequently royal, and pervasively masculine terms in which the Bible speaks of peace? These questions cannot be answered by the rigorous and critical exegesis of the biblical texts alone; they demand serious moral and theological reflection as well. But that reflection will be substantially aided by exegetical studies of the kind included in this series.

In the present volume, a number of scholars concerned with the study of peace and Scripture have assembled to honor the life work of Perry Yoder (Hebrew Bible scholar) and Willard Swartley (former New Testament editor of this series, among other accomplishments). These contributors—colleagues, students, collaborators, and others who follow Yoder and Swartley—join with them here in serious investigation of Scripture. This collection is diverse and ambitious. For church and academy, for anyone curious about what Scripture has to say about peace and violence, it delivers focused study of a wide range of texts across the Testaments. As such, this work contributes to and expands the purposes of the series.

Studies in Peace and Scripture is sponsored by Institute of Mennonite Studies, the research agency of the Anabaptist Mennonite Biblical Seminary. The seminary and the tradition it represents have a particular interest in peace and, even more so, an abiding interest in the Bible. We hope that this ecumenical series will contribute to a deeper understanding of both.

Laura L. Brenneman, New Testament Editor

Ben C. Ollenburger, Old Testament Editor

Foreword

For three years in the early 1980s, on an evening in late autumn, a man handed out twenty-dollar bills to people in hotel rooms in different American cities. The rooms were meeting rooms, the people were Mennonites attending the annual meeting of the American Academy of Religion (AAR) and the Society of Biblical Literature (SBL), and the man was Willard M. Swartley. Dr. Swartley was then professor of New Testament (NT) at AMBS—now Anabaptist Mennonite Biblical Seminary—and director of the Institute of Mennonite Studies (IMS), the research agency of AMBS, and the twenty-dollar bills came from IMS coffers. But Willard neither embezzled the money nor scattered it without purpose. He and IMS offered this modest stipend, an amount much more modest now than in 1980, to help make it possible or more attractive for Mennonite scholars to gather for an evening of conversation before the AAR/SBL meetings began. Out of these conversations, funded by twenty-dollar bills generously distributed, the IMS series Studies in Peace and Scripture (SPS) was born. But not right away, and not directly.[1]

Under the direction of AMBS professor C. J. Dyck, IMS had earlier initiated a significant program of research and publication in sixteenth-century Anabaptism, a program whose fruit has been the series Classics of the Radical Reformation. Its first volume, published in 1973, was John Howard Yoder's translation and annotation of Michael Sattler's writings.[2] That series continues, with the 2010 publication of *Jörg Maler's Kunstbuch: Writings of the Pilgram Marpeck Circle*. Upon succeeding Dyck as director of IMS, Swartley hoped to bring about a monograph series in biblical studies of similar scholarly quality, and from an Anabaptist/Mennonite perspective.[3]

---

1. I rely on conversations with Willard Swartley, documents in the AMBS archives, and my own memory.

2. *The Legacy of Michael Sattler.*

3. AMBS archives: Swartley letter to Josephine Ford, 24 November 1982.

That hope grew stronger with the 1984 appointment of Perry B. Yoder, a scholar equally adept in Hebrew and Greek, as Swartley's colleague in the AMBS biblical studies department.

A year before his appointment to the AMBS faculty, Perry Yoder published an article, "Toward a Shalom Biblical Theology," in the initial volume of *Conrad Grebel Review*. Yoder observed that Mennonite theologians, systematic and biblical, had not attended substantively to peace or pacifism or nonresistance in their published work, which depended on and imitated confessional and theological traditions in which peace had no prominent place, if it had any place at all. The result, Yoder claimed, was "schizophrenia": assumptions about and commitments to peace, but theologies that were at odds with both the assumptions and the commitments. Yoder insisted: "The ortho*praxis* of peace must be based on an ortho*doxy* of peace."[4] To this end, he proposed a "biblical theology," to be constructed around cardinal compass points: "creation, covenant, community, cult, cross, and consummation."[5] Among all those *c*-words, Yoder stressed especially *king*ship, and especially the close biblical association between kingship and justice.[6]

Perry Yoder's thinking about biblical theology, and specifically a *shalom* biblical theology, combined productively with Willard Swartley's continuing hopes for a monograph series. Further conversation, provoked and enabled by Willard's profligate and effective twenty-dollar handouts, but carried on otherwise as well, complicated and finally made impossible the project of *a* biblical theology. But Yoder's article, among other things, and Swartley's hopes for collaborative publication, led to a symposium, in the summer of 1985, sponsored by IMS and directed by Swartley, on the subject of kingship and the Bible. The participants included both Swartley and Yoder, along with David Rensberger (Interdenominational Theological Center), Gerald Gerbrandt (Canadian Mennonite University), and me (then at Princeton Theological Seminary). The symposium generated enthusiasm for further work, further collaboration, and publication.

Discussions about a monograph series on peace and scripture continued in the late 1980s among a small editorial council, led by Willard Swartley, that convened at annual SBL meetings. That small group agreed that the IMS monograph series should focus explicitly on peace and the Bible, and should favor exegetical studies, while defining *peace* rather broadly. At the same time, Swartley, as IMS director, continued to pursue concrete plans

---

4. Yoder, "Toward a Shalom Biblical Theology"; italics mine.

5. Ibid., 45.

6. Ibid., 47–49.

for such a series. Anticipating—as he had done as early as 1982—that the first volume would be a collection of previously published essays on peace, or *shalom*, most of them translated from German, Swartley continued soliciting permissions and requesting comment from authors. One letter (18 March 1987), to Claus Westermann of Heidelberg, among the best known and most highly regarded Old Testament (OT) scholars at the time, addressed him as "Professor of New Testament." The archives do not include a reply from Westermann. It also bears—it requires—mentioning that Willard neither wrote the letter himself nor signed it. Delegation always carries risks.

In the volume—*The Meaning of Peace: Biblical Studies*—for which Westermann's essay was solicited (successfully, it turned out), its editors, Perry Yoder and Willard Swartley, brought together in one volume a number of seminal articles and essays originally published in German. Walter Sawatsky, another AMBS colleague, prepared the initial translation of the book's chapters. Westminster John Knox Press published the book in 1992. This was not, however, the first SPS volume. Earlier in the same year, 1992, Westminster John Knox, a Presbyterian press, published the inaugural volume of SPS—*The Gospel of Peace: A Scriptural Message for Today's World.* The book's author, Ulrich Mauser, from Germany, was then professor of NT at Princeton Theological Seminary, after serving as professor and dean at Pittsburgh Theological Seminary—two Presbyterian schools. A Presbyterian press published a book by a Reformed theologian at a Presbyterian seminary as the first volume in a series on peace and scripture sponsored by a Mennonite seminary. These first two volumes gave substance to the promise that the SPS series would be ecumenical.

Westminster John Knox published (also in 1992) one additional book in the series—*The Love of Enemy and Nonretaliation in the New Testament*—another multiauthor volume, this one edited by Willard Swartley. Since 1992, SPS has been independent of a specific press. Eerdmans, Herald Press, Cascadia, Pandora, and IMS itself, have published subsequent volumes.

Willard Swartley served as NT editor of SPS until his retirement from AMBS, in 2004. His magisterial work, *Covenant of Peace: The Missing Peace in New Testament Theology and Ethics*, published by Eerdmans, appeared two years later, as volume nine of SPS. Laura Brenneman, a graduate of AMBS and of Durham University, and lately associate professor of religion and director of peace and conflict studies, Bluffton, University, succeeded Willard as NT editor.

Late in 2011, Eerdmans published Darrin W. Snyder Belousek's book, *Atonement, Justice, and Peace: The Message of the Cross and the Mission of the Church*, which stands with Swartley's *Covenant of Peace* as a monumental achievement. IMS, and the editors of SPS—especially Laura Brenneman, and former NT editor Willard Swartley—contributed to the publication of Snyder Belousek's book, which he hoped would be part of the SPS series. Although Eerdmans initially resisted this identification, *Atonement, Justice, and Peace* is SPS volume ten. Further, Baker Academic Press published *A Peaceable Hope: Contesting Violent Eschatology in New Testament Narratives*, by David Neville, an Australian scholar. It is volume eleven in SPS, a series that began with Willard Swartley passing out twenty-dollar bills in hotel meeting rooms, Perry Yoder writing about biblical theology, and a serendipitous—a providential—combination of vision, conviction, and friendship.

Ben C. Ollenburger

Acknowledgments

I am grateful for the support of many colleagues—scholars and friends—who pulled together to bring this book to fruition. In this project of many years it has been an honor to work closely with my coeditor, Brad Schantz, and with Institute of Mennonite Studies managing editor Barbara Nelson Gingerich; without these astute and stalwart companions, there would be no *Struggles for Shalom*.

My thanks also go to the Institute of Mennonite Studies at Anabaptist Mennonite Biblical Seminary (Elkhart, Indiana), sponsor of the Studies in Peace and Scripture series. Wise counsel and encouragement from my series coeditor, Ben Ollenburger, and IMS director Mary Schertz came at the right moments to keep this project on track.

It has been a particular honor to work with twenty-four fine authors who share passion and perspective in biblical studies and peace studies. They are co-workers, indeed, in more than this book.

My appreciation goes to David Neville, associate professor of theology at Charles Sturt University (Canberra, Australia), for generative interaction with my chapter, as well as for his recent monograph, *A Peaceable Hope* (SPS 11, Baker Academic, 2013), with which several of this book's authors engaged.

I would have been at a loose end without research assistant and indexer Lydia Nofziger, student at AMBS, whose biblical scholarship and sunny disposition were—in equal parts—instrumental in moving the work along.

Finally, *Struggles for Shalom* is thoroughly a thanksgiving for the life work of biblical scholars, peace advocates, church activists, and inspirational educators Perry Yoder and Willard Swartley. We who have joined you in writing this book are a small representation of the people whom you've motivated to teach and preach peace. We thank you for your witness in church and academy.

Laura L. Brenneman
May 1, 2013

xix

Abbreviations

1 En.	*1 Enoch*
1Q28b	*Rule of the Blessings* (Appendix b to 1QS)
1Qap Gen^{ar}, 1Q20	*Genesis Apocryphon*
1QH^a	*Hodayot*^a or *Thanksgiving Hymns*^a
1QpHab	*Pesher Habakkuk*
1QM	*Milḥamah* or *War Scroll*
1QS	*Serek Hayaḥad* or *Rule of the Community*
2 Bar.	*2 Baruch (Syriac Apocalypse)*
2 Esd	2 Esdras
4Q161	Pesher Isaiah^a
4Q169	Pesher Nahum
4Q171	Pesher Psalms^a
4Q174	*Florilegium*
4Q175	*Testimonia*
4Q212	Letter of Enoch
4Q252	*Commentary on Genesis A*
4Q285	*Sefer Hamilḥamah*
4Q420	*Ways of Righteousness*^a
4Q504	*Words of the Luminaries*^a
4Q544	Visions of Amram^b ar
4Q545	Visions of Amram^c ar
4QMMT^a	*Miqṣat Maʿśê ha-Torah*^a
11QT^a	*Temple Scroll*^a
AB	Anchor Bible
ABD	*Anchor Bible Dictionary*
ACCS	Ancient Christian Commentary on Scripture
ACNT	Augsburg Commentaries on the New Testament
Adul. amic.	*Quomodo adulator ab amico internoscatur*
ALD	*Aramaic Levi Document*

ALASP	Abhandlungen zur Literatur Alt-Syren-Palästinas und Mesopotamiens
AMBS	Anabaptist Mennonite Biblical Seminary (formerly Associated Mennonite Biblical Seminary)
Amic.	*De amicitia*
AnBib	Analecta biblica
Ant.	*Jewish Antiquities*
ANTC	Abingdon New Testament Commentaries
AOTC	Abingdon Old Testament Commentaries
ASTI	*Annual of the Swedish Theological Institute*
BCBC	Believers Church Bible Commentary
BEATAJ	Beiträge zur Erforschung des Alten Testaments und des Antiken Judentums
Ben.	*De beneficiis*
Bib.	*Biblica*
Bibl. hist.	*Library of History*
BibInt	*Biblical Interpretation*
BTCB	Brazos Theological Commentary on the Bible
BZAW	Beihefte zur Zeitschrift für die alttestamentliche Wissenschaft
CD	Cairo Genizah copy of the *Damascus Document*
CEB	Common English Bible
CEV	Contemporary English Version
CBQ	*Catholic Biblical Quarterly*
CBQMS	Catholic Biblical Quarterly Monograph Series
CGR	*Conrad Grebel Review*
CH	*Church History*
CMBC	Canadian Mennonite Bible College
CMU	Canadian Mennonite University
Contempl.	*De vita contemplativa*
COS	*The Context of Scripture*
CRR	Classics of the Radical Reformation
CurTM	*Currents in Theology and Mission*
DJD	Discoveries in the Judean Desert
DSS	Dead Sea Scrolls
ECDSS	Eerdmans Commentaries on the Dead Sea Scrolls
EDNT	*Exegetical Dictionary of the New Testament*
EMU	Eastern Mennonite University
Ench.	*Enchiridion*
Ep.	*Epistulae morales*; *Epistles*
ERT	*Evangelical Review of Theology*

ESV	English Standard Version
ET	English translation
Eth. eud.	*Eudemian Ethics*
Eth. nic.	*Nicomachean Ethics*
ExAud	*Ex auditu*
FF	Foundations and Facets
Frat. amor.	*De fraterno amore*
FRLANT	Forschungen zur Religion und Literatur des Alten und Neuen Testaments
GUPEA	Studia Graeca et Latina Gothoburgensia
HB	Hebrew Bible
HBT	*Horizons in Biblical Theology*
HSM	Harvard Semitic Monographs
HTR	*Harvard Theological Review*
HTS	Harvard Theological Studies
HUCA	*Hebrew Union College Annual*
Hypoth.	*Hypothetica*
ICC	International Critical Commentary
IMS	Institute of Mennonite Studies
Int.	*Interpretation*
ITC	International Theological Commentary
JATS	*Journal of the Adventist Theological Society*
JBL	*Journal of Biblical Literature*
JHS	*Journal of Hebrew Scriptures*
Jos. Asen.	*Joseph and Aseneth*
Joüon	*A Grammar of Biblical Hebrew*
JPS	Jewish Publication Society
JSNTSup	Journal for the Study of the New Testament: Supplement Series
JSOT	*Journal for the Study of the Old Testament*
JSOTSup	Journal for the Study of the Old Testament: Supplement Series
JSPL	*Journal of the Study of Paul and His Letters*
JSPSup	Journal for the Study of the Pseudepigrapha: Supplement Series
JTS	*Journal of Theological Studies*
Jub.	*Jubilees*
J.W.	*Jewish War*
KJV	King James Version
KTU	*Die keilalphabetischen Texte aus Ugarit*
LCBI	Literary Currents in Biblical Interpretation

LCL	Loeb Classical Library
LEC	Library of Early Christianity
Leg.	*Laws*
LHBOTS	Library of Hebrew Bible/Old Testament Studies
LNTS	Library of New Testament Studies
LS	*Louvain Studies*
LXX	Septuagint
m. Ber.	*Mishnah Berakot*
MCC	Mennonite Central Committee
MQR	*Mennonite Quarterly Review*
MT	Masoretic Text
MWC	Mennonite World Conference
Nat.	*Naturalis historia*
NET Bible	New English Translation
NIBCOT	New International Biblical Commentary on the Old Testament
NICNT	New International Commentary on the New Testament
NICOT	New International Commentary on the Old Testament
NIDB	*New Interpreter's Dictionary of the Bible*
NIGTC	New International Greek Testament Commentary
NIV	New International Version
NIVAC	New International Version Application Commentary
NovT	*Novum Testamentum*
NRSV	New Revised Standard Version
NT	New Testament
NTL	New Testament Library
NTS	*New Testament Studies*
NTT	New Testament Theology
NZSTh	*Neue Zeitschrift für Systematische Theologie und Religionsphilosophie*
OBT	Overtures to Biblical Theology
Or.	*Orationes*
OT	Old Testament
OTL	Old Testament Library
Paideia	Paideia: Commentaries on the New Testament
Pol.	*Politica*
Pr Man	Prayer of Manasseh
PSB	*Princeton Seminary Bulletin*
Pss. Sol.	*Psalms of Solomon*
RB	*Revue biblique*

RSV	Revised Standard Version
RTR	*Reformed Theological Review*
SBL	Society of Biblical Literature
SBLEJL	Society of Biblical Literature Early Judaism and Its Literature
SBLWAW	Society of Biblical Literature Writings from the Ancient World
SHBC	Smyth & Helwys Bible Commentary
Sib. Or.	*Sibylline Oracles*
Sir	Sirach/Ecclesiasticus
SNTSMS	Society for New Testament Studies Monograph Series
SNTW	Studies of the New Testament and Its World
Somn.	*De somniis*
SP	Sacra Pagina
SPCK	Society for Promoting Christian Knowledge Publishing
SPS	Studies in Peace and Scripture
SR	*Studies in Religion*
STAR	Studies in Theology and Religion
STDJ	Studies on the Texts of the Desert of Judah
SVTP	Studia in Veteris Testamenti Pseudepigraphica
Symp.	*Symposium*
TDNT	*Theological Dictionary of the New Testament*
Them	*Themelios*
THNTC	Two Horizons New Testament Commentary
TJ	*Trinity Journal*
TNK	Tanakh
TynBul	*Tyndale Bulletin*
UCOP	University of Cambridge Oriental Publications
Virt.	*De virtutibus*
Vision	*Vision: A Journal for Church and Theology*
VT	*Vetus Testamentum*
VTSup	Vetus Testamentum Supplements
WBC	Word Biblical Commentary
Wis	Wisdom of Solomon
WUNT	Wissenschaftliche Untersuchungen zum Neuen Testament
ZAW	*Zeitschrift für die alttestamentliche Wissenschaft*

1

Peace and Violence across the Testaments

Laura L. Brenneman

Is violence the antonym of peace, as implied by the title of this book? I remember my former professor, Willard Swartley, posing this question. It is one to which he and I both return in this volume. Indeed, it is appropriate to recall it here, as this book honors two scholars, Swartley and Perry Yoder, who have thought about this question, among many others, in the study of peace and Scripture. Grateful for their work, I and the other contributors to this volume vigorously interact—and sometimes disagree—with their proposals. We are, after all, biblical scholars, that often irksome breed who delight in the contours of Scripture, rough and smooth. As an introduction to the present collection, I briefly consider meanings of peace and violence, propose the importance of a peace hermeneutic in biblical study, and preview the essays.

DIMENSIONS OF PEACE AND VIOLENCE

What are peace and violence, and how are we using these terms here? The authors in this book use these words in different ways. However, most of them use *peace* to signify a fullness of something rather than an absence of violence. The "absence definition" is how people typically think of peace. The critique of this view is that it is rather insubstantial and does not promote creative thinking about how to make positive change. Through research and experience in areas of conflict, peace practitioners demonstrate that lasting peace is most clearly indicated by the presence of justice in society. So peace can be described in two ways, as positive peace and negative peace.[1] Negative peace—what the absence definition points to—is the lack of violence or its threat. Positive peace is an environment where resources for health, personal and community development, and happiness are commonly available (i.e., a condition of human flourishing). I believe that theologians and biblical scholars can benefit from knowing more about the conceptual models of peace that conflict transformation and resolution practitioners are developing.[2]

In his 1987 book, Perry Yoder notes that his experience in the Philippines shaped a new perspective. His project about *shalom*, started before he lived in the Philippines, changed as he was confronted with questions about what peace means in contexts of poverty and oppression. Very generally, Yoder characterizes peace as "a goal for which we should strive."[3] In claiming that peace has a wider meaning than lack of violence, Yoder describes discomfort with the "middle-class luxury"[4] of seeing peace narrowly, as "the avoidance, personally or corporately, of doing physical violence,"[5] which may allow people to believe that they are not involved in global violence. Yoder's critique sharpens: "We have become too involved with criticizing violence and not involved with peacemaking—working to transform the present structure of injustice and violence into structures of peace and equity."[6] Yoder's *Shalom* book grew out of his experience of listening to suffering people. His reading of the Bible was sensitized by their perspectives, and they influenced his conclusion that shalom as portrayed in the Bible is "active, it is struggle to bring about social, structural transformation. There should be no compromise with the evils of oppression and exploitation which impoverish, make helpless, and destroy human beings."[7]

1. An early and influential description of positive and negative peace is found in Galtung's 1969 "Violence, Peace, and Peace Research." While Galtung has written much since then and his observations spark debate, this stands as a classic essay in peace studies.

2. An excellent place to begin one's acquaintance with such resources is the Center for Justice and Peacebuilding's publications website (http://www.emu.edu/cjp/publications/faculty-staff/).

3. Yoder, *Shalom*, 1.

4. Ibid., 3; see also his essay in this volume.

5. Ibid., 2.

6. Ibid.

7. Ibid., 144.

Swartley's work shows basic agreement with Yoder's, particularly in his robust definition of peace;[8] however, his critique is not so pointedly against violence within social structures as it is concerned with the insidious quality of evil. With Scripture as his reference point, Swartley demonstrates that violent language often depicts the gospel of peace's confrontation with and destruction of evil. This gives peace its fullness of definition; it is the active campaign waged against all that opposes God. The NT witness is that "Jesus comes to render evil powerless over human life";[9] indeed, his resurrection is proof of this victory.[10]

Violence, like peace, has various dimensions, and appeal to peace research provides definitional clarity. In its most common usage, violence refers to direct (or overt) destructive actions, from a punch to verbal abuse to acts of warfare. The broader terminology of structural violence, however, refers to the often invisible systems that hinder human flourishing. In theological terms, structural violence is everything that works against God's intended shalom for the world.[11] It is invisible to the extent that economic, legal, political, social, and cultural systems and patterns are unquestioned. But it is not invisible to all people, as those who are poor and in nondominant social groups are aware.

For Galtung, violence can be intended, unintended, manifest, and latent. Each of these types of violence can be personal and structural in nature; further, personal and structural violence can have physical and psychological aspects, which are perpetuated with objects or without objects.[12] There is also a correlation between peace and violence: When there is an absence of direct violence, there is the presence of negative peace. When there is no structural violence (or social injustice), there is positive peace.[13] Following this reasoning, in order to understand peace well, we must understand violence (and vice versa). I believe Perry Yoder's contribution is to make this point as a biblical scholar, growing from his study of Scripture with sensitivity to the experience of those daily experiencing structural violence.

One final "take" on violence can further situate Swartley's work in this conversation. Robert W. Brimlow, in a rigorous meditation on just war, describes violence as "the expression of the arrogance of selfhood," acting as

---

8. See his essay in this volume and *Covenant of Peace*.

9. *Covenant of Peace*, 50.

10. Ibid.; see esp. the chaps. on Paul and Rev.

11. One finds a similar perspective throughout *Shalom*, clearly stated on 119: "Peacemakers live in the conviction that God does will shalom."

12. Galtung, "Violence, Peace, and Peace Research," 173.

13. Ibid., 183.

if "I were alone to act upon the universe [and thus as if] I have the power of God and I am God. That is the sin of violence."[14] This description of sin (which he also terms "evil") captures the sense of revolt against God's will that is Swartley's antonym for peace in the Bible. Brimlow, a philosopher, posits violence as the ultimate rebellion against God. It is putting oneself and one's desires ahead of all others and in the place of God. If one accepts Brimlow's articulation, it is easy to see how evil (rebellion against God) and violence (exercising the power to act as if only I matter) are intimately connected. As the common refrain of biblical wisdom literature expresses it, the fool is the one who oppresses others and acts as if there is no God;[15] the wise one ascertains the pattern of God's will and the shalom justice therein.

THE CASE FOR A PEACE HERMENEUTIC

So—according to this logic—to read Scripture wisely is to discern the pattern of God's shalom justice. This, I contend, has been the consistent goal of Swartley's and Yoder's work and is the aim of the current project.

In a recent book, David Neville calls for a hermeneutic of shalom to accompany the church's interpretive rules of faith and love in order to achieve "theological-moral . . . interpretive adjudication" in cases of ambiguity in biblical texts.[16] This preference is justified, says Neville after a thorough examination of the Gospels, Acts, and Revelation, because "shalom has intrabiblical theological sanction and, from the perspective of human flourishing, has more intrinsic moral meaning than violence ever could."[17]

With Neville, I believe that biblical texts (not only those of the NT) offer ample support for taking a peace hermeneutic as a theological-moral adjudicating lens. The essays in this volume attest to this, as do the collection of works by the honorees and by other contributors to these pages.[18] However, I will push a bit further. I think that those of us in the academy and in churches who have a peace hermeneutic occupy a particular social location. It seems impossible to maintain that peace is a marginal concern in the Bible, and ridiculous to say that the church—an entity tasked with the proclamation of hope in a world of violence—need not be an outspoken

14. Brimlow, *What about Hitler?* 134.

15. And why the "fear of the Lord is the beginning of knowledge" (Prov 1:7a NRSV).

16. Neville, *Peaceable Hope*, 244–45.

17. Ibid., 245.

18. Many of the contributors' works can be found in the bibliography. See also Swartley's forthcoming entry on *peace* in *The [Oxford] Encyclopedia of the Bible and Ethics*.

advocate of peace. Thus, those of us with the distinction of being trained "peace readers" need to take our places as conversation partners in the church and the academy, for those who long for concrete resources in their "peace arsenals" and, perhaps more significantly, for those who do not espouse a peace hermeneutic.

But are peace churches, and particularly the ecclesial descendants of the Anabaptists, doing this?[19] Mennonite World Conference (MWC), an association of Anabaptist-related congregations, recently conducted a survey of a hundred member churches that asked, "How is your church doing in its desire to be a Peace Church?" The results reveal that peace churches worldwide are creatively articulating their peace identity, but also that their contexts pose significant challenges; "all respondents indicated a need for additional resources and resourcing as they engage their desires to be Peace Churches."[20] The Mennonite Church USA's assessment shows both growth of and continuing need for biblical and theological peace understandings in its member churches. In particular, the denomination noted concern that local members are sometimes unable to articulate an account of peace as a "part of a whole web of commitments [for people and communities] formed in the image of Jesus."[21] As a Mennonite biblical scholar and peace educator, I see this as a call to additional work.

A RICH TAPESTRY

Perry Yoder and Willard Swartley's combined years—nearly a century—of teaching, scholarship, and service to the church extend a tradition of excellence and engagement. Both men practice and teach meticulous study of texts in context. Both have been dedicated churchmen. And both are devoted to peace education. The differences between them are vast; for the purposes of this volume, however, twenty-three colleagues, former students, friends, and others influenced by their scholarship add their essays to

19. Anabaptists of the sixteenth century who refused to act violently toward enemies chose to do so because they were convinced by Christian Scripture. Thus Mennonites, descendants of these Anabaptists, are classified both as conservative in their high view of the authority and trustworthiness of Scripture (see e.g., Article 4 in *Confession of Faith in a Mennonite Perspective*) and radical in a commitment to pacifism. See also Murray, *Biblical Interpretation*.

20. "Mennonite World Conference Peace Commission Peace Audit," online at http://www.mwc-cmm.org/, accessed 10 November 2012. This report is based on self-assessments by twenty-one member churches, not a large sample but a geographically representative one. A noticeable gap is in reporting from church conferences in Africa.

21. Stoner, "How Are We Doing?" 45.

the honorees' own in order to demonstrate our appreciation for their shared laser-like focus on biblical texts' lessons of peace. We submit our work as thanks for their dedication to a robust peace hermeneutic.

The essays in this book vary in scope and kind, but all grapple with particular questions of peace or violence raised in the study of Scripture. Perry Yoder's essay sets a challenging lens through which to examine the rest of the book. He contends that Mennonite scholars have shifted in their accounts of the violence of God from a canonical approach (i.e., God is sometimes violent) to a "biblical" one in which God cannot be violent because Jesus is nonviolent. Yoder suggests four areas of additional study for biblical peace scholarship, particularly with attention to justice.

Ben Ollenburger examines texts that portray God as acting violently and creatively, texts that challenge a portrait of a peaceful creation. Ollenburger writes that while he finds God to be the God of peace, this peace is expressed in God's activity both as creative gift-giver and as opponent to "the power of nothing."

Next, Andrea Dalton Saner challenges Millard Lind's classic formulation, "YHWH is a warrior" from Exod 15:3.[22] She argues that this is not the primary understanding of God's name in Exodus and, further, that right speech about God matters because it guides Israelite and subsequent human response.

In her chapter, Wilma Bailey takes on English translations of the Hebrew Bible (HB) that contain more violence than is warranted by the original. Bailey believes that peace churches, in their resistance to violence in Scripture, have favored the NT over the HB because they accept "violence added" translations. Bailey highlights Exod 21 and Josh 6 to show how the HB is best read in the contexts of the ancient recipients.

Paul Keim posits that questions about idolatry are significant for contemporary audiences, not only biblical authors. Idolatry in the biblical tradition has to do with allegiance, loyalty, and faithful worship of God. Whereas Christians today may suppose that the battle against idols has been won, Keim disagrees, suggesting that the Bible's warning about the "sequencing of allegiances" is still appropriate.

In a look at Ezekiel's portrait of Pharaoh and Egypt as a chaos monster, Safwat Marzouk argues that it functions as Israel's double, serving as a warning of "the loss of boundary and as a sign for religious assimilation" (68). Further, Marzouk suggests that Ezekiel's "othering" of Egypt raises questions for peace churches about sectarian boundary maintenance.

---

22. Lind, *Yahweh Is a Warrior.*

Brad Schantz finds that the odd occurrence of the non-Israelite figures Noah, Danel, and Job in Ezek 14:12–23 advances the rhetorical aims of Ezekiel as a whole. Although the named figures experience divine deliverance, they do not provide hope of intercession (as do ancestral heroes [cf. Jer 15:1–3]) for the doomed audience.

In an exegetical study of Eccl 3:1–8, Doug Miller provocatively pokes at the truism that there is a time for war. Pointing out ambiguity in the poem, Miller shows that Qohelet has more than one thing to say about time: God has ordered the world, although that order is only partially comprehensible to humans. However, the wise will distance themselves from materialism and individuality, as a way to confront oppression.

Steven Schweitzer describes Chronicles as a book that steers a course past traumas by employing images of shalom. Schweitzer sees the story of Hezekiah's Passover (2 Chron 30) as paradigmatic for a shalom-making leader: come to collaborative decisions with the people, allow the spirit of reconciliation to guide the process, and permit what "seems right" to the people to trump formal procedure. Thus constructive shalom in Chronicles is shown through unconventional methods of restoring right relationships.

In "Sex, Knowledge, and Evil," Jackie Wyse-Rhodes examines connections between disorder, violence, and evil in the Enochic tradition. By expanding the Genesis account of violence, the *Book of the Watchers* portrays humans as willing accomplices in the spread of evil; they are also creatures with great potential. In particular, if humans live in step with the natural order—which is generally obedient to God's will—humans can have peace now and be assured of a happy future.

In another examination of violent language, Dorothy Peters observes that there is "conversational tension" in the DSS: they are permeated with both a yearning for peace and a desire to participate in divine vengeance. Peters compares this conversation within the scrolls with sword language in sixteenth-century Anabaptist literature. Peters finds that both groups see God as the only authorized judge, and both are reticent about sectarian sword-wielding.

Swartley's essay opens the second part of the book in a pursuit of definitional clarity about peace and violence in the study of NT texts. He presents six definitions of peace in the NT and lays out pressing theological-hermeneutical issues of method for biblical peace research. Swartley concludes that the peace-promoting message of the NT is relevant in equipping people to withstand and transform violence, which is instigated by the evil one.

In an examination of the relationship between peace and righteousness, Tom Yoder Neufeld asserts that the NT promotes the virtues of meekness and long-suffering alongside aggressive pursuit of love of God and others. This "super-righteousness" is rooted in God's character, epitomized by Jesus, consistently demonstrated in the scriptural tradition, and the necessary practice of all recipients of God's kindness. Further, Yoder Neufeld discerns a danger in losing sight of the biblical thread of God's patience with enemies as historic peace churches move from a basic posture of nonresistance toward nonviolent activism.

Paul Yokota examines the Gospel of Matthew's use and interpretation of royal messianic texts to cast Jesus's humility, compassion, and non-military posture as messianic. In addition, Matthew widens the scope of typical messianic texts as additional proof for Jesus as Messiah. Yokota asserts that a further interest of the Gospel is to show the Messiah as a uniquely divine being.

In the next two chapters, David Rensberger and Mary Schertz examine Gospel texts that challenge a "shalom-centered" view of Jesus. Rensberger questions the interpretation that Jesus's temple action is an act of violence, i.e., an enraged Jesus whipping a crowd of animals and moneychangers. Instead, Rensberger finds resonance in Mark and John (despite their different portrayals), showing Jesus's action as prophetic, not violent.

Schertz's difficult passage is Luke 22:35–38, a text with multiple interpretations. After analysis of the narrative structure of the wider context of Luke 22:31–62, Schertz suggests that Jesus's prayer in verses 39–46 shows a genuine struggle between use of holy war and nonviolent acceptance of his crucifixion. Schertz concludes that the prayer represents an integration of the two choices: "Jesus will suffer and die on a cross as God's [ultimate] holy warrior. . . . who is paradoxically not violent" (see 204 below).

Jo-Ann Brandt also recognizes a problem in NT scholarship in its tendency to use Greco-Roman notions of peace as a foil to biblical shalom. Instead, she argues, the early church drew from Greek and Roman discourse on friendship in development of concepts of salvation and reconciliation. Rejecting a sharp contrast between Christian and Hellenistic thought, Brant contends that Christian belief in peace as forgiveness, atonement, and reconciliation is informed by the Greek and Roman views of genuine friendship.

In a study of Anabaptist-Mennonites' use of Acts, Joshua Yoder describes it as a "treasure trove" for teachings on proper relationships between church and society. Through a survey of selected texts from sixteenth-century Anabaptists and influential twentieth-century scholars Guy F. Hershberger, John Howard Yoder, Perry Yoder, and Willard Swartley, Joshua Yoder finds that Acts has been significant in shaping Anabaptist-Mennonites' views of politics. Further, some of these interpretations remain relevant for contemporary discussions of Acts in the church and the academy.

Gordon Zerbe poses the question, are religion and Scripture inherently violent? Zerbe's main concern is the Pauline corpus, taking Phil 3:2—a passage often accused of violence—as a test case. He suggests that methods more varied than those of historical criticism should be employed for "rhetorical flexibility" and relevance. Zerbe sees Paul's texts as having "ambiguous potential and multivalent character" but a directionality for peace and justice.

Reta Halteman Finger also examines conflict in Paul's writings, particularly in the Corinthian correspondence. Conflict exists not only in the church and between Paul and certain factions of the church, but also, as Finger perceives, in Paul's preaching of the gospel. In promoting fictive kinship groups, Paul disrupts patron-client relationships for the churchgoers in Corinth. Rather than backing off when they balk, Paul presses them, arguing that unity in the body of believers comes only after social reorganization.

In another essay about unity, Chris Marshall explores the link in Eph 4:1–6 between peace and ecclesiology. The passage, influenced by significant Pauline thought, exhorts the church to "live a life worthy of the calling to which they have been called" (Eph 4:1). The practice of living the unity of Christ's body is, Marshall says, "a foretaste of universal reconciliation" (266).

Jacob Elias detects a Pauline theology of peace in 2 Thessalonians, even amid language evocative of holy war. Elias considers the apocalyptic tone to be reassuring to people in a hostile environment. The recipients are reminded that the resources of communal resilience and faithfulness to God provide sustenance, and that God will ultimately triumph over opponents.

In his chapter, Michael Gorman claims that there is more to Revelation than scenes of violence. Gorman sees in the book several theologically significant dimensions of shalom. Although some blame Revelation for Christians' unpeaceful and unfaithful way of being church, Gorman contends that if read rightly, Revelation "has the potential to help restore the church as a community of shalom in anticipation of the new creation God has promised" (290).

Finally, Nancy Heisey, former president of MWC, levels a challenge to North American and European scholars to broaden our frame of reference and become conversant with biblical peace scholarship happening in the global south. Heisey highlights three Mennonite scholars who draw on biblical themes of peace in their work. She argues that southern authors, often outside the guild of biblical studies, have been elevating the themes of peace, reconciliation, and love of enemies.

As this preview shows, the essays in this volume vary in topic and tenor. For those interested in the interaction between study of Scripture and perspectives on peace, this book will be a rich tapestry with cohesive themes and contrasting threads. Despite difference, the authors testify together about how Willard Swartley and Perry Yoder have stimulated conversation for many years about peace and Scripture. We submit this book in gratitude and humble hope that it pushes the conversation further.

PART 1

Peace and Violence
in the Hebrew Bible

2

Mennonite Peace Theology and Ethics

Biblical or Canonical?

Perry B. Yoder

In making a case for nonresistance or pacifism, earlier Mennonite scholars denied neither the "violence" of God or the retributive justice of God as presented in the biblical account (e.g., in the exodus). Recently, however, some Mennonite scholars have claimed that a nonviolent or pacifist position needs a nonviolent or pacifist God. This claim is based on their understanding of Jesus's crucifixion and atonement. This recent theological presumption requires a shift from a canonical perspective of the older works to a more narrowly focused one, one focused on Jesus's death and their interpretation of it.

The aim of this essay is twofold. First, I will illustrate this paradigm shift in some recent writings by Mennonite theologians and ethicists. Then I will make several tentative suggestions for further study by biblical scholars. My depiction of earlier and later Mennonite peace scholarship will of necessity be brief, but I believe it will reflect views that were or are held by many scholars, pastors, and laypersons within the North American Mennonite church.[1]

---

1. The labels to use for the various Mennonite groupings are confusing when writing about the past. I will use (Old) Mennonite Church for one group and General Conference Mennonite Church for another. Canadian Mennonites deserve their own label. I confess that I have not mined each group equally for this survey, which is illustrative rather than exhaustive.

GOD'S PREROGATIVES AND OURS: SHIFTING VIEWS IN SOME MENNONITE THEOLOGY

Guy F. Hershberger

I begin with Guy F. Hershberger's *War, Peace, and Nonresistance,*[2] a work commissioned and supported by (Old) Mennonite Church peace leaders and authorized by the denomination's "Peace Committee" to make the case for Mennonite nonresistance. This work was written during the Second World War and was to serve an educational purpose for the denomination. While written by an "Old Mennonite," it has become an important work within the larger Mennonite peace tradition.[3]

In chapter 2, "Peace and War in the Old Testament," Hershberger explains his understanding of the canon's story. Following the fall of humankind, God made concessions, such as civil law, on account of human sinfulness. Thus in human society people must act sinfully to punish—such as carrying out capital punishment as in Gen 9:6 (p. 21). However, such concessions were not the ultimate or primary will of God that would be revealed in Jesus Christ.[4]

God's primary will was for Israel not to fight. This we see from the example of their deliverance at the Reed Sea (Exod 14), as well as in God's primary command to them concerning their coming occupation of the land of Canaan. If Israel is obedient to God, then God will send an agent before them to drive out the inhabitants before them (Exod 23:30–33). However, Israel did not remain faithful either at Sinai or in the wilderness trek that followed. Because of their sin, God, through God's permissive will, allowed or commanded Israel to fight. These wars express not the primary will of God but God's permissive will working through sinful society to bring about God's ends (30–35).[5]

---

2. Hershberger, *War, Peace, and Nonresistance.* I am using the 3rd ed., which includes a "perspective" written by J. R. Burkholder, dated 1991. Hereafter, authors will be cited in text.

3. See "War, Peace, and Nonresistance," chap. 5 in Schlabach, *War, Peace, and Social Conscience,* 117–62, for a masterful account of this book's contexts, sources, and content. See the account in Stutzman, *From Nonresistance to Justice,* chap. 2, "A Place to Stand (1908–1942)," 49–94, for a broader view of these times within the (Old) Mennonite Church.

4. Jesus's teaching on divorce serves as an example of the difference between God's primary will and the remedial necessity of law allowing for divorce.

5. He notes God's use of the Assyrians to punish Israel (Isa 11). We could also refer to Cyrus, God's messiah, whose conquests were aided by God for God's own ends (Isa 45).

From Hershberger's reading of the canon he concludes:

(1) "The perfect covenant of the New Testament restores human conduct to its rightful place where it was before the fall" (16).

(2) In the meantime, because of Israel's sub-Christian level, we find God's permissive will, which allowed Israel to fight (34). Consequently,

(3) the warfare that we find in the HB is set aside by Jesus, and Christian conduct is now guided by God's primary will. In Jesus we find a restoration of what God intended from the beginning.

This change between the two testaments "is due to *a change in human character and in the human will*, and *not a change in the fundamental character and will of God*" (26; italics added).[6] Just as we find God's wrath and punishing judgment in the HB, so we find them in the Greek scriptures. Hershberger calls attention to the story of Ananias and Sapphira in Acts 5. He notes that God commands Christians to non-vengeance while reserving vengeance for God alone (Rom 12:19). His conclusion is that "punishment is *the prerogative of God*[7] alone" (44; italics added). Later, in the context of quoting Rom 12:19–21, he writes, "*Thus there is no contradiction between the Christian ethic of love for others and God's wrath and judgment*" (51; italics added). It is God's primary will and character that bind the canon together.

Paul Peachey

The notion that God has special prerogatives and thus acts in ways forbidden to humankind, along with the view that Jesus begins a new moral age, is found prominently in Mennonite and related peace statements of the post-World War II era. I will give one example. The historic peace churches and the International Fellowship of Reconciliation prepared a statement for the World Council of Churches Amsterdam assembly in 1952.[8] This statement makes reference to dispensations—the dispensation of providence versus the dispensation of redemption—to explain why Christians are called to a pacifist way of life (86).

Following a critique commissioned by non-pacifist members of the assembly, a "Continuation Committee" drafted a further statement that was

6. He cites Mal 3:6.

7. Ollenburger, "Yahweh's Exclusive Prerogative," chap. 4, in *Zion* 87–144, presents the basis for this concept in the Zion Psalms and Isaiah.

8. The textual references in the following refer to page numbers in Durnbaugh, *On Earth Peace*.

published in its final form in 1958. This statement, whose major author was Paul Peachey, a Mennonite sociologist, tackled the issue of justice that had been raised by responders. Two major points are set forth:

(1) God's *ṣedeq* (righteousness) is redemptive and normative for human justice. As an example of God redemptive justice, the exodus of Israel from Egypt is cited (113). God's righteous redemptive justice may involve the judgment or "violence" of God (a divine prerogative).

(2) In the HB we find a fallen society and non-Christian ideas of justice (Hershberger's "permissive will"), such as *lex talionis* (114). The statement's conclusion is: "The Church is not called to work for either justice or peace using methods not founded in God's righteousness and mercy" (115).

Millard Lind

This traditional position has been supported by biblical scholars. Millard Lind, in his monograph *Yahweh Is a Warrior,*[9] extends the insights of Hershberger. To put Lind's argument in a nutshell: God fights for Israel so that Israel does not have to fight. Warfare is God's prerogative. Israel is to be quiet and wait for God's deliverance. Human warfare represents not only a lack of trust in God but a usurping of God's own prerogative. It was exactly because Israel's God was a God of war that Israel should have been a people of peace. Yahweh as warrior is *negative* evidence for participation in warfare rather than a positive argument, as might be thought. The iconic example for Lind is found in Exod 14 and the battle at the Reed Sea. When Israel is terrified by the approaching Egyptian army, Moses calms them saying, "Do not be afraid, stand firm, and see the deliverance that the Lord will accomplish for you today; for the Egyptians whom you see today you shall never see again" (Exod 14:13 NRSV). It is God's victory—not Israel's—that is celebrated in Exod 15. God is a warrior. God's people are not. For Lind, "Yahweh is a man of war" is an underpinning of biblical pacifism.

---

9. Lind, *Yahweh Is a Warrior.* This work was included in The Christian Peace Shelf, works selected by a committee whose chair was appointed by MCC and whose members came from the Brethren in Christ, General Conference, Old Mennonite, and Mennonite Brethren churches.

Waldemar Janzen

Canadian Mennonite scholar Waldemar Janzen wrote three articles on war in the HB, which form part of a collection of his writings, *Still in the Image: Essays in Biblical Theology and Anthropology*. In the third of these articles, which seems most salient for our discussion, Janzen begins with the issue of theodicy that is inherent to monotheism.[10] How can a single God who is ruler of the universe allow the evil, suffering, and injustice we experience in the world? Why do the wicked prosper and the righteous suffer? Why does God allow wars that destroy innocent civilians—young children and babies, for example? Why are these wars fought by the poor in a society and not by the ones profiting from them? Evil and its subset war are theological problems for the whole of scripture.

In the middle of this essay Janzen points to two striking aspects of war in the HB:

(1) Human participation in war is deemphasized. God, not Israel, is responsible for victory. We do not find statues of military heroes in the Bible. Gideon erects an altar to God rather than "cashing in" on his victory.

(2) God's victory will usher in the peace that God wills and promises to Israel. It is God, not Israel, who will establish the peaceful kingdom. In this context, Janzen argues that God has the same character in both testaments. "Jesus never denies, but rather assumes, that the one sovereign God rules the whole world and is thus, in the last analysis, responsible in some sense for the wars and violence of the Roman Empire, including his own crucifixion" (207).

Gordon Zerbe

Mennonite NT scholars have also supported the view of God as having the prerogatives of judgment and retribution. Gordon Zerbe, in a careful study of Rom 12:14, 17–21,[11] discusses Paul's notion of divine justice within the literary and social context of Romans. In the section titled "Warrants of the Exhortation," he argues that Paul's warrants for the exhortation to return good for evil rather than taking vengeance are grounded in the divine prerogative to avenge and repay evil. Christians are to be nonresistant, but God is not. This perspective of Paul, based on a quotation from the HB, is

---

10. Janzen, "Christian Perspectives," 193–211.

11. Zerbe, "Paul's Ethic," in *Love of Enemy*, ed. Swartley, 177–222.

in line with his eschatological expectations: God will dispense retributive judgment in the future (Rom 5:9, for example).

Willard Swartley

Willard Swartley, in his article "God's Moral Character as the Basis of Human Ethics: Foundational Convictions,"[12] argues that God's moral character is for justice. A God who does not act for justice is not on the side of victims (386). In the end it is human violence that moves God to action and brings God's punishment on human actors. "To put it bluntly, God's vengeance, however executed, stands against human violence" (395). But for Christians, it is *the nature of God as revealed in Christ* that is our guide. In the end, it is the nonviolence of Jesus, not the wrath and vengeance of God, that is normative for Christian action.

Harry Huebner

Some Mennonite theologians and ethicists, however, hold such a dual ethic to be unacceptable. Harry Huebner, in his article "Christian Pacifism and the Character of God," sets out to refute the traditional point of view described above. He proposes a "divine-human-moral-continuity model" (260). His basic thesis is that our ethic is based on who God is, on the character of God. Consequently there can be no dualism between God's character, as seen in God's actions, and ours. There are no divine prerogatives. We learn God's character from what God has done—from the acts of God recorded in Scripture (252). But these reputed actions must be sorted and selected, since not all "acts of God" in Scripture are really acts of God and therefore do not demonstrate the character of God. Instead, we look for a pattern in the actions ascribed to God, and on the basis of this pattern we determine which acts show us the character of God and which do not (267). But in fact, the definitive nature of God's being or character[13] we learn from "the Christ event."[14] This act of God allows us to determine which acts attributed to

12. Swartley, *Covenant of Peace,* 377–98.

13. Huebner seems to use the words *being* and *character* interchangeably, a move that is theologically problematic. Normally God's being or essence is not reduced to God's character. Being is about who God is; character is about how God "normally" acts—what God does—which is Huebner's main concern.

14. "Since Jesus shows us the moral character of God, we must reconstruct our understanding of God's acts from the standpoint of the character of Jesus" (267). In the writing of those who make a theological argument for God's nonviolence, the notion

God in Scripture are not God's doing.[15] Huebner does not give us examples of which "acts of God" are wrongly ascribed to God, but from his emphasis on suffering, forgiveness, and love, we could expect that the exodus from Egypt would be among them.[16] The bottom line is that as Christians our ethic must be "rooted in the character of God," which is to be no different, in principle, from our character. Consequently, "the very content of our actions is to emanate from the virtues of God which we are called to make our own" (268). For Huebner the message of this version of the biblical story is clear. We can learn, for example, that God is more concerned with how change is brought about than that change actually happens (268). Or we find that "the biblical story tells us that God wills to rule the world through the servant community" (270).[17]

J. Denny Weaver

J. Denny Weaver in *The Nonviolent Atonement*[18] likewise asserts that God is a nonviolent God. Consequently, traditional views of the atonement could be accepted only "if one is willing to defend the compatibility of violence and retribution with the Gospel of Jesus Christ" (7). The Mennonite tradition as described above did, in fact, hold to both the retribution of God and to nonviolence for the one following Jesus. It would thus have been helpful for Weaver to have shown how the hermeneutics and assumptions of the preceding tradition were in error. As for the retribution of God, Weaver writes: "Jesus made it clear that statements about the retribution of God were really a declaration of what those who reject the rule of God bring on themselves. Their sin turns upon them, and in effect, they judge themselves. Declarations of judgment make clear the consequences of

---

of the "Christ event," "the story of Jesus," and "the gospel of Jesus" are frequent terms. These terms seem to refer to normative theological constructs. Here the "event" of the cross shows, apparently, the character of Jesus and thus the character of God.

15. It is perhaps ironic that this article was motivated by the nationalistic claims of a Jew and Muslim. Neither would accept an argument based on Jesus's deity and crucifixion.

16. Such acts of justice and liberation involve judgment, and in the case of the exodus, the wiping out of the Egyptian army. However, Huebner also affirms that we cannot ignore the acts of God previous to Jesus, or at least some of them (267).

17. As a student of Bible I find it difficult to find texts that explicitly voice these views. I can find many that do not—Isa 2:1–5 being the first to come to mind. God rules over all the nations directly, not through a "servant community."

18. Weaver, *Nonviolent Atonement*.

rejecting God."[19] In contrast, God is a God of love who offers the sinner forgiveness.[20] Thus, expressions like "wrath of God" actually boil down to "logical consequences"—"you do the sin, you get the punishment." It is sin, not God's justice and consequent judgment, that brings punishment on the wrongdoer. What God does instead is love and forgive sinners.

FOUR AREAS FOR FURTHER STUDY

Given the dichotomies between the earlier tradition of biblical scholar-ship sketched above and the positions taken by some later theologians and ethicists,[21] what is the Bible scholar to do? I would suggest four areas that apparently need additional consideration, emphasis, and integration into a base for pursuing peace. My hope is that this approach might be helpful to the overall enterprise.[22]

The Nature of Jesus's God

First, the nature or character of *Jesus's God* might be more carefully teased out from the texts themselves. It is not obvious from a plain-sense read-ing of the Gospels that Jesus's God was in fact or in principle nonviolent. Jesus does not seem shy about mentioning the coming judgment of God on those who resist the kingdom. It will go better for Sodom and Gomorrah in the day of God's judgment than for those who reject the disciples and their proclamation of the kingdom (Matt 10:15; also 11:24 and Luke 10:12). In the face of suffering for the sake of the gospel, Jesus reminds his followers, "fear the one who is able to destroy both soul and body in hell" (Matt 10:28 NET).

---

19. Ibid., 41.

20. See also p. 78, where Weaver discusses the justice and mercy of God. God's judg-ment or wrath means we are in bondage to sin—our natural condition. God's justice seems to be God's noninterference with the wages of sin rather than any act on God's part.

21. For a theological critique of Weaver's position and others sharing this trend, see Snyder Belousek in *Atonement, Justice, and Peace* and "Nonviolent God," 49–70. A history of the discussion can be found by following the footnotes.

22. The following comments are based on a "simple, plain-sense reading" and are tentative. They aim to illustrate possible lines of study which would call into doubt the new paradigm. The areas of suggested study would also help us understand the conti-nuity of the canon and provide a context for understanding Jesus within the context of this continuity.

In Matt 26:51–53 we find one of Jesus's entourage defending Jesus with his sword. Jesus rebuked him saying, "Do you think that I cannot call on my Father, and that he would send me more than twelve legions of angels right now?" (Matt 26:53 NET). That would be twelve Roman army units, or approximately 72,000 angels. This is reminiscent of 2 Kgs 6, in which an army of fiery horses and chariots were ready to protect Elisha from the Syrian army.[23] In neither case were they activated, but the fact of their presence indicates that God's army was on standby, ready to act in a decisive way. Calling on God to act by a heavenly military is seen as a real option, in contrast to the disciples' use of the sword.[24]

So it is with the "Son of Man" in the eschatological judgment scene in Matt 25:32–42. The Son of Man acts as judge and consigns people "into the eternal fire prepared for the devil and his angels" (Matt 25:41 NRSV). As opposed to the earthly Jesus, the Son of Man is a heavenly figure who participates in the transition from this world to the world to come. For Jesus, the transition to the next world is marked by divine intervention and judgment rather than nonviolence.[25]

The Theocentric Perspective of the New Testament

Second, the theocentric perspective of the NT itself needs more publicity—or substantiation. The NT frequently speaks of Jesus/Christ as either the subject of God's action or as God's agent. Peter's speech placed at Pentecost is the church's first sermon (Acts 2:14–35); it is thoroughly theocentric. The description of Jesus begins in verse 22: "Jesus of Nazareth, *a man attested to you by God* with deeds of power, wonders, and signs that *God did through him* among you" (Acts 2:22 NRSV; italics added). It ends with these words: "Therefore let the entire house of Israel know with certainty that *God has made him both Lord and Messiah*, this Jesus whom you crucified" (Acts 2:36 NRSV; italics added).[26]

For Paul, Jesus illustrates God's love for us: "But *God demonstrates his own love* for us, in that while we were still sinners, Christ died for us. Much

23. In the case of Elisha, like that of Jesus, this heavenly army was not invoked. Instead Elisha, unlike Jesus, prayed that God would blind the Syrian army. They were then led to Samaria and the Israelite king fed them and then released them.

24. In Rev 20:9, we find fire coming down from heaven and annihilating those besieging the saints.

25. This apocalyptic framework for understanding the Jesus of Greek Scriptures may need more attention by pacifist scholars.

26. See also the christological hymn in Phil 2, which ends with a similar declaration in vv. 9–11.

more then, because we have now been declared righteous by his blood, we will be saved through him from God's wrath. For if while we were enemies we were reconciled to God through the death of his Son, how much more, since we have been reconciled, will we be saved by his life?" (Rom 5:8–10 NET; italics added). Note Paul's "inconsistency"—Jesus's death illustrates God's love of enemies, but yet this same God can show wrath.

Finally, we may cite from 2 Corinthians: "All this is *from God*, who reconciled us to himself through Christ, and has given us the ministry of reconciliation; that is, in Christ *God was* reconciling the world *to himself*, not counting their trespasses against them, and entrusting the message of reconciliation to us. So we are ambassadors for Christ, since *God is making his appeal* through us; we entreat you on behalf of Christ, *be reconciled to God*" (2 Cor 5:18–20 NRSV; italics added). For Paul, in this passage God is the actor to whom we are to be reconciled. Christ is God's agent to accomplish God's reconciliation with the world, a very theocentric point of view.

A Canonical Basis for Peace and Justice

Third, we need to work on a canonical basis for peace and justice rather than a "biblical" one. The latter approach is neater: a few key verses can be cited and from that foundation a position can be argued. This type of argument suits polemics. A canonical argument, which theoretically includes the entire canon as its context, is messy—more variegated and nuanced and marked by humility. We may not make sense of it all; there will be loose ends. But it would bring a corrective to proof texting—selecting what suits the argument and treating as invalid texts that do not—and the tunnel vision that results.[27]

27. Contrast Huebner's critique of canonical criticism, in "God and Pacifism," 271–72n47. His objection is that "the Bible cannot read itself, and is not canon until it is read by a faithful community. Hence how it is read must at least to some degree be determined by that community." The danger with canonical criticism is in " 'democratizing' its truth at the expense of depreciating its power in forming a community capable of being the church." This formulation seems misleading. A text can be accepted as authoritative without ever having been read—a dictionary or the rules of a game come to mind. Going by custom or tradition, one can play tennis without ever having read the rules of the game. One could also play "tennis" without a net. But is it tennis? Who decides, the "faithful community" of some tennis players who have decided that this is the way the game should be played? Or is an appeal made to the "unread" rules of the game to bring a corrective to their understanding of the game?

Further, isn't the concept of "a faithful community" really a myth used to defend one interpretation against others? Which Winnipeg community has the right to determine how the game is played or how the canon is read? How does such a community validate its authority apart from "because we say so"? In reality, we find congregations and

The problem with the God of the canon is that God is God. God's being cannot be limited by definition, nor can God's character be logically represented. Scripture represents the dilemma of thinking about a radically free God by positing seemingly contradictory attributes of the Divine.

Moses on Mount Sinai wishes to know the character or nature of God.[28] God promises Moses at least a partial vision (Exod 33:18–19). But first God commands Moses to descend the mountain and carve out two stones to replace the ones Moses broke. On these new tablets God will write the "words" which were on the first set. After carving out two tablets, Moses climbs Mount Sinai for his fateful meeting with God. But before writing anything on the tablets, God declares God's own character: "The Lord passed before him and proclaimed: 'The Lord! the Lord! a God compassionate and gracious, slow to anger, abounding in kindness and faithfulness, extending kindness to the thousandth generation, forgiving iniquity, transgression, and sin; yet He does not remit all punishment, but visits the iniquity of parents upon children and children's children, upon the third and fourth generations'" (Exod 34:6–7 TNK).[29] This is a theological statement about the character of God. The ethical statement for Israel is the "ten words" revealed on Mount Sinai. Israel is to follow the will of God. God's attributes are not a model for human behavior, but instead acquaint Israel with the character of their God.[30]

The notion that God's will is our ethical guide can be found in many places in scripture. One representative passage must do. In the Lord's Prayer we find "Your kingdom come. Your will be done, on earth as it is in heaven" (Matt 6:10 NRSV). This notion may be a distant echo of Isa 2:5: "O House of

individuals expressing a wide range of views. Denominational conventions thus may decide by majority vote how to understand the Bible on an issue such as homosexuality. It is difficult to think of a better way to "democratize" interpretation at the expense of its authority.

28. The text reads, "He said, 'Oh, let me behold Your Presence!'" (Exod 33:18 TNK). What is meant exactly by *kābôd* is not readily apparent, but it seems to have to do with the nature of God.

29. Although God metes out retribution, the God of retribution can be appealed to for grace and forgiveness. Notice the intercessory prayer of Moses: "The Lord! slow to anger and abounding in kindness; forgiving iniquity and transgression; yet not remitting all punishment, but visiting the iniquity of fathers upon children, upon the third and fourth generations. Pardon, I pray, the iniquity of this people according to Your great kindness, as You have forgiven this people ever since Egypt" (Num 14:18–19 TNK). God then pardoned the people. Our confusion is in thinking God must be either one way or the other. The God of retribution is also the God of faithfulness, compassion, and mercy, much to Jonah's disgust in Jonah 4.

30. To be sure certain individual attributes of God, such as holiness, are to be characteristics of the Israelites as well.

Jacob! Come, let us walk by the light of the Lord" (Isa 2:5 TNK). God's people are to do God's will, now. Following God's will is known as discipleship.

God's Justice and God's Wrath

Fourth, the notion of God's justice in connection with the "vengeance of God" and the "wrath of God" needs clarification and expansion. God, as a God of justice, is assumed by the biblical record. Abraham's rhetorical question, "Shall not the Judge[31] of all the earth do what is just?" (Gen 18:25 NRSV) is a basic presupposition. God's justice is not always sure, because God may forgive. Jonah is a classic example of the latter.

The God of justice is the court of last resort for those who cannot obtain justice within human society. This is the cry we hear in the psalms of retribution. God's judgment will set things right. Rather than "vengeance," a better translation for this action of God is "retribution," as in, "God of retribution, Lord, God of retribution, appear!" (Ps 94:1 TNK). The God who is the sole sovereign of the universe surely will give justice to those who are suffering, will break the forces of oppression, and will deliver the weak and powerless. Indeed, "These passages imply (in a situation of uttermost threat!) an abandonment of private revenge and a total surrender to him who judges righteously. In no instance is the satisfaction of feelings of hatred of embittered people at stake. The prayer for vengeance is the prayer for victory of lawfulness and the revelation of the God of the covenant, who while judging, keeps his word (Pss 58:11; 79:10; 94:1; 149:7). . . . Without God's vengeance there is no justice (Ps 58:12) and no future (Deut 32:43; Ps 149:7–9)."[32]

The tradition of the oppressed, the persecuted, and powerless calling for God's retribution is continued into Greek scriptures. In the book of Revelation we find the souls of the saints who had been slaughtered crying out, "Sovereign Lord, holy and true, how long will it be before you judge and avenge our blood on the inhabitants of the earth?" (Rev 6:10 NRSV). Later, the elders around the throne finally begin to see God's justice: "We give you thanks, Lord God Almighty, who are and who were, for you have taken your great power and begun to reign. The nations raged, but your wrath has come, and the time for judging the dead, for rewarding your servants, the prophets and saints and all who fear your name, both small and great, and for destroying those who destroy the earth" (Rev 11:18 NRSV). Then

---

31. The word *šōpēṭ* can mean judge or ruler. This verse could be translated, "Will not the ruler of all the earth do what is just?"

32. Peels, "*NQM*," *NIDOTTE* 3:155; see his monograph, Peels, *Vengeance of God*.

in chapter 16:5–6, we have angels saying: "You are just, O Holy One, who are and were, for you have judged these things; because they shed the blood of saints and prophets, you have given them blood to drink. It is what they deserve!" God is pronounced just and holy because God acts as judge giving "what they deserve." Finally, the people are even to celebrate, to rejoice over, the fall of Babylon (Rome): "Rejoice over her, O heaven, you saints and apostles and prophets! For God has given judgment for you against her. Then a mighty angel took up a stone like a great millstone and threw it into the sea, saying, '*With such violence Babylon the great city will be thrown down, and will be found no more*'" (Rev 18:20; italics added).

God's judgment may be deferred until the end of this age, but it will come, and the saints will seek it and look forward to it. Surely our peace theology and ethics should have a concern for justice and room for prayer to God for justice. Otherwise "peace" may be a middle-class luxury and part of the ideology of oppression.[33]

33. As students from other parts of the world have repeatedly reminded me, "Of course you are for 'peace.' You profit from oppression every day."

3

Creation and Violence

Ben C. Ollenburger

In his book *Covenant of Peace,* Willard Swartley makes a strong case in favor of the claim that the Bible does not—hence, we should not—attribute
violence to God, who hates violence.[1] Wrath, vengeance, and punishment
God does exhibit and perform, according to Swartley, and does so on behalf of *shalom,* along the lines of Perry Yoder's capacious definition of that
Hebrew term in his seminal treatment of it: *Shalom, the Bible's Word for
Salvation, Justice, and Peace.* But violence? In these pages I propose to treat,
very briefly, some biblical texts that seem to portray God acting creatively
but violently, including Pss 74:13–17, 77:14–20, and Isa 51:9–11. A contrast
is often drawn between these texts and God's nonviolent creation in Gen 1,
and the contrast sometimes assumes moral significance. But what counts,
or does not count, as violence? For that matter, what counts as creation?
May pursuing these questions in the pages that follow count as small trib-
ute to Willard Swartley and Perry Yoder, treasured friends and respected
colleagues.

Many biblical scholars and theologians claim that passages like those
from Psalms and Isaiah listed above—I will call them *contra chaos* texts—
have to do not with creation but with providence, and thus with God's
governance of the world. That is, they are not concerned with absolute
beginnings or the origin of all things.[2] While it is not obvious what does

---

1. Swartley, *Covenant of Peace.*

2. I addressed the matter in "Isaiah's Creation Theology," 54–71. Walton's and van

and does not fall into the category (or under the concept) *thing*, neither is it obvious why the Latin(ate) term *creatio(n)* should mean only absolute beginnings and origins. It acquired such a meaning under the pressure of early Gnostic and then Christian theology and the emerging doctrine of creation out of nothing, grounded scripturally in Gen 1, among other texts.[3] Whether that chapter, or the Bible itself (cf. John 1:1–3; Rom 4:16–25), can or should bear the weight of *creatio ex nihilo* remains outside our focus here, even though the category or the concept *nothing* shares with *thing* the same lack of obviousness, or self-evidence, as to its (possible or necessary or absence of) extension. Furthermore, it may turn out that the *nothing*—best serving the theological (hence, scriptural) case for *creatio ex nihilo*—comes to expression in texts like those listed above. In any case, in the long history of Christian theology, creation and providence have shared an intimate relationship. The Puritan theologian William Ames (1576–1633) expressed it this way: "The efficiency [productive work] of God may be understood as either creation or providence."[4] Borrowing Ames's terms, we may ask whether God's efficiency as creation (Gen 1) proceeded without violence, and thus differently from—in contrast with, and in opposition to—God's violent efficiency as providence (Ps 74).

GOD CONTRA CHAOS

Psalm 74 employs the language of Canaan. In verses 1–11 and 18–23, the community urges God (Elohim) to remember God's dwelling, Mount Zion, in light of the destruction and desecration of the sanctuary—presumably by Babylon's army under Nebuchadnezzar II—and to act in response to this devastating event. In common with other and older ancient texts, the prayer understands the disaster to mean that God has abandoned in anger both his dwelling and the community itself: "the sheep of your pasture" (v. 1).[5] Why

Wolde's work productively complicate what "to create" means, and what creation does, in the Bible (cf. Walton, *Genesis 1 as Ancient Cosmology*; van Wolde, *Reframing Biblical Studies*).

   3. See May, *Creatio ex Nihilo*, 76–83, on Basilides and the Basilideans.

   4. Ames, *Marrow of Theology*, 100. Pannenberg asks "whether the term 'creation' may be reserved for the beginning of the world or whether we must expound it as the epitome of God's creative action in world history" (*Systematic Theology*, 2:12). Contemporary biblical scholarship, in a different conceptual environment, might differentiate between "protological" and "cosmological" texts, as does Blenkinsopp ("Cosmological and Protological Language").

   5. *Lament for Ur*, a Sumerian text from ca. 2000 BCE, lamenting the destruction of that city by the Elamites, similarly complains that the god Enlil (among other deities) has "abandoned his cow-pen, and let the breezes haunt his sheep-fold." The lament

has this come about? The framing question, "Why?" directed to God in verses 1 and 11a—why have you rejected us forever and your anger smokes (v. 1), and why do you "hold back your hand" (i.e., why do you not act in power?)—issues in an imperative, "Make an end!" (v. 11b).[6] The imperatives continue in verses 18–23; they include "Remember!" (vv. 18, 22), "Rise up!" (v. 22), and "Do not forget!" (v. 23). The first in this series of imperatives, "Remember!" (v. 18), echoes verse 2, "Remember your community," but the exhortation in verse 18 continues by urging the Lord—YHWH—to remember that "the enemy taunts, and a senseless people reviles your name." The lamenting questions, "Why?" in verses 1 and 11a, and the plea for God to remember in verses 2 and 18 (and 22), join with the plea for God/YHWH to act in 11b and 18–23 in framing the confession of an individual in verses 12–17—an individual who *does* remember, and who reminds God of God's primordial (*miqqedem*) deeds as King and (hence) Creator, acts of creation performed against primordial forces.

The psalm describes these forces as aquatic in nature (Ps 74:13–15):

> It was you[7] who divided by your might Sea (*yām*);
> You smashed the heads of the dragon[8] on the waters.
> It was you who crushed the heads of Leviathan (*liwyātān*);
> You gave him as food to wild animals.
> It was you who broke open well and stream.
> It was you who dried up rivers (*nahărôt*) ever-flowing.

It may seem surprising that the psalm, rather than urging God to act against contemporary and imperial military forces, instead recalls God's primordial action against mythological chaotic forces and urges God to that kind of action in the present. The destruction wreaked by a mundane historical force, Babylon's army, returns to view subsequently (v. 18). But the situation described in the psalm's first section (74:1b–11) is one in which, because of God's wrath and, hence, absence (v. 9), chaotic, anti-creation powers appear to have prevailed. The psalm's speaker in verses 12–15 thus reminds God that it was *you* who brought about cosmic order in the first place, and only *you*—acting again as Creator, on behalf of your people and

---

for Urim, line 1. ETCSLtranslation : t.2.2.2, http://etcsl.orinst.ox.ac.uk/cgi-bin/etcsl.cgi?text=t.2.2.2&charenc=j#.

6. On the verb here, see Hossfeld and Zenger, *Psalms 2*, 240–41.

7. The emphatic independent personal pronoun, "You," occurs repeatedly in this passage, and my wooden translation aims to reflect this and other features of the Hebrew syntax.

8. I understand the plural *tannînîm* as intensive, with Joüon §136f.

your dwelling—can restore it in the calamitous present, when chaotic forces prevail.

The psalm's deployment of aquatic imagery to name the chaotic forces—e.g., sea, dragon, Leviathan, river(s)—draws on a long antecedent tradition. Texts from Ugarit, centuries earlier, attest this imagery, including one in which the goddess Anat speaks (*KTU* 1.3 iii–iv.38–42):

> Did I not strike El's beloved, Yam [sea]?
> Did I not finish off Nahar [river], god of the great waters?[9]
> Did I not muzzle the dragon . . . ?
> I struck the twisting serpent,
> The coiled one of seven heads.

All of the aquatic objects of God's primordial action in Ps 74:13–14 were deities, or their personified powers, in the Ugaritic texts.[10] Those texts also name Leviathan—the twisting, coiled, seven-headed serpent (*KTU* 5.1.1)—who also appears in Isa 27:1:

> On that day, YHWH will punish with his hard, great, and
>   strong sword
> Leviathan the slithering serpent,
> Leviathan the twisting serpent,
> And the dragon that is in the sea (*yām*).

What Ps 74 *remembers* as God's primordial action as Creator, and urges God to repeat in the chaotic present, Isa 27:1 *promises* as YHWH's eschatological act "on that day." Both draw on the language of Canaan in speaking of God as Creator.[11] They do so because achieving creation, or restoring it, entails the displacement of Canaan's gods. The rhetoric of Ps 74:13–14, with its repeated "It was *you*," testifies to the latter point. *Canaan* is, of course, a metaphor.

The Targum, or Aramaic translation/interpretation, to Psalms inter-prets Ps 74:13–14 in reference to the crossing of the sea in the exodus, so that the dragon of verse 13 is explained as the Egyptians, and the Masoretic Text's "heads of Leviathan," in verse 14, become in the Targum "the heads of

---

9. Taking *rbm* as elliptical for *mym rbm,* "mighty waters." See Smith, "Baal Cycle," in *Ugaritic Narrative Poetry,* 168n67, and see below, on Ps 77:20.

10. Exactly what counts as a deity or a god, or what *god* means, in ancient texts is less obvious than we tend to assume. See regarding Mesopotamia, for example, Barbara Nevling Porter, *What Is a God?* At Ugarit, Yam (*yammu*)—i.e., Sea—was included in the "assembly of gods" and received sacrifices (*KTU* 1.148.9).

11. As does the Apocalypse, in Rev 12:3; 13:1; 17:3, 7, 9, speaking of the dragon or beast with seven heads.

the soldiers of Pharaoh." This appropriation of the so-called *Chaoskampf*[12] to the exodus narrative, and especially to the poetic rendering of it in Exod 15, occurs within the OT itself, as in Ps 77, which, like Ps 74, opens with a complaint to God about God's absence or forgetfulness (vv. 2–10) and proceeds to recall God's acts in the past. Again, the imagery is aquatic: the waters saw God, and the deeps (*těhōmôt*) quaked (v. 16). Storm imagery follows, with lightning and thunder and earthquake, before the sea (*yām*) and "mighty waters" (*mayim rabbîm*) appear, in verse 20. While these references echo both Ps 74 and the Ugaritic Baal Cycle, here in Ps 77 the imagery is expressly oriented to the crossing of the sea in the exodus, as verse 21 makes explicit: "You led your people like a flock by the hand of Moses and Aaron." All of this displays God's strength, the work of God's arm/power (vv. 15–16).

While the aquatic imagery of Ps 77 lacks an explicit association of redemption (v. 16) with creation, their combination is explicit in Isa 51:9–11. There, the same "arm" of the Lord is urged to awake and put on strength, and once again the reference is to the past (v. 9). In that primordial past (*kîmê qedem dōrôt 'ôlāmîm*), "Was it not you who cut in pieces *rahab* and who pierced the dragon?" (v. 9). Rahab (*rahab*, masculine gender)—not to be confused with the prostitute Rahab (*rāhāb*) of Josh 2, who aided Joshua and Israel's conquest of Jericho—can be taken as the equivalent of Leviathan. Further, the rhetorical question, "Was it not you?" is equivalent to the repeated "It was *you*" of Ps 74, both of which deny the rhetorical character of—and answer no to—the repeated question, "Did not I?" of the Ugaritic text quoted above.[13]

GENESIS 1, CONTRA?

In their portrayal of God's action as Creator, the texts I have quoted from Psalms and Isaiah differ from, and can seem to be at odds with, the pacific, nonviolent, sometimes merely *verbal*, oracular way in which God brings about an ordered world in Gen 1 (or in Ps 33:4–7). J. Richard Middleton has stressed the differences, pitting Gen 1 against the *contra chaos* texts and granting Gen 1 normative status. His argument on behalf of this grant is

12. The existence in the OT of a *Chaoskampf* (battle against chaos) motif, first advanced by Gunkel, has been debated for decades. Molin denied its existence in 1977, "Motiv vom Chaoskampf," 13–28. Tsumura mounts more recent criticisms in 2005, *Creation and Destruction*.

13. Ugaritic lacks an interrogative particle of the sort that appears in the Hebrew of Isa 51:10. The Ugaritic particle *la*, which begins each sentence I translated "Did I not?" could also be interpreted as an asseverative, "Surely I did." In either case, it is a strong affirmation.

twofold: (1) The infrequent biblical depiction of God battling against and conquering, or sometimes subduing, the forces of chaos "seems to enshrine violence as the quintessential divine action." (2) The portrayal of God as thus engaged in combat "is highly problematic for those who believe that the canonical portrayal of God ought to be paradigmatic for the human exercise of power."[14]

We need linger over argument (1) only long enough to point out the non sequitur: it hardly follows from the fact of biblical depictions of God's battle against chaos that these enshrine divine violence as the essential divine action (leaving aside the clichéd "quintessential"). In Ps 74, the governing conception is of God "working salvation on [in the midst of] the earth" (v. 12b). The same conception, related expressly to the primordial and paradigmatic exodus, governs both Ps 77 and Isa 51. All three texts, along with Isa 27:1, enshrine the reality that "working salvation" or achieving an exodus—primordially, historically, or eschatologically—is neither a merely human possibility nor one accomplished against merely mundane powers. Against cosmic powers—on behalf of creation, on behalf of salvation, on behalf of Israel, and on behalf of God's own self—God, in these biblical texts, performs acts we see as violent, though the Bible calls them great acts of judgment/justice. The object—the victim—of those actions is water. But Ps 74 employs ancient mythological language and imagery in depicting water as a force, a cosmic power hostile to God and creation, a power that has mundane allies and agents, a power that God—Israel's God and no other— defeated (or took captive) in establishing the world's order (primordially against powers and their agents that appear in the NT), and an order that Ps 74:16–17 describes and ascribes to God. Creation-and-salvation is the essential divine action.

Middleton's second argument—the portrayal of God engaged in combat "is highly problematic for those who believe that the canonical portrayal of God ought to be paradigmatic for the human exercise of power"—evokes a mixed response. Yes, the portrayal of God engaged in combat poses a problem for those believing that

(a) "the canonical portrayal of God ought to be paradigmatic for the human exercise of power"; and that

(b) the "canonical portrayal of God"—apart from the *contra chaos* texts— provides such a noncombative, nonviolent divine paradigm.

But we should rush to embrace neither (a) nor (b).

Regarding (a): the canonical texts do not offer a uniform view of the relationship between God's "exercise of power" and that of humans. The

14. Middleton, "Created in the Image of a Violent God?" 342.

two cannot be systematically correlated in such a way that God's exercise of power could be uniformly paradigmatic. In many instances the relationship is asymmetrical: God's exercise of power stands in an asymmetrical relation to the action(s) required of humans.[15] Exodus 14 serves as an example. In verses 13–14, in the context of the exodus and countering the people's fear and their complaints, Moses instructs the Israelites, "Do not fear, stand by, and witness the salvation of YHWH. . . . YHWH will fight on your behalf." It bears mentioning that the following poetic account, in Exod 15, employs language and imagery familiar from the biblical *contra chaos* texts, and from Ugarit, but in such a way that the sea, rather than an enemy to be conquered, is instead Yahweh's ally in conquering the Egyptians. Returning to Exod 14, the end of the chapter reports that the Israelites did indeed witness the salvation of Yahweh against the power (hand) of Pharaoh (v. 30)—that they did witness the "mighty power" (hand) of Yahweh, and that they both feared and "had faith" (*wayya'ămînû*) in Yahweh—and in his servant, Moses (v. 31).

This faith or belief or trust in God becomes, in Isaiah, a positive injunction (e.g., Isa 7:9b) by way of stressing the asymmetrical, even antithetical, relation between God's exercise of power and the action—faith/trust (Isa 28:12; 30:15) and, thus, the practice of justice (1:16–17; 14:32)—required of Judah's nobility. In Isaiah, God the King acts as Zion's creator and defender in exercising what I have called God's "exclusive prerogative."[16] It is exclusive precisely in reserving to Yahweh alone the prerogative to secure Zion's defense. Above, commenting on the *contra chaos* texts, I remarked that "working salvation" is not, at least in their context and conception, a human possibility. That impossibility comes to count also as a proscription against the myth of God as simply paradigmatic of or for the human exercise of power. God, who says "vengeance is mine" (Deut 32:35; Rom 12:19; Heb 10:30), is not subject to such a simplistic and anthropocentric reduction and projection. The portrayal of God acting violently against chaotic forces (Isa 8:9–10; 10:24–34; 17:12–14), while proscribing superficially prudential measures of national security (Isa 22:8–11; 30:1–3; 31:1–3), may be problematic, and on more than one level, but it is thoroughly canonical. And it is, definitively, *not* paradigmatic for the exercise of human power. In this vein, Willard Swartley refers to the "offense of this category distinction between God's prerogative and our obedience," urging us not to stumble over it.[17]

15. Lind, *Yahweh Is a Warrior.*

16. Ollenburger, *Zion,* chap. 4.

17. Swartley, *Covenant of Peace,* 398.

Early in this essay I asked: What is violence? Does Gen 1 avoid it? Genesis 1:2 names a totality—the earth—devoid of life and hostile to it, a severe emptiness. About the earth, nothing more can be said here. Earth can only be named and equated with a vacuous void, whether like that of a lifeless desert (cf. Deut 32:10) or of an equally lifeless, damp, unformed mess. As this totality, the earth lacks both universals and particulars; it is without individuals or substances or accidents. The KJV's rendering of *tōhû wābōhû* as "formless and void" captures its sense (or its character as absence), except that the component terms are nouns, not adjectives. The totality earth cannot—yet—be described by adjectives or by phrases, not yet having been created. *This—tōhû wābōhû*—the earth then "was."[18]

The verse (Gen 1:2) continues with reference to an encompassing *darkness* over the *deep*, and the wind (power/force) of God sweeping over the *waters*. The terms in italics name (non)entities that, in this context, stand (as it were) in the way of creation, including precisely the creation of earth. They do not mount active opposition; they are not here actors, as Leviathan and Rahab, Sea and River(s) may be imagined to be—to have been—in the Psalms and Isaiah and Job. They stand, inert, in the way. But already among them, in the stasis of un-creation, and immediately over the waters, sweeps an alien and disruptive force, the *rûaḥ ʾĕlōhîm*—the spirit/power/wind of God. The participial form of the verb (*mĕraḥepet*, "sweeping"), combined with the vocabulary and complex syntax of Gen 1:1–3, suggests that the Elohim to which *rûaḥ* is bound as the subject of the participle is the same Elohim named in verse 1, and that the "sweeping" of Elohim's *rûaḥ* is incipient of the creation (*bārāʾ*) announced in verse 1 and inaugurated verbally—orally—by Elohim's initial and initiating speech (v. 3). That speech, Elohim's self-directed "Let there be light," marks and constitutes an imperious, imperial—a sovereign—and violent interruption in, and intervention against, the inchoate and static totality that Elohim proceeds to invade. Darkness is not annihilated, and neither the deep nor the waters. But the anti-creation stasis, the life-inhibiting silence that they constituted, along with the earth's then being *tōhû wābōhû*—all of this is conquered by the violence of speech. As Rolf Rendtorff puts it: "The 'weapon' God employs in Gen 1 is the word."[19] It is the violence of God's speech, then also God's consequent actions of making and dividing, separating—forming particulars, individuals, bodies, substances, organisms, and binary oppositions as well—that destroy the silent and, in its own totalizing way, violent stasis of *tōhû wābōhû* and darkness and the deep and the waters, and brings about

---

18. The copula with a temporal sense (Joüon §154m).
19. Rendtorff, *Theologie des Alten Testaments*, 2:8.

in its (not their!) stead a dynamic, lively, life-filled earth, both habitable and inhabited, the subject of infinite adjectives and phrases.

The proffered contrast between the *contra chaos* texts and Gen 1, on the subject of violence, fails to present us with a purely nonviolent portrait of God in the latter. The richly mythological and poetic depiction of God the Creator in Ps 74, drawing on the language of Canaan, makes its violence graphic and dramatic, in the manner of a cartoon. The poetic and liturgically constructed Priestly account in Gen 1, with its forward glance into history, exhibits its own violence. By what means, what instrument, what weapon did God the Creator crush and smash mythic, monstrous, aquatic heads (Ps 74:13–14)—heads and (a) dragon(s), *tannînîm*, that Gen 1:21 says God *created*—and what is the "hard, great, and strong sword" of Yahweh (Isa 27:1) but God's, the aniconic YHWH's, *speech*? The promised shoot and branch from Jesse will rule justly on behalf of the poor and oppressed, and (just so?) will also "strike the earth with the rod of his mouth, and by the power [*rûaḥ*] of his lips he will slay the wicked" (Isa 11:1, 4). This *messianic* capacity both to rule justly and to strike the earth with mouth and lips—with speech—to directed, lethal effect, derives from the endowment of the *messianic* shoot/branch with God's spirit and power—with the *rûaḥ yhwh* (Isa 11:2).[20] That same spirit, that wind, that force . . . was it not sweeping over the waters at creation? Was it not the same "spirit" that rested on the speaker in Isa 61:1–2 and on Jesus in Luke 4:18–19? The power signified by *rûaḥ*, the spirit of God, is that of God's speech, God's word, which does what God desires and brings about that for which God sends it (Isa 55:10). It is sharper than any sword (Heb 4:12; cf. Eph 6:17). It crushed primordially—will crush eschatologically—the heads of Leviathan, and it pierced a dark and life-denying stasis—*earth*—with light and life.

IN PLACE OF A CONCLUSION

In consequence of this *tu quoque* (more precisely, *id quoque*) response— "But so is Genesis 1!"—to criticism of the *contra chaos* texts and their violent imagery, I make two suggestions. First, neither the resistance of Leviathan nor the stasis of *tōhû wābōhû* is "self-cancelling," to borrow a term from Miroslav Volf.[21] I have employed the Greek term *stasis,* because it can refer to "the rest, pause, halt, or standing still . . . in-between opposite 'changes' and in-between contrary motions, movements, processes, functions, or forces in

---

20. Cf. Rev 19:5, which combines the sword of the servant's mouth (Isa 49:2) with the "rod of iron" from Ps 2:9.

21. Volf, *Exclusion and Embrace,* 298. Volf uses the term with reference to evil.

action"[22] (cf. the LXX in Deut 28:65; Josh 10:13), and also to active dissent, opposition, sedition, or insurrection (Mark 15:7 and Luke 23:18–19, 25, re: Barabbas; Acts 15:2). God's action as Creator can thus be considered an intervention against *stasis* in both Ps 74 and Gen 1, which describes creation, not simply *ex nihilo*, but *contra nihilo*: against the power of nothing—the power of darkness (*ek tēs exousias tou skotous* Col 1:13).

Second, contemporary theologians ranging from Miroslav Volf to David Bentley Hart, and from Wolfhart Pannenberg to John Milbank, have insisted, on various grounds, including Trinitarian ones, on an original situation of peace . . . of peaceful creation. Bentley Hart, for example, refers to "the myth of chaos" and acknowledges that "some biblical language" could lend support to this myth, this "picture." But he insists on the difference between "God's transcendent act of giving being to what is not"—that is, creation—and, on the other hand, "the oscillating play of finitude's forms and forces within creation (especially fallen creation)."[23] These remarks return us to the beginning. Nothing in the Bible stands in the way of original peace, or of God's *transcendent* act of giving being to what was not. But the Bible presents God the Creator creating—acting as Creator—*in medias res*: in the midst of things from the beginning . . . a beginning also defined by God's creating. At the same time, the Bible refuses—so its human voices refuse—abstraction and distraction that would reduce horror and tragedy and profound evil to "the oscillating play of finitude's forms and forces within creation," in defense of God.

God is indeed the God of peace (Rom 15:33, etc.), in creation and in providence. And "the God of peace will soon [*en tachei*] crush Satan under your feet" (Rom 16:20). This head-crushing God of peace . . . this is *God*? Indeed.

---

22. Loeb Dieter, "Stasis," 241.

23. Hart, *Beauty of the Infinite,* 257.

4

"YHWH Is a Warrior" Reevaluated

(Exodus 15:3)

Andrea Dalton Saner

Millard Lind's *Yahweh Is a Warrior* remains a significant work of OT scholarship. In it, Lind argues that the confession "YHWH is a warrior" (Exod 15:3) shaped Israel's political structure and approach to warfare. But what of the reference to the divine name in this verse? In an attempt to shed light on some of the theological issues involved in making the claim that "YHWH is a warrior; YHWH is his name"[1] I offer a canonical reworking of Lind's reading of the Song at the Sea (Exod 15). Seen from a canonical perspective and as commentary on the divine name, this statement is secondary to the texts of Exod 3:14–15 and 34:6–7. Furthermore, these texts have in view both God's self-revelation and the nature of true human response to that revelation. This does not negate, but rather enhances, our understanding of theological language as "reality depicting."[2]

---

1. Biblical quotations are from the NRSV, although I have substituted "YHWH" for "Lord" here for clarity and for continuity with Lind's title. Additionally, though it has become conventional for Christians to write out, and pronounce, the name "Yahweh," I have retained the four consonants in translation as a reminder that the Hebrew text handles this name uniquely, with great reverence.

2. Soskice, *Metaphor and Religious Language.*

EXODUS 15 AS A FOUNDATIONAL WITNESS

Lind summarizes his main points as follows: "(1) that Yahweh as God of war fought for his people by miracle, not by sword and spear; (2) that this method of Yahweh's fighting affected Israel's theo-political structure in a fundamental way; and (3) that Yahweh's warfare was directed not only against Israel's enemies but at times against Israel herself, in such cases not by means of miracle but by the armies of Israel's enemies."[3] In support of these points, Lind argues that the Reed Sea traditions of Exod 14 and 15 are vital for the development of political structure in Israel. These texts attest to the Lord's victory through a miracle of the natural world, while Israel keeps still. Throughout the periods of judges and kingship, the Reed Sea conviction remained alive: even when Israel fought, she did so ineffectively, for only Yahweh can secure victory.

Further, against the contemporary trend in OT scholarship,[4] Lind argues that Israel's understanding of holy war dates very early, to the experience of the Exodus and the writing of Exod 15 within a century of that experience.[5] Lind proceeds historically, from the Reed Sea traditions and the rest of Exodus; through conquest texts, the book of Judges and Davidic traditions; to later kingship and prophetic texts (including Gen 1–11). He then concludes with the Deuteronomic writings. Throughout, Lind argues that the normative witness of Israel to Yahweh as warrior and the appropriate political structure that stems from this witness continue throughout these diverse periods in Israel's history, even as the witness becomes muffled by kings who hire private, standing militias and disregard limits on monarchal power.

As a historical argument, Lind's work could be critiqued. The poems in Exod 15 could be ancient, but arguing that is a matter of distinguishing between true archaic forms and later writing that employs archaisms for stylistic reasons,[6] and of determining the referent of the Lord's dwelling place in verses 13 and 17.[7] Lind follows Freedman in arguing for a rather early

---

3. Lind, *Yahweh Is a Warrior,* 23.

4. These "Type A Interpretations" include those of Schwally, Pedersen, von Rad, and Miller. Ibid., 24.

5. Ibid., 47.

6. Dozeman, *Commentary on Exodus,* 336–37.

7. Houtman, *Exodus,* 2:241–42.

date,[8] though the text has led other scholars to propose later dates ranging from the time of David/Solomon[9] to *ca.* 200 BCE.[10]

Even if Lind's dating of Exod 15:1–21 does not hold, his reading could be reframed canonically. Regardless of whether poetic and narrative accounts of the sea crossing were written early in Israel's history, these witnesses were placed in a foundational context in the OT canon. For this reason, these texts remain important for reflection on the theological basis for political structures in Israel. Moreover, Lind's work lends itself to such reworking.[11] Though Lind is interested in a diachronic approach, he often attends to large segments of text, resisting the tendency of diachronic criticisms to divide texts into smaller and smaller units for consideration. For example, Lind strays from the standard approach of dividing 1 Sam 8–12 into "anti-kingship" (8:4–22; 10:17–27; 11:14—12:25) and "pro-kingship" sources (9:1—10:16; 11:1–13).[12] He follows Tsevat[13] in seeing the components of the story as a unit, moving between meetings (8:4–22; 10:17–27; 11:14—12:25) in which the issues are discussed, and actions (9:1—10:16; 11:1–13). Rather than viewing the text as a compilation of politically divergent sources, Lind perceives its literary coherence.[14] Likewise, on the subject of the Exodus, Lind emphasizes the point on which the J and P narratives agree: that "the action was that of Yahweh alone who by an act of nature delivered his people from the Egyptian army."[15] Though Lind acknowledges that the written traditions of the OT had long and complex histories, he not infrequently suggests that the enduring voice of the text is that of its received form.

8. Lind, *Yahweh Is a Warrior,* 47.

9. Gressmann, *Mose und Seine Zeit,* 408.

10. Strauss, "Das Meerlied Des Moses—Ein 'Siegeslied' Israels?" For a range of dates later than Lind's, see de Vaux, "Revelation of the Divine Name YHWH," 242.

11. This point holds despite the fact that in a canonical reorientation, Deuteronomic materials and Gen 1–11 would need to be addressed at points in the book other than where they currently stand.

12. Lind, *Yahweh Is a Warrior,* 100.

13. Tsevat, "Biblical Narrative."

14. Lind, *Yahweh Is a Warrior,* 100.

15. Ibid., 55.

EXODUS 15:3 IN CANONICAL PERSPECTIVE[16]

Lind's reading of Exod 15 is rich in many respects. He describes well the character of the Lord's victory and its effect on the concepts of holy war, kingship, and Israel's relationship with her neighbors. The Lord's victory is complete and comes without any action on Israel's part. This poem employs the ancient Near Eastern vocabulary of holy war, but alters it; the words no longer call to mind only ancient Near Eastern mythology, but also recall the particular experience of the Exodus. Furthermore, "Yahweh the warrior becomes Yahweh the king" (v. 18).[17] However, the relationship between God and king developed differently in Israel than in the rest of the ancient Near East. The Lord's exclusive action and victory in Exod 15 suggest Israelite rejection of human kingship. Lind writes that "outside of Israel the experience of divinity in history was god *and* king. Within Israel the experience of divinity in history was Yahweh *versus* king."[18] If God is king, then there is no other king in Israel (cf. Judg 8:23; 1 Sam 8:19–20).

Though Lind's emphasis on political structure in Israel is fruitful, such a narrow focus causes Lind to ignore important elements of the text, elements that might help one explore "What, in short, is the theological significance, as the Old Testament views it, of portraying even Yahweh as a warrior?"[19] Exodus 15:3 reads not only, *yhwh 'yš mlḥmh* ("YHWH is a warrior") but also, *yhwh šmw* ("YHWH is his name"). However, Lind does not mention the second half of the verse. He argues that the ancient Near Eastern concept of God as a warrior differs significantly from the OT witness, but the next step would be to ask: How does this transformed understanding of the divine warrior fit within the context of other statements about God in the OT? What is the nature of the reference to the divine name in this text, and how might it influence our understanding of the Lord as a warrior?

Taken as a whole, Exod 15:3 invites the reader to consider Yahweh as a warrior within the context of other references to the divine name in the

16. By *canonical perspective,* I mean that which considers first the received form of the biblical text. Because of limitations of space in this essay, I attend only to the most immediate context of the book of Exodus; a more thorough analysis would consider references to the divine name elsewhere in the Pentateuch, OT, and two-testament Scripture.

17. Ibid., 50.

18. Ibid., 52; emphasis original.

19. Miller, Review of *Yahweh Is a Warrior*, 394. Miller's point, in light of Schleitheim, is that the sword has a purpose outside the rule of Christ; Lind does not seem to consider this.

book of Exodus. These references are manifold,[20] but two crucial texts are Exod 3:13–15 and 34:5–7. To these we now turn.

EXODUS 3:13–15

In his question (v. 13), Moses seems to request more information, either about how the people are to address God, or about God's character.[21] The response that follows gives both the name—"YHWH"—and an explanation of the name; this response suggests an application beyond the immediate context of Moses's mission. Thus Walter Moberly identifies the question as a form of "child's question,"[22] which is intended to instruct future generations of Israelites. Indeed the verse seems to present the question of under what name—what understanding of God's nature—the Israelites will be able to trust God not only to deliver them from Egypt but to continue to deliver them, post-Egypt.[23]

The forms in both verse 14a (*'hyh 'šr 'hyh*, "I am who I am" or "I will be who I will be"[24]) and verse 14b (*'hyh*, "I am" or "I will be") resonate with the language of 3:12 and 4:12, implying again that the Lord will be with Moses. However, 3:14 suggests much more than this. The *idem per idem* formula

20. In Exodus, texts that refer to the name of Yahweh, either through the use of *šm* ("name") in reference to Yahweh, or through a phrase that emphasizes the being or action of Yahweh under this name, include also 5:2; 6:3; 7:5, 17; 8:10 [Heb. 8:6], 22 [Heb. v. 18]; 9:14, 16, 29; 10:2; 12:12; 14:4, 18; 15:3, 11, 26; 16:12; 20:2, 5, 7; 23:21; 29:45–46; 33:19; 34:14.

21. If the author(s) believed that the Hebrews did not know the name Yahweh prior to the time of Moses, then perhaps this question is merely a means of introducing the issue. However, in keeping with our canonical approach, we will not address whether the Israelites knew the name YHWH prior to the time of Moses, or whether source distinctions adequately account for the continuities or discontinuities between this text, Exod 6:2–3, and, e.g., Gen 4:26. For readings that deal with these questions while attending to the final form of the text, see Moberly, *Old Testament;* and Seitz, "Call of Moses."

22. Moberly, *Old Testament,* 20.

23. The wider narrative demonstrates that the purpose of deliverance from Egypt is a particular type of freedom: freedom to be the people of God, worshiping God in accordance with the law. Yahweh's command to Pharaoh gives purpose to their freedom: "Let my people go, so that they may worship me" (Exod 7:16; 8:1 [Heb 7:26], 20 [Heb 8:16]; 9:1; 10:3; cf. 5:1), and thus the revelation at Sinai fulfills the revelation at Horeb (Exod 3:12).

24. Some scholars have argued that the most natural translation of the MT of v. 14a is "I am the one who is," as in the LXX *egō eimi ho ōn*, but this is not a majority opinion. See Lindblom, "Noch Einmal die Deutung"; Schild, "On Exodus III 14"; de Vaux, "The Revelation of the Divine Name YHWH," 69. For critique of this translation, see Albrektson, "Words and Meanings."

is used, according to S. R. Driver, "where either the means, or the desire, to be more explicit does not exist" (e.g., Exod 16:23 and 33:19).[25] In this case, God is attempting to explain something that is profound, if not inexpressible. "I will be who I will be" is not sheer open-endedness or arbitrariness but true freedom; God will be who God chooses to be. Further, the *idem per idem* formula, much like the cognate accusative, adds emphasis to the statement.[26] However, the use of *hyh* ("to be") is wordplay, or paronomasia, not etymology, because it is not clear that *yhwh* ("YHWH," v. 15) is from this root.[27] At the level of interpretation or commentary, rather than definition or etymology, repetition of *'hyh* ("I will be") in verse 14 suggests that this term is not merely rhetorical but also substantially significant.[28]

So, in what sense should we understand verse 14 as suggesting that the name of God has something to do with being? Perhaps we cannot be more specific than to say that, in the sense of "being with," God is profoundly *for* the Hebrew people while simultaneously existing in perfect freedom, as the only one who can determine God's own being and name. As Karl Barth eloquently writes of "I am who I am,"

> There is therefore no objective definition that we can discover for ourselves. We might say of this revelation of His name that it consists in the refusal of a name, but even in the form of this substantial refusal it is still really revelation, communication and illumination. For Yahweh means the Lord, the I who gives Himself to be known in that He exists as the I of the Lord and therefore acts only as a He and can be called upon only as a Thou in His action, without making Himself known in His I-ness as if He were a creature.[29]

God is known only by self-revelation, only by being personally involved—as subject, not as object—in human recognition of God.

The text of verse 15 looks both back, to the patriarchs, and forward, to the coming generations. Here, the name YHWH, only alluded to in verse 14, is given and identified with the God of Abraham, Isaac, and Jacob; Yahweh is none other than the God of Abraham's family. Whether the intended subject of verse 15b is simply "YHWH" or the longer "YHWH, the God of your

---

25. Driver, *Notes on the Hebrew Text*, 185–86. Cf. Joüon §158O.

26. Moberly, *Old Testament*, 77.

27. As Beitzel demonstrates, there is no consensus on the root of YHWH. Beitzel, "Exodus 3:14 and the Divine Name"; *contra* de Vaux, "The Revelation of the Divine Name YHWH," 67.

28. Freedman, "Name of the God of Moses,"153; Moberly, *Old Testament*, 77.

29. Barth, *Church Dogmatics*, 2/1:61.

fathers, the God of Abraham, the God of Isaac, and the God of Jacob" is of little consequence, for the longer form is understood in the name itself; Yahweh *is* the God of the fathers. This name will be the name by which the people will call on God forever.

Thus the movement from verse 14 to verse 15 is one from divine freedom to manifestation, from hiddenness to accessibility. The God who is known as subject can nevertheless be called on; yet calling on this God ought never become manipulation or conjuring, as it is contingent on God's will. Moreover, that divine freedom is the subject of the initial answer may suggest that this is not a qualification of the Lord's responsiveness to his people but rather the reason for it. The Lord will choose whom the Lord will choose, and the Lord's will to deliver Israel is not dependent on anything outside himself. Moses should have confidence in this mission because Yahweh, who is ultimately free, stands behind it.

EXODUS 34:5–7

In response to Moses's request to see the glory of the Lord (Exod 33:18), God says that he will declare the name "YHWH" before Moses (Exod 33:19). In Exod 34:5–7 this promise is fulfilled, but only after the nature of this revelation has been qualified: since "no one shall see [the Lord] and live" (33:19b), the Lord will protect Moses from seeing God's face, but Moses will be able to see God's back (33:20–23). The text suggests that these statements are metaphorical, since God is not concretely, physically manifest (as in, e.g., Gen 18 and 32).[30] Even if "face" and "back" govern the qualification in chapter 33, the revelation in chapter 34 is much more concerned with the name and Yahweh's character. Moreover, the metaphor presents a series of allusions: "face" refers to how the Lord will lead Israel (33:14) and foreshadows the shining of Moses's face (34:29ff.), and "back" is the obvious counterpoint to "face."[31]

In Exod 34:5, the revelatory moment begins with a descending cloud, which is associated with the glory of the Lord in Exodus (16:10; 40:34–38). The remainder of verse 5 can be read as a heading for what follows in verses 6–7, indicating that this declaration is constitutive of Yahweh proclaiming the name "YHWH."[32] The Lord then proclaims the name "YHWH" twice,

---

30. On Gen 18 and 32, see Hamori, *When Gods Were Men.*

31. Moberly, *At the Mountain of God,* 82.

32. I take Moberly to be correct that Yahweh is the subject of *wyqr'* in both v. 5 and v. 6. Ibid., 86; cf. Cassuto, *Commentary on the Book of Exodus,* 439. Though Childs suggests that an earlier version of the narrative had Moses as the subject of both verbs

perhaps for emphasis, and as a confessional statement.[33] To Cassuto, the double statement, not unlike the "I am who I am" of 3:14a, suggests that "it is impossible to define His nature in any other words."[34] The Lord declares the formula,[35] as in Exod 3:14–15, but different from 15:3.

The end of Exod 34:6 repeats the terms of 33:19b, "a God merciful and gracious." Further, "YHWH" is "slow to anger, and abounding in steadfast love and faithfulness" (34:6b). In contrast to the form the confession takes in Exod 20:5–6, here the merciful elements are placed first, in extended form, as they are the more prominent features of the declaration in this context. Further, in the Decalogue, the primary contrast is between those who keep the commandments and those who do not. However, chapter 34 emphasizes the Lord's character rather than human obedience. On the one hand, Yahweh is "keeping steadfast love for the thousandth generation" and "forgiving iniquity and transgression and sin," and on the other, "yet by no means clearing the guilty, but visiting the iniquity of the parents upon the children and the children's children, to the third and the fourth generation" (34:7). Rightfully, the Decalogue forefronts obedience to the commandments; however, when these commandments have been broken (chap. 32), the issue turns exclusively to God's character.

Though the Lord's compassion and forgiveness are highlighted, his judgment is not ignored. Why not? On the basis that theological speech includes an element of faith (namely, appropriate human response to divine revelation), Moberly describes the role of the reference to punishment, in this text, as working "to clarify that YHWH's forgiveness is truly forgiveness, not leniency, still less moral indifference."[36] If God will always forgive, then obedience is unnecessary—such an attitude could not be held by one with an adequate understanding of the nature of God. God is fundamentally merciful, but his mercy is not truly confessed if it is presumed upon (cf. Rom 6:1–2). Rather, "the unparalleled emphasis upon divine mercy and forgiveness is simultaneously accompanied by an implicit control to prevent the words from being misunderstood and misused."[37] God's self-revelation

in v. 5, he concedes that the flow of the current narrative suggests Yahweh is the subject of v. 5b. Childs, *Book of Exodus*, 603.

33. Durham, *Exodus*, 453.

34. Cassuto, *Commentary on the Book of Exodus*, 439.

35. From a form-critical perspective, Dentan observes that, as a third-person declaration, the formula is liturgical, and could have originally been from the perspective of an individual worshiper. Dentan, "Literary Affinities," 37. Yet in this literary context, Yahweh is clearly the speaker.

36. Moberly, "How May We Speak of God?" 200.

37. Ibid.

to Moses concerns not only what one can rightly say of God but also guidance for human response to this revelation.

READING EXODUS 15:3 WITH EXODUS 3:13–15 AND 34:5–7

Our canonical reading has shown that *"YHWH is a warrior" is not the primary understanding of God's name offered in Exodus.* While Exod 15:3 mentions the divine name, the text does not try to explore the meaning or nature of the name, as do Exod 3:13–15 and 34:6–7. The literary phenomenon of the question in 3:13 and the dual pronouncement of the name in 34:6 (following the introduction in v. 5) heighten the reader's expectation of revelation regarding the name. The function of the name in 15:3 differs; "YHWH is a warrior" is not the proper name of God, nor is it offered as primary means for understanding the name.[38] Also, there are other literary indicators that 3:14–15 and 34:6–7 are more theologically significant texts than 15:3: the former are spoken by God on the mountain, the latter by Moses and the children of Israel at the sea.

Further, our canonical reading has demonstrated that *right speech about God guides particular types of responses.* Exodus 3:14–15 concerns not only the name of God but also how one can call on this name (not as an object to be manipulated but as acting, revealing subject). Likewise, we have argued that 34:6–7 has in view human response to God's mercy. This resonates with Lind's argument that "YHWH is a warrior" is foundational to political structure in Israel. The truth of the statement "YHWH is a warrior" includes a particular type of response to that truth—namely, that God's people must trust in the Lord to defend them, rather than amassing military power.[39]

However, these points require further clarification. I have suggested that Exod 3:13–15, 15:3, and 34:5–7 cultivate certain types of responses to God and critique other types of responses, while also referring to God directly. Put differently, through the texts, God speaks of God's own self.

---

38. The reference to the divine name in this verse seems to function emphatically; "warrior" truly describes something that is at the heart of who God is. Cf. "YHWH, whose name is Jealous" (Exod 34:14).

39. Exodus 15:3 is not about humans fighting in the name of Yahweh but about the nature of Yahweh as the one who fights for his people. *Contra* Houtman, who writes, "Only if one does battle in his name . . . can one confidently await the outcome" (*Exodus*, 2:280). Human warfare may be the context of the other text biblical texts that Houtman cites (Ps 20:1 [Heb. v. 2], 5 [Heb. v. 6]; 68:4 [Heb. v. 5]; 1 Sam 17:45–47; see also Isa 63:16), but it is not envisaged in Exodus 15.

Questions of reference and biblical interpretation are too great in number and significance to be resolved here, and yet they are felt acutely. Possible implications of the statement "YHWH is a warrior" seem in tension with the emphasis on divine mercy so prominent in chapter 34. Further, questions of reference arise from canonically reframing Lind's reading. While Lind could imagine that particular biblical texts refer to the faith of Israel at a particular point in its history, an approach that primarily considers the text in its received form both suggests and requires a different understanding of reference.[40] While I can only scratch the surface of the issues in this essay, I want to suggest that a realist approach to theological language is a valid possibility even in the case of reading Exod 15:3 as a call to trust in God rather than take up arms.

THEOLOGICAL LANGUAGE, METAPHOR, AND REALISM

In *Metaphor and Religious Language,* Soskice argues for a "critical realist" approach to religious language. Soskice wants to retain the traditional sense that theological language is "real" or "reality depicting." In other words, such language is not merely affective (that is, expressing human response, emotional or behavioral), but it identifies something that is true about God. In fact, it is the truth of theological language as "reality depicting" that gives it affective power.[41] Yet, Soskice avoids naïve realism by distinguishing between reality depiction and direct description,[42] claiming that "we do not claim to describe God but to point through His effects, and beyond His effects, to Him."[43] Our theological speech is never complete and ever open to the possibility of modification through further revelation. Despite being guided significantly by Scripture and tradition to use certain types of language about God, the Christian realist must admit to the possibility of being wrong or having one's mind changed.[44]

Moreover, speech about God genuinely depicts reality even as it is informed by the context in which it is spoken. For the Christian, this means

---

40. It is not fully satisfying to identify the primary sense of the text as self-referential, as constituting a narrative rather than pointing beyond itself. For one discussion of the challenges of reference facing narrative interpretation and postliberal theology, see Placher, "Paul Ricoeur and Postliberal Theology," 35–52.

41. Soskice, *Metaphor and Religious Language,* 109.

42. Ibid., 148.

43. Ibid., 140.

44. Ibid.

that any claim that "YHWH is a warrior" presumes the Exodus context, the prophets' conviction that the Lord fought even *against* Israel, and Christ's final conquering of evil. To apply Soskice's point about biblical metaphors to the example in question: "To explain what it means to Christians to say that God is [a warrior] requires an account not merely of [warriors], but of a whole tradition of experiences and of the literary tradition that records and interprets them."[45] Though metaphors can be used to say what one can say in no other way,[46] their meanings build over time through use in community. At the same time, this metaphor need not be understood in the sense of holy war,[47] because the metaphor is not directly descriptive; tradition can critique itself.[48]

Through commentary on the name of God, Exodus witnesses to Yahweh who is with Israel, responding when Israel cries out, delivering the Israelites from their enemies, and forgiving when Israel breaks the covenant. At the same time, the book names this God as one who cannot be manipulated or conjured, whose perfect freedom ultimately determines who God will be and how God will be known. In the context of this story and the faith communities that live by it, we can truly say "YHWH is a warrior; YHWH is his name," and in doing so, point to the God in whom we trust to protect and keep us in his love, even as we "keep still" (Exod 14:14).

45. Ibid., 158.

46. Ibid., 93–95.

47. I mean "holy war" in the sense of Cahill's criteria: "identification of violence with the Christian mission" and "self-righteous abandonment of restraint in war" (Cahill, *Love Your Enemies*, 123).

48. This point seems crucial for a church that believes in the reality of repentance and forgiveness.

5

Violence Added

A Study of Insertions of Violence into English Translations of the Hebrew Bible

Wilma Ann Bailey

For most of the two thousand-year history of the translation of the Bible, the task has been done by men who—by virtue of their education and place in the community—controlled the ways people understood and interpreted the text. In the case of the English Bible, until the second half of the twentieth century the dominant translations were products of the state church or mainline denominations, which also controlled the political structures and established the social norms in English-speaking societies. The translators were usually well-educated. They were also—by virtue of their station in life, class, and affluence—representatives of those in power and authority. Their mindset was the mindset of those who use their power to interpret texts in ways that support their worldview.

The thesis of this essay is that because of the worldview of the translators, the OT in some English translations has become more violent than the original Hebrew text. This is not to argue that there is no violence in the original text. There is plenty of that. Rather, it argues that translations—by the words chosen in translation—insert a greater degree of violence into some texts. This is significant because those insertions can cause a loss in nuance or shifts in the intent of the text. Additionally, the historic peace churches have never produced a Bible translation of their own, one reflecting the less violent worldview of those committed to peace and justice.

Typically, peace church persons read the Bible through the lens of dominant-denomination translators. The prevailing strategy of the peace churches vis-à-vis violent texts has been either to ignore them or to dismiss them as perhaps valid in a pre-Christian era—to accomplish the purposes of God—but no longer applicable to contemporary life.[1] These strategies assume that translator-interpreters are correct in a general sense. It also assumes that people were more violent in ancient times than today, and that we have evolved into more peaceful people, a stance recently articulated by Steven Pinker and Joshua S. Goldstein.[2] If the latter assumption is true, then the argument may be put forth that translating texts into violent language is justifiable because people were simply more violent in the past. But is it appropriate? As interpreters of ancient texts, we must first, to the greatest extent possible, try to read texts as the ancient readers and interpreters would have read them. The violence that we interpolate may not have been their intent. It may be our own.

A case in point is Jonah's sermon to the Ninevites in Jonah 3:4. In English translations, it becomes a dire warning. Translating into modern English, the Matthew Bible (1537) reads, "There are yet 40 days and then will Nineveh be overthrown."[3] The Geneva Bible (1560) proclaims, "Yet forty days and Nineveh shall be overthrown." The 1611 King James Version (KJV) continues the trend: "Yet forty days and Nineveh shall be overthrown." The Jewish Publication Society (JPS) version of 1985 translates, "Forty days more, and Nineveh shall be overthrown!" The Revised Standard Version (RSV) of 1952 interprets similarly, "Yet forty days and Nineveh will be overthrown!" The New Revised Standard Version (NRSV) of 1989 has: "Forty days more, and Nineveh shall be overthrown!" In contrast to these, the New International Version (NIV) reads, "Forty more days and Nineveh will be overturned." The latter lacks the exclamation point and the violence connected to the word *overthrown.* Although the NIV is in the minority, it is the better translation of the Hebrew word *nehpaket,* because it supports and anticipates the irony in the message. Nineveh will indeed be overturned, but not in the way that Jonah expects. All the people repent, so they are not destroyed. The "overthrown" translation can anticipate only one thing, the

---

1. See Handy, "Peaceful Kansas Mennonites," 29, 30.

2. Pinker, *Better Angels of Our Nature*; Goldstein, *Winning the War on War.*

3. See Table 5.1.

destruction of the city. The word *overturned* can be interpreted to mean "destroyed" or "converted." Jonah does not know what is going to happen, so he sits opposite the city to find out. This suggests that his sermon was ambiguous, uncertain, even to him. The book of Jonah is full of irony and humor. These nuances are lost in the dominant translations.

A longer text that tends to be translated into more violent language than the text warrants is Josh 6, often referred to as the "Battle of Jericho," a title that prejudices the interpretation of the story toward enhanced violence. Joshua 6 is preceded literarily by several ritual actions: circumcision, Passover, and the shedding of sandals before Yahweh's representative. The last is said to have taken place at Jericho. There Joshua sees a man standing before him with a drawn sword in hand. The image is of one who is prepared for aggression. Joshua asks whether the man is with "us" or with "our enemies." The man does not directly answer Joshua's question. Rather, he responds that he is a "leader of the host of Yahweh."[4] When Joshua asks for instructions about what he is to do, the man replies, "Strip your shoe from your feet because the place where you are standing is holy" (Josh 5:15). This is the same instruction given to Moses in his encounter at the burning bush (Exod 3:5). After Moses sheds his sandals, God self-identifies: "I am the God of your fathers, the God of Abraham, the God of Isaac, and the God of Jacob" (Exod 3:6). In the Joshua narrative, one is prepared for a similar declaration, but it came earlier. What Joshua expected to be a fight on the part of God's messenger is instead transformed into a ritual act.

Many scholars think that the Jericho narrative of Josh 6 was used as and intended to be a ritual, not an actual event,[5] commemorating the Israelite conquest of the land. It was to be an ideal representation of how the Israelites were to have taken the land. It follows a series of other ritual acts, and its position in the text assumes that it is to be placed with them rather than with the battles that follow.

The sentence that transitions into the Jericho scene (Josh 6:1) implies that the people in Jericho are aware of the Israelites at their gates: they are taking defensive measures, the gates are closed, and no one is entering or leaving. The Israelites meet with no resistance, according to the story as it is told in Josh 6. After the walls fall down, they simply enter the city and slaughter all of the people, oxen, sheep, and donkeys, sparing only Rahab, her family, and certain metal objects. The Jericho narrative perhaps served as an idealized model of how the land should have been taken, as opposed

---

4. All translations are the author's unless noted otherwise.

5. See Creach, *Joshua*; Hamlin, *Joshua*; and Bratcher and Newman, *Translator's Handbook*.

to how it was actually taken: the native inhabitants should have been wiped out and no Israelites should have died.

However, there is a problem with matching this story to the intent stated in the first chapter of Joshua. The intent was for the Israelites to inhabit *the land,* and the land would be *given* to them by God, not *taken* from the native inhabitants. Moreover, in the story the Israelites do not inhabit Jericho. They destroy it, abandon it, and burn it. (This should be interpreted as an act of *ḥerem*—a word used by Joshua in the text—that gives to God the firstfruits of the land, removing it from the possibility of profane use.) Lastly, Joshua intones a curse on anyone who rebuilds Jericho. We should also note that a solecism states that the preserved metals were placed in the "treasury of the house of YHWH" (6:24). "House," in relation to the word "YHWH," in biblical Hebrew refers to a temple. However, there was no treasury of the house of Yahweh at this point; according to ancient Israelite historiography, an Israelite temple is not built until the time of Solomon. Therefore, this is not a literal account but a reenactment of an idealized conquest of a Canaanite city from the perspective of a later time when the Israelites were no longer in control of the land.

Without question, the conquest is presented as happening in a violent manner, but it becomes even more so in the hands of translators.[6] The "battle" narrative begins with Yahweh informing Joshua that Yahweh has given Jericho and its king into his hand along with the *"gibbôrê haḥayil."* The latter phrase can refer to warriors, but it is also used in the HB to refer to the prominent men in a community.[7] It would be just as accurate to translate it here as "strong, competent men." Moreover, commentators on the Masoretic text suggest that this phrase is a gloss that was added later. It does not appear in the Septuagint (the early Greek translation of the HB) or in Roman Catholic translations. The phrase is syntactically awkward, placed at the end of the sentence without the expected indicator that it is a direct object of the verb "have given." It may have been added to the text to imply that the Israelites faced opposition from a fighting force. These men are not mentioned again in the narrative.

In verse 3, men called "the men of the battle" play a role at Jericho. Since Israel does not have a trained professional fighting force, we assume that this is a reference to men who will participate in the fighting but in the text their role is limited to the ceremonial part of the event. These men are to surround the city and circle it one time for six days. This is their only role.

6. For a translation comparison, see Table 5.2.

7. See 1 Sam 9:1; 16:18; 1 Kgs 11:28; 2 Kgs 15:20; and Ruth 2:1, where the phrase refers to wealthy men, competent men, or men of valor.

They are not said to participate in the invasion itself. The people themselves take all the action, when the walls have fallen.[8] In addition, there are seven priests carrying seven horns before the ark. On the seventh day, they are to circle the city seven times and the priests will blow the horns. When the sounds of the horns are heard, all the people will shout a great shout and the wall of the city will fall and the people go up.

This simple text becomes considerably more violent in the hands of English translators of the Bible. For example, in verse 2 the NRSV has the city handed over to "its king and soldiers," "soldiers" being the translation of "*gibbôrê haḥayil.*" The English word *soldiers* connotes a trained professional fighting force. In verse 3, instead of "walk around" the city, as the Hebrew reads, the NRSV uses the military term "march." "Men of the battle" becomes "warriors." Verse 4 repeats the word "march" where "circle" or "go around" appears. The NRSV ends verse 5 with all the people "charging"— again a military term—into the city. The Hebrew has them "going up" into the city. The phrase *go up* is frequently used in the ritual language associated with pilgrimages to Jerusalem.[9]

Neither the "men of the battle" nor Jericho's "strong, competent men" play any role in the actual battle. The ones who participate in the "battle" are repeatedly called "the people" (*hā'ām*). This deliberate designation is especially important at a later time—perhaps during the postexilic era—when various factions are vying for influence and power within Israel. The land was taken by all of the people, not one specific group nor an elite group, and so it belongs to all.

Another phrase that is frequently translated into more violent language than the Hebrew text intends is found repeated throughout Exodus 21. The phrase is *môt yûmat.* This syntactical construction is well represented in the HB. The first word is an infinitive absolute, followed by a finite verb, a hophal imperfect (prefix) third masculine singular. This verbal construction is considered emphatic. The base meaning of the verbal stem is "die." One might translate the phrase literally as, "dying, he will be caused to die." Matthew's Bible reads "shall die for it." Geneva has "he . . . shall die the death." The King James translators rendered this as "he . . . shall be surely put to death" (21:15). The TNK has "he . . . shall be put to death." The NRSV and

<hr>

8. In v. 20, it is clear that the people, not the "men of the battle," capture the city. This is probably meant to symbolize that the land belongs to all the people of Israel, not just to Joshua or the men of the battle.

9. The chart at the end of the essay illustrates the progression from ordinary to more militaristic language in the translation of Josh 6. The addition of specifically military language occurs in twentieth-century translations.

the NAB have the same "shall be put to death" reading, while the NIV is more explicit, interpreting the phrase as "must be put to death."[10]

The Hebrew phrasing leaves open both *how* this person will die and *at the hands of whom*, if an outside person or being is involved. At issue is the question: Is the human community ordered to execute the person who strikes father or mother, or is it suggesting that God will bring about the death of this person? Or is it even possible that the text is simply implying the person will die as a result of the deed itself? It is unclear. The Hebrew is perhaps deliberately ambiguous because the aim is to stress the seriousness of the offense. In a traditional society in which individuals could not well survive on their own, to reject one's parents—and therefore the knowledge and tools and resources needed for survival—would be to bring a death sentence on oneself. The English translations, however, overwhelmingly favor the death penalty for this offense, portraying an execution by the human community.

From these examples, one can see that the choice of words used in translating from Hebrew to English loses nuances of the original language and can change the meaning of the text—and therefore its use—in significant ways. In the apocryphal book that shares his name (often called Ecclesiasticus), Jesus Ben Sirach warns of the change in meaning that may come with translation. In the second century BCE, it cautions, "For what was originally expressed in Hebrew does not have exactly the same sense when translated into another language. Not only this work, but even the law itself, the prophecies and the rest of the books differ not a little as originally expressed" (RSV).

Historically, Anabaptists have primarily focused on the NT and interpreted Scripture through the nonviolent life and teachings of Jesus Christ. Consequently, they have not been overly troubled by the violent texts of the OT and they have rarely challenged the dominant society's translations of them. But as the old adage affirms, "Translation is interpretation." With the translations, Anabaptists have too often accepted interpretations of the OT made by the dominant society. The problem is that these translations—made by those in power—reflect the worldviews of those in power and support its institutions and ethic. Particularly when it comes to issues of violence, those who have the power to threaten and carry out those threats have looked (and may look) to the Bible for justification and models. However, the HB emerged in and was given to a community that was not dominant in the ancient Near East. The Jews and other remnants of ancient Israel were under the hegemony of Assyria, Babylon, Persia, Greece, and Rome. As a people in

---

10. See also Table 5.3.

the minority and without power, their interpretations of biblical texts would have differed to some degree from readings of the same texts undertaken by those in power. As a starting point, we ought to recover those early interpretations by being as faithful as possible to the Hebrew texts.

Table 5.1. Translation comparisons: Jonah 3:4

Hebrew	author	NRSV	NAB	JPS	NIV
Nineveh *nehpaket*	Nineveh will be overturned.	Nineveh shall be overthrown!	Nineveh shall be destroyed.	Nineveh shall be overthrown!	Nineveh will be overturned.

Author's Translation of Jonah 3:4

Jonah began to go into the city, walking one day, and he called out, "Yet forty days and Nineveh will be overturned."

Table 5.2. Translation comparisons: Joshua 6:1–5

Verse	2	3	3	4	5
Hebrew	*gibbôrê ha-ḥayil*	*sabbōtem*	*'anšê ham-milḥāmāh*	*tāsōbbû*	*'ālû hā'ām 'îš negdô*
Matthew's	men of war[A]	compass	men of war	go round about it	ascend up every man before him
Geneva Bible	strong men of war	compass	men of war	going round about	shall ascend up every man straight before him
KJV (1611)	mighty men of valor	compass	men of war	go round about	shall ascend up every man straight before him
ASV	mighty men of valor	compass	men of war	going about	the people shall go up every man straight before him
NIV	fighting men	march around	armed men	march around	the people will go up every man straight in
JPS	Warriors	march around	troops	march	the people shall advance, every man straight ahead
NRSV	Soldiers	you shall march	warriors	you shall march	all the people shall charge straight ahead
REB	Warriors	march	fighting men	making the circuit	the army will advance, every man straight ahead
NAB	n/a	circle	soldiers	march	they will be able to make a frontal attack
The Inclusive Bible	brave warriors	encircle	troops	march around	the people will advance with everyone surging forward straight ahead

A. The spelling in Matthew's Bible, the Geneva Bible and the KJV of 1611 has been modernized throughout the essay.

Author's Translation of Joshua 6:1–5

1. Jericho was closed and had been closed before the Israelites. No one was going out or coming in. 2. YHWH said to Joshua, "See, I have given Jericho, its king and prominent men into your hand. 3. All of the men of the battle

will circle the city, going around the city one time. Thus you will do six days. 4. Seven priests will carry seven rams' horns before the ark. And on the seventh day, you will circle the city seven times and the priests will blow the horns. 5. And it will happen, at the sound of the rams' horn, all the people will shout a great shout and the wall of the city will fall under it. All the people will go up, each before it."

Table 5.3. Translation comparisons: Exodus 21:15

author	Dying, he will be caused to die
Matthew's	He . . . shall die for it
Geneva	He shall die the death
KJV	He . . . shall be surely put to death
TNK	He . . . shall be put to death
NRSV	Whoever . . .shall be put to death
NAB	Whoever . . . shall be put to death
NIV	Anyone . . . must be put to death

Author's Translation of Exodus 21:15

One who strikes his father or his mother will certainly be caused to die.

6

No Other Gods

Allegiance and Identity in the Nation State

Paul Keim

He removed the high places, broke down the pillars, and cut down the sacred pole. He broke in pieces the bronze serpent that Moses had made, for until those days the people of Israel had made offerings to it; it was called Nehush-tan. (2 Kings 18:4 NRSV)

INTRODUCTION[1]

My grandfather once told me that he did not think it was right to refer to money or celebrities as idols. It is not an idol unless someone bows down and worships it, he insisted. As a dutiful grandson I kept my peace. But as a budding seminary student, I attributed his attitude to a lack of theological imagination. Surely, I thought, there are compelling parallels between the impieties of modern secular society and the sin of idolatry so vehemently condemned in the Bible.

In the intervening years I often pondered my grandfather's words. Even if his view was informed by an austere biblicism, he may have been making a point, however inadvertently, about the danger of applying terminology too broadly and loosely. If anything and everything can be called

---

1. This essay is offered in fond appreciation of Willard Swartley and Perry Yoder.

an idol, how do we distinguish what is truly idolatrous from those things that are merely alien, disgusting, or wasteful? Even as the word is applied analogically to the varied impieties of modern life, its use runs the risk of undermining our appreciation for its tangible antecedents in antiquity. Ultimately, this overuse may trivialize the legitimate concerns of the biblical writers for the sanctity of the first and second commandments. What is the relationship between the idolatry of the biblical polemic and the idolatries of contemporary ethical discourse—whether formal or popular? Is it possible to determine where one's ultimate allegiance lies?

The text from 2 Kgs 18 quoted above depicts a religious object destroyed during the reforms of Hezekiah. Along with hilltop shrines, votive, stele and iconic asherah-poles that are condemned and removed, the reformist king also crushes a "bronze serpent" of Mosaic vintage, which he ironically dubs Nehushtan,[2] because "the people of Israel had made offerings to it." Though biblical scholars have long considered the object in question to have been the cult image of an unnamed healing deity once associated with the Yahwistic cult,[3] the narrative gives the impression of a previously sanctioned (Mosaic) cultic object (Num 21:8–9) that had come to be declared illicit by virtue of the acts of worship directed toward it. The tradition of the Nehushtan provides a convenient starting point in our assessment of biblical passages dealing with the prohibition of idolatry, and the possible significance such passages might have in a contemporary settings.

The idea of biblical monotheism and the enduring functionality of idolatry as a pejorative accusation against false religion (and things foreign) continue to influence contemporary debates about the ethical and moral dilemmas of modernism.[4] A variety of putative trends—from secularization to consumerism to militarism to civil religion—have evoked the charge of idolatry and calls by religious leaders for a return to the pure monotheism of the Bible. One does not need to dig far into the biblical text, however, to realize that this idealized picture of biblical monotheism belies both the history of Yahwism in ancient Israel and the complex symbiosis (syncretism) that characterized the beliefs and ritual practices reflected in all aspects of biblical literature. From Mosaic torah-ism to Trinitarian synthesis, the Bible reflects echoes of past (or passing) theological legacies and the assimilation of new loci of ultimate concern.

2. A play on the words for bronze/copper (*něḥōšet*) and snake/serpent (*nāḥāš*).

3. See Curtis, "Idol, Idolatry."

4. I am using this term loosely to refer to those aspects of contemporary culture that represent conscious rejection of ancient and classical modes of thought and belief, especially in matters of religion, but broadly in terms of world view and moral discourse, and the putative displacement of divine prerogatives by anthropocentric concerns.

It is certainly not unusual in contemporary religious discourse to hear accusations of idolatry directed against various elements of modern culture and religion. A quick online search finds such accusations leveled against "modern day idols" such as: greed, drugs and leisure;[5] materialism, pride and humanity;[6] and even environmentalism.[7] There are many others. To what extent do such accusations accurately reflect the biblical teaching about idolatry, and how do they function effectively to shape contemporary Christian ethics?

IDOLATRY IN THE BIBLE

At its most tangible, idolatry is presented in the Bible as the worship of alien gods and/or the use of cultic images.[8] Both are closely associated in the ancient code of the Ten Words.[9] But as biblical literature and history show, the struggle of Israelite religion with idolatry exhibits a complex and sustained development.[10] Initially, the priests and prophets of ancient Israel are presented as railing against the use of images and warning against the tempting inducements of rival gods. Eventually, the implications of exclusive loyalty to Yahweh are taken to a logical conclusion in the reforms of the Deuteronomic school: even in cases where the images were, putatively, part of longstanding practice within the Yahwistic cult (cf. household gods of Genesis 33; Gideon's priestly garment of Judg 8:27; the ark of the covenant as narrated in 1 Sam 4–6), they are rejected in the reformist program. Any practices that might possibly be construed as similar to the cult practices of other deities are considered dangerous and off limits.[11] As a matter of fact, the monotheism of the Bible is never absolute, never static, and never unambiguous. Whether one assumes an early pristine Israelite monothe-

5. Source: http://preachersfiles.com/modern-day-idolatry/.

6. Source: http://www.gotquestions.org/idolatry-modern.html.

7. Clauson, "Environmentalism: A Modern Idolatry," http://www.reformed.org/webfiles/antithesis/index.html?mainframe=/webfiles/antithesis/v1n2/ant_v1n2_environ.html.

8. See Rosner, "Concept of Idolatry."

9. The sum of the first two commandments is clear: There shall be no worship of any god other than the God of the ancestors, identified with YHWH, and there shall be no use of images and idols to worship any god, including God.

10. Smith expertly traces this history in *Early History of God*.

11. In place of the more value-laden term "syncretism," Smith documents a process of "convergence and differentiation" within the Yahwistic cult, whereby deities and worship practices were alternately associated with the cult of Yahweh and disassociated from it.

ism later corrupted by Canaanite paganism and its iconographic cult, or a gradual evolution via monolatry to monotheism, the process of engagement against illicit forms of worship is a constant—one might even say essential—part of Israelite religion.[12]

The biblical terminology used to refer to divine images is robust and variegated. Some of the terms are derived from the way the object was made: *pesel* from a root meaning "to hew"; *massēkâ* meaning "poured out, molten."[13] Some denote the innate character of representation: *tabnît* "copy, pattern," *dĕmût* "likeness," and *tĕmûnâ* "form, shape." Other terms are derogatory euphemisms based on wordplay: *gillûlîm* (whatever its etymology) sounds like the word for "dung" or "dung balls"; *ʾĕlîlîm* sounds like the adjective for "weak"; *šiqqûṣ* "something detestable, like ritually unclean animals"; *tôʿēbâ* "abomination"; *hebel* "insubstantial, vaporous"; *šeqer* "something deceptive or false"; *šāw(ʾ)* "empty, vain"; *mipleṣet* "causes trembling." In light of the implicit devaluation expressed by these latter terms, it is not difficult to imagine that even the words denoting method or material of construction, or function of representation, expressed a degree of derogation for the objects themselves, the deities they represented, and those who used them.

In their masterful study of biblical idolatry and its legacy, Halbertal and Margalit describe the elements that came to represent this most foundational of Israelite sins.[14] They lift out a number of characteristics of idolatry and idols in the Bible. When one looks at the functionality of idolatry in the Bible, it is clear that, among other things, accusations of idolatry help to define the "other" and thus become part of identity formation. Those who worship "idols" are not we, and those "deities" whom *they* worship are not *our* gods, and the way *they* worship is not *our* way. Idolatry is about identity; it helps to identify a boundary for a community of faith. In this way, at least, accusations of idolatry continue to function effectively in contemporary moral discourse. As James Brenneman summarizes, "The arguments about idolatry are often disguises about claims to truth over against accusations of falsehood."[15]

Idols also represent ways the deity or deities they represent can be controlled and manipulated. Waldemar Janzen describes this potential of images in the following way: "The images were not always conceived of as

12. James Brenneman makes reference to the same historical ambiguity to raise an important point about the difficulty of defining idolatry and the contours of Israelite monotheism from the biblical record. See his article, "Sequencing Allegiances."

13. These and the ones that follow are from Curtis, "Idol, Idolatry."

14. This section of the article is dependent on the discussion in the first three chapters of *Idolatry*, by Halbertal and Margalit.

15. Brenneman, "Sequencing Allegiances," 6.

being fully coextensive with the gods, but they represented the gods' presence realistically. Consequently they could be manipulated, through offerings, incantations, processions, and the like, to do the worshipers' will."[16] Even if we concede that the ancients were capable of sophisticated understandings of the relationship between deity and image,[17] the danger exists. From the high culture of ritual cult images to the myriad magical machinations of amulets, fetishes, emblems, and representations, it is in part the very tangibility of the images that makes us feel in control and able to grasp God's will and get a grip on secure outcomes.[18]

The metaphysics of idolatry as sin was not about the inherent danger or evil of visual representations per se. Images, albeit abstract and stylistic, were part of the worship of Yahweh in ancient Israel.[19] According to Halbertal and Margalit, idolatry was associated with monotheism, not primarily in a metaphysical sense, but in the sense of exclusive loyalty, allegiance, and devotion. The primary sin of idolatry was violation of the exclusive bonds of loyalty pledged by the people to God, and vice versa. In fact, as Halbertal and Margalit point out, the theology of idolatry begins with the highly personal nature of Israel's God. They assert: "According to the anthropomorphic concept of God, which is characteristic of biblical faith, idolatry is a sin within a system of interpersonal relationships, a sin analogous to those [that] people commit with respect to other people, such as betrayal and disloyalty."[20] The sin of idolatry assumes that the God of Israel is personal and enters into relationship with human beings in ways that lend themselves to the analogy of friendship, treaty, marriage. So, idolatry as a sin is first and foremost an act of disloyalty to Yahweh. Correspondingly, the conceptual world of biblical polemic against idolatry is shaped by analogies from personal relationships. Accordingly, the primary metaphor for idolatry is adultery, the most intimate of interpersonal betrayals. This metaphor of marital jealousy

---

16. Janzen, *First Commandments,* 18.

17. Jacobsen, "Graven Image."

18. Halbertal and Margalit note the acceptability of verbal images and prohibition against visual images in the Bible, but do not attempt to defend or rationalize the contrast. Whatever its ultimate origins, the prohibition of cultic images apparently did not preclude the acceptance of visual "art"; cf. Curtis, "Idol, Idolatry," *ABD* 3:376–81, esp. 379, which refers to an article by J. Gutmann.

19. The accoutrements of hilltop shrines, asherah poles, priestly garments, and pedestal calves are well known from the earlier stages of Israelite religion. Only later were some of these condemned by various reformers.

20. Halbertal and Margalit, *Idolatry,* 1.

emphasizes the personal nature of Israel's God and has little bearing on the later issue of the metaphysical question of the existence of other gods.[21]

In this context, classical prophecy further developed the metaphor of Israel's relationship to God as wife to husband. Hosea gives poignant expression to the image of Israel as an unfaithful wife. The effect is personal and painful. The marital infidelity is portrayed as a kind of wantonness that is both shameful and brings destruction in its wake. The insult to the "husband" is worse than mere prostitution in this case, because, as Halbertal and Margalit write, "the fee is always being paid with the husband's money, as he is the sustainer of the world."[22] Jeremiah recasts Hosea's metaphor, emphasizing both the early devotion of bride Israel for her divine husband, and also overtly politicizing it with reference to Israel's expedient treaties with Egypt and Assyria. Ezekiel eroticizes the metaphor to emphasize the element of shame, reiterating the specific acts of treachery from Israel's history that constitute the harlotry. The religious and political components of the disloyalty become indistinguishable.

Exploring the metaphor of marriage/adultery can provide useful tools for theological reflection on what might constitute idolatry, or its moral equivalent, today. In Israelite society, though married men were allowed some sanctioned interaction with women other than their wives, in law there were clear cases (at least theoretically) of adultery in which third parties witnessed the act and provided testimony (Num 5:13; cf. John 8:3). However, adulterous behavior that did not meet this standard was more difficult to discern and adjudicate.[23] What then were the triggers for violation of the boundary of exclusive allegiance to the wife? What came to be embedded in culture as improper, immoral, or at least impolitic, even if legally blameless?[24] As Ezekiel pointed out long ago, idolatry is not necessarily accompanied by the overt display of cultic images, but may be a matter of internalizing, rationalizing, and attempting to nullify competing allegiances. In his admonition of the elders of Israel in exile who came to him for a word from the Lord while "taking their idols into their hearts and placing their iniquity as a stumbling block before them" (Ezek 14:4), the discernment of the community and the judgment of God are called for.

21. This theme is eventually addressed by the late classical prophets.

22. *Idolatry*, 13.

23. Thus the forensic ordeal of the Sotah in Num 5:11–31 for cases in which a wife is suspected of adultery, but "there is no witness against her since she was not caught in the act" (v. 13).

24. Jesus's encounter with the Samaritan woman evokes the surprise of the disciples who find him conversing with a woman in public, perhaps reflecting a common social taboo.

Does the second commandment's prohibition of idolatry have any relevance in the modern world? If the actual worship of other gods in my grandfather's sense is no longer a clear and present danger in contemporary Christian ethics, how should accusations of idolatry in the extended sense of "competing loyalties" be evaluated? Waldemar Janzen defines the locus of concern in this way: "Our ultimate allegiance today is also claimed by immanent, this-worldly powers and forces: political states and empires; ideologies such as Marxism, fascism, capitalism, but also democracy if it makes imperial claims; sports, movies, and other forms of entertainment, including music; academic disciplines, such as the natural and social sciences, but also rigid theological systems that attempt to fully explain God's inherently mysterious nature. In sum, any aspect of creation can become idolatrous."[25] For Franz Rosenzweig, polytheism in the modern world meant "the worship and apotheosis of transient values and objects, all of which should be subordinate to the true God." How we might balance the competing claims for our loyalty in the modern world is the theme of the case study to follow.

GOSHEN COLLEGE AND THE NATIONAL ANTHEM DEBATE

Goshen College (GC), a small liberal arts institution owned by the Mennonite Church, was recently engulfed in a controversy about playing the national anthem before selected athletic events.[26] In the course of the year-long process in which constituent members of the community passionately debated the relevant issues, the theme of ultimate allegiance constituted a kind of moral foundation for those opposing the anthem. Though the tenor of face-to-face conversations on campus remained civil, the less guarded rhetoric of competing Facebook pages revealed more disturbing examples of calling into question the moral integrity of the competing position.[27] Against the background of this unfolding controversy, James Brenneman, president of the college, published an article on the theme of allegiance and idolatry that addressed this latter concern. With reference to this statement, I would like to pursue some of its themes and reflect on the issue of

25. Janzen, *First Commandments*, 22.

26. For a summary of the controversy and its outcome, see http://www.goshen.edu/anthem/.

27. The clearest and most balanced of the formal statements about the controversy remains Liechty's "National Anthem Debate," an editorial in the *Journal of Religion, Conflict, and Peace*.

"sequencing our allegiances" as a metaphor for navigating the treacherous waters of faith and citizenship from a biblical/theological perspective.

Brenneman charts the difficulty of comparative idolatries, and in particular what he calls the costly price of pure monotheism. Put succinctly, it is much easier to see (and condemn) the idolatry in the beliefs and practices of the Other than it is in one's own. Brenneman uses the core Deuteronomic teaching against idolatry to make the point that those from aniconic traditions, who believe themselves safely beyond the grip of idolatry, may nevertheless be guilty of its practice. Though he does not apply it directly to the anthem controversy at GC, the timing and theme of the article make it clear that it was intended to speak to that situation and to the broader cultural attitudes it manifested.

Using the book of Deuteronomy's prohibitions against idolatry, Brenneman first reaffirms the moral obligation to oppose the militarism and consumerism of our society. He notes some of the difficulties, even in these areas, of maintaining a purist ethic in a context where the modern military is less concerned about the numbers of human beings engaged in warfare and much more dependent on money to fund the deadly new weapon technologies. Conscientious objection to participation in the military—itself no longer a foregone conclusion in Anabaptist communities—no longer represents an adequate ethical response to the dilemma posed by the ideology of modern warfare. Even just war theory has been similarly challenged to keep abreast of the innovations of current warfare.

As for consumerism, there are also challenges for those concerned with living according to a distinctly Christian ethic. During times of economic downturn—or when Christians from sectarian traditions were able to maintain a sense of "distance" from the broader society, living modestly and sustainably—it was easier to convince ourselves that we were being faithful stewards of God's gifts, and that our lives were not organized around the building of wealth and the consumption of goods. Yet many of us have become wealthy. Perhaps we refrain from ostentatious displays of our well-being and security, but we have a vested interest in things as they are.

It is on the third principle that Brenneman brings his critique to greatest effect. In the glib sense that we have been able to maintain a kind of ideological purity and theological biblicism, Brenneman is able to show how self-justification is an equally serious problem within the moral framework of the Deuteronomist. This is a difficult position to rationalize, and it touches on a sore spot for Anabaptists. As long as we remained relatively separate from broader society, including other Christians, it was possible for us to maintain the sense that we were being faithful over against the beliefs and practices of our neighbors, whether Christian or not. When it came to

Christian support for war or the ostentatious display of wealth, it was not difficult to see oneself as more faithful, more biblical, and more in touch with God's will for the world. But as our isolation has eroded over the past century, we have found ourselves in the middle of the world (where we had always been), but now engaged with other Christians in issues of mutual interest and support. It was harder to dismiss the ethical and moral practices of other Christians, most of which had long histories of Christian tradition behind them. It also became clear that elements of the old ethic were simply self-serving rationalizations for practices that no longer spoke meaningfully to the challenge of the modern situation (cf. "nonswearing of oaths" where "affirming" has the same legal status as "swearing").

Having challenged some of the past complacency of our ethical system, we find ourselves asking essentially the same set of questions from a different position. What does it mean to be faithful in the modern world? What if we give up our complacency and our self-righteousness, our sense of entitlement and our theological pride? Where does that leave us? Are there new lines to be drawn, or is the whole enterprise of drawing lines and declaring certain things off limits to be discarded? What should a Christian ethic for the twenty-first century look like? There are several aspects to these questions that I would like to address. Using Brenneman's starting point, I will try to both contextualize and refine his discussion, and suggest that we must maintain a sense of boundaries and continue to exercise our moral discernment. As we reconsider our approach, we may discover that some cherished past practices no longer speak meaningfully in the present circumstances. If that is the case, then we must decide what attitude and practices should characterize a Christian community concerned about keeping ethics at the center of its understanding of the gospel.

THE ISSUES AT STAKE

> And the people bowed and prayed, to the neon god they'd made
> . . .[28]

In navigating the treacherous waters of contemporary ethical discourse about the meaning of monotheism, the insidious forms of modern polytheism, and accusations of idolatry, Brenneman insists that perspective matters and that sequencing our allegiances is inevitable. In his editorial about the Goshen controversy, Liechty exhibits exemplary sensitivity to context

---

28. Paul Simon and Art Garfunkel, "The Sounds of Silence," *The Sounds of Silence*, Columbia Records, 1965.

throughout and qualifies many of his observations and conclusions in the direction of inclusion. Brenneman and Liechty may be right in arguing that the time has come for us to reevaluate our insistence on what have arguably been sectarian practices. Singing the national anthem to the flag may not in and of itself represent a danger to our beliefs or to our continued commitment to pacifism and reconciliation. When kept in the proper context, it may be set aside, albeit in slightly altered fashion, in favor of other important values like hospitality and welcoming the stranger. Liechty's rationale here is particularly cogent and convincing.[29]

But taken within the broader context of the threats of patriotic nationalism in this country, it is fair to ask the question whether such practices are as harmless as they might seem. When our children are constantly inundated with the ideology of the (righteous) state, encouraged to support it by a form of civil religion akin to Christianity, called to engage in just wars against its enemies, to consider its (and their?) own civilization superior to others (American exceptionalism), and to pursue a practice that uses military might to impose its will on the world, one could argue that such inconsequential acts as singing the anthem before sporting events, or pledging allegiance to the flag, represent real threats over time to the integrity of a biblical and prophetic voice of faith and reason.[30]

The language of "pure monotheism" in this context strikes me as tendentious—something of a straw man easily dispatched—though I recognize and appreciate its rhetorical function in Brenneman's essay. The ethical monotheism of the sixteenth-century Anabaptists had a strong Christological focus. The issue for them was not so much whether to follow this one god as opposed to some other god but whether to follow one Lord more than another lord. Whether or not there were other gods in the world was not a matter of undue concern, but it was clear that there were other "lords" in the world, lords who made ethical demands on their Christian subjects as Christian magistrates. Earthly rulers were thought to have a legitimate, ordained function, and the social ethic or politics of Anabaptism, as I understand it, was not theocratic. Obedience (or rather, cooperation) was to be rendered unto Caesar up until the point at which the state reached beyond its mandate. And the state did reach beyond its mandate, often in the name of God. Social and political obligations were not sequenced but

---

29. Liechty does qualify his rationale with a soul-searching concern about the unforeseen dangers of the "slippery slope."

30. This is especially the case for a community of like-minded believers who find themselves in the midst of a prolonged identity crisis characterized by greater assimilation into broader society and its values, yet not ready to give up all of their group's traditional distinctives.

integrated in a field that required moral discernment at those points where the prerogatives of one set of obligations conflicted with those of another. Sometimes the differences could be negotiated, sometimes not. At the point where competing claims are intractable, noncooperation becomes a moral necessity.

Most of the time we function with overlapping sets of allegiances: to spouse, families, occupation, school/town, faith/church, and nation. We tend to live our lives as if the allegiances inherent in these roles constitute a coherent whole. However, we notice these overlapping claims on us in those times when the demands or obligations of one seem to conflict with the demands of another: employee and parent; member of society and independent moral agent; member of faith community and citizen of the nation. The problem with the language of sequencing is that it implies the moral equivalence of *any* belief or practice subordinate to a professed allegiance to God. Confessions such as "God and Country," or even "Allahu Akbar," may adequately give expression to such a notion. But we dare not neglect the moral question of what ultimate allegiance to God consists. Certainly, "to imagine that [one's] own moral decency, inherent goodness, or doctrinal purities, were reasons for having received a homeland from God, would be idolatry of the worst kind."[31] But to caution against the "placing the peace of Christ above a relationship with Christ, or reifying pacifism above Christ, our Peace,"[32] seems to rob the theological confession of its ethical heart. As Liechty rightly asserts, "We need to think of hospitality as an aspect of the lordship of Christ, *alongside* allegiance rather than beneath it."[33] It is the integration of these values—not their sequencing—that holds out the hope of living faithfully in idolatrous times.

31. Brenneman, "Sequencing Allegiances," 5.

32. Ibid., 6.

33. Liechty, "National Anthem Debate," 13; italics added.

7

The Paradoxical Monstrification of Egypt in the Book of Ezekiel

Violence, Impurity, and the Other

Safwat Marzouk

When compared with the rest of the prophetic books of the OT, the book of Ezekiel includes the largest collection of oracles against Egypt found in a single book (Ezek 29–32). These oracles proclaim divine judgment over Egypt by employing rich images and interweaving diverse themes. Prominent among these themes is the portrayal of Pharaoh/Egypt as a monster of chaos.[1] In Ezek 29:2–3 and 32:1–2, the prophetic word exercises its power as it embodies Pharaoh not as a human being but rather as a monster that lies in its rivers. Snatched and thrown into the wilderness, the monster's body is dismembered and left abandoned and unburied so that wild animals and birds may feast on it (Ezek 29:4–5; cf. 32:3–5).

To be sure, Ezekiel is not the only biblical tradition that portrays Egypt/Pharaoh as a monster (cf. Isa 51:9–10). As a way of explaining this phenomenon of portraying Egypt as a monster throughout the OT, John Day posits that "the Old Testament allusions to Egypt as Rahab or the dragon probably arose as a result of the oppressive role that Egypt played toward Israel before the Exodus, and that the use of this imagery was also conditioned by the fact

---

1. For a fuller treatment of the subject, see my dissertation, *"Not a Lion but a Dragon."*

that the heart of the Exodus deliverance actually took place at the sea."[2] The problem with this explanation when applied to Ezekiel's monstrification of Egypt is that Ezekiel's memory of the exodus, as I will explain below, does not center on the notion of oppression and slavery, nor does Ezekiel speak of Yahweh parting the sea and defeating the Egyptians by the sea (Ezek 20:7–8).

Most interpreters of the book of Ezekiel correctly read the severe judgment in Ezek 29–32 against Egypt in the historico-political context of the alliance between Egypt and Judah prior to the fall of Jerusalem in 587 BCE.[3] Although it is clear to the reader of the book of Ezekiel that the political situation of the sixth century is critical to understanding Ezekiel's severe criticism of Egypt, I believe that the political coalition for the prophet is a thin veneer over the religious chaos that prevailed in the life of the people of Israel before and during the time of the exile. Many commentators have pointed out the significance of the political alliance, but the connection between the meaning of the political alliance and the imagery of the monster has gone unexplained.[4]

I believe that the paradoxes that constitute and characterize the category of *monster* are what prompt the prophet Ezekiel to portray Egypt as a monster. As I will explain below, a monster represents simultaneously something that is similar and different, same and other. Furthermore, although the monster is often violently defeated, it continues to exist and is even resurgent. Thus, I argue that in the book of Ezekiel, Egypt functions as Israel's double: a symbol for the loss of boundary and a sign for religious assimilation. Yet in the same book, Egypt suffers the violence of being Otherized, embodied as a monster, defeated, and its body dismembered by Yahweh. Despite this near annihilation, Egypt, in Ezekiel's rhetoric, is not entirely obliterated. Rather, it is kept at bay, hovering at the periphery, questioning Israel's identity.

THE MONSTER AS ABJECT

In order to unpack the category of the monster, I will appeal to the work of Julia Kristeva and the notion of "abjection." In McAfee's words, Kristeva's work, *Powers of Horror: An Essay on Abjection*,[5] "takes the reader back to

---

2. Day, *God's Conflict*, 96. For a similar explanation see Wakeman, *God's Battle*, 74, and Blenkinsopp, *Isaiah 1–39*, 414.

3. See for example, Eichrodt, *Ezekiel*, 399; and Zimmerli, *Ezekiel 2*, 105.

4. See for example, Odell, *Ezekiel*, 371; and Tuell, *Ezekiel*, 199–201.

5. Kristeva, *Powers of Horror*.

the brink of how subjectivity is constituted in the first place, that is, to how a person comes to see him- or herself as a separate being with his or her own borders between self and other."[6] Following Jacques Lacan, Kristeva suggests that the infant, who is born with no sense of borders between self and other, and who shares a unitary sameness with the mother, constitutes his or her identity (his or her "I") through the process of abjection.

In an interview, Kristeva defines abjection as a "revolt of the person against an external menace from which one wants to keep oneself at a distance, but which one has the impression that it is not only external menace but that it may menace us from inside. So it is a desire for separation, for becoming autonomous and also the feeling of an impossibility of doing so."[7] We see here the paradox of the process of abjection. Because the infant and the mother share in a unitary sameness, when the infant abjects the mother, it abjects part of itself. There is a necessity to expel the danger, whether external or internal, that threatens the identity and the borders. At the same time, there is a sense of fear that this expulsion is impossible. The paradox of abjection goes further in that there is a tension between the need to completely exclude the abject, and the reality that it is never utterly annihilated.[8] The abject continues to question the person's sense of distinct and proper identity. Therefore, the notion of abjection is not an event; it is process that continues to take place throughout the person's life.[9]

This process of abjection is not just related to individual infants; it is also related to how communities and groups of people constitute their identity. By initiating rituals of abjection, societies reconstruct their identities by abjecting the impure and the polluted.[10] Societies abject the one who—or that which—"disturbs identity, system, order. What does not respect borders, positions, rules. The in-between, the ambiguous, the composite."[11] We can see here affinities between the monster and the abject as posited by Kristeva. "The horror monster signifies abject terror because it violates cultural categories, disrespects organizing principles, and generally serves to present a chaotic alternative to the place of order and meaning, socially as well as biologically."[12] Both—the monster and the abject—question one's

---

6. McAfee, *Julia Kristeva*, 45.

7. Baruch and Serrano, eds., "Interview with Julia Kristeva," 135–36.

8. McAfee, *Julia Kristeva*, 46.

9. Kristeva, *Powers of Horror*, 2. See also McAfee, *Kristeva*, 46.

10. "A combination of anthropology and psychoanalysis now appears to squeeze out the kind of sociological framework based on a dichotomy between individual (subject) and society" (Lechte, *Julia Kristeva*, 162). See also Oliver, *Reading Kristeva*, 56.

11. Kristeva, *Powers of Horror*, 4.

12. Magistrale, *Abject Terrors*, 7. Further connections between the abject and the

sense of identity and order. The monstrous and the abject suffer the drastic association with utter Otherness, yet they are not a complete Other; prior to the initiation of abjection they were part of an imaginary union with the self. Even after being abjected, and even though firmly excluded through rituals, they hover at the periphery. They are not completely annihilated.

WORSHIPING EGYPTIAN IDOLS AS A MARKER FOR BOUNDARY TRANSGRESSION: EZEKIEL 20

After revealing himself in Egypt to the Israelites as their god, Yahweh commands the Israelites to no longer defile themselves by worshiping Egyptian idols: "Cast away the detestable things your eyes feast on, every one of you, and do not defile yourselves with the idols of Egypt; I am the Lord your God" (Ezek 20:7; see also vv. 8–9).[13] Yahweh commands the Israelites in Egypt to throw away the detestable things their eyes feast on. The word *šqwṣ* stems from the root *šqṣ* "feel loathing or abhorrence." The term is used twenty-eight times in the OT, nine of these occurring in the book of Ezekiel (5:11; 7:20; 8:10; 11:18, 21; 20:7, 8, 30; 37:23). In various texts in the OT the term is used independently to designate detestable things in the religious sense (cultic, ritual, improper worship, etc.—e.g., Ezek 20:30). This religious connotation is usually nuanced by adding the words *glwlym* or *twʿbwt* (Ezek 5:11; 7:20; 11:18, 21; 20:7, 8; 37:23). In Deut 29:13, Moses reminds the people of Israel about their time in the land of Egypt and their journey through the different lands that led them to the borders of the promised land. Moses points out that "you have seen their detestable things and their idols of wood and stone, of silver and gold, that were in their midst." Like Deuteronomy, Ezekiel acknowledges the fact that the Israelites have seen "detestable things" and "idols" in the land of Egypt. However, unlike Deuteronomy, Ezekiel claims that the Israelites themselves worshiped these idols and the detestable things.

In the second part of the command in Ezek 20:7, Yahweh urges the people, "Do not defile (*ṭṭmʾw*, *hithpael*) yourselves with the idols of Egypt." The word *glwlym* ("idols") is Ezekiel's favorite word with which to designate idol worship. This term is used forty-eight times in the OT, thirty-nine of these in the book of Ezekiel (eight times in chap. 20 alone; vv. 7, 8, 16, 18, 24, 31, 39 [twice]). Ezekiel 20:7–8 warns the Israelites—prior to the exodus— about being defiled by worshiping the "idols of Egypt" (*glwlym mṣrym*). Although the etymology of the word *glwlym* is ambiguous, Bodi suggests that

---

monstrous female in horror literature are discussed by Creed, *The Monstrous Feminine*.

13. All biblical quotations are taken from the NRSV unless otherwise indicated.

the semantic field of the root *gl/gll* includes two meanings: "roundness" and "excrement." Thus interpreters understand the word to literally mean "dung balls."[14] If this suggestion is true, then Ezekiel's point is emphatic: these idols are worse than a heap of round stones, they are dung balls that defile (*ṭm'*) those who worship them.

The Israelites rebelled and refused to obey Yahweh; that is, they continued to worship the idols of Egypt. Yahweh declares, "But they rebelled against me and did not listen to me; not one of them cast away the detestable things of their eyes, nor did they forsake the idols of Egypt" (Ezek 20:8). In wrath, Yahweh decided to lead them out of Egypt (Ezek 20:9). Yahweh did so not because they were oppressed but because of their shared elements of identity with Egypt. Israel worshiped the idols of Egypt; they shared the same idols. Assimilation had taken place between Israel and Egypt. They possessed shared aspects of identity.[15]

Oppression and slavery are not the conditions of the Israelites in the land of Egypt, according to Ezekiel's account of the exodus. Instead, the focal point is their transgression and rebellion at the point of their constitution as a nation, prior to their exodus from Egypt. For Ezekiel, the constitution of Israel as a nation took place in Egypt while Israel was engulfed in the chaos of idolatrous practices. The context of the Israelites in Egypt prior to the exodus was like the primordial water prior to the creation: chaos all around, loss of boundary, and formless identity.[16]

The chaos that Egypt represents in the religious life of Israel is resurgent. Idolatry does not just start in Egypt; Ezekiel's text suggests that it keeps coming back, reappearing in the religious life of Israel. Although the Israelites are led out of Egypt, the land of idols, the issue of idolatry is not completely solved. We read in Ezek 20:16 that this same generation worships idols in the wilderness. The symptoms of the rebellion of the Israelites

14. Bodi, "Les gillûlîm chez Ézéchiel." See also Joyce, *Ezekiel*, 90, and the discussion in Kutsko, *Between Heaven and Earth*, 33–34.

15. The identity of the Israelites was in question because they disobeyed Yahweh and refused to cast away the idols of Egypt. Odell writes, "The Israelites rebel against this divine command, and their failure to give up the idols signifies rejection of their holy identity as the people of Yahweh" (Odell, *Ezekiel*, 250).

16. Ezekiel is unique in claiming that the Israelites worshiped idols in Egypt prior to the exodus. For further discussion see Block, *Ezekiel 1–24*, 629; and Levitt Kohn, "With a Mighty Hand and an Outstretched Arm," 166. Josh 24:14 speaks about the idols of Egypt and Mesopotamia. However, Ezekiel is not concerned, at least in chap. 20, with the idols of Mesopotamia. Egypt occupies his imagination. In the book of Exodus the rebellion took place in the wilderness, as attested in the golden calf incident (Exod 32). The chaos of idolatry and the rebellion of the Israelites, according to the prophet, originated in Egypt (cf. Ezek 23:3–5).

reappear in the wilderness. Egypt has been left behind; nonetheless, its impact still haunts the Israelites. The second generation, which was led into the promised land, also defiles itself with the idols of their ancestors (Ezek 20:24). Again, the symptoms of the rebellion of the Israelites, which started in Egypt, resurface in the land. Whereas Egypt geographically is at a great distance, its primordial, chaotic influences keep coming back. The political alliance between Egypt and Judah is a thin film under which lies the religious chaos of idolatry that originated in Egypt, but also returns to the fore in the sixth century BCE.

COMBAT BETWEEN YAHWEH AND EGYPT, THE MONSTER

In the first oracle against Egypt, dated to January 587 BCE, during the final siege of Jerusalem,[17] Yahweh addresses Pharaoh, "I am against you, Pharaoh king of Egypt, O great dragon (*htnyn hgdwl*)[18] who is lying down in the midst of its Nile branches" (Ezek 29:3). The divine command to the prophet, "Set your face" (Ezek 29:2), anticipates the opposition between Yahweh and Pharaoh. Although Pharaoh seems to possess power, his power is by no means comparable to that of Yahweh. The unequal power relation between the two contributes to the creation of the monstrous body ascribed to Pharaoh. The body is constructed by the prophetic discourse; the prophetic word exercises Yahweh's power over Pharaoh by assigning him the identity of a monster.[19]

17. Parker and Dubberstein, *Babylonian Chronology*.

18. In Ezek 29:3 and 32:2, the Hebrew word that is translated dragon/monster is *tnym*, where we would expect *tnyn* (cf. Gen 1:21; Isa 27:1; 51:9; Jer 51:34). I take the word to refer to a *tnyn* ("dragon") and not to "jackals" (sing. *tn*). This reading is supported by multiple Hebrew manuscripts that read *tnyn*, a variation that is reflected in the Targum (*tnyn'*) and the LXX (*drakonta*). Furthermore, the adjective *hgdwl* ("the great"), which describes the dragon that lies in the Nile, is in the singular, denoting a singular noun.

19. Scholars have debated whether the word *tnyn* has a mythological referent (so, to be translated specifically as "dragon") or whether it is demythologized (and thus to be understood as a terrestrial creature, such as a crocodile). The latter translation ("crocodile") would provide a geographically specific, localized nuance, giving the creature an Egyptian color, but the mythic translation ("dragon") would universalize the creature's geographic range. Even if the text does indeed describe a crocodile, this is not necessarily a raw demythologization, describing only a mundane reptile. In fact, the ancient Egyptians spoke mythologically of a crocodile-god named Sobek as the god of the Nile (Wilkinson, *Complete Gods and Goddesses*, 218–20). In other words, even if Ezekiel had a crocodile in mind, this does not automatically imply that he is demythologizing the *Chaoskampf* motif by referring to a local animal.

Not only does Ezekiel exercise Yahweh's power over Pharaoh by ascribing to him the body of a monster, Ezekiel also deconstructs Pharaoh's claims. Pharaoh is criticized on account of his claim: "My Nile is my own; I made it for myself." Between Pharaoh's claim and the prophetic word that Ezekiel is about to proclaim, we have a "speech war" between the prophet and the monster. "Ezekiel has created a literary structure admirably suited to directing the battle of opposing ideological forces, and the balance is heavily weighted in God's favor."[20] It is a combat in which discourse constructs reality. Ezekiel quotes Pharaoh's claim as the owner—and even the creator—of the Nile and its channels, the source of life in Egypt.[21] Through this opposition, Ezek 29:1–3 skillfully sets the stage for the combat between Yahweh and the monster of chaos. Thus the reader anticipates the first attack from the divine warrior, Yahweh.

The first divine offense against this *great* monster, which glorifies itself, is placing hooks in its jaws. The expression "I will put hooks in your jaws" is also used in Ezek 38:4 to speak of the judgment of Yahweh against Gog of Magog: "I will turn you around and put hooks into your jaws, and I will lead you out with all your army." The idea in both passages is to emphasize that the semi-divine, mythic opponent—the monster Egypt in chapter 29 and the mythical figure Gog in chapter 38—is under the control of Yahweh. Although the jaws of this creature are probably the most powerful parts of its body, they become the site on which Yahweh manifests his power (cf. Job 40:26). Ezekiel describes in great detail what befalls the body of the monster of chaos: Yahweh dismembers its body. This dismemberment underlines the divine ability to annihilate the monster, that is, Egypt. Divine sovereignty is inscribed directly on the body of the monster.

The combat between the monster and Yahweh moves to the wilderness and the open field. The body of the monster will be thrown on the face of the open field, not to be gathered ('*sp* and *qbṣ*; *niphal*). The use of the *niphal* here denotes the isolation of the monster and the absence of anyone who would have concern for the monster of chaos. The semantic nuance in Ezek 29:5 is that the monster will die and will not be properly buried, thus bringing dishonor on Pharaoh and all of Egypt. Besides being dishonored, the body of the dead monster is left unburied and on the face of the field for another purpose. In Ezek 29:5b, Yahweh will offer its carcass as a food for "the beasts of the earth" and the "birds of the sky." "The carcass lying in the desert is

20. Davis, "And Pharaoh Will Change His Mind," 231.

21. A Scarab of Thutmosis III reads, "The Nile is at his service, and he opens its cavern to give life to Egypt" (cited in Greenberg, *Ezekiel 21–37*, 612). For more connections between the Pharaoh and the Nile, see Frankfort, *Kingship and the Gods*, 57–60, 194–95.

eagerly seized by birds and wild beasts which complete the work of destruction, thus shattering human pride."[22]

IS THE MONSTER UTTERLY ANNIHILATED?

Egypt, according to Ezekiel, is a monster that poses a threat to Israel's religious identity. Given the danger that Egypt represents, the prophet speaks
of a divine struggle against this monster of chaos. In the struggle, Yahweh
defeats and dismembers the body of the monster (Ezek 29:3–5; 32:1–5). Although the struggle gives the impression of eradicating the existence of the
monster through the annihilation of its body, we are confronted with Egypt's
ongoing survival, as the prophetic oracles continue to unfold. The prophet
Ezekiel speaks of Egypt's continuing existence when he proclaims that
Yahweh will restore the Egyptians after sending them into a period of exile
(Ezek 29:13–14). Yahweh announces, "I shall gather (*qbṣ*; *piel*) Egypt from
among the nations where they were scattered" (Ezek 29:13). This positive
remark regarding Egypt's survival is perplexing. Zimmerli writes, "One cannot suppress the question why precisely with regard to Egypt there should
be recounted this sacred, saving postscript which keeps Egypt's name from
extinction, whereas there is no such postscript with regard to all the other
groups to which the foreign oracles were addressed."[23] Of the seven nations
who fall under the divine judgment in Ezekiel (chaps. 25–32), Egypt is the
only one that is promised a return from the exile and a continued existence.

By comparison, the rest of the nations fall under divine judgment
without any promise of restoration. As a matter of fact, some of these nations are said to completely perish; they will not be remembered or exist
anymore (Ammon in 25:7, 10; 21:32; Moab in 25:10; Edom in 25:13; the
Philistines in 25:16; Tyre in 26:21; 27:36; 28:19). In the case of Ammon,
Yahweh declares, "I will cut you off from the peoples and I will make you
perish from the lands; I will destroy you" (Ezek 25:7). Along with Ammon
goes Moab; Yahweh will deliver both of them into the hand of the people
of the East. Although the oracle in Ezek 25:8–11 is concerned with Moab,
the prophet declares that Moab and Ammon will have the same fate, and
they will not be remembered anymore. "As a possession I will give it [Moab]
along with Ammon to the people of the East, for the Ammonites will not be
remembered among the nations anymore" (Ezek 25:10).

---

22. Eichrodt, *Ezekiel*, 404.

23. Zimmerli, *Ezekiel 2,* 115. For a similar observation, see Greenberg, *Ezekiel
21–37*, 613; and Block, *Book of Ezekiel*, 144–45.

To be sure, this language of annihilation and eradication was also pronounced against Egypt. When Yahweh dismembers the body of the monster, Yahweh intends to eradicate Egypt through shameful death (Ezek 29:4–5; 32:4–6). Furthermore, in Ezek 23:27, Yahweh declares, "So I will put an end to your lewdness and your whoring brought from the land of Egypt; you shall not lift up your eyes to them, and you shall not remember Egypt anymore." Though Yahweh declares that a nation such as Ammon will not be remembered among the nations, here in 23:27 Yahweh's concern is that Egypt should not exist anymore in the communal memory of Israel. Yahweh will put an end to the lewdness of Judah and its desire for relationship with Egypt; Judah will not *remember* Egypt *anymore*. In a sense the prophet declares that Yahweh will annihilate the influence of Egypt on Israel through eradicating the *memory* of Egypt from the communal memory of the Israelites.

However, the book of Ezekiel itself betrays this goal because it contains the largest corpus of oracles against Egypt in the whole prophetic section of the OT. In other words, the reader of the book cannot forget Egypt because it occupies so much space in the book. This observation raises questions: What is so peculiar about Egypt that despite the chaos it perpetuates, it continues to exist? And how can we explain the tension between the desire to completely annihilate Egypt (and its memory) and the fact that it continues to exist?

The prophet optimistically wishes to annihilate Egypt and put an end to Egypt's threat to Israel's religious identity. At the same time, the prophet realistically (though implicitly) acknowledges that this annihilation is impossible. Israel needs Egypt in order to define itself. Zygmunt Bauman suggests that "society can only define itself against its strangers."[24] A complete annihilation of Egypt would leave Israel without an Other against which to construct its identity. Caught between the danger and the necessity Egypt's existence, the prophet hopes for a complete annihilation of the memory of Egypt, while knowing that Egypt must exist in order for Israel to formulate its own identity. Ellen Davis asserts, "Egypt is too central to Israel's history."[25] Therefore, if Egypt must exist, the boundaries between Egypt and Israel must be strongly defined and maintained.

In Ezek 29:14–16, the prophet proclaims Yahweh's plan to minimize Egypt's influence on Israel. Yahweh will accomplish this in two ways, according to this text: Egypt will be restored to its southern borders, and it will

24. Bauman, "What Prospects of Morality," 12. See also the treatment of the category of "stranger" in Bauman, *Postmodernity and Its Discontents*, 17–45, cited in Sharpe, *Foucault's Monsters*, 2.

25. Davis, "And Pharaoh Will Change His Mind," 235.

be a lowly nation. In other words, in terms of empirical geography Egypt will occupy the southern part of its land; it will be at a great distance from Israel. Furthermore, on the political level, Egypt will be a lowly nation. As such, it will not interfere in the internal politics of surrounding nations, and it will not be a source of confidence for the Israelites.

RESTORING EGYPT TO ITS SOUTHERN ORIGIN

The prophet proclaims that after forty years Yahweh will gather and collect the Egyptians.[26] Yahweh will restore the Egyptians from captivity to be restored to Pathros, which is described as the southern part of Egypt and their land of origin. As a location, Pathros is mentioned in several places in the OT (Isa 11:11; Jer 44:1, 15; Ezek 30:14). These references inform us that Pathros designates the southern part of ancient Egypt. The name Pathros comes from the Egyptian name *pa ta rsy,* "the Southland."[27] During the time of Ezekiel, Egypt was governed by the Saite dynasty, which ruled in the delta area. The presence of Egyptian power in the delta area poses a temptation to the Judahites, as a possible source of help from their southern neighbors. Thus when Yahweh restores Egypt to its southern part (Pathros), the distance between Egypt and the Levant will be maximized.

EGYPT AS A LOWLY KINGDOM: MINIMIZATION OF POLITICAL POWER

In addition to creating this physical distance between Egypt and Israel by pushing Egyptian borders southward, Ezekiel proclaims a political minimization of the power of Egypt. Egypt will become a lowly kingdom, a nation with minimal political power. The Hebrew word *šplh,* translated above as "lowly," describes the way Yahweh portrays Egypt—namely, as a "low kingdom," and perhaps as a vassal state (29:14).[28] In Ezek 17:14 the same expres-

26. Minj argues that returning to Pathros has theological significance; for him it "signifies both their territorial and political restoration, which is equally linked to their historical origin. However, it has an important theological significance, which means bringing them back to the Lord through inner conversion of their hearts" (Minj, *Egypt the Lower Kingdom,* 192). I believe that the emphasis on Pathros in Ezekiel lies in creating greater distance between Judah and Egypt. Restoring Egypt to its southern origin is not an act of salvation. It is, rather, an act that aims at maintaining the boundaries between Judah and Egypt; in this way Egypt will not be a power to which the Israelites look for security.

27. Baker, "Pathros," 178.

28. See Tsevat, "Neo-Assyrian and Neo-Babylonian Vassal Oaths," where it is

sion was employed to speak of the kingdom of Judah as a "low kingdom": "so that it would become a lowly kingdom (*mmlkh šplh*) and not lift itself up, and that by keeping his covenant it might stand." The context of the latter verse is the Babylonian imperial subjugation of the exiled Judean royal family, and of a Judah that was made a "low kingdom," that is, a Judah turned into a vassal nation. Ezekiel's prophecy against Egypt will put limitations on the geography that Egypt imagines for itself and will also turn Egypt into a vassal nation subjugated to Babylon. Yahweh turns Egypt—once an empire—into a small colonized nation.

THE RESULT OF THE GEOPOLITICAL MINIMIZATION

Distancing Egypt to the far south and disempowering it not only removes it as a source of temptation, infidelity, and occasion for divine punishment, it also grants Israel a safer and more secure world. In fact, the security of Israel is a key theme in Ezekiel's oracles of salvation. This is the theme of Ezek 28:24–26, an oracle interpolated immediately after the oracle against Sidon and right before the oracles against Egypt. The oracle focuses on the security that will be granted Israel's returnees from exile. In this short oracle, the word *bṭḥ* ("to trust, to be secure") is repeated twice (28:26).[29] Then in the last segment of the first oracle against Egypt, when Yahweh minimizes both Egypt's political power and its geographical space, Egypt will not be a source of "trust or security" (*bṭḥ*) for Israel (29:16). Both of these statements concerning Israel's security (28:26; 29:16) are preceded by similar oracles regarding the restoration of both Egypt (29:13) and Judah from their places of exile (26:25). The repetition of *bṭḥ* throughout these passages highlights the conviction that Israel will be more secure if Egypt is at enough distance that Israel does not trust in it: boundaries between Egypt and Israel will be maintained and the chaotic power of Egypt kept at bay.

---

suggested that "lowly kingdom" is a technical term for "vassal state."

29. The word *bṭḥ* ("to trust, to be confident, or to rest safely") is used in Ezekiel to describe Jerusalem in her wickedness before the exile (Ezek 16:15; Jerusalem trusted in her beauty) and to describe the state of the inhabitants of Israel after the return from the exile. In Ezek 34:25, 27–28, Yahweh promises to make those returning from exile rest "safely" (*lbṭḥ*) in Israel. These verses prepare the way for the account of Gog of Magog in Ezek 38–39, who attempts to attack those who are resting "safely" (*lbṭḥ*) in the land of Israel.

IMPLICATIONS FOR PEACE STUDIES

Ezekiel's rhetoric concerning Egypt, and especially his portrayal of Egypt as a monster, raises important questions and implications for churches that advocate peace. Ezekiel's construction of Egypt as a threat to the identity of the people of Israel is ironic. The prophet who rejects political alliance between Egypt and Judah against Babylon—and deems it idolatry—ordains the geopolitical upheaval of the exile by allying Yahweh with the imperial power of Babylon (Babylon is the divine agent of judgment). In his complex context, the prophet seeks to make sense of the crisis of the exile by defending divine justice, portraying Babylon as a divine agent, and blaming the people for their cultic and moral impurities. In contrast, we often think that the world makes better sense when it is divided clearly between good and evil: Yahweh and Babylon on one side and Egypt and Judah on the other. The messiness of the exile and Ezekiel's own interpretations, however, teach us that we are better off when we let *none* of the characters off the hook.

The community of faith is surrounded by a culture whose prevalent worldview is structured by binary opposites (us versus them, insiders versus outsiders) and constructed by drawing the tightest possible borders and boundaries (ethnic, racial, religious, sexual, etc.). This worldview perceives the Other as monsters, and even demons, that threaten the purity of the community of faith. These monsters must be excluded at any cost, even if it entails violence. Another worldview advocates the polar opposite: peace by the erosion of difference and by opening up boundaries and eliminating all borders. This worldview normalizes the Other, suggesting that no difference exists between the self and the Other. In contrast to these two worldviews, the paradoxical category of the monster (*monstrare,* "reveals") opens up a new, third avenue in understanding how the community of faith relates to those who are deemed Other: our faithfulness to God is best mediated through negotiating both sameness *and* difference in our relation with the Other. Violence against the Other or violence against one's own identity will not bring about peace. To use Richard Kearney's language, peace has a better chance when one recognizes oneself as another and the Other as another self.[30]

---

30. Kearney, *Strangers, Gods and Monsters,* 80.

8

"These Three Men"

Another Look at Ezekiel 14:12–23

Brad D. Schantz

In Ezekiel 14:12–23, questions surround the mention of the three figures Noah, Danel, and Job.[1] While most commentators agree that the overall focus of this unit is Ezekiel's definition of divine retribution, they do not agree on why these three figures are mentioned. Part of the issue is the text's claim that they alone will be saved *bṣdqtm* "by their righteousness." This *ṣdqh* is interpreted variously. Some consider it a type of contagious, personal virtue that saves those around them, a view similar to the one evident in Gen 18:22–33 in Abraham's argument with the Lord regarding Sodom.[2] Others argue that the men's righteousness is their intercessory ability to perform works of deliverance, like Moses's prayer in Num 14:11–25 that prevents the destruction of the Israelites.[3] Still others argue that the men's righteousness is related to the fact that they are non-Israelite paragons of virtue; mention of them universalizes or generalizes the concept of retribution.[4]

---

1. The name Danel is used to signify the likelihood that the character being referred to in Ezekiel is a legendary Danel figure as found in the tablets from Ugarit, and not the Daniel of the HB.

2. Eichrodt, *Ezekiel: A Commentary*, 188.

3. Cooke, *A Critical and Exegetical Commentary on the Book of Ezekiel*, 153.

4. See Greenberg (*Ezekiel 1–20*, 257–58) and Zimmerli (*Ezekiel 1*, 314–15). Zimmerli actually combines the contagious righteousness with the universal nature of the men. Joyce calls them "paragons of virtue" and notes they "are in some sense international figures" (*Ezekiel*, 125). Block thinks they are all "paradigms of virtue," but argues

The position of this essay is that none of these interpretations are fully accurate. Rather, this essay argues that the three men are being mentioned primarily for rhetorical effect, not because of any single unifying character-istic or act that all three performed. In fact, the unit's use of these figures at this location relates directly to how the book of Ezekiel—as a whole—refers to ancestral and mythological characters and events. Noah, Danel, and Job are used in this passage as general non-Israelite intermediaries whose sto-ries echo both deliverance and divine destruction. They are named instead of figures such as Moses, Samuel, Abraham, and David in order to prevent *any* hope of miraculous or prophetic mediation.

The above thesis is reached in three steps. First, the unit itself is exam-ined, structurally and thematically. Second, the unit is examined in its im-mediate context. This includes comparing it and its context with its parallel unit in Jer 15:1–3. Finally, the unit is examined in relationship to the larger book of Ezekiel, paying close attention to Ezekiel's overall use of ancestral and mythological characters and events.

EZEKIEL 14:12–23

Ezekiel 14:12–23 appears to be composed of two sections, verses 12–20 and verses 21–23. Modern critical study of this unit within Ezekiel varies in its views of the passage's unity; verses 12–20 are usually allowed to stand as original to the prophet Ezekiel, but verses 21–23 are not always viewed as original. In the first section, the revelatory announcement of verse 12 is followed by four subunits of two verses each. The content[5] and cycle of each subunit are so repetitive in form and constituent parts that Zimmerli was prompted to refer to them as "monotonous . . . only slightly varied in detail."[6] Greenberg presents an alternative view. He notes that despite each being composed of seven similar statements, they are all uniquely ordered and therefore prevent monotony and introduce freshness.[7] Greenberg's analysis is compelling: both the repetition and the variation help emphasize the point that if a land sins against God and he punishes it, even if (three) esteemed, righteous persons were in it they would save only themselves.

---

that they are Israelite (*Book of Ezekiel*, 446–48).

5. (1) A disaster from the deity is said to be sent as punishment, (2) then the three men are mentioned, and (3) then some form of a statement highlights that they will save only themselves.

6. Zimmerli, *Ezekiel 1*, 312.

7. Greenberg, *Ezekiel 1–20*, 260.

Verses 21–23 are marked off by a second revelatory formula at the beginning of verse 21, *ky kh 'mr 'dny yhwh* "For thus says the Lord God."[8] There appears to be a shift in form and content. The form initially follows the previous four scenarios: disaster is named and the Lord's purpose in it (*lhkryt mmnh 'dm wbhmh* "to cut off from it man and beast"), and divine retribution is still in focus. But the theoretical offender ("a land") is replaced by an actual entity ("Jerusalem") and the exception to the case changes dramatically: the three men disappear and suddenly a *nwtrh* "remnant" or a *plṭh* "escapee" appear in their stead. In fact, the escapees are sons and daughters, ostensibly contradicting the previous three scenarios where sons and daughters are examples of those who will not be saved by the three men. These breaks in the form and content are why many scholars argue for the secondary nature of verses 21–23.[9] Again, Greenberg contends that the differences between verses 12–20 and verses 21–23 are intentional, and they help unify the text. He states, "The break in the formulation of his dealing with Jerusalem conforms with the surprising contradiction be-tween the doctrine of the cases and the fate of Jerusalem's inhabitants. The organic relation of the contradiction to the doctrine comes out not only in its troublesome use of 'sons and daughters,' but in its deliberate avoidance of any form of *nṣl* 'save'—for which *ytr* 'be left,' *plṭ* 'survive' and *yṣ* 'come out' are substituted."[10]

In regard to the text's unity, Greenberg's reference to "the surprising contradiction" is helpful. Stylistically, reversal of imagery and expectation (and/or inclusion of seemingly disparate imagery and expectation) occurs in several places in Ezekiel. Schwartz has argued that throughout the book, restoration is presented as part of the punishment.[11] Similarly, God's prom-ise to uphold his covenant (normally a good thing) at the end of chapter 16 is unmistakably bad news for the hearers: it will cause them to be ashamed. A related observation has been made in regard to the vision of bones in Ezek 37:1–14. Fox contends, "God uses a sort of reverse enthymeme. He does not proceed from a common, unspoken premise. Rather, he contradicts a universally accepted premise and constructs a new syllogism that directly confronts the people's unconscious, deep-rooted syllogism."[12] Arguably, the elements of surprise and reversal of common-held imagery and expectation are rhetorical devices employed throughout the book of Ezekiel.

8. Translations are the author's, unless otherwise indicated.

9. Zimmerli omits only 22b–23a as secondary (*Ezekiel 1*, 316).

10. Greenberg, *Ezekiel*, 260–61.

11. Schwartz, "Ezekiel's Dim View," 55–56.

12. Fox, "Rhetoric of Ezekiel's Vision," 12.

Verses 21–23 share two other details with verses 12–20. First, the theme of sons and daughters in place of the three men functions as more than a surprise; it also carries over the theme from verses 12–20. Second, the form of the closing unit (vv. 22–23) shares a parallel with the opening unit (v. 13)—both contain four verbal actions.[13] In verse 13, God is described as (1) stretching out his hand, (2) breaking its staff of bread, (3) sending famine upon it, and (4) cutting off from it man and beast. Verses 22–23 also contain a foursome, but these are actions taken by or on the people. The people are told that (1) they will see, (2) they will be chagrined,[14] (3) they will be chagrinned a second time, and (4) they will know.

Even if verses 12–23 are a single unit, the question of the three men remains. Were these three men specifically chosen, and if so, why? What role does their mention play? Are they simply props in the theoretical argument? The text suggests that the latter might be possible. The whole unit is set up as a theoretical situation, '*rṣ ky tḥṭ'-ly lm'l-m'l* "a land, if it sins against me by acting faithlessly. . . ." At this point an examination of the immediate context is instructive.

THE IMMEDIATE CONTEXT

The role of this unit in its immediate context is initially unclear, partially because of uncertainty regarding where the larger unit begins. The book of Ezekiel is often broken into three large units—chapters 1–24 (judgment), chapters 25–32 (oracles against the nations), and chapters 33–48 (restoration and hope)—though some scholars argue for smaller units.[15] As the text now stands, the temple visions end at the close of chapter 11 and chapter 12 begins with the prophet performing two sign-acts (12:1–20).[16] The end of chapter 12 then addresses visions, and chapters 13:1—14:11 contain three units regarding the issues of false or improper prophets, prophecies, visions, and/or inquiring of the deity. Following Ezek 14:12–23, there are then three

---

13. None of the other scenes contain more than three actions by God.

14. This translation attempts to capture the sarcastic nature of the use of *nḥm*, following Schwartz's discussion of the use of this verb in Ezekiel. Schwartz, "Ezekiel's Dim View," 53–54.

15. Sweeney suggests (in an unpublished handout distributed in a private lecture, 10 November 2005) that chaps. 8–19 are a subsection of the book of Ezekiel. Sweeney's outline is enlightening, but it does not adequately delineate the detail in this section of Ezekiel.

16. The first involves the baggage of an exile, while the second involves trembling while eating, signifying fear and uncertainty.

chapters relating to Jerusalem (15–16) and rulers who influence her (17).[17] Chapter 18 uses a proverb of the people to raise the theme of divine retribution for a second time in the book.

The connections of Ezek 14:12–23 to the chapters that follow are clear. The themes of Jerusalem's wickedness and coming destruction are expounded in detail throughout chapters 15 and 16, and to a degree in chapter 17. Additionally, the theme of divine retribution is picked up again in chapters 18 and 33. Furthermore, the terminology of *m'l* "acting faithlessly or treacherously" is also picked up in chapters 15, 17, 18, 20, and 39.[18] In contrast, direct links to preceding texts are not so obvious. There are a few, but most are confined to chapter 12.[19] Zimmerli also pointed out a formal connection between 14:1–11 and 14:12–23: both share a parallel reworking of the same type of casuistic legal form.[20] However, strong ties are not immediately obvious.

At this point, an examination of the thematic and contextual parallels of Ezek 14:12–23 and Jer 15:1–3 is helpful. Scholars have long noted the correspondence of these two texts. Zimmerli remarked, "The connection between the reference to the four powers of judgment and Yahweh's refusal to listen to prayer, even the prayers of great men of piety, sets Ezek 14:12ff in such a striking relationship to Jer 15:1–3 that *we cannot regard it simply as accidental*. Since Ezekiel's familiarity with sayings of Jeremiah is not to be denied in other places (especially chap. 23), *we may conclude that here he also is dependent*."[21] He goes on to point out that Ezekiel—though familiar with and at times dependent on sections of Jeremiah—always develops such texts to his own end. If these observations are accurate, then the issue of reliance and development becomes even more instructive when one compares the larger context of the Jeremiah text to that of the Ezekiel text.

Jeremiah 14 begins with a description of a great drought affecting the land (*'rṣ*). Then in Jer 14:11–12, the Lord tells the prophet, "Do not pray for the welfare of this people. Although they fast, I do not hear their cry, and although they offer burnt offering and grain offering, I do not accept them; but by the sword, by famine, and by pestilence I consume them."[22] This command is followed by a dialogue between the prophet Jeremiah and the Lord

---

17. Allusions are made both to Israelite and Babylonian rulers.

18. Ezek 15:8; 17:20; 18:24; 20:27; 39:23, 26.

19. Ezek 12:1–20 mentions exile, destruction, and the desolation of Jerusalem; 12:16 mentions sword, famine, and pestilence; and 12:19–20 name the inhabitants of Jerusalem as facing desolation.

20. Zimmerli, *Ezekiel 1*, 302–3, 312.

21. Ibid., 313; italics added.

22. Translation taken from the NRSV.

regarding the prophets whom the Lord did not send (Jer 14:13–14). Then an oracle of punishment follows, set against these prophets and the ones to whom they prophesy (Jer 14:15–16). This is followed by a cry of woe (Jer 14:17–22) and then the parallel text of Jer 15:1–3. In this text the Lord announces that *'m-y'md mšh wšmwl lpny 'yn npšy 'l-h'm hzh šlḥ m'l-pny wyṣ'w* "if Moses and Samuel stood before me, my intention would not change upon this people: send (them) from before me, and let them go forth!" The punishments of "plague" *dbr*, "sword" *ḥrb*, and "famine" *r'b* follow, and then a lament over Jerusalem's pending destruction (Jer 15:5–9). In this context Moses and Samuel are presented in contrast to the false prophets of the previous chapter; they are true prophets, great ancestral prophets who had the power to intercede with the Lord regarding the people.

The context of Ezek 14:12–23 is conspicuously parallel. Though no prohibition is given to Ezekiel about praying for the people, the preceding three units (Ezek 13:1–16, 17–23, and 14:1–11) are all about prophets and visions or divine inquiries. Like the context in Jeremiah, here false prophets are condemned (both male ones and women performing prophet-like activities), as are elders who seek prophets inappropriately. As in Jeremiah, the prophets and the people inquiring of them will be punished (Ezek 14:9–11). Then the Ezekiel text mentions three heroes in an apparent shift to a new theme, God's divine retribution (Ezek 14:12–23). In these scenarios of a hypothetical land sinning against God, God claims he would desolate it even if these three esteemed figures of antiquity were in it.[23] The focus of the text then shifts back to the city of Jerusalem and its punishment by the Lord. The following chapters of Ezekiel (chaps. 15–17) go on to describe Jerusalem's worthlessness and coming destruction.

The comparison reveals that even the larger contexts of Jer 15:1–3 and Ezek 14:12–23 contain the same sequence of themes.[24] This suggests that this larger unit of Ezekiel was also dependent on the context of Jer 15:1–3. If so, then it is possible that these three men play a similar role to those in Jeremiah. Yet it must be kept in mind that the book of Ezekiel develops texts for the writer's own purposes. So, what is similar and what is different? In Jer 15:1–3, Moses and Samuel are presented as ancestral prophetic intercessors

---

23. All three afflictions mentioned in Jer 15—plague, sword, and famine—are used by Ezekiel, in reverse order. Wild or evil beasts (*ḥyh r'h*) are added—in the second cycle—as a fourth affliction.

24. Though details vary throughout the larger contexts of each passage, both Jer 14–15 and Ezek 13–17 deal with, in the same sequence, the topics of prophets (not sent by God), punishment (of the prophets and/or prophet-related activities and those who inquire of them), certain men whose presence does not save those around them, and Jerusalem and its pending destruction. Both the MT and the LXX of Jeremiah are parallel at this point.

of Israel, whose presence did not sway the Lord from destruction. As commentators have often and correctly noted, apparently something similar is true of Noah, Danel, and Job; all three figures intervened in some way to change their deity's course of action. Genesis 8:20–21 describes Noah as offering sacrifices to the Lord after the flood. It is the smell of those burnt offerings that prompts the Lord's promise to never again destroy the world with a flood. In the Ugaritic Aqhat myth, Danel's performance of daily sacrifices influences Baal to grant Danel whatever he asks or prays for. When Danel mourns his son's death for six years, Baal dries up the land. It is only in the seventh year, when Danel stops mourning and offers sacrifice, that Baal again sends rain and the land is restored.[25] In Job 42:7–9, Job's prayers—as well (apparently) as Eliphaz's sacrifice of seven bulls and seven rams—are what prevent God from destroying his companions. Even in light of the presence of these men, God will not relent from carrying out his destruction.[26] In fact, extensive destruction or desolation plays a key role in all three stories.

So what is different between Jeremiah's men and Ezekiel's men? The first difference most commentators underscore is that the three men in Ezekiel are not Israelites. Then interpreters search for some other feature that would explain the mention of the three. Some advocate for their stated righteousness.[27] Others propose that the key detail is their attempts to save their children.[28] Still others suggest that the three (non-Israelites) are mentioned in order to universalize or generalize the principle of divine retribution.[29] But none of the explanations are entirely satisfactory.[30] A more satisfying observation is implied by the contextual comparison to Jeremiah: the most prominent detail that these men hold in common is that *they are not*

25. See Pardee, "The 'Aqhatu Legend."

26. The latter point is another similarity between the stories: each is laden with destruction. In Noah's story, the world is destroyed. Danel's son is murdered and the land is desolate for six years. Job's health, family, and possessions are utterly destroyed.

27. This highlights that Danel and Job are both described as caring for widows and orphans. However, this explanation is not as convincing with regard to Noah. Though he is described as "a completely righteous man in his generation" *'yš ṣdyq tmym hyh bdrtyw* (Gen 6:9), no extant texts describe Noah as performing specific righteous acts, let alone caring for widows and orphans.

28. This option is tempting, since sons and/or daughters are prominently named in every story. But as readers well know, only Noah saved his children. Neither Danel nor Job saved their children from death.

29. See n4 above.

30. One explanation that has not been adequately explored is whether these men share some priestly quality or role, such as offering sacrifice. With Ezekiel's priestly orientation, such a connection might be insinuated.

prophets. Rather, they are simply well-known, ancient, non-Israelite persons who at some point displayed the ability to influence the deity. It appears that the book of Ezekiel diverges from Jeremiah's characters—Moses and Samuel—in order *to remove the prophetic nature* of the intercessors, but not their intermediary ability or the stories of destruction.

But why the avoidance of prophets? Moreover, why did Ezekiel or the editor of Ezekiel not reference other nonprophet ancestors like Abraham? In fact, the hypothetical situation of Ezek 14:12–23 has much in common with the Abraham and Sodom episode of Gen 18:16–33. Did Ezekiel or the editor of Ezekiel not know the character or the myth of Abraham, or did the stories not yet exist? Or does the book of Ezekiel exhibit other consistencies in its choice of ancestral characters? These questions prompt us to consider the larger work of Ezekiel.

THE UNIT IN THE BOOK OF EZEKIEL

One issue to consider in the book of Ezekiel is the extent to which it reflects awareness of ancient events and people. Examination of the book suggests that the writer (or editor) was conscious of a number of earlier Israelite events and figures, besides Noah, Danel, and Job. Though Moses and Samuel are never mentioned, the book refers to stories they appear in or objects with which they interacted: chapter 20 refers to the deliverance from Egypt, and the temple visions describe in detail the ark of the covenant. Regarding Abraham, maybe the most illuminating allusions are those in chapter 16, where the book demonstrates familiarity with the tale of Sodom. Sodom is paraded as a sinful sister of Jerusalem and Samaria, but Abraham is not mentioned. This is surprising because the book in its present form is aware of a figure named Abraham; in chapter 33 his name appears in the mouths of those left in the land.[31]

Another issue to consider is the location of references to ancestral figures in the book as a whole. Of the major ancestral Israelite figures, only three ancestors are mentioned as individuals: Abraham, David, and Jacob. Two of them, Abraham and David, are not mentioned until late in the book. In fact, neither is mentioned until after the fall of Jerusalem is announced in Ezek 33:21–22. Immediately after Jerusalem's fall, Abraham's name surfaces in the mouth of "the inhabitants of these waste places in the land of Israel" *yšby ḥḥrbwt h'lh 'l-'dmt yśr'l* (Ezek 33:24). But he is not mentioned again. David is mentioned a few times, but even his name is confined to two

---

31. Chapter 33 is one of three units (besides chaps. 14 and 18) that discuss the issue of divine retribution.

locations, chapters 34 and 37.[32] The only ancestor who is named as a person prior to the fall of Jerusalem is Jacob, in Ezek 28:25,[33] and this verse is often attributed to a very late hand in the redaction of the book of Ezekiel.[34] It appears that—besides one late reference to Jacob in Ezek 28:25—no ancestors are mentioned as individuals until after the fall of Jerusalem,[35] and even then their appearance is tempered.

CONCLUSION

The preceding examination indicates that though aware of ancestors and ancestral stories, the book of Ezekiel severely limits their use. It mentions significant Israelite ancestors only after Jerusalem's destruction, and then sparingly. Even when apparently relying on other ancestral Israelite stories or texts, it leaves out the honored ancestors. And when the book uses rhetoric similar to that of the book of Jeremiah, it chooses characters that fit its purpose: the ancestral prophetic intercessors of Jeremiah are removed, and nonprophetic foreigners whose stories hint at both intercession *and* destruction are employed. For the book of Ezekiel, the characters (and stories) of Noah, Danel, and Job offer the least amount of hope that human intervention can influence the deity. If restoration occurs, it will only happen when the deity decides to initiate it.

32. Ezek 34:23, 24; 37:24, 25. Even then, Schwartz asserts that the future Davidic king is presented as a "legate, a puppet king . . . a liturgical figurehead" (Schwartz, "Ezekiel's Dim View," 61).

33. The name of Jacob appears four times in Ezekiel (Ezek 20:5; 28:25; 37:25; 39:25). In Ezek 20:5, Jacob's name is used as part of a title for the children of Israel, *lzr' byt y'qb* "to the seed/descendants of the house of Jacob." The latter three occurrences can be read as referring to the ancestral *individual* of Jacob, but only 28:25 can be construed as possibly occurring before the fall/destruction of Jerusalem.

34. Joyce considers Ezek 28:24–26 one of several late additions (*Ezekiel*, 180). See also Zimmerli, *Ezekiel 2*, 100–101.

35. Even if Ezek 28:24–26 is not a late insertion, it is quite possible to read the Jacob reference in Ezek 28:25 as referring to the nation or children of Israel and not to Jacob the individual.

9

Should We Take Time for War?

Moral Indeterminacy in Qohelet's Poem

Douglas B. Miller

According to Ecclesiastes 3:8, there is "a time for war, and a time for peace."[1] This brief phrase, found within the well-known time poem of Ecclesiastes (3:1–8), is interpreted by many to mean that war, though horrific, is at certain times an appropriate, even divinely approved, course of action.[2] To justify such a thesis, I propose, would require establishing one or more of the following: divine determination, divine approval, or the author's commendation of the war element. I will argue that none of these three can be sustained, particularly due to the moral indeterminacy of elements within the poem.

TIME AS A WISDOM THEME

The quest among ancient Near Eastern sages to discern the right time for specific actions and events is well documented. Within the Bible, Prov 15:23 urges: "To make an apt answer is a joy to anyone, and a word in its time, how good it is!" and in 25:11, "A word fitly spoken is like apples of gold in a

---

1. Translations of biblical texts are the author's.

2. See, for example, Craigie, *Problem of War*, 93, 111–12; Kaiser, *Ecclesiastes*, 65; and Fredericks, "Ecclesiastes," 117. Many commentaries pass over the issue of contemporary relevance in regard to the poem's elements, including war, though some insist that the poem is not prescriptive (see discussion below).

setting of silver." The sages also addressed the importance of being prepared for challenging times (Prov 24:16; 27:10) and their disappointment with those who are not reliable in such circumstances (Prov 25:19). Not to know one's time might elicit divine discipline (Jer 8:7–10). Wisdom knows the outcome of seasons and times (Wis 8:8), and to know the appointed times is to be wise (Job 39:1–2; 1 Chr 12:33 [Eng. v. 32]). Such understanding included awareness that each person had a designated time for death (Job 15:32). For many of the ancient teachers, the "aim of wisdom instruction was, in large measure, the recognition of the right time, the right place, and the right extent for human activity."[3]

Into this intellectual milieu came Qohelet's poem.[4] Following the Teacher's royal investigation, with its gloomy assessment of pleasure, wisdom, and work (Eccl 1:16—2:23), and the only slightly more hopeful perspective of 2:24–26, the start of chapter 3 takes a new look at human existence through the dimension of time. Qohelet previously compared human activity to the cycles of the natural world (1:3–11) and acknowledged the mysterious and arbitrary actions of the Deity (1:13–15). He now examines God's relation to timing in the activities of life. Although there are connections to the previous unit, this section (3:1–15) is unified by its attention to the sovereignty of God in overseeing events. The theme is further developed in the area of judgment (3:16–22). The latter paragraph resumes the issue of fate raised in 2:12–17, and the conclusion regarding pleasure (in 3:22) both reinforces 3:13 and reaffirms 2:24–26.

THE TIME POEM ITSELF

The poem begins with the statement, "For everything there is a season, and a time for every matter under heaven" (Eccl 3:1).[5] The terms *season* (*zĕmān*) and *time* (*'ēt*) have received much attention.[6] To summarize the current consensus, these terms are roughly synonymous, particularly as Qohelet

---

3. H. H. Schmid quoted in Rad, *Wisdom in Israel*, 159. Cf. also Sir 1:23–24; 4:20, 23; Hos 13:13; and Pss 1:3; 37:13; 119:126.

4. The book's author, that is the first-person voice speaking from 1:2 through 12:8, will be referred to as Qohelet, the Teacher, and the Sage throughout.

5. With few exceptions, there is little debate concerning the translation of the poem. With their consistent rhythmic syntax, these verses share characteristics of both a poem and a list (Whybray, "Time to Be Born," 469–70). Some interpretations understand v. 1 to be a thematic prose introduction to the poem (RSV, NRSV, NJPS, NJB), while others read it as verse and part of the poem (T/NIV, NKJV, NLT, NCV, NAB). See the discussion in Linafelt and Dobbs-Allsopp, "Poetic Line Structure."

6. See Barr, *Words for Time*; Wilch, *Time and Event*; Brin, *Concept of Time*.

employs them.[7] They both indicate identifiable periods of time, more than the passing of time. The term *zĕmān* (only here in Ecclesiastes) can indicate an annual ritual or an appointment (cf. Esth 9:27; Neh 2:6). The term *ʿēt* (employed exclusively through the rest of the poem and book) is used more broadly of a segment of time (a king's reign), periodic events (winter), sporadic events (a time of famine), and potential events (circumstances best for harvest).[8] Wilch's summary is apt:

- Qohelet does not have moments of time in mind but *occasions* or *situations*.

- He does not mean critical or decisive occasions, but rather *all* occasions.

- He does not mean only situations for decision but *all* situations that are presented in the daily course of life, e.g., emotional reactions and passive experiences as well as decisions for a particular activity.[9]

To conclude verse 1, the word *ḥēpeṣ* (matter, pleasure, desire), in its later usage, is a general term indicating something that occurs.[10] All these occur "under heaven," that is, the realm of normal human existence.

The poem then lays out fourteen pairs of elements: birth and death, breaking down and building up, weeping and laughing, and so on. The exact nature of the polarities is debated. Some call them *merism*, a pairing by which a totality is expressed through contrasting parts (e.g., near and far, old and young). Birth and death seem to qualify (= all of life) but not the others (does weeping and laughing = all emotions?). Another approach is to label these as *opposites,* because the elements cannot be done simultaneously (e.g., embracing and not embracing). Yet a mother can die giving birth (v. 2), and in a conversation, some are silent while others speak (v. 7). It is best, with Fox, to understand the list to imply totality by giving

7. This is also the consensus concerning their translation equivalents in the LXX, *chronos* and *kairos* respectively. Wordplay and synonymity are part of Qohelet's literary style. See Miller, *Symbol and Rhetoric*, 15–18; Sasson, "Wordplay in the OT."

8. As Fox explains, "'*ēt* does not in itself indicate the notion of 'appointment,' of the designation of a certain moment or period in advance" (Fox, *Time to Tear Down*, 198n12).

9. Wilch, *Time and Event*, 122.

10. Most scholars date the book to either the fifth or the third centuries BCE. Those favoring a preexilic provenance for the book incline toward a meaning of "wish" or "choice" in 3:1 (Fredericks, "Ecclesiastes," 108), based on the meaning of the root *ḥēpeṣ* ("to choose or delight in") as evident in Eccl 8:3. The noun occurs elsewhere in Eccl to mean "pleasure" (5:3 [Eng. v. 4]; 12:1) but in late Hebrew may also mean "matter, business" (as in 3:1, 17; 5:7 [Eng. v. 8]; 8:6; 12:10). The former meaning of the noun does not fit well in 3:1, 17: Qohelet is not addressing only pleasures, nor are all elements in the time poem a matter of choice.

a broad range of examples, all of which are in some sense opposite to the other though not all in the same way.[11] Completeness is also indicated by the number of elements: *seven* double pairs.

The syntactic pattern in verses 2–8 is the noun *'ēt* (time) plus verbs in the infinitive construct. In all but three cases, these infinitives are preceded by the preposition *lĕ*.[12] Considering that the final two elements are nouns (war and peace), it is best to consider the infinitives as gerunds, and to translate "a time for mourning" rather than "a time to mourn," and so on. This is analogous to the use of *lĕ* in verse 1: "a time *for* every matter."[13] Even so, we are left with five different possibilities for the meaning of *'ēt* plus infinitive construct. They are:

1. Actual: something that regularly happens apart from human involvement: "the time of evening" (Gen 24:11); "at the (seasonal) time for the mating of the flock" (Gen 31:10).

2. Actual: something involving humans that happens apart from human choice: "the time for her delivery (of a child)" (Gen 38:27).

3. Potential: time for something that *should* happen, a *moral or religious obligation*: "the time for seeking the Lord" (Hos 10:12); "the time for building the house of the Lord" (Hag 1:2; cf. 2 Kgs 5:26).

4. Potential: time for something that *should* happen, a *socially appropriate or strategic choice*: "the time when women go out to draw water" (Gen 24:11; cf. 29:7); "the time for the giving of Merab . . . to David" (1 Sam 18:19); "the spring of the year, the time of the going forth of kings (to battle)" (2 Sam 11:1; 1 Chron 20:1).

5. Actual: God's actions, past or future: "the time for the coming of [the Lord's] word" (Ps 105:19; cf. Ps 102:14 [Eng. v. 13]; Zeph 3:20).

In the time poem, there are no events from category 1; all concern human activity. Category 2 items include those in verse 2a (dying and giving birth),[14] but also healing (v. 3) and losing (v. 6). Nothing clearly connects with category 3, something with a moral or religious obligation; however, relevant poem elements could include building (v. 3, e.g., God's house, Hag 1:2), and seeking (v. 6, e.g., the Lord, Jer 29:13; Hos 3:5) or keeping (v. 6, e.g., a religious feast, Exod 12:17; God's covenant, Exod 19:5). Category 4,

11. Fox, *Time to Tear Down*, 194.

12. The exceptions are at v. 4b and v. 5aβ.

13. Seow, *Ecclesiastes*, 160.

14. Contra NRSV, NIV, and many others, the phrase does not mean "being born" but "giving birth" (Blenkinsopp, "Another Interpretation," 56–57; Seow, *Ecclesiastes*, 160).

appropriate or strategic actions, seemingly involves the majority of the items: planting, weeping/laughing, mourning/dancing, silence/speaking, and many more.

For present purposes, two important considerations remain: (1) whether war (and peace) should be included in categories 3 or 4, and (2) whether any or all of the list fits into category 5, divine action. On these two matters the poem itself is completely ambiguous. Despite a common assumption, the poem does not declare divine direction or prescription of the elements. Perhaps in reference to the phrase "under heaven," the Targum inserts the word *bḥyr* (chosen) to signify that each time is divinely appointed.[15] Supplementation is also necessary to resolve the moral ambiguity of the elements. One cannot assess love, hate, tearing down, and building up without more information. Loving the *good* is ethical, but loving the *wrong* is unethical, similarly for hating evil as opposed to hating one's neighbor. Breaking down someone's home or building a pagan shrine would be wrong, but tearing down an unsafe structure or building something useful could be good. The Targum and the midrash resolve the moral uncertainty by additions and explanations. Examples from the Targum include "kill *in battle*," "rend *a garment over a dead person*," and "hate *the guilty*"; from the midrash, embracing *the righteous*, keeping silent *during a time of mourning*, and applying the whole poem to God's actions on behalf of Israel.[16]

We note in passing that several proposals have been made for the poem's stand-alone message as well as for subthemes within the poem. None has won consensus, and none is determinative for addressing our concern for Qohelet's comment about war.[17] The variety of interpretations given the time poem further testify to its ambiguity apart from a larger literary context. We consider now the significance of the context in which we find the poem.[18]

---

15. "A time chosen to embrace," etc. Levine assesses the Targum as permeated with the influence of astrology, reflected in its use of the term *mazal*, a kind of fate influenced by the Deity. See his discussion of determinism in the Qohelet Targum (Levine, *Aramaic Version of Qohelet*, 75–76, as cited in Knobel, *Targum of Qohelet*, 29). Translations of the Targum in this essay are from Knobel.

16. Cohen, *Midrash Rabbah: Ecclesiastes*.

17. Plausible themes for the poem as a whole include war and sexuality. On the latter, and esp. the treatment of 3:5, see Brenner, "M Text Authority." See also A. Wright, "For Everything There is a Season"; Loader, "Qohelet 3,2–8."

18. On the distinction between the poem as an isolated piece and Qohelet's use of it, see Gordis, *Koheleth*, 228.

QOHELET'S USE OF THE POEM

When we turn to the question of how Qohelet employs the poem in the book, what we find suggests that the poem was likely borrowed or adapted by the Teacher rather than composed by him.[19] Terms and phrases found in verse 1 and in the question of verse 9 are found elsewhere.[20] But half of the twenty-eight elements are never mentioned again in the book, and six more just once or twice. Only eight are mentioned outside the poem three times or more.[21] Even when Qohelet mentions the poem elements elsewhere, he typically does not evaluate them. For example, though death receives a negative assessment, especially because it conspires against justice (e.g., 2:14–16; 8:10–15), war is recounted twice elsewhere without comment (8:8; 9:11).[22] On the question of war, then, the function of the poem within the book is crucial.

In this regard, we need to pay close attention to Qohelet's style. As for other sages, ambiguity is an important part of the Teacher's rhetoric through which he challenges his audience to discern the true from the false, the wise from the unwise. As Wilson explains,

> the purposeful use of ambiguity is a way of reminding the reader that wisdom observations usually reflect part, not all, of the truth. In other words, what is being asserted from one viewpoint might need to be qualified by other perspectives. . . . Deliberate ambiguity does not mean uncertainty of meaning. Rather, it is simply to identify a feature of the text that invites the reader to re-read the text in order to arrive at the final meaning. The meaning is, in fact, richer when it affirms two aspects which

19. Whybray, "Time to Be Born," 480. Other sections where this may be the case include 7:5–6; 10:2–3; 10:12–15; and 12:1–7.

20. According to Krüger, the structure of 3:1–9 mirrors that of 1:3–9 (Krüger, *Qoheleth*, 75).

21. Eight items mentioned three times or more: birth, death, planting, seeking, losing, keeping, speaking, and loving. Six mentioned once or twice: breaking down, building up, laughing, mourning, hating, and war. Fourteen items not found elsewhere in the book: plucking up, killing, healing, weeping, dancing, throwing and gathering stones, embracing and refraining from embracing, throwing, tearing, sewing, keeping silent, and peace. Other matters for which Qohelet states approval (community, 4:9–12) or *dis*approval (oppression, 4:1–3) are missing from the poem.

22. In 8:8, "no discharge from the battle," Qohelet does not speak of the inevitability of war but uses an analogy to claim that wicked oppressors will not escape judgment in the same way that the wealthy can escape war by hiring someone to take their place (Seow, *Ecclesiastes*, 282–83). The anecdote recounted in 9:11–18 celebrates the power of wisdom over weapons of war to overcome a besieging enemy, though we are not told how (negotiation?).

may be in tension with each other, but which are both equally true to life.[23]

For this reason, we should not be surprised that the poem (taken on its own) is susceptible to more than one interpretation.[24]

Qohelet has more than one thing to say about time: God has ordered the world, and it is best to comply with that order; yet God has also ordained that humans only partially understand. He introduces the topic with a poem that, by itself, may be interpreted in a variety of ways.[25] The discussion of time raises other points concerning God, humanity, and their relationship.

Another of Qohelet's strategies is to introduce a poem or event and then to comment on it (e.g., 1:3–8, followed by 1:9–11; also 4:1–3 with 4:4–12; and 6:1–2 with 6:3–6). Thus we must stay alert to possible reflections on the poem—as well as thematically related material—elsewhere in the book. In the case of the time poem, there is double commentary. In the first (3:9–15), Qohelet calls into question the value of the human activity represented in the poem. He affirms that God has arranged appropriate times for things, but then has hidden the plan from mortals by placing a sense of eternity or perpetuity (ʿôlām) within them. Qohelet counsels enjoyment and doing good, while stating that God acts to motivate awe of the divine. The second commentary (3:16–22) takes up the theme of human wickedness with the consolation that God will judge at the appropriate time. God tests humans to demonstrate that they are dust. The Sage declares existence after death to be unknowable and counsels enjoyment of work.

A brief overview will need to suffice concerning Qohelet's other teachings about time.[26] In 7:17, he counsels not to be wicked or a fool, lest one's time of death arrive prematurely. Section 8:1–9 employs ʿēt three times. In 8:5–6, it is twice combined with mišpāṭ to indicate that judgment will come at an appropriate time. One can be encouraged that unjust rulers cannot

23. Wilson, "Artful Ambiguity," 364.

24. For my understanding of the rhetorical strategy in the book—credibility, critique, and counsel—see Miller, "What the Preacher Forgot." Elements employed with ambiguity include the symbolic use of *hebel* (vapor, "vanity"), his use of questions, and his use of double entendre. See Wilson, "Artful Ambiguity"; Johnson, *Rhetorical Question*; and, for a very different understanding of the book's rhetoric from my own, Salyer, *Vain Rhetoric*, esp. chap. 3.

25. Wilson demonstrates this in regard to the opening poem in Ecclesiastes: "The same words can indicate both the regularity of nature and the apparent pointlessness of human activity. Both interpretations pass the wisdom test of ringing true to the sage's experiences and observations of the world" (Wilson, "Artful Ambiguity"). Similarly, Fox, "Indeterminacy," 175.

26. A total of forty occurrences for Qohelet's preferred word for time, ʿēt, twenty-nine of these in the time poem itself.

circumvent the day of death, though oppression is a present reality (8:9). Qohelet's strong commendation of enjoyment in 9:7–10 urges for it "in every time." This is best understood not as a challenge to the time poem at 3:4–5 (times for weeping/laughing, mourning/dancing); rather, Qohelet cites coming death to provide urgency to his counsel. In 9:11–12, Qohelet thrice refers to time as part of his concern for death: "no one can know their time" (v. 12) and all have the same fate. Finally, in 10:17, Qohelet congratulates those whose rulers feast at the right time, for "strength and not for drunkenness."

As Schultz notes, each occurrence of ʿēt subsequent to the time poem seems to refer back to the poem: 3:11, to express frustration that humans are not clued in to God's activities; 3:17, to be encouraged that justice will happen at the right time; 7:17, to show that the time of death is not completely predestined; 8:5, 6, 9, again concerning the time of judgment (as in 3:17); 9:8, showing that some things transcend specific times; 9:11–12, again concerning death; and 10:17, of rulers alert to appropriate times.[27] There is no reason to doubt that Qohelet has a consistent approach to time. It remains to determine how that is best described.

FOUR QUESTIONS, FIVE ANSWERS

The poem in chapter 3 has become a focal point concerning major philosophical questions addressed to the book. Scholars agree that Qohelet insists on God's control to some extent and that this involves complications for human beings. The extent of that control is debated. The intersection of God's oversight with human choice and their relationship to the twenty-eight elements of the time poem raises key questions:

1. *Is God's oversight a strong or a weak determinism*? *Weak* means that God allows for human choice to some extent.

2. If it is weak determinism, *are these actual events or potential events*? *Potential* means that God does not impose them, but allows them and may invite some or all to happen.

3. *Is there strong, medium, or weak human agency*?

4. *Does God approve of all these events or not*?

These questions have led to five major positions for interpreting Qohelet's use of the poem.

27. Schultz, "Sense of Timing," 260–62.

Position 1. Strong determinism, actual events, God-approved

All twenty-eight poem elements are parts of God's plan for the universe. Humans cannot change anything. Humans are puppets "appointed" for activities; they do not make their own choices.[28]

  Problems: For Qohelet, God is capable of operating this way (1:15; 7:13; cf. Prov 16:1, 9, 33; 19:21; 20:24; 21:31). Yet his rejection of strong determinism is evident in fifty direct instructions (imperatives and jussives with the negative particle) in addition to less direct instructions, e.g., his use of "better than" sayings to counsel enjoyment of God's good gifts (2:24–26; 8:15, et al.). Humans have some choice and can expect to be held accountable for these choices (3:17; 5:5 [Eng. v. 6]). The tension between divine sovereignty and human choice is not a problem to which Qohelet devotes much space: it is part of life's reality for which he gives counsel, assuming that humans can choose some ways that are better than others. Qohelet's confidence that God will sovereignly judge the wicked is even a source of encouragement in the midst of experiences that suggest otherwise (e.g., 3:17; 8:10–14).

Position 2. Weak determinism, actual events, God-approved, weak human agency

All elements are parts of God's plan for the universe. Humans have only the ability to cooperate with events and circumstances in order to help make them happen. From this perspective, the question of 1:3/3:9 urges mortals to consider how few choices they have in face of a controlling Deity.[29]

  Problems: This allows for some human choice, but not enough. Qohelet conducts experiments and explorations (notably in 1:12—2:26) that seem unhindered by divine orchestration. Other indicators are that humans have sought out *many schemes* (7:29) and are capable of dying before their *time* (7:17), suggesting that both God and humans can cause a change in the

---

28. "All events have a time when they will occur . . . God determines when this is. . . . man cannot change the course of events," the early position of Fox (Fox, *Contradictions*, 191), cf. also Murphy, *Ecclesiastes*, 39; Kaiser, "Determination und Freiheit." Schoors claims to embrace Fox's early position, yet insists this does not mean absolute predetermination or exclusion of a limited human freedom for action, represented by my option 2 (Schoors, *Preacher Sought*, 115).

29. Fox's more tempered view (Fox, *Time to Tear Down*, 197). One version of this approach is to assess Qohelet as a wealthy sage, depressed and resigned to the inequities of life but conveniently so because of his own relative comfort; Qohelet sees injustice but is impotent, even though the poem itself actually allows for a call to struggle against injustice (Song, "Asian Perspective").

time.[30] More positively, humans are capable of making their relationships and work better (4:1–12).[31] Schultz addresses the question of determinism in the poem by showing how Qohelet elsewhere encourages his readers to make the most of their time. After 3:11, which affirms God's role in the times announced in 3:1, all subsequent occurrences of the term *ʿēt* (time) involve Qohelet's admonitions to his readers: the call to enjoy life (3:16–22); warning of premature death (7:17); astute decisions to make at a time of injustice (8:1–9, *ʿēt* 3x); preferred ways to live in light of death (9:7–12, *ʿēt* 4x); and the call for a nation to rejoice when it has leaders who feast at the appropriate time (10:17).[32]

Position 3. Weak determinism, potential events, God-approved, strong or medium human agency

An appropriate time is "appointed" by God for mourning, dancing, and so on. All poem elements are part of the way God made the universe operate and are desirable from God's perspective. Strong human agency says that mortals should astutely take advantage of this awareness: to make one's life as successful as possible, recognize the appointed times and act in complementarity with them. Even times of giving birth, dying, and healing, though not chosen by the immediate participants,[33] may require appropriate responses from others who are involved. Alternately (medium human agency), the poem challenges its audience to comply correctly with the occasions to the extent that they are able, though not all may happen appropriately because of human ignorance or failure. Though some have argued that emotions (weeping, laughing, mourning, loving, hating) are not under one's control, these have an actional dimension (subject to choice)

---

30. Frydrych, *Living under the Sun*, 120–21.

31. Rudman argues that Qohelet resolves the problem of evil and human freedom as did Cleanthes, the Greek Stoic: "the righteous are stated to be under God's deterministic control, while the wicked are said to act outside it" (Rudman, *Determinism*, 198). However, Qohelet's struggle with the Deity has more to do with making sense of the divine plan than with solving the problem of evil and human freedom (6:12; 8:17; cf. 7:20, 29).

32. Schultz, "Sense of Timing," 260–62. Note also in the Psalms how God can be praised for being a refuge in a *time* (*ʿēt*) of trouble, without assuming that the Deity was somehow also the source of the trouble (Pss 37:19; 62:8). It is true that elsewhere God is given credit for both good and ill (e.g., Exod 4:11).

33. Though see Hos 13:13.

and likely involve the educational agenda of training to respond to situations with emotional appropriateness.[34]

Problems: The strong human agency version of this approach falls within the traditional wisdom perspective on time and is plausibly the message of an original poem borrowed or adapted by Qohelet. However, in its extant form the items listed do not emphasize human initiative. It seems odd to include matters over which people have little control (birth, death, healing, losing) if the poem concerns human initiative for success; in fact, very few of the elements (planting, building, gathering stones, seeking, speaking) lend themselves to such strategizing. Externally, Qohelet's commentaries following the poem (3:9–15; 3:16–22) suggest that his use of the poem is parody-like. In the first, (1) he raises the question whether humans actually accomplish much of value, even if they do the right things at the right time (3:9; cf. 1:3),[35] and (2) he insists that God has arranged matters so that mortals cannot be consistently sure what God is doing in this world (3:11; cf. 9:11–12). Human agency is restricted. However, even the "medium human agency" version of this approach falters because it is not clear that all elements are to be embraced as part of a divine plan.

To pause for a moment, positions 1, 2, and 3 argue that all twenty-eight items in the poem align with divine approval.[36] But several factors call this into question. The terms for time in the thesis statement of 3:1, 'ēt and zĕmān, do not in themselves require that the elements in the poem be matters of divine approval.[37] Elsewhere Qohelet commends certain actions

34. Contra Eaton, "Events and characteristic seasons of time are imposed upon men: no-one chooses a time to weep" (Eaton, *Ecclesiastes*, 77). See also Rudman, *Determinism*, especially chaps. 5 and 6. This excessively affective approach to emotion seems inconsistent with the more actional nature of Hebrew terms such as *love* (e.g., Deut 6:5) and *hate* (e.g., Exod 20:5), esp. in the wisdom literature (Prov 8:36; 28:16; 29:3).

35. In 3:9–15, Qohelet uses the Hebrew word *'āsāh* (to do) seven times. Verse 9 asks rhetorically what the human gains for all that the human *does* (*'āsāh*). The next verses emphasize that *God* is the primary actor, the one who *does* various things. The concern for futility after a detailed list of polarized events aligns with the ancient Mesopotamian *Dialogue of Pessimism* in which a servant and his master ponder the positive and negative entailments of diametrically opposite actions (Pritchard, *ANET*, 437–38).

36. Translations often promote this assumption, translating the infinitives as "to kill," "to seek," and so on, implying purposes with which humans are expected to comply. The NET of the LXX translates *kairos*, the LXX term corresponding to 'ēt, as "right time," so that there is a "right time to kill" and a "right time for war."

37. Contra Rudman, the opening statement in Eccl 3:1—"a time for"—does not declare that "God's deterministic control extended over every aspect of existence" (Rudman, *Determinism*, 124). Examples in the five categories of syntax identical to 3:1 illustrate a variety of options (above), and Rudman's attempts to establish this claim from elsewhere in the book do not convince.

(so they must be in some sense "good," e.g., 2:24–26; 3:13, 22; 11:1–6) and warns against others (5:5–6 [Eng. 5:6–7]; 7:17). Yet the Teacher does not presume to know all that is desirable from God's perspective (6:12). His statement of human ignorance in 3:11 does not affirm divine approval of the poem's elements; rather, it expresses confidence in God's ultimate plan, whatever that might be.[38]

The author, as part of the book's rhetoric, has presented a text that can legitimately be interpreted in more than one direction or from more than one perspective. In recognition of this, the final two positions posit that the poem's elements are things that happen, yet not all are desirable, even from God's perspective, though they may ultimately serve God's purposes.[39]

Before looking at the final two positions, it is helpful to consider briefly the impact of several distinct approaches to Ecclesiastes. In general, it is striking how little these "lenses" affect the interpretation of a given pericope.[40] Certainly, for those who understand the author to be a cynic, the places where Qohelet gives advice are taken as ironic or otherwise diminished (such as in Eccl 4:9–12). But in most places the subunit itself is not so drastically affected. Thus, all readers hear a weariness and futility in the opening poem (1:4–11) and discern a strong assertion that human knowledge has severe limits, especially in portions of the book's second half (e.g., 6:10–12; 7:23–29; 8:16–17).

But the time poem *is* one of the sections treated differently according to one's perspective on the book as a whole. The earlier, and more pious, approaches (Qohelet is perceived as piously apologizing for bad behavior) admonish obedience to God's will and ways as the message of the poem.[41] Those who hear the author as a bitter cynic (Qohelet is complaining about how God made the world) tend to hear the poem stating that humans have little or no productive opportunities in the face of a deity who controls the

---

38. Fox, *Time to Tear Down*, 210; cf. Sir 39:33.

39. "Since the author does not present these details from a moral point of view, the time here is not that which is morally right, but that which, be it morally right or not, has been determined by God, the Governor of the world and Former of history, who makes even that which is evil subservient to His plan" (Delitzsch, *Proverbs, Ecclesiastes, Song of Solomon*, 684).

40. For a description of five major approaches, and the significance for each of the term *hebel* (vapor, traditionally "vanity"), see Miller, "What the Preacher Forgot," 115–21. For present purposes, the two precritical approaches are collapsed and referred to as "pious," the third as "cynic," and the fourth and fifth together as "recent," the latter being those who espouse an instructive rhetoric for Qohelet's work rather than primarily a venting of frustration (cynic approach), yet which also reject the simple piety and other-worldly spirituality of the precritical approaches.

41. See the examples cited in Wright, *Proverbs, Ecclesiastes, Song of Solomon*, 217–28.

listed options.[42] More recently, interpreters have credited Qohelet with espousing some relative advantage—namely, that opportunities for pleasure
or for avoiding some of life's problems may be accomplished by astute decisions.[43] Within this perspective lies the potential for recognizing the moral
indeterminacy of the poem's list. The pietist and cynic approaches rule this
out by their attitude toward Qohelet's work overall.

Position 4. Weak determinism, potential events, not all God-approved, strong human agency[44]

God places limits on human choice, yet God calls mortals to distinguish
good from evil. *Humans do God's work* as they counter the wrong things and
do the right things.[45]

Problems: Although the basic analysis regarding the uncertainty of
God's approval of the time poem's elements is correct, and although Qohelet
is concerned about injustice *and* has something to commend in that regard
(e.g., 4:1–12),[46] Qohelet's counsel is primarily focused on helping people
navigate a frustrating and tragic world.[47] He is not a prophet and does not
call people to accomplish divine work, which is profoundly mysterious
(8:17). The emphasis Qohelet places on the power, immutability, and mystery of divine ways (e.g., 1:13–15; 3:14; 5:1–6) makes it awkward to consider
that the Teacher is inviting his readers to join with the Deity to accomplish
God's plans.

Position 5. Weak determinism, potential events, not all God-approved, medium human agency

God places limits on human choice. Yet, by being alert to what is happening,
humans can respond so that their lives are more likely to be better. Ecclesiastes

42. See, e.g., Crenshaw, *Ecclesiastes*, 92; Barton, *Ecclesiastes*, 97.

43. See, e.g., Seow, *Ecclesiastes*, 172; Fox, *Time to Tear Down*, 206.

44. Provan insists—though without explanation—that the list is descriptive of human existence in general and not prescriptive (Provan, *Ecclesiastes/Song of Songs*, 89).
Similarly, see Longman, *Ecclesiastes*, 118.

45. Tamez, *When the Horizons Close*, 61.

46. See esp. Miller, "Power in Wisdom."

47. Qohelet urges his audience (1) to acknowledge and accept the nature of human
existence, (2) to reject bad assumptions and strategies in regard to these realities, and
(3) to adopt better ways of responding to them. See specific descriptions of each of
these categories in Miller, *Ecclesiastes*, 32.

11:6 is especially telling: because one cannot be sure of the times, one should show initiative both morning and evening to make prosperity more likely. I believe this position to be most faithful to Qohelet's work. God has crafted a world in which certain things are allowed to happen, but Qohelet does not indicate that God directs or prescribes all of the poem elements. Qohelet has a discernible set of values toward which he seeks to motivate his audience, and a set of practices that he hopes his audience will avoid. But a comparison of poem topics to themes in the book overall makes it evident that the poem elements were not chosen to align either with Qohelet's values or with his criticisms. Qohelet's assessment of each element must be considered on its own.

SUMMARY AND CONCLUSION

We have seen that the time poem by itself is ambiguous on the concerns of this essay: whether the poem's elements are divinely directed, divinely prescribed, or commended by the author. On the latter, we discovered that the author does not typically evaluate or commend the poem elements.

Regarding divine involvement, we considered five models for the role of the poem in Qohelet's work. The diversity is due in part to Qohelet's artful ambiguity, and in part to different perspectives concerning the book as a whole. Though there is consensus that Qohelet presents God as having significant control over human existence, there is not agreement on its extent. Divine direction is only sustainable in the first two positions. Divine prescription requires a demonstration that each of the elements is divinely approved, a perspective assumed by the third position. Since we have seen that this is not demonstrable for more than a few elements, nor are more than a few even commended by Qohelet, I argued (also in view of the problems of position 4) for the fifth position.

In a tragic and paradoxical world, Qohelet presents his own version of a wisdom ethic. He takes on problematic understandings, such as superficial naturalism (1:4–11), workaholism (4:1–8), naïve political optimism (4:13–16), and religious triumphalism (7:15–18). In the time poem (3:1–8), he rejects the excessive optimism of the traditional sagely vision for time. Yet he still believes that there are appropriate times for certain things, including God's judgment (3:17).[48] He also contends that part of the human

---

48. Similarly, Treier concludes (regarding the time poem) that "a moderately prescriptive interpretation is best: the Sage favors an ordered life in which, when possible, one acts at the time made clear by divine wisdom. On the occasions when discernment is difficult, we must rest in the times being established 'under heaven'—even, perhaps,

dilemma is that we cannot know what God is up to, and thus wisdom itself is limited (3:11).

Although he evaluates some issues and makes reference to war among other aspects of human experience, Qohelet's assessment of war is uncertain. Perhaps he decided that war was too far removed from the choices of the ordinary person to warrant counsel. At any rate, the simplistic truism, "Ecclesiastes says that there are appropriate, God-approved occasions for war," must be rejected. The book never says this, and a sustainable interpretation to this effect is only possible within certain contested perspectives on the book and the poem.

This does not mean, however, that the Teacher has nothing constructive to offer in regard to the question of war or issues related to war. He astutely addresses injustice, power, and oppression. He acknowledges the human contribution to injustice (3:16; 4:1–3; 5:7–11 [Eng. vv. 8–12]; 10:16–17) and counsels those on the bottom of society to practice prudence when dealing with royalty (8:1–9; 10:20). The wise person uses tools such as calmness in the face of anger (10:4) and speech that is cautious and ambiguous (10:16–20). Qohelet does not counsel those at the higher end of society about how to gain and hold on to power, though he seems disturbed at the prospect of the poor and ruling classes switching roles (10:5–7, revolution?). In chapter 4, he identifies individualism and materialism as roots of oppression, and advocates for simplicity and community. Though any confidence Qohelet has for the resolution of oppression lies within the middle classes who are his audience, he expects few to embrace his cause. The wise, however, will commit to these values, even though wisdom is vulnerable and there is no guarantee of success against the abuse of power (4:13–16; 9:13–18). They will practice generosity (11:1–2) and take a right stance toward righteousness, wisdom, and the fear of God (7:15–18).[49]

the times to be confused as well as the times to act with conviction" (Treier, *Proverbs and Ecclesiastes*, 155).

49. On Qohelet as both conservative and radical when it comes to issues of power and oppression, see Miller, "Power in Wisdom," 170–73.

10

The Concept of *Shalom* in the Book of Chronicles

Steven Schweitzer

The biblical concept of *shalom* is multifaceted. In their important works, Perry Yoder and Willard Swartley presented compelling cases for the breadth and depth of this central theological concern in the HB and in the NT.[1] Helping to move the conversation away from a simple negative understanding of shalom (peace is when something—namely, war—is missing), Yoder and Swartley argue for a comprehensive and constructive approach to the nature of shalom. They both argue that shalom is peace, but it is not only the absence of war. Rather, it involves individual, communal, societal, and national features. Building on their foundational analyses, this essay will investigate the concept of shalom in a biblical text that is deeply invested in portraying a creative and constructive vision of shalom—the book of Chronicles.[2]

---

1. Yoder, *Shalom*; Swartley, *Covenant of Peace*. It is my privilege to offer this essay in honor of Perry Yoder and Willard Swartley.

2. This essay builds on the method and analysis of Chronicles in my book, *Reading Utopia*, which emphasizes the "better alternative reality" posed by the book, but without explicit connections to the concept of *shalom*.

A DEFINITION OF SHALOM

The Hebrew word *shalom* has a wide semantic range. At least fourteen meanings for the word have been identified: a simple greeting (literally, granting someone or inquiring about someone's shalom),[3] harmonious relationships between individuals or groups, a nonanxious presence in the midst of fear or uncertainty, peace/harmonious relationship with God, a blessing from God, prosperity (typically in material forms), righteousness and justice, safety and security, absence of war and violence, well-being, wholeness, dying well, something good and favorable, friendship or companionship (or alliance).[4] From this list, it is clear that the fundamental expression of shalom concerns relationships, whether material or social, and in various types: intrapersonal, interpersonal, intercommunal, or between humanity and the divine. Shalom refers to the presence or existence of right relationships, not simply the absence of destructive ones.

Shalom is not simply a state without negative practices; it exists when other positive qualities are present, such as righteousness and justice and rest. In many cases in the biblical text, this depiction of shalom is a reflection not of the current reality but of what should be the case for the individual or the community. Many stories and statements in the HB serve as negative examples, either as violations of shalom or as illustrations of what a society looks like when shalom is not present. This is true of various genres: in narrative, law, prophetic oracles, and wisdom literature. It is also the case in every time period represented by the biblical texts. In holding out positive examples, shalom often calls for something beyond the present, to something that should be but is not yet manifest. It holds out a vision for things as they ought to be, often in tension with the status quo and its tendency toward oppression. In this respect, the concept of shalom often forms part of the prophetic hope for a future that removes the inequities and failures of the present. In the end, depictions of shalom are not bound to any genre, time period, or social context in the biblical material.

ASPECTS OF SHALOM IN CHRONICLES

The book of Chronicles provides a perspective on Israel's history different from the one presented in the books of Samuel and Kings. Among the many purposes of the storyline in Samuel-Kings is a concern to explain the crisis

---

3. This is still reflected in Modern Hebrew's use of *shalom* as a greeting; the same is true in the related Arabic use of *sala'am*.

4. Leiter, *Neglected Voices*, 22–28.

of the Babylonian exile, the event that ends the book of Kings and hangs as a shadow over the entire narrative. The book seems to answer these questions: How did we get into this mess [the exile]? and What went wrong that this disaster befell our people? There is little hope and there are few positive comments about what went right; instead, the focus is on what went wrong. The conclusion of the book, with its "muted hope" of the continuation of the Davidic line in the release of King Jehoiachin from prison (2 Kgs 25:27–30), lacks any real sense of how to reconstitute society in the aftermath of the forced migration, only a suggestion that the story is not yet over. The books of Samuel and Kings are a "negative" history, of what not to do and how things fell apart. As the people live in exile, this account both explains how the current trauma occurred and how to avoid it in the future. However, there is not much in Samuel and Kings to build on when that community has returned to the land and begins to recreate a society that is constructed to succeed (as opposed to not failing).

In contrast to its main source,[5] Chronicles provides a view of Israel's history that focuses on what went well, and on hope for a new society built on principles different from those that led to failure. Written sometime in the postexilic period and likely in the transitional fourth century BCE,[6] this book addresses different questions: Where do we go from here? and How can we create a society that will last and not just survive but thrive? Thus, Chronicles moves from explaining the past crisis to constructing a way forward, one that moves past the trauma of exile to new possibilities. The new community needed a new history, a new story from which to draw inspiration for creating a new future.[7] As part of this rewriting, the Chronicler[8] offers many images of shalom—of a society that embraces the positive

---

5. Chronicles draws heavily on the books of Samuel and Kings in its presentation of Israel's history, sometimes copying it verbatim, and other times deleting, expanding, or rearranging the order of the contents. See the detailed treatments by McKenzie, *Chronicler's Use,* and Kalimi, *Reshaping of Ancient Israelite History.*

6. The precise date of Chronicles is a matter of dispute, though there is broad agreement on the general window of the late fourth or early third century BCE. Apart from the complexity of the textual variants in the postexilic segment of the Solomonic genealogy in 1 Chr 3:17–24, there is nothing that requires dating the book past the transitional period from the Persian to Hellenistic eras (Knoppers, *1 Chronicles 1–9,* 116; Schweitzer, *Reading Utopia,* 3–5).

7. In the face of disaster, communities often need to recover a different past or a different collective memory in order to formulate an identity that will give them a better position from which to start over.

8. In referring to the Chronicler, I intend the single author of Chronicles, almost certainly male, who is responsible for nearly all the book's content, while allowing for minor late additions, following the general arguments presented by Japhet, "The Supposed Common Authorship of Chronicles and Ezra–Nehemiah Investigated Anew";

qualities of these various relationships between individuals and groups and between the people and God.

The word *shalom* itself appears twelve times in Chronicles.[9] In line with some of the common uses in other biblical texts, the word is used as a greeting (five times: 1 Chr 12:17, 18 [3x]; 18:10), for a "good" death (once: 2 Chr 34:28), and for safety and security especially in returning safely from battle (four times: 2 Chr 18:16, 26, 27; 19:1). The remaining two occurrences of shalom (1 Chr 22:9; 2 Chr 15:5) are the most interesting and will be explored more closely.

In 1 Chr 22:9, David reflects on Solomon's birth. There is an explicit pun on his name: he will be the one who brings rest and his name will be Solomon (*šlmh*), who will receive peace (*šlm*) from God for the people of Israel.[10] Solomon is the exemplary, even ideal, figure in Chronicles.[11] In contrast to the depiction of Solomon in Kings, the portrayal of Solomon in Chronicles completely omits Solomon's failures at the end of his reign (1 Kgs 11). Solomon is without sin, without failure, and wholly commendable in this book. As is well known, the Chronicler similarly "cleaned-up" the reign of David (notably, omitting the Bathsheba and Uriah episode in 2 Sam 11–12 and all the intrigues in his reign that follow in 2 Sam 13:1—23:7), but the Chronicler did not eliminate all David's shortcomings. David still confesses his sin in the census incident (1 Chr 21:7) and he states twice—claiming divine revelation—that the reason for his disqualification to build the temple is his own guilt in shedding blood in warfare (1 Chr 22:8; 28:3).[12] Thus, David can function as a repentant sinner in Chronicles

Williamson, *Israel in the Books of Chronicles*; Williamson, "Composition of Ezra i–vi"; and Kalimi, *Reshaping*, 407.

9. It should be noted that Chronicles is rarely mentioned or cited in the books by Yoder and Swartley, and not at all by Leiter (see their indices). When it does appear, it is only in a list of "other verses" that support the main point being made by recourse to some other text. While the depiction of shalom is consistent with its portrayal in other biblical books, the Chronicler's vision for shalom does have unique features and is worthy of consideration on its own.

10. This pun on Solomon's name is not found in Samuel-Kings. This can only reinforce the emphasis the Chronicler places on Solomon as the "man of peace" in his unique depiction of the monarch.

11. See the fuller treatment of Solomon in my *Reading Utopia*, 81–88.

12. Contrast the similar statement in Kings (1 Kgs 5:3–4, which has Solomon tell King Hiram of Tyre that the reason is David's preoccupation with war (that is, he was too busy, and the situation, with its constant conflict, was too tenuous). There is no judgment against war itself in the text from Kings, simply the practical recognition that David's attention needed to be elsewhere in securing his kingdom.

and as a utopian ruler, but he is not perfect.[13] Solomon, on the other hand, escapes any criticism in Chronicles.

The contrast between father and son could not be more direct than in David's own words to Solomon in 1 Chr 22:8–9, which state that David will not build the temple because of his warfare and shedding blood, but Solomon will build the temple, will not engage in war, and will experience shalom. This contrast between the great warrior and the one who does not need to fight and is therefore superior is part of the Chronicler's larger commentary on war and peace.[14]

The views of war and peace in Chronicles have been much discussed.[15] The purpose of this essay is to present an account not of the Chronicler's view of war but of his view of shalom, of which only one part is his attitude toward war. Therefore I will only summarize how the Chronicler presents an understanding of war.[16] The Chronicler seems to advocate a militaristic policy that could be expressed something like this: Israel may defend itself—which may or may not be successful—but attacking surrounding nations is a *great risk* for the continued existence of the people, especially given the uncertainty about chances for success; even what may appear to be an immediate success may become a miserable failure. With no guarantee of victory in battle or of the ability to preserve national independence when it has been attained, the postexilic Israelite community should *not* seek to engage in war, expand the boundaries of the territory, or overthrow the political powers to whom the community is currently subject. Instead, religious reforms are to be carried out within the territory in which the people currently exercise some influence, without attempting to expand the sphere of influence into surrounding areas through military action.[17] Theologically,

---

13. Knoppers, "Images of David," 57–76.

14. In this context, the repeated association of Jesus as "son of David" may refer not to a comparison with David, but with the *son* of David, Solomon. In the Second Temple period, Solomon was perceived as a magician who brought about healing and exorcism of demons (see, for example, *Testament of Solomon*; Torijano, *Solomon the Esoteric King*, 6). Almost every time this title is used for Jesus by others in the Gospels, they are seeking divine healings and deliverance from demons, especially in Matthew (Matt 20:29–34//Mark 10:46–52//Luke 18:35–43; Matt 9:27–34; 12:22–32; 15:21–28). The claim by Jesus that someone or something "greater than Solomon" is also suggestive (Luke 11:31).

15. Niditch, *War in the Hebrew Bible*, 139–49; Rad, *Holy War in Ancient Israel*, 129–31; Wood, *Perspectives on War*, 58–59; Davies, "Defending the Boundaries," 43–54; Heard, "Echoes of Genesis," n.p., http://www.jhsonline.org/Articles/article_24.pdf; Knoppers, "Jerusalem at War," 57–76; Wright, "Fight for Peace," 150–77.

16. The details supporting this summary can be found throughout my discussion of the Davidic monarchy in *Reading Utopia*, 76–131.

17. This, of course, is in direct contrast to the actions of the Maccabees a few

as demonstrated by the narratives in Chronicles, war can never produce authentic and lasting peace.[18] Peace is a gift of God that human agency cannot fully actualize of its own accord, as repeatedly illustrated in Chronicles. Thus, when viewed as a whole and in direct contrast to many of the prevailing views during the centuries of the Second Temple period, the Chronicler advocates a pacifistic, quietistic attitude, particularly in rejecting offensive actions in the present situation.

The other significant instance of the term shalom in Chronicles occurs during the reign of Asa in 2 Chr 15:5. A prophet named Azariah speaks about a time in Israel's past—the precise referent is difficult to determine, but it most likely alludes to the period of the conquest or Judges[19]—when the people were "without the true God, and without a teaching priest, and without law" so that there was no shalom and the people lived in fear and danger. Azariah continues to encourage King Asa, who engages in reform of the people's worship and the removal of idols (2 Chr 15:2–19). As a result, the land experiences no war for many years. There is an explicit contrast between the people "seeking God" with all their hearts in their worship, and the practices of the past and their failure to do exactly this. In this particular passage, several key elements of the Chronicler's vision for shalom come together:

1. the centrality of worship at the temple in Jerusalem;

2. the actions of righteous kings to restore proper worship;

3. the importance of music, singing, and instruments in expressions of worship;[20]

4. the continuing prophetic voice calling the people to repentance and to action;[21]

5. the inclusion of individuals from the northern tribes who remain faithful to Yahweh in worship at Jerusalem;[22]

centuries later in their violent revolt, their military expansionism, and their forced imposition of the practice of Judaism in those areas (1 Macc 2:46; Josephus, *Ant.* 13.257–58, 318–19).

18. Compare the helpful and provocative treatment of "Post-Violence Peace" as discussed by Leiter, *Neglected Voices*, 51–67.

19. Japhet, *I & II Chronicles*, 718–21.

20. See my discussion on music, singing, and instruments in *Reading Utopia*, 159–64.

21. See my excursus on prophecy (ibid., 43–46).

22. See also, 2 Chr 11:13–17; 30:1–22.

6. the emphasis on the condition of the heart in committing oneself to God; and

7. the "democratization" of leadership, so that the king does not act unilaterally but consults and works collaboratively with other leaders or the people as a whole in making decisions.[23]

Each of these elements contributes to the depiction of shalom experienced during the "faithful" part of Asa's reign. In contrast, in the final five years of his reign he fails to seek God, takes money from the temple treasury to form a military alliance with Aram (trusting in military might instead of God), imprisons (in a rage) the prophet who speaks against him, and acts harshly toward the people (2 Chr 16:1–12).[24] Thus, as Asa moves away from the appropriate practices and attitudes that promoted its presence, the shalom brought to the people is undone.

These two contrasting uses of shalom in the book reveal a great deal about the Chronicler's overarching theological concerns that echo and repeat throughout his portrayal of Israel's past. From this point, it is worth moving beyond instances of the word *shalom* to the details of a representative text that demonstrate most fully the Chronicler's vision of shalom as the manifestation of right relationships: the account of Hezekiah's Passover in 2 Chr 30.[25]

First, this chapter begins with the king, Hezekiah, taking counsel with the officials and all the assembly in Jerusalem. In the book of Kings, the monarch almost always acts alone. Throughout Chronicles, good or model rulers consistently work in tandem with the people, making decisions collaboratively. As noted above, scholars have labeled this the "democratization tendency" in the book. The ruler does not legislate from on high but instead demonstrates sensitivity to the insights and wisdom of the community.[26]

---

23. See Ben Zvi, "Book of Chronicles," 271–74; Japhet, *Ideology of the Book of Chronicles*, 416–28.

24. In contrast to Asa's "crushing" the people, both David and Solomon are said to have executed justice and righteousness (*mšpṭ wṣdqh*) for the people (2 Sam 8:15//1 Chr 18:14; 1 Kgs 10:9//2 Chr 9:8, respectively). In addition to one reference to Josiah (Jer 22:11, 15–17), David and Solomon are the only kings in the entire HB acclaimed as having engaged in this activity, a necessary feature of shalom; see, Yoder, *Shalom*, 24–38. In addition, there is envisioned explicitly a future king who will replicate these ideals; see, e.g., Isa 9:2–7; 11:1–9; 16:4b–5; 32:1; Jer 23:5; 33:15.

25. I have come to view this particular text as the lens through which I read the entire book, seeing in its details a sophisticated and relevant theological statement.

26. Those in the Anabaptist and Pietist traditions might hear in this, appropriately, an echo of the concept of the priesthood of all believers.

Second, this community decides to celebrate the Passover festival during the second month (2 Chr 30:2, 13, 15). The Torah, the authoritative law, explicitly requires that it be observed in the first month and that those who fail to follow the written regulations should be cut off from the people (Exod 12:43–49; Lev 23:4–8; Num 28:16–25; Deut 16:1). So, the proper thing to do would be to wait nearly a full year for the appropriate time to celebrate. But they do not. Instead, explicit disobedience to the literal command regarding timing for the festival "seemed right" to them. There is no appeal to the Torah, tradition, or new revelation. Instead, the community makes a decision given their present circumstance. This phrase finds an intriguing echo in Acts 15, at the Jerusalem Council.[27] In this new situation, when the early Christians were arguing over the inclusion of the Gentiles, they did not quote authoritative texts to support their decision.[28] They argued from their experience—what Paul, Barnabas, and Peter, among many others, had seen. The letter sent by these leaders to the churches explaining the theological rationale for why Gentiles should be included states plainly: "It seemed good to the Holy Spirit and to us." In this, there is no logical exegesis of Scripture and no appeal to tradition; rather, they appeal to experience and sensitivity to the movement of the Spirit in their present, perhaps drawing implicitly on the precedent set forth in 2 Chr 30.

In this provocative chapter in Chronicles, why did the community feel it should worship at the wrong time? Because of practical concerns: the time had passed, the priests were not in the proper state of ceremonial purity, and the people had not gathered in Jerusalem on time. In light of this delay, Hezekiah and the people decide to send letters[29] to the people of Israel still living in the northern part of the land asking them to join in the celebration. Two points are worth noting: first, according to the book of Kings, no Israelites were living in the northern kingdom during Hezekiah's reign. In the account found in 2 Kgs 17, *all* the people were deported by the Assyrians, and non-Israelites were resettled in the area. The text in Kings is explicit about this point. These "lost tribes" of the north are no longer to be identified with Israel, according to the narrative in Kings. Israel is now equated with the southern tribes, and more precisely, with those sent

---

27. I wish to thank my colleague Loren Johns for suggesting this possible connection between 2 Chr 30 and Acts 15.

28. Those present who wanted to continue the practice of requiring circumcision could point to a text from the Torah that explicitly links circumcision with inclusion and the failure to be circumcised as a reason for exclusion from the people of God (Gen 17:1–14).

29. Perhaps this is another subtle link between Acts 15 and 2 Chr 30: the use of letters to convey the radical decision.

into Babylonian exile. Chronicles tells a different tale: not all Israelites were deported, and they retained their identity as Israel, the people of God. Their identity was not lost. Chronicles never rejects the people of the northern kingdom.[30] Instead, Chronicles extends hope to these people, inviting and including them, not rejecting them.

However, only a few northerners came; most laughed the messengers to scorn. Those few who did come were moved by humility to accept this invitation of hospitality, a stark change after more than 250 years of hostility between the northern and southern kingdoms. Humility and having a "true heart" is clearly one of the chief virtues in Chronicles (2 Chr 12:6–8; 29:10, 31, 34; 31:20–21; 33:12, 23; 34:26–28). Pride is the chief sin in the book, repeatedly and explicitly condemned (2 Chr 25:29; 26:16; 32:26; 36:12).[31] In this situation that emphasizes motivation and internal disposition, 2 Chr 30:12 further states that the "hand of God" gave the people "one heart" to come together. This depiction of unity redefines Israel: faithfulness is defined by allegiance to God, not to political regimes or endogamy.[32]

As 2 Chr 30 continues, these northerners come to celebrate, but another problem arises: there are not enough priests and not enough time for these northerners to go through the cleansing rituals that would allow them to participate. Again, the community could simply wait (they are a month late anyway, remember!), but they do not. This text seems to revel in the violations of Torah in this Passover event. At least three times it mentions the improper time of observance; it notes that the priests and Levites were ashamed, that the people were not ritually clean, that the Levites functioned as priests rather than as the priests' assistants [as they should according to the Torah (vv. 16–17)], and that the unclean northerners actually ate the Passover in explicit violation of the written commands of God in the Torah (v. 18). The text seems excessive in its desire to point out all the improper practices.

In response, Hezekiah does not offer a reprimand. There is no prophetic word of condemnation for violating the authoritative Torah and no warning of impending judgment for their actions. Instead, Hezekiah prays a simple prayer: "The good Lord pardon all who set their hearts to seek God,

30. While Chronicles was once connected by scholars to the negative view of the north that is clearly expressed in Ezra-Nehemiah, this link is no longer held. When Chronicles is examined on its own, it becomes clear that the book contains a much more positive view of the northern tribes; see, further, my *Reading Utopia*, 9–10, 53–60, 71–75.

31. Steven McKenzie identifies pride as the "basic cause of sin" in the book (*1–2 Chronicles*, 57).

32. On this as a significant theme throughout Chronicles, see my *Reading Utopia*.

the Lord the God of their ancestors, even though not in accordance with the sanctuary's rules of cleanness" (v. 19). Several points are worth noting. First, the actions are not following the rules and Hezekiah does not try to hide this or explain it away. Hezekiah acknowledges that this practice does not match the prescriptions, but it does reflect the principles that lie behind them. Second, Hezekiah calls on the "good Lord" (*yhwh ḥṭwb*). This is significant. In the entire HB, this is the only place where the divine name is paired with "good" as an attributive adjective. The phrase "God is good" is extremely common, especially in the Psalms, but this is the only time the phrase "the good Lord" is used to describe God.[33] This linguistic point serves as a major theological statement: the appeal is to God's inherent ethic and person, to the true character of the divine, and to the hope for mercy and grace that comes from God's goodness.

How does God respond? Does God smite them, reject them, or send a prophet to straighten them out? No, in contrast to what may be expected, God hears Hezekiah's prayer and heals the people. God transforms them. Hezekiah does not and cannot do that. God acts in accordance with God's character. God hears Hezekiah's simple prayer, offered in humility, and apparently approves of this event, despite (or on account of?) all its technical failures. And the response of the people? Exuberant and excessive joy in celebrating together, by "all who set their hearts to seek God." The condition of the heart trumps formal practices, even written authoritative texts with precise procedures.

"Seeking God" is the ambiguous phrase used in Chronicles to indicate authentic worship and the quest for the divine.[34] It is never defined and never limited. It is a multivalent phrase that resists categorization. It remains open, suggesting a variety of actions as valid theological and spiritual expressions. The idea suggests numerous means of reaching out to God, rather than a quick-and-easy, sure-proof program to be replicated. In this text, as throughout the book of Chronicles, the notion of simply replicating the past in the present for an assured result is flatly rejected. Authentic theology requires adaptation, without completely leaving the past behind. Furthermore, Chronicles celebrates innovation, commends creativity, and extols the virtue of change. Rather than say "this is how it has always been" or "the tradition teaches" or even "the Torah [the Bible] says," Chronicles invites its readers into a world where continuity and innovation work together

---

33. The "Lord is good" (*yhwh ky ṭwb* or *ṭwb yhwh*) occurs several times (e.g., Jer 33:11; Nah 1:7; numerous times in Psalms; 1 Chr 16:34 [citing Ps 106:1]; and 2 Chr 7:3).

34. See Begg, "'Seeking Yahweh,'" 128–41; Endres, "Theology of Worship," 165–88; and Graham, "Setting the Heart," 124–41.

in unresolved tension and the messiness of reality, and in the formation of theology in the midst of uncertainty and shifting realities of the present. God is still "the God of the ancestors," as Hezekiah calls out in his prayer. There is still continuity with the past, but new circumstances require new approaches and creative theological statements about the divine, such as reaching out to those often excluded, breaking some rules while finding the principles behind them to be more important, and recognizing that the community (rather than the isolated individual) provides the best context for doing theology.

All this comes together as a rather provocative development in the concept of shalom. This chapter presents the restoration of right relationships between leader and people, between people excluded and those in the center of power, and between God and humanity. Perhaps most interestingly, this restoration happens not on the basis of rigid observance of the Torah but in actions that highlight the priority of the condition of one's heart over the written authoritative rules. Right relationships have been restored in an unconventional and potentially subversive manner. The book of Chronicles does not give its readers all the answers to theological questions, but the entire book offers a means and a model for those who stop to ponder its theological perspective and work together in pursuit of truth, seeking to live out the principles of shalom in this world.[35] The view of shalom in Chronicles adds to the theological complexity of the term and to our understanding of the scope of God's vision for wholeness and peace in a wide variety of right relationships.

---

35. That many of these theological positions also find echoes and affirmations in the NT is not without significance. While the Chronicler is not Jesus, and this utopia ("better alternative reality") for the people is not identical to the ones found in the NT, the book exists on a trajectory that moves from the Old Testament to the New. It also serves to reject, yet once again, common false dichotomies set up between the Testaments.

11

Sex, Knowledge, and Evil

Violence and Peace in the *Book of the Watchers*

Jackie Wyse-Rhodes

INTRODUCTION

The reported marriages between divine beings[1] and human women—preserved in Genesis 6:1–4 in what appears to be a fragment of tradition—crops up again in expanded form in the *Book of the Watchers*, one of the earliest known works of Jewish apocalyptic literature. The *Book of the Watchers* is the first of five books that make up *1 Enoch* and dates to the third century BCE. Though the account in Genesis focuses primarily on the divine-human marriages and their progeny, the Enochic literature displays a more complex set of interests, exploring not only the nature of these sexual unions but also the acquisition of knowledge and the onset of violence on the earth (and the relationship of each to the other).

In this essay, I will explore ways the *Book of the Watchers* expands on the mythic fragment in Gen 6, paying attention to the manner in which

---

1. The divine beings are called the "sons of God" in Genesis and "Watchers" in later works like *1 Enoch* and *Jubilees*.

this later text[2] judges the actions of the Watchers negatively[3] and links their disorderly conduct to the proliferation of violence on the earth. In the end, I will argue that the *Book of the Watchers* links violence to the introduction of evil into the world in a way distinct from the book of Genesis.[4]

Violence and Peace in Genesis 6:1–4

Unlike the *Book of the Watchers*, Gen 6:1–4 does not explicitly address issues of violence and peace:

> When people began to multiply on the face of the ground, and daughters were born to them, the sons of God saw that they were fair; and they took wives for themselves of all that they chose. Then the Lord said, "My spirit shall not abide in mortals forever, for they are flesh; their days shall be one hundred twenty years." The Nephilim were on the earth in those days—and also afterward—when the sons of God went in to the daughters of humans, who bore children to them. These were the heroes that were of old, warriors of renown. (Gen 6:1–4 NRSV)

In its immediate context in Genesis, these four verses constitute an odd mythic fragment, nestled between (but not explicitly connected to) the preceding tales of creation and the subsequent tales of worldwide flood. Readers of the book of Genesis have already been drawn into stories of human violence (Cain and Abel) and human hubris (the tower of Babel); cities have been established as centers of flourishing civilization, technology, and the arts; genealogies abound. But here in chapter 6, a new and fragmentary narrative breaks onto the scene, different in tone from the material that has come before.

The unions described in Gen 6:1–4 are not ordinary marriages; this is the only instance in the Hebrew canon in which divine beings marry human beings. Yet these marriages are described in much the same way as other marriages in the HB: the divine beings' regard for human women is

2. Some have argued that the book of Genesis uses the *Book of the Watchers* as a source. I find it more convincing that the *Book of the Watchers* expands upon the mythic fragment preserved in Genesis, perhaps drawing on oral tradition as well.

3. The *Book of the Watchers* portrays most of the Watchers' actions in a negative light. The *Book of Jubilees*, which retells Genesis and parts of Exodus, and is dated to about a century later, portrays the Watchers' pedagogical endeavors positively, while judging their sexual unions with human women as wicked.

4. This is not to say that the *Book of the Watchers* was necessarily intended to serve as a polemic against Genesis. The two books do, however, provide different answers to certain theological questions, such as the nature and origins of evil.

presented neutrally, as physical attraction. Furthermore, the progeny produced by these marriages are portrayed exceptionally, as heroes.[5]

Setting aside the exceptional nature of divine-human marriage itself, questions linger, especially regarding women's agency and the nature of the progeny produced by these divine-human unions. One unknown is whether the daughters of humans assented to their unions with the divine beings. Looking at the language of marriage in Genesis more broadly,[6] these women seem to have no more or less agency than participants in ordinary "earthly" marriages. In both cases, men are said to "take" (*lqḥ*) women.[7] One possible (yet oblique) reference to violence is the fact that the children of these unusual unions are said to be *gb(w)rym*—"warriors" or "strong ones"—a word that may imply violence but is more clearly indicative of might and heroism.[8] Violence or coercion may play a latent role in this story, but no more so than in other biblical stories of women being given and taken in marriage, or in stories of warriors and heroes among the Israelites.

The following pericope—describing the onset of the worldwide flood—includes one explicit reference to violence. Gen 6:5 makes it clear that the flood was initiated in response to wickedness and corruption.[9] These claims are followed by the only overt reference to violence in Gen 6: "and violence covered the face of the earth" (6:11b). This summary statement describes, in general, the state of affairs on earth that led to God's re-making of the world (arguably another violent act). Though violence is present in Gen 6, the link between the first four verses in chapter 6 and the violence named in the ensuing flood story is tenuous at best. In contrast, violence is prominently featured in the *Book of the Watchers*. In fact, it is explicitly linked to the origins of evil in the created order.

5. In placing these verses just prior to the account of human corruption that led to the flood, the redactor may have hoped that the reader would associate the actions of the divine beings with the subsequent moral chaos on earth. However, these negative valuations surpass the text's explicit meaning and entail judgment on the reader's part. In and of themselves, the only judgments these verses make are positive ones.

6. Cf. Gen 12:19; 24:67; 25:1.

7. Rape is usually indicated with additional, harsher verbs. See, for example, Gen 34:2, in which Shechem is said to lay with Dinah "by force" (NRSV). The text reads *wyqḥ 'th wyškb 'th wy'nh* "and he took her and he lay with her and he humiliated/vexed/oppressed her."

8. For example, in 1 Sam 14:52, *'iš gibbôr* is used in parallel with *'iš ḥayil*, phrases that can be best interpreted as "man of strength" and "man of honor." However, in passages such as 1 Sam 21:17, 2 Sam 20:7, and 2 Kgs 24:16, *gb(w)rym* is used in a military context to refer to warriors.

9. In Gen 6, while wickedness itself infests the human heart and its violent desires, "corruption" (Gen 6:11) is the word used to describe the state of the earth as a result of human violence.

VIOLENCE AND PEACE IN THE BOOK OF THE WATCHERS

In the first chapters of the *Book of the Watchers*, the message given to erring humankind can be summed up in the phrase: "There will be no peace for you" (*1 En.* 5:4–5). The dearth of peace that follows in the wake of human disobedience stands in stark contrast with the orderly and obedient actions of the natural world. In *1 En.* 2–5, a wisdom poem and nature hymn that helps introduce the *Book of the Watchers*, the natural world is extolled as a model for human righteousness and morality. Humans are commanded to contemplate all God's works, which "do not alter their paths" (2:1):[10] these include luminaries, seasons, trees, seas, and rivers. In contrast, humans are criticized for not standing firm; unlike nature, humans have strayed from the paths God intended for them. Rather than praising God's mastery of the natural world, as is common in the biblical psalms and some prophets,[11] this hymn extols nature itself for its inherent righteousness, exemplified by its orderliness. Prior to this wisdom poem, the righteous are promised peace; following it, disobedient humankind is told: "There will be no peace for you."

The lack of peace proclaimed in the opening wisdom poem plays itself out in the narrative that follows, the *Book of the Watchers* proper. The onset of violence is triggered by the acts of the Watchers: they descend, marry, beget, and teach—and chaos ensues. Though the divine beings in the *Book of the Watchers* are villains, they are not purely evil; rather, these angels are multifaceted, possessing complex motivations for their actions. For example, the Watchers are depicted as marrying human women not only because of physical attraction but also because they desire to share in the human comforts of companionship and child-rearing (*1 En.* 6:1).[12] Though such motivations for marriage appear normal, the forbidden nature of the Watchers' desire is made manifest in their children's bodies; their progeny grow increasingly monstrous with each generation, and they violently and catastrophically devour life on earth. Additionally, in the *Book of the Watchers*, the divine beings—now given individual names—are portrayed as teaching heavenly secrets to humans, each apparently offering instruction within his own area of specialization (including medicinal arts, sorcery, the mixing of cosmetics, and the forging of weapons). So not only do the illicit unions result in violent children but violence is also portrayed as one

---

10. Translations of *1 Enoch* taken from Nickelsburg and VanderKam, *1 Enoch*.

11. Among others, cf. Pss 24, 33, 89, 104; Jer 10:13.

12. On this position, see Carol Newsom, "Genesis 2–3 and 1 Enoch 6–16," 15.

subject of the Watchers' forbidden teachings: presumably, human beings are taught to forge weapons so that they might engage in warfare. The Watchers' curriculum, consisting of "stolen" mysteries (*1 En.* 16:3), thus leads to violence proliferated by humans against one another.

The Watchers know that their decision to descend is "a great sin" (*1 En.* 6:3), but they proceed nonetheless. Later, when the disastrous consequences of their actions become apparent, the Watchers plead for mercy (*1 En.* 13). They summon Enoch, the prophetic seer and apocalyptic intermediary, to intercede with God in their behalf.[13] Yet in the end, their disregard for the divinely mandated order of things is irreparable. By seeking marriage, they are chasing after a "double dose" of immortality, both through their nature as immortals and through their progeny. God will not pardon this blatant attempt to have their cake and eat it too (*1 En.* 15:5–6).

The rash actions of the Watchers—both sexually and pedagogically—breached the boundaries between earth and heaven in a manner explicitly condemned by the *Book of the Watchers*. The reader might sympathize with the Watchers' desires for families and human connection, but God makes it clear that the Watchers can never be vindicated (*1 En.* 15–16) and the effects of their disordered actions can never be fully eradicated. Though the Watchers' descendants are wiped out in the global flood, their progeny's devilish spirits are immortal and cannot be killed; they remain on earth forever, continuing to lead humankind astray (*1 En.* 15:8–11).

The Watchers are not the only ones blamed for the cosmic catastrophes that result from their actions. Annette Yoshiko Reed notes that *1 En.* 11–16 includes three accounts of angelic wrongdoing—chapter 7, chapter 8 and 9:6–10.[14] In chapter 7, the Watchers alone are blamed for the illicit sexual unions and the propagation of forbidden knowledge. But in chapter 8, the fault is shared between angels and humans: though the angels teach humans forbidden arts, human men are responsible for promulgating that knowledge among their wives and children, and human women are blamed for "leading astray" the Watchers (8:1b). If read chronologically, chapters 6–11 suggest that the Watchers bear initial guilt, while the humans—complicit in spreading the knowledge or in engineering the Watchers' sexual unions—bear a secondary measure of guilt. Though the Watchers are consistently blamed for ushering evil into the world, it is apparent that they found in humankind willing accomplices and eager students.

---

13. This plot point is echoed in the fragmentary *4QGiants* from Qumran.

14. Reed, *Fallen Angels*, 29–37.

The violence initiated by the Watchers causes both human beings and the earth to cry out in suffering, and angels hear and respond.[15] In *1 En.* 8:4, in the wake of the violence and destruction wrought by the Watchers' monstrous descendants, we read: "(And) as men were perishing, their cry went up to heaven." In 9:1, four archangels hear the cries of the earth itself, and in response, they "look down" and see blood being shed and lawlessness being wrought upon the earth (described as "without inhabitant"). Here, the results of illicit unions are bloodshed and profligate unrighteousness. Just as peace was linked with righteousness in *1 En.* 2–5, bloodshed is linked with unrighteousness in *1 En.* 8–9. In this way, the *Book of the Watchers* implies that a lack of peace involves the presence of violence and unrighteousness, and it may also anticipate the judgment that follows.

Indeed, the righteous long for judgment in the *Book of the Watchers*. In 8:10, the souls of those who died cry out and "make suit" against their earthly enemies. These souls cannot cease their keening until lawless deeds are eradicated from the earth. The text makes clear that as long as violence and disorder rule the earth, there will be no peace for the righteous, not even after death. This reinforces the refrain from *1 En.* 2–5, "There will be no peace," and it rings as a word of judgment, but not necessarily regarding the fate of the dead. Rather, a lack of peace is a this-worldly description of the events that follow in the Watchers' wake.

The *Book of the Watchers* does offer a way back to peace, suggesting what must be done for a world devoid of life in the wake of violence. To begin, it includes visions of the punishment of the fallen Watchers. However, in order for peace to return, punishment is not sufficient; the earth must be cleansed by a flood. Unlike Gen 6, in which God's motivation for sending the flood is not explained in detail,[16] here the necessity for a worldwide flood is apparent. By the time God sends the flood in *1 Enoch*, there is simply no good green earth left. A flood is the only way to push creation's reset button and allow the earth to return to its original, orderly, and obedient ways. In the *Book of the Watchers*, the flood functions like an intentional forest fire, destruction that is necessary so future generations may thrive.

The thriving of all life is at the heart of *1 Enoch*'s hopeful imagery for the new creation. In 10:18–29, after "the end" (which here refers to the flood), a complete and glorious restoration will take place. Once again nature will be

15. This is reminiscent of the earth crying out after receiving the blood of Abel, signaling to God that the first death (and the first act of violence) had taken place (Gen 4:10).

16. In fact, God's reasons for sending a flood are confusingly similar to God's reasons for never sending a flood again. Both times, God's reasoning is that "the inclination of the human heart is evil from youth" (Gen 6:5b; 8:21).

orderly and obedient, just as in *1 En.* 2–5. God will say to the angels: "Open the chambers of blessings which are in the heavens" (*1 En.* 11:1),[17] and the earth will soak them in. Furthermore, we are told in 10:17 that one result of the flood will be the ability of humankind to bear children *in peace*. In the *Book of the Watchers*, a peaceful existence is affiliated with renewal and restoration of the earth, and with the proliferation of righteousness and order.

In the end, the *Book of the Watchers* makes a variety of claims about peace and violence:

- Peace has its place among the righteous.
- Peace is associated with the orderly manner in which the world is meant to function.
- Violence is associated with disobedience and illicit boundary crossings.
- Living in accord with what is permitted leads to peace.
- Living in rebellion against what is permitted results in violence.

READING THE BOOK OF THE WATCHERS

Some have argued that the *Book of the Watchers* is most intelligible when read as a polemic against the Hellenistic rulers of the day: the activity of the Watchers symbolizes the havoc wreaked by certain emperors, and the invective against human/divine marriage reflects concerns about religious purity.[18] If such concerns were present in the minds of the ancient writers, it would make sense to frame them within the context of an ancient, cosmic, antediluvian narrative. But these stories are more than allusions to the contemporary political climate of their first writers and readers. Additionally, they are enduring myths that reveal deep anxieties about evil, its introduction into the cosmos, and the resultant fate of humankind and the whole earth. As such, the book has much to say to readers today.

How do we read "mythic" texts like this—texts about our origins—especially when the text in question has been widely (with the exception of the Ethiopic Orthodox Church) regarded as noncanonical? Though the *Book of the Watchers* is not Scripture for most Christians today, in the centuries following its writing it was considered an important and authoritative text both by the Jewish community at Qumran and by NT writers (such as the

17. In *1 Enoch*, heavenly chambers are also depicted as storehouses for natural elements, like rain, snow, and hail. Perhaps the "blessings" referred to here also call to mind the regularity and order with which the natural world, as a model for humankind, is supposed to function.

18. Nickelsburg, *1 Enoch 1*, 169–70.

author of Jude).[19] Moreover, the *Book of the Watchers* is rooted in the book of Genesis, and seeks to interpret it. For these reasons, it is illuminating to read this text for the moral and ethical commitments that it reveals, and to evaluate its ancient claims in light of modern concerns about violence and peace.

One example of such a reading would compare the locus of responsibility for evil's origins according to the two books. Unlike Genesis, the *Book of the Watchers* locates some of the responsibility for evil in the heavens themselves, with the Watchers' activity. Evil descends from the heavens, and humans collaborate with it gladly. This is particularly significant insofar as the *Book of the Watchers* rejects an interpretation of Gen 2–3 that locates the origins of evil precisely (and uniquely) in Adam and Eve's human capacity to choose evil over good. Rather, the *Book of the Watchers* reflects a more complex moral and theological anthropology, explicitly blaming heaven for the introduction of evil into the world, while also implicitly linking heavenly evil to the Watchers' desire to live a human life. This can be read as an assumption on the writers' part that the nature of evil is in some way inextricable from human nature,[20] while paradoxically lifting up the human condition as something so good that even heavenly creatures envy it.

The world is a messy place in the *Book of the Watchers,* but when it functions as intended, it is also a place of order and predictability. Even the most extensive villainy—that which results in the earth's very destruction— can be instructive, warning humankind about the consequences of choosing chaos. If humankind chooses to model itself after the natural world—which is normally steadfast in its obedience to God's commands (*1 En.* 2–5)—then humans have a real chance to live in peace in the present, and to assure themselves a happy fate in the future. In this way, *1 Enoch* portrays humans as having great potential. However, *1 Enoch* also makes clear that humans tend to deviate from God's paths. The natural world is instructive here as

---

19. Numerous manuscripts of *1 Enoch* were found among the DSS at Qumran, and Jude 14–15 quotes *1 En.* 1:9. For more on Jude, see VanderKam, *Enoch and the Growth of an Apocalyptic Tradition*, 110.

20. Later traditions pick up on this assumption, since human agency in choosing evil is increasingly highlighted. The *Book of Jubilees* accepts the interpretation of Gen 2–3 that links human choice with the origins of evil. In *Jubilees*, it is clear that humankind corrupts the Watchers, while the *Book of the Watchers* incorporates some traditions in which the Watchers corrupt humankind, and others in which humans participate with the Watchers in a kind of mutual corruption. By the time apocalyptic works such as the *Life of Adam and Eve* and the NT book of Revelation were written, the figure of Satan, though not found in Gen 2–3, becomes associated with the serpent of Eden, and evil becomes divorced from the activity of heavenly beings.

well, for if nature deviates from God's paths, it serves as a sign that judgment is imminent. Humans would do well to heed nature's warning.

In spite of the disastrous results of human-divine relationships in the *Book of the Watchers,* the book depicts properly ordered interaction between heaven and earth as something to be desired. This is especially evident in the book's portrayal of Enoch's heavenly journeys, and the interdependent relationship they reveal between the heavens and earth (*1 En.* 17–34). During Enoch's heavenly journeys, he is acquainted with all the secrets of the heavens.[21] Most of these "heavenly mysteries" are linked to natural and meteorological phenomena that are in significant part "earthly"—the storehouses for precipitation, the gates for the winds, and the courses of the stars. In other words, *1 Enoch*'s portrayal of the heavens themselves reveals an integral relationship between earth and heaven. Regarding Enoch himself, his mediating role between the earthly and heavenly realms leads to his "angelization"—if not his "divination"—and he is eventually named Son of Man, a heavenly title (*1 En.* 74:14). It becomes clear from the descriptions of Enoch and his journeys that when the intermediary is righteous (as in rightly ordered) and the orderly nature of the cosmos is not breached, earth and heaven interact symbiotically. Together, the heavens and the earth function as one organism; neither is healthy if the other is ill.

A careful reading of the *Book of the Watchers* also sheds light on (unanimously) canonical literature.[22] When reading Genesis, modern readers may wonder if a worldwide flood was a just method of dealing with a corrupt and violent world. The *Book of the Watchers* offers one way the ancients made sense of what might seem like a drastic measure on God's part. In the book, the destruction of the cosmos happens long before God sends the deluge; the earth had already been made void by violence. Its interpretation of Gen 6 is that the destruction of the world was wrought not by God but by disobedient heavenly and human beings and the violence resulting from their chaotic and disorderly behavior. In this case, it is easier to understand why a drastic "re-creation" was God's next move. In the same way that God formed the cosmos from what was "formless and void" in Gen 1, God re-formed the cosmos from a similarly formless situation in the *Book of the Watchers.*

21. Many are strikingly similar to the forbidden curriculum taught by the Watchers.

22. Foremost to remember is the fact that the *Book of the Watchers* emerged from the same world as some of our later biblical literature, especially the vision reports in the book of Daniel. Additionally, by acknowledging the diversity of views even in the ancient world—a diversity that is preserved within the Bible itself and intensifies when biblical texts are placed in conversation with extra-biblical texts—we can enter into an ancient dialogue about evil, violence, and its effects on the created order.

Furthermore, more clearly than in Genesis, the *Book of the Watchers* links the introduction of evil in the world with the onset of violence. The order of the cosmos, which in Genesis was breached by individuals and a serpent, is here breached by the heavenly beings and humankind in partnership. Evil dawns collectively, and it results in violence and destruction. In Genesis, it takes but one generation for the first act of violence to take place (when Cain kills Abel). In the *Book of the Watchers,* it takes multiple generations for evil to take root; violence overwhelms the whole earth in waves, again and again. In Genesis, the earth inexplicably becomes a violent place, pre-deluge. In the *Book of the Watchers,* violence is cultivated from generation to generation, until the earth can take it no longer, and God's re-creation by way of the flood is the only feasible solution.

The exception to all this violence and disorder is the natural world, which stands firm and does not participate in any of the evil acts in the *Book of the Watchers*: rivers flow, as they are designed to flow; stars course through their designated paths; winds blow in and outside of proper gates. Nature only reels out of order at the hand of violence perpetuated upon it by the descendants of the forbidden unions between the Watchers and humans, when appetites become disordered and distinctions are disrespected. As such, the natural world is portrayed as both an innocent bystander and a victim. As a bystander, later in *1 Enoch* it is called on to give testimony against the evils of humankind at the time of final judgment. Just as humans are called on to observe the natural world in *1 En.* 2–5, *1 En.* 100:10–11 reveals that the natural world has been observing the deeds of humankind all along, and it is on the testimony of the created order that humankind is finally judged.

At the heart of the *Book of the Watchers* lies a belief in a symbiotic relationship between heaven and earth, in which the "halves" of the cosmos are an essential unity, and humans are just one element in the greater chain of order and disorder, of obedience and disobedience, of all that keeps the world turning day after day, season after season, year after year. When humans and nature follow God's ordained paths and play their correct role in the universe, all life can prosper and thrive. Humans are instructed to learn from what was created before them, and from what excels in obedience beyond what they can hope to imitate. The long-term well-being of humankind is directly linked to the well-being of nature. Just as earth and heaven are an ecosystem of one, so are humans and the natural world.

CONCLUSIONS

Looking to ancient texts for answers to modern questions about peace and violence is an endeavor fraught with complexity. The passing of centuries is more than enough to make us foreigners to these old texts with whom we seek to have a conversation. However, when we bring to the *Book of the Watchers* our own urgent questions about violence, destruction, and peace, we are not unlike the ancients. Though the ancients' impetus for writing the Enochic stories differs from our contextual impetus for reading them— our modern questions about climate change, ecology, or creation care were likely unknown in the ancient world—we share with the ancients a concern about the ways misguided human (and divine) actions can lead to violence. They, like us, were working to make sense of how evil had invaded the earth in the first place, and they, like us, were also faced with urgent choices about their loyalties—to faith communities, cultures, and empires. When faced with such pressing questions, we would do well to consider what the ancients had to say, not the least being that genuine care for the created order transcends "stewardship" and instead calls on us to observe, contemplate, and ultimately emulate the natural world's faithfulness to God's plans and purposes.

With the decline of the Enochic traditions, much was lost to later Jewish and Christian communities. However, the *Book of the Watchers* still offers itself as a potential conversation partner to communities of faith who are interested in living out an environmental ethic molded by both convictions regarding the rejection of violence and a theological model that places peace at the center of God's creative endeavors in the world. This relatively unknown and largely noncanonical book offers us a vision of a recreated, renewed, and flourishing cosmos which is as compelling as the eschatological visions in biblical literature: a restored creation in which the stars answer when God calls them (*1 En.* 69:21) and humans are invited to take their place in a cosmos united by its oath of praise to God (*1 En.* 69:25).

12

The Sword in the Dead Sea Scrolls and Sixteenth-Century Anabaptism

Dorothy M. Peters

The God of Israel has called out a sword against all the nations,
And by the holy ones of His people He will do mightily.

(*WAR SCROLL* XVI, 1)[1]

Holding righteous indignation in reserve,
they are masters of their temper . . .
very ministers of peace.

(JOSEPHUS, *JEWISH WAR* 2.135)

Thereby shall also fall away from us the diabolical weapons of violence
—such as sword . . .
The sword is an ordering of God outside the perfection of Christ.

(FROM *THE SCHLEITHEIM BROTHERLY UNION*, ARTICLES 4, 6)[2]

---

1. English translations of the DSS adapted from Wise, Abegg, and Cook, *The Dead Sea Scrolls*; Hebrew and Aramaic from DJD and "Qumran, Non-biblical Manuscripts," *Accordance Bible Software*.

2. Yoder, *Legacy of Michael Sattler*, 38–39.

INTRODUCTION[3]

The Dead Sea Scrolls (DSS) were rediscovered in the aftermath of World War II, when the Middle East was caught in the ebb and flow of bloodshed and violence. A Bedouin shepherd chased a goat into a cave above Qumran near the Dead Sea. Throwing a rock into the cave, he heard the sound of breaking pottery and found clay jars containing the first of more than 900 Hebrew, Aramaic, and Greek scrolls that would be extracted from eleven caves over the next ten years (1946–1956).[4] Bloodshed and violence also characterized the centuries between the third century BCE and 70 CE, when the scrolls were being composed, copied, and collected. Therefore, it is not surprising that the scrolls are permeated not only with a yearning for peace and justice but also with a desire to participate in divine vengeance and judgment, whether with the sword sheathed or with it unsheathed.[5]

The first part of this chapter introduces the people of the DSS and the conversational tension between their desire for vengeance and their ethic of nonretaliation. The second part introduces their questions: In *whose* hand did the sword belong, *how* was the use of the sword authorized, against *whom* could it be wielded, *when* would it be used, and *how* might God's people live among the nations and with one another when the sword was sheathed? The third part offers a brief comparative example of conversations about the sword among sixteenth-century European Anabaptists.

THE PEOPLE OF THE DEAD SEA SCROLLS

Upon the discovery of the DSS, the similarities between the internally, self-identified *Yaḥad* ("Community") (1QS II, 24; cf. CD XX, 32) and the Essenes known from the external, classical sources were immediately

---

3 This study was funded by a Social Sciences and Research Council of Canada Postdoctoral Fellowship and a Harold Hyam Wingate Fellowship at the Oxford Centre for Hebrew and Jewish Studies, University of Oxford.

4. Finds included more than 200 biblical scrolls, copies of *Jubilees, 1 Enoch*, Tobit, Ben Sira, the *Damascus Document* (CD), and *Aramaic Levi Document* (*ALD*), plus previously unknown songs, rulebooks, commentaries, calendar texts, and rewritten scripture. For excellent overviews of the Dead Sea Scrolls, see VanderKam and Flint, *The Meaning of the Dead Sea Scrolls*; and Davies, Brooke, and Callaway, *The Complete World of the Dead Sea Scrolls*.

5. "Sword" or *ḥereb* was variously understood as a literal weapon or metaphorically as generalized enemy-initiated violence or the "sword of God." Other weapons listed include the short sword (*kydwn*), "spear" or "lance" (*ḥnyt; rmḥ*), "bow" (*qšt*), "arrow" (*ḥṣ*), "darts of battle" (*zrqwt mlḥmh*), and "weapons of war" (*kly mlḥmwtm*).

apparent.[6] Pliny the Elder located the "solitary tribe of Essenes" near the Dead Sea (*Nat.* 5.15.73), and the immersion pools, dining room, plaster tables, and inkwells at Qumran fit well with a scribal community. A picture emerged of a developing sectarian movement that differentiated itself from the ruling priestly establishment in Jerusalem. Both internal and external texts confirmed initiation rituals including oath-swearing and a lengthy probationary period. Fully inducted members enjoyed the pure food and drink in closed table fellowship meals. Some lived in communities as celibates, shared personal property, imposed stricter Sabbath regulations on themselves, practiced the ban for community discipline, and were known to care for the needy and strangers. If the *Yaḥad* of the Dead Sea Scrolls were not Essenes, at the very least their members resembled the Essenes more closely than other known Jewish groups.

Vengeance and Nonretaliation: Conversational Tensions

According to Josephus, the Essenes were "ministers of peace" (*J.W.* 2.135), and Philo notes that they did not make weapons of war (*Good Person* 78). During initiation, they swore to "do no harm to anyone" but to "hate the wicked" (*J.W.* 2.139, 142), while not objecting to self-defense. For example, Essenes carried arms for protection against brigands (*J.W.* 2.125), and "John the Essene" was a military commander (*J.W.* 2.567; 3.11).

Consistent with Josephus's description, the *Community Rule* taught restraint from returning evil for evil and the pursuit of others only for good (1QS X, 17–20). Yet as "Children of Light" they were to hate the "Children of Darkness" (1QS I, 9–10), a hatred for the "Men of the Pit" that was meant to be concealed until an eschatological Day of Vengeance when they expected to "attack the wicked" (1QS IX, 21–23).

Jewish scholar David Flusser was troubled by this concealment of hatred by a group viewed by outsiders as ones who "loved people to an extraordinary degree" but whose nonretaliatory behavior was motivated by a desire to hasten God's "bloody and terrible vengeance." In an effort to resolve the tensions inherent in this strange ideological mixture of hatred, hospitality, nonretaliation, and deferred vengeance, Flusser proposed the existence of peripheral Essenes who rebelled against the "Essene doctrine of hatred" and were filled with "universal love."[7]

6. See Taylor, "Classical Sources."

7. Flusser, "Hatred through the Love." Cf. Hippolytus's documentation of Essenes who refused to hate their enemies and prayed for their persecutors (*Elenchus* 9.23); for evidence that Hippolytus was "Christianizing" Josephan sources, see Taylor, "Classical

Others have differentiated the Essenes or *Yaḥad* synchronically and diachronically, presupposing that any given "group" possessed a univocal ideology at any given point in space and time. For example, J. T. Milik proposed that Essenes developed Zealot-like tendencies at a late stage of their existence, becoming a "centre of military resistance."[8] Others have fit the seemingly disparate elements into variously constructed frameworks. So, Gordon Zerbe's model of "eschatological tension" holds the "prohibition of retaliation" together with the "sometimes passionate interest in vengeance."[9] Alex Jassen has observed that the sectarian "rhetoric of violence" effectively empowered those disempowered before Rome's military might and Jerusalem's powerful priesthood. This *infusion* of a violent worldview was simultaneously *defused* by the delay of all punishment until the legitimatized eschatological battle.[10]

Recent studies of the archaeological and manuscript evidence suggest that the Qumran community was just one of many settlements of a larger *Yaḥad* or Essene movement which was in ongoing conversation with unifying, codifying centers, such as Jerusalem, but which exhibited individual variations in thought and practice.[11] Therefore, the DSS may be read as a multivocal record regarding various "sword" questions as discussed and disputed among various Essene settlements throughout the history of the movement.

THE SWORD IN THE DEAD SEA SCROLLS

In Whose Hand the Sword? God, Angels, and Humans

Apparently unauthorized by God, the wrong kind of angel holds the sword in the Enochic *Book of the Watchers* when Asael puts weaponry into human hands by teaching them to make metal swords (*1 En.* 8.1). *Jubilees* clarifies this problematic tradition by stating that it was God who introduced the sword to the sons of the angels so they would smite one another with it (*Jub.* 5.7–9). Human enemies, known by the sobriquet *Kittim,* destroyed "many people with the sword, including boys, adults, old men, women, and children" (1QpHab VI, 8–12; cf. Hab 1:17). More satisfying for God's people

Sources," 186.

8. Milik, *Ten Years of Discovery*, 95–97.

9. Zerbe, *Non-Retaliation*, 135.

10. Jassen, "Dead Sea Scrolls and Violence."

11. Schofield, *From Qumran to Yaḥad*, 65; cf. Collins, *Beyond the Qumran Community*, 10. Cf. Philo (*Hypoth.* 11.1) and Josephus (*J.W.* 2.124).

were the enemies who used their swords to destroy one another. For example, a psalm-contemporizing commentary interpreted "May their sword pierce themselves!" (Ps 37:14–15) as a reference to the "wicked" of Ephraim and Manasseh," handed over to the "wicked Gentiles" (4Q171 1_2 II, 15–20). Elsewhere, the sword—pre-authorized against Israel for covenant violations—was like a restorative "chastisement" administered by father to his firstborn son (4Q504 1_2R III, 6–9).[12]

In the hands of God's people, the sword was reaffirmed in their *past* history and authorized for the *future*. In Deuteronomy, Moses had spoken in the third person on behalf of God (Deut 13:12–15). However, the *Temple Scroll* places the words into God's mouth, "concerning on[e of your cities that] *I* am giving you to in[dwell]" (11QTᵃ LV, 2–8); now it was God who directly and explicitly authorized *ḥerem*. The sectarians also expected a *future* "Branch of David" to control "all the peoples" with his sword in the "Last Days" (4Q161 f8_10 17–21) and the wicked to be "handed over to the sword" at the coming of the "Messiah of Aaron and of Israel" (CD XIX, 6–11). Yet, the "literal" sword is surprisingly elusive even in the liturgical *War Scroll* describing an eschatological battle and filled with trumpets, banners, priestly prayers, battle formations, and intricate descriptions of artistically designed weaponry, including the shield, lance, and "short sword" *kidon* (*kydwn*) (1QM V, 3–7). God calls out a "sword against all the nations" (*qr' ḥrb*); however, when the infantry comes within throwing range, it is not a sword (*ḥereb*) that each one raises but his more generic "weapon of war"(*kly mlḥmtw*) (1QM XVI, 1–7; cf. 1QM IX, 7–8; XV, 2–3). Indeed, the nearest that any *War Scroll* warrior would get to the *ḥereb* was the inscription on his throwing dart, "The blade of a sword devours the slain of wickedness by the judgment of God" (1QM VI, 1–3).

How Was the Sword Authorized? Revelation, Scripture, and Idealized Archetypes

Sword and Revelation

Within the DSS, impending judgments are divinely revealed in various ways. Visionary, archetypical characters such as Enoch (*1 En.* 1; 10.1–3) and Noah (1Q20 VI, 14–16; XIII, 9–XV, 23) transmit revelation received from angels, dreams, and visions. Judgments recorded on heavenly tablets are revealed to Moses through an angelic messenger (*Jub.* 23.22–32). In the Aramaic texts, dreams and visions are the favored revelatory means,

---

12. See Lev 26:25; Jer 34:17–18; and Ezek 17:19–21.

whereas the Hebrew texts reflect a developing back-to-Torah movement in which inspired interpretation contemporizes the authoritative scriptures, demystifying God's intentions and purposes for his people (e.g., 4Q169 3_4 IV, 1–4; cf. Nah 3:10).

Sword and Scripture

Before the Bible was a book and when authoritative writings were written on individual scrolls, a generous exegetical flexibility concerning judgment and the sword was noted by the sectarians. In Genesis and Exodus, God sends the flood on the earth, fire on Sodom and Gomorrah, and plagues on Egypt, all unassisted by Noah, Abram, and Moses.[13] Later, God would wield the metaphorical sword for covenant violations (Lev 26:25). Yet, although judgment by flood, fire, and plague could easily be imagined as coming solely from the hand of God, a sword normally required help from a human hand.

While copying a scroll of Deuteronomy, the scribe would see the *ḥerem* command authorizing Israel to put cities to the "edge of the sword." But when copying a scroll of Judges, he would see Gideon shouting, "A sword of the Lord and of Gideon!" while he and his company held only trumpets, jars, and torches, and the Midianites wielded the sword against one another (Judg 7:19–22). David appears swordless before Goliath, only picking up his enemy's sword to finish off the already fallen, dying giant (1 Sam 17:39–51). Though David is praised for leading his armies on successful military campaigns (1 Sam 18:7), the priestly editorial disqualifies David from building the temple because of the blood he has shed (1 Chr 28:3).[14]

One of the most intriguing hermeneutical strategies from the Second Temple period is the re-formation of biblical characters into diverse archetypes representing the idealized beliefs and praxis of each interpreter's community. Those emphasizing divinely enacted judgments favor recasting the stories of Enoch (*1 Enoch*) and Noah (*Genesis Apocryphon*), while those emphasizing human participation favor a sword-carrying Levi (*ALD*). The scriptural portrayals of David are varied enough that groups could identify simultaneously with the vulnerable and swordless David before a gigantic adversary (1QM XI, 1–2) *and* with a future, militant "Branch of David."

---

13. For a history of traditions study of Noah and his role in divinely enacted judgments, see Peters, *Noah Traditions*.

14. Cf. God's destroying angel holding the "sword of the Lord" and confronting David for taking a census of sword-carrying males (1 Chr 21:11–30).

In Genesis, the purely negative portrayal of Levi's sword as a "weapon of violence" (*kly ḥms*) demanded creative exegesis.[15] In *Joseph and Aseneth*—not preserved in the scrolls—Levi prevents Simeon from striking Pharaoh's son with a sword and repaying evil for evil. Yet the sword as an instrument of divine vengeance is affirmed when Levi confronts Pharaoh's son who was plotting to kill Joseph: "Behold, our swords are drawn. . . . With these two swords the Lord God punished the insult of the Shechemites" (*Jos. Asen.* 23.7–17). Later Levi seeks to heal the wound of Pharaoh's son, telling Benjamin that they would be friends with Pharaoh's son and that Pharaoh would be like their father (*Jos. Asen.* 29.4).[16]

Jubilees affirms the use of the sword against Shechem by explaining that Dinah had been "a small girl, twelve years of age" who was "taken by force" (*Jub.* 30.2) Elsewhere Levi's words—"I was eighteen when I killed Shechem and destroyed the workers of violence (*l'bdy ḥms'*), I was nineteen when I became a priest" (*ALD* 12.6–7a)—imply that this action credentialed him as priest and that it is the Shechemites, not Levi, who are characterized as violent. Levi's prayer for God's "wall of peace" to surround him (*ALD* 3.11) and the angelic vision about a "kingdom of peace" in contrast to a "kingdom of the sword" (*ALD* 4.9–10) both serve to anchor Levi securely to the "covenant of peace" known from Mal 2:4–5, while distancing him from the "violence" associated with him in Genesis.[17]

Against Whom Would the Sword Be Wielded? Identifying the Enemy

In Genesis, Esau lives by the sword (Gen 27:40). *Jubilees* goes further by vilifying Esau, linking him linguistically to Noah's generation because of his evil inclination (*yṣr*) and ways of "violence and evil" (*ḥms wrš'*) (*Jub.* 35.9–14; cf. Gen 6:5–13). Esau's own actions—defiling marriages, breaking oaths, denouncing brotherhood, and attacking Jacob with 4000 sword-bearing men—effectively authorize the use of the "sword" against him. Jacob eventually kills Esau, but he does so by shooting an arrow and not with a sword (*Jub.* 37.15–38.2).

---

15. Gen 49:5–7; 34:25–26.

16. Zerbe suggests that *Jos. Asen.* portrays an archetypical Simeon who prefers an armed response while Levi exhibits a preference for non-retaliation. Zerbe, *Non-Retaliation*, 95.

17. Translation and reconstruction from Greenfield, Stone, and Eshel, *Aramaic Levi Document*, 131.

In sectarian texts, the enemy is identified most distinctly in dualis-tic terminology drawn from a common stock of Jewish Scriptures and re-accentuated.[18] The protagonist "Children of Light" expect to attack the antagonist "Children of Darkness, the army of Belial" in a future, eschato-logical war (1QM I, 1–2; cf. 1QS I, 9–10).[19] At the end of Week 7—in the *Apocalypse of Weeks*, representing the author's own time—the "witnesses of righteousness" expected to "uproot the foundations of violence." In Week 8, they would be given a "sword" to "execute righteous judgment on all the wicked" (4Q212 1 IV, 12–17; cf. *1 En.* 91.11–12).

When? The Sword and Eschatology

Generally, weapons of war are affirmed when legitimately used in Israel's *past* and in a carefully circumscribed *future*. The *Apocalypse of Weeks* re-stricts the sword in righteous hands to the imminent future, and the *Animal Apocalypse* adds an "end date"; after the "sheep" kill the "wild beasts," the sword is to be brought back and sealed up in the house of the Lord (*1 En.* 90.19, 34). Krister Stendahl's rhetorical question most famously describes the motivation for deferring private vengeance: "With the Day of Vengeance at hand the proper and reasonable attitude is to forego one's own vengeance and to leave vengeance to God. Why walk around with a little shotgun when the atomic blast is imminent?"[20]

If not the Sword, then What? The Sword Sheathed

Living Peacefully among the Nations

Not all the DSS portray adversarial relationships with Gentiles. The Ara-maic writings in particular include more positive portrayals. Levi instructs his children and grandchildren to study wisdom as Joseph did, so that they will be honored and find "a brother and friend" in other lands (*ALD* 13.6–10). In *Visions of Amram*, war closes the border between Egypt and Hebron for forty-one years where Amram is visiting. When the borders re-open, Jochabed does not join Amram in Hebron. Instead, Amram desires to return safely to Egypt, which implies that the Israelites were happily settled there (4Q545 1a_b II, 16–18; 4Q544 1 1–9). In the *Genesis Apocryphon*, the

18. Newsom, *Self As Symbolic Space*, 10–11.

19. On the terminology of protagonists and antagonists in the *War Scroll*, see Schultz, *Conquering the World*.

20. Stendahl, "Hate, Non-retaliation, and Love," 344.

king's councilors bring gifts in exchange for Abram's "knowledge of goodness, wisdom, and righteousness," and Abram teaches them from the "book
of the words of Enoch" (1Q20 XIX, 23–25). After Sarai is forcibly seized,
God afflicts every male in the king's household with impotence, but Abram
lays hands on the king, exorcising the spirit and removing the plague. In
gratitude, the king bestows on Abram, Sarai, and Hagar many gifts of silver
and gold, linen and purple-dyed garments (1Q20 XX, 1–34).

   These retellings of scriptural stories convey the possibility of peaceful,
mutually beneficial relationships between Israel and the nations. However,
when the purity or safety of the family is threatened, several options were
presented as available. In the *Genesis Apocryphon*, God takes the vengeance
initiative on Abram's behalf, as in Genesis, whereas—in *ALD*—Levi's un-
sheathing of the sword against Shechem is legitimized. Yet to say that these
interpretative narratives are two different "answers" to the vengeance debate
would be too simplistic. In Shechem, the children of Jacob use their military
strength against a disabled opponent. In Egypt, they are helpless before a
powerful foreign king. Taken together, the narratives instruct the children of
Israel to pick up the defending sword when they are able and authorized to
do so, while reassuring them that God will wield the sword when the people
are powerless. That said, the Abram archetype in *Genesis Apocryphon* hints
rather strongly at the benefits of leaving vengeance in God's hands! Abram's
nonretaliatory response means that he is called on to act in an intercessory
and healing role in Egypt. He in turn grows rich from the wealth of Egypt.

Discipline within the Community and Dispute with Outsiders.

Religious conflicts among the *Yaḥad* were resolved without the use of lethal force. Penalties, a temporary ban, and permanent expulsion from the
community could be administered for infractions (CD IX, 23; 1QS VI,
24—VII, 25). Active protests were made against religious and political adversaries outside the community, orally and in writing. More conciliatory
in tone was the *Halakhic Letter* that discussed disagreements about priestly
purity laws (4QMMTᵃ). Songwriters interpreted suffering theologically by
framing scriptural lament motifs with thanksgiving (*Thanksgiving Psalms*).
Additionally, ordinary sectarians performed cursing ceremonies for those
"foreordained to Belial" (1QS II, 4–18) and assigned sobriquets to their enemies, including "Man of the Lie" and "Men of Mockery."[21] The most drastic
option, of picking up the sword in religious and political conflicts, was exercised by the priestly Hasmonean family in their violent war of resistance

---

21. Collins, *Use of Sobriquets*.

against the Seleucid Antiochus IV Epiphanes and their forced circumcision of Hellenized Jews.[22] This family of priests was bitterly opposed by the *Yaḥad*. A commentary on Habakkuk protested violence and oppression of the poor by the Wicked Priest (likely the High Priest), the principal adversary to the "Teacher of Righteousness" (1QpHab VIII, 1–13).

For the Essenes, being swordless may have been the most pragmatic and, indeed, the only survivable option for a group with little power and unskilled in the ways of war. Yet the ways they rewrote their history reveal a preference for the pen over the sword as an implement of judgment: an archetypical Enoch bore witness, in writing, to the wickedness of angels and humans until judgment day (*Jub.* 4.16–26), an archetypical "Jacob learned writing" while "Esau . . . learned war" (*Jub.* 19.14), and the Teacher of Righteousness himself was imagined as a latter-day Habakkuk, recording divine revelations in anticipation of coming judgments (1QpHab VI, 12–VII, 14).

(A BRIEF EXCURSION TO) THE "SWORD" IN SIXTEENTH-CENTURY ANABAPTISM

Those at home in the world of sixteenth-century European Anabaptism may already have noticed similarities with the DSS.[23] This briefest of excursions compares the two movements in only the broadest of strokes, reserving a more complete discussion of the various complexities for another time.[24]

Generally speaking, both movements were spread over scattered settlements in various geographical areas. Also, members originally tried to influence the mainstream religious groups from which they emerged,

---

22. The Hasmoneans' chosen archetype was a zealous Phinehas (Num 25:6–15; 1 Macc 2.23–68; 3.18–19; 2 Macc 5.1–4). Cf. Zealots (Josephus's "Fourth Philosophy"), notorious for violence (*Ant.* 18.9–10, 23–25; *J.W.* 2.651).

23. See Regev, *Sectarianism in Qumran*. I am grateful for this comparison of the "ideological characteristics" (e.g., millennial views, marriage restrictions, and community property) of the Qumran sect with what Regev calls other "introversionist sects." Although Regev accounts for neither the polygenesis of the Anabaptist movement nor its diversity or complexity, this study is a useful platform from which to move toward more nuanced studies.

24. These observations are part of a larger study, currently underway by the author. Particularly helpful for study of the sword in the DSS and sixteenth-century Anabaptism is the method of Gerald Mast's and his rhetorical analysis of Anabaptist confessional texts. He proposes that rhetorical instabilities may be evidence of unstable negotiations between the church community (*Gemeinde*) and civil authority (*Obrigkeit*); specifically, the "rhetorical movement" in articles 4 and 6 of *The Schleitheim Brotherly Union* reveals practical arguments about the controversial issues of separation and the sword. Biesecker-Mast, *Separation and the Sword*, 24, 97–108.

even as they became increasingly differentiated and marginalized. Many from both movements rejected the use of the sword for religious coercion. A nonretaliatory ethic was articulated and practiced by at least a segment of the movements, and the overlap in the range of nonlethal, word-dependent strategies of responding to conflict is striking.

Only fragments of the "sword conversations" in the DSS have survived damage from cave worms and rodents. In contrast, the relative richness of the Anabaptist record makes it useful for framing new questions for the scrolls and as a lens through which to view them. Specific identifiable beliefs and practices can be attributed to specific people (a luxury not enjoyed by scholars of the DSS!). Those who wielded or refused to wield the literal sword or the metaphorical sword of the magistrate can be identified and something said about their social-political locations, adversaries, and the toleration or persecution they experienced. The record can be studied to identify their eschatological views, the means by which they received divine revelation, and their favorite Scriptures and biblical characters. If correlating patterns emerge between any of these elements and a particular sword ideology, one can search for similar patterns among the DSS. Where different patterns emerge, one might explore how contributing factors differ. For example, the Anabaptists appealed to Jesus as an exemplar and to NT scriptures on loving one's enemies and blessing those who cursed one (Luke 6:27). In contrast, in the extant DSS, the *Yaḥad* possessed no authoritative command to love and bless their enemies.

The Anabaptist example may also be helpful in proposing possible scenarios in places where the DSS are silent. For example, it is not known whether the *Yaḥad*'s eschatological imaginings sufficiently defused the desire for vengeance or whether it inflamed some who subsequently picked up the sword when given the opportunity.[25] During the sixteenth century, affirmed by the revelatory dreams of the "Strasbourg prophets," Melchior Hoffman predicted the imminent destruction of the godless, the end of the world, and the return of Christ. He counseled the suffering church to refrain from taking up arms and to wait, instead, for God's judgment. After Hoffman's imprisonment in 1533, his followers engineered an ideological shift in his eschatology, moving the bearing of arms from their *future* to their *present*. Bernard Rothman appealed to the "reign of David," arguing that it could only begin after God's people picked up the sword. Anabaptists already possessed influence in Münster but now gained and maintained control of the city by means of violence. Under the leadership of Jan Matthijs and Jan

---

25. The manuscript and archeological records are silent about whether any numbers of Essenes sought or attained political or religious power outside their own movement.

of Leyden, rebaptism was mandated, private property banned, and rebels punished by execution.[26]

This Anabaptist narrative reveals several elements correlating to and potentially contributing to the ideological shift of timing from the future to the present: a social location in which the previously marginalized group had already gained some influence, an appeal to a military Davidic archetype, and an eschatological worldview that was encouraged through dreams and visions arousing hopes for the imminent arrival of the visible kingdom of God on earth. The *Yahad*'s fervent, eschatological hopes—together with its (temporary) nonviolence—bear resemblance to the thinking of Melchior Hoffman. The sectarians were receptive to revelation from dreams and visions and certainly appealed to the biblical David as an archetype for an expected kingly, messianic figure who would wield the sword at the head of Israel's armies. In light of the Anabaptist example, it is possible to conjecture that *if* the priestly Essenes had recognized a realistic opportunity to obtain religious control with the use of force, the eschatological views of at least some may have shifted rapidly. Still, the consistency with which the sectarians self-consciously entrenched themselves on the margins as the suffering and poor ones whom God would rescue (1QH^a 2:27; CD 19:9) suggests that these Essenes would have experienced opposition by the traditionalists. Even if some eventually mounted a resistance against the Romans who swept through their settlements around 70 CE, they would have been ill-prepared to resist long. If any believed that the last days had come, they were disappointed.

CONCLUSIONS

The sword conversations in the DSS reveal that beliefs about vengeance and nonretaliation continued to be a live issue throughout the history of the Essene movement. Yet there were general unifying tendencies in thought and practice that distinguished the Essenes from other Second Temple Jews such as the Maccabees and the Zealots. The sectarians understood that vengeance and judgment belong to God, the one who ultimately authorizes and powers the sword in whatever hand it is found. They generally affirmed the just use of weapons by their past ancestors and hoped to participate with God in executing judgment in future. However, the continual deferment of an active, physical role into the ever-receding eschatological future, and

---

26. For a convenient summary of the ways Melchiorite ideology was variously interpreted, see Biesecker-Mast, *Separation and the Sword*, 162–99.

the practice of nonlethal alternatives for resolving conflict in the meantime, made for a *de facto,* if not ideological, "peace position" in the present.

The DSS betray a reticence to placing the sword (*ḥereb*) in the hands of present and future *Yaḥad* sectarians that goes far deeper than pragmatic preference. There are several possible explanations. First, priestly Jews conceivably had an aversion to hand-to-hand combat because of the fear of impurity that would arise from corpse contact. Like an archetypical Jacob in *Jubilees* or the imagined *War Scroll* warriors, they could visualize themselves as battle participants while maintaining purity by simply hurling darts or arrows. Second, the sword (*ḥereb*) was a two-edged metaphor linked both to their enemies and to God. On one hand, *ḥereb* may have become too contaminated by connotations of enemy "violence" and "bloodshed." Alternatively, the "sword of God" may have become a theophoric for the "hand of God" and therefore unsuitable as weapon to be held in human hands.[27] Finally, these priestly Jews were also scribes. Although they did not wield *swords* of judgment, they did not hesitate to write and speak *words* of judgment. Their written testimonies, spoken curses, and inscribed darts may well have been the response of Jacob, in writing, to the sword of Esau.

---

27 So Brian Schultz, private communication, 23 December 2011. See 1QM I, 14–15; XI, 11–12; XVIII, 1–3; cf. Isa 31:8.

PART 2

Peace and Violence
in the New Testament

13

Peace and Violence in the New Testament

Definition and Methodology

Willard M. Swartley

Much has been written on peace and violence in the NT. Michel Desjardins' book-length treatment of both topics seeks to treat each topic extensively and even-handedly.[1] The bulk of the contributions on peace and/or violence may be classified as:

- book-length studies, including essay collections, devoted to peace;[2]
- book-length contributions on violence, with peace as well;[3]
- contributions that treat peace in relation to war;[4]
- treatments that discuss peace in relation to pacifism as a theological-political stance or view;[5]

---

1. Desjardins, *Peace, Violence.*

2. Foremost here are Wengst, *Pax Romana*; Mauser, *Gospel of Peace*; Janzen, *Der Friede im lukanischen Doppelwerk*; Swartley, *Covenant of Peace.*

3. Notable here are Edwards, *Jesus and the Politics of Violence*; Desjardins, *Peace, Violence*; Tite, *Conceiving Peace and Violence*; Yoder Neufeld, *Killing Enmity*; Frankemölle, *Friede und Schwert.*

4. Swartley, "War and Peace in the New Testament." See bibliography for more.

5. Swartley, chap. 3 in *Slavery, Sabbath, War, and Women.* See the book's bibliography for more.

- the numerous dictionary or encyclopedia articles on either topic;[6]

- the many treatments of one or both topics in books (articles, not listed for space) that address the NT as part of the Bible as a whole;[7] and

- ancillary topical studies that bear directly on peace-promoting and/or violence-promoting emphasis in the NT.[8]

As the compendium of bibliographical entries—not intended to be exhaustive, and certainly not in all languages—in each of these categories demonstrates, many rich contributions to the topic have already been made. This article addresses two layers of issues: first, definitional clarity for both *peace* and *violence* in NT studies, and second, methodological issues that are also theological-hermeneutical in nature.

DEFINITIONAL CLARITY

What is meant by *peace* and *violence*? Often, the antonym for *peace* is assumed to be *war*, with the practical implication that pacifism is opposed to "just war," to some extent, and altogether to the crusade. But in this book the antonym of peace is violence. Just as in the OT *shalom* is not an exact antonym to war but rather to evil,[9] so we must question whether war

---

6. Among them are Foerster, "*Eirēnē*"; Klassen, "Peace" (1992); "War" (NT); "Peace" (1995); "Peace" (1986); Swartley, "Peace" (2003); "Sword" (2003); "Violence, Violent" and "War" (2003); "Peace" (2009) and "Sword" (2009); "Peace" (2011); "War" (1997).

7. Notable here are Eller, *War and Peace*; Swaim, *War, Peace, and the Bible*; Tambasco, ed., *Blessed Are the Peacemakers*; Yoder and Swartley, eds., *Meaning of Peace* with key German articles (Erich Dinkler's is especially important); also in Swartley, ed., *Love of Enemy*, chap. 10 by Luise Schottroff; Winn, *Ain't Gonna Study War No More*; Longman III and Reid, *God Is a Warrior*; Boyd, *God at War*; Wood, *Perspectives on War*; McDonald, *God and Violence*. Contributions that span OT-NT-Christian history into the twentieth century are: Pawlikowski and Senior, *Biblical and Theological Reflections*; Miller and Gingerich, eds., *Church's Peace Witness*; Goeringer, *Haunts of Violence*; Reimer, *Christians and War*; Long, ed., *Christian Peace*.

8. Numerous studies on atonement, salvation, love of enemy, historical Jesus, or on specific texts (e.g., Sermon on the Mount), justice, the "powers," et al., have bearing on peace and/or violence. Examples are Borg, *Jesus*; Klassen, *Love of Enemies*; Swartley, ed., *Love of Enemy*; Zerbe, *Non-retaliation*; Wright, *Jesus*; Marshall, *Beyond Retribution*; Stassen and Gushee, *Kingdom Ethics*; Wink, *Naming the Powers; Unmasking the Powers; Engaging the Powers*; Gingerich and Grimsrud, eds., *Transforming the Powers*; Gorman, *Inhabiting the Cruciform God*. Most important is Snyder Belousek, *Atonement, Justice, and Peace*.

9. In 2 Sam 11:7, David asks Joab about the *shalom* of the war. Also, negotiated treaties after wars make *shalom* between nations (Deut 20:10–12; Josh 9:15; 10:1, 4; Jdg 4:17; 1 Sam 7:14; 1 Kgs 5:12). Evil (*rah*) is that which opposes God. Violence is handmaid to evil (cf. Gen 6:5, 11; note also the summaries of many kings of Israel who

or violence is the antonym to peace in the NT. To put the point sharply, with regard to violence, one NT text speaks of the "kingdom of God" as "righteousness and peace and joy in the Holy Spirit" (Rom 14:17),[10] whereas another text connects the coming of the kingdom of God with violence (*biazomai/biastes*; Matt 11:12). What this latter text means is "not that the kingdom brings or condones violence but that the kingdom coming sets up violent reactions by those who refuse or subvert its message; it also causes Satan's fall (Luke 10:1–20)"[11] as the gospel of peace is proclaimed (10:5–10)! To confound the matter, the kingdom of God brings peace but also occasions violent response! Hence Jesus, who came proclaiming the kingdom of God, ends up *crucified*. The gospel of peace means standing for the truth, which may provoke violence (cf. the Gospels' passion narratives, especially John's).

René Girard's contributions on violence illumine the relationship between peace and violence. The gospel of peace is ever at odds with and also exposes violence that is endemic to human nature, as human history and myths universally attest.[12] But the gospel of peace seeks to overcome evil with good and halts violence by holding captive its fomenter: the evil one, Satan, devil, and demons. Thinking that Scripture should avoid "battle" imagery is to misunderstand Scripture at its core (see titles in n7, especially Boyd). The antonym of peace is evil (personified as Satan or Devil). The petition in the Lord's Prayer, "Deliver us from evil," is at the center of this definitional challenge. We do not pray "Deliver us from violence," but "Deliver us from evil" (or, in the Eastern Christian tradition, "Deliver us from the evil one"), since the evil power foments the evil and violence in the human heart and history.

In sum, any treatment of violence in the NT must take into account the Scripture's own conception of what violence is and its origins. This begs for full-book treatment.[13]

Defining *peace* in the NT is not simple either, even after book-length treatment of peace in all the NT literature (Swartley, *Covenant of Peace*).[14] At least six denotations arise from the one hundred occurrences of peace,

---

did *evil* in the sight of God).

10. All biblical quotations are taken from the NRSV unless otherwise indicated.

11. Swartley, "Violence, Violent," 520 (see n6 above).

12. For understanding Girard and his impact on biblical studies, see the essays in *Violence Renounced*, ed. Swartley.

13. Boyd has done this in his two books *God at War* and *Satan and the Problem of Evil*. This latter volume complements *God at War* (see n7).

14. For more, see Swartley, *Covenant of Peace*, 419, 123–51, 155–70, 189–219, though the entire book contributes complementary perspectives.

in its noun, verbal, and compound forms, in the NT. In the NT, peace may refer to

1. relationship between God and humans arising through salvation in and by Jesus Christ;

2. a simultaneous peace among humans, breaking down walls of enmity (note Yoder Neufeld, *Killing Enmity*) such that peace is thus also *reconciliation* (cf. Eph 2:13–18 with 2 Cor 5:17–20);

3. Christ's new creation peace, creating an alternative community to the Pax Romana, and thus

4. a peace with sociopolitical dimension, evident especially in Luke-Acts, but also in Paul and in all NT lordship titles of Jesus Christ;

5. peace with cosmic dimensions, clearest in Col 1:20 ("through Christ God was pleased to reconcile *all things,* whether in earth or in heaven by *making peace* through the blood of his cross"), uniting *all things* in Christ (Eph 1:10), and creating a new heavens and earth (Rev 21:1); and

6. peace that stills the human spirit, giving confident hope amid adversity and imprisonment (the noun form of the verb *keep, phrourō,* in Phil 4:7 is similar to the noun for prison *guard,* whom Paul knew well).[15]

This peace—guarding heart and mind—contrasts to the farcical political cry of "peace and security" (1 Thess 5:3). *Jesus's* peace contrasts to the peace the world gives (John 14:27) and is possible because Jesus has *conquered* the world (16:33).

METHODOLOGICAL AND THEOLOGICAL-HERMENEUTICAL CONSIDERATIONS

At least five issues are crucial in adequately treating peace and violence in the NT:

1. To what extent does the work take into account the historical-critical method that, among other factors, sets the treatment of peace and/or violence in the NT in its contemporaneous historical-cultural setting?

2. To what extent does the treatment of either topic consider a larger theological scope or semantic field of either violence or peace? Or, put another way, is the contribution based mainly on statistical data (frequency and context-significant uses of peace and/or violence) or does

---

15. Minear, "The Peace of God," 125–26. This is an excellent, perceptive article.

it also seek to understand peace and/or violence in relation to larger theological and ethical *topoi*?

3. Are the texts under consideration on peace and/or violence in the mode-form of command or principle? Or are they a paradigm type, emerging sometimes from stories, such as the parable of the Good Samaritan? Or are they embedded in a symbolic world, culturally and/or theologically?[16] Further, is the moral action culturally descriptive in its contemporary world, morally regulative, or morally imperative? Are the moral injunctions intended to connect hermeneutically and authoritatively to the reader? Are they descriptive and/or prescriptive of the Christian moral life?

4. When texts constrain morally, what warrants that appeal? For example, do texts appeal to eschatological expectations for warrant, or do they appeal to God's nature or Christ's model and thus assume a degree of imitation, or a nonsynergistic relation between God and the faith community (e.g., Rom 12:19)? Alternatively, do they appeal to some form of law, the Decalogue, or Jesus's summary of it in his double love commandment?

5. To what extent do we take into account contemporary cultural sensitivities in interpreting texts pertinent to peace and violence? For example, Desjardins considers Paul's command that women be veiled violence (not all agree that the word should be translated "veil"). Whence the warrant for this? Here consideration number one comes into play: Was veiling in that culture a form of violence? *Whose* value system is regulative, and for what ends are such judgments made?

THE HISTORICAL AND CULTURAL CONTEXT

Understanding texts of any time period, in any type of literature, is aided significantly by taking into account the relationship of a given topic to its historical and cultural setting. To make the point sharply, consider Desjardins' exposition of peace in the NT alongside Wengst's. Desjardins (and Tite, tacitly) says he is not using a historical-critical method and thus does not compare the NT witness on peace with the Pax Romana, and its peace with its horrendous physical violence and subjugation of peoples and nations.

---

16. These modes of appeal function to warrant ethical proposals. See Hays, *Moral Vision*, 208–9.

The outcomes of these two contributions are quite different. Wengst identifies seven acclaimed features of Pax Romana[17] and then contrasts this array to the peace of Jesus Christ: "The Pax Romana was not really a world of peace" but ended with the empire's limits, enforced by armies and oppression of its subjects.[18] Desjardins and Tite do not consider the violence of the empire as context for understanding the NT peace witness. Desjardins does, however, list many terms occurring in the NT that reflect the reality of military presence and empire domination as the cultural setting of NT Scripture. In addition to thirty-two occurrences of general terms for "quarreling and fighting," he identifies ninety-seven encounters with military terms (among which are *stratia* and *strateuma* for armies, *strateia* for military campaigns, *stratologein* for gathering of armies, *antistrateuesthai* for battling with other armies, *stratopedon* for troops, *stratiotes* for soldiers, *sustratiotes* for fellow soldiers, and six types of weapons and armor (four of which appear in Eph 6:13–17; the other two, *thorax* and *romphaia*).[19] This vocabulary, "to a large extent, is a reflection of the military environment in which first-century Christians lived."[20] Desjardins acknowledges that the early Christians lived within a military culture and borrowed everyday language from that culture for describing and communicating the gospel message. But he does not adequately evaluate this latter point when assessing whether the NT is more peace promoting than violence promoting.[21]

Because Desjardins and Tite fail to consider the significance of the historical and cultural setting of Christian origins, and the communication dynamics of the gospel message within that culture, they overlook how the gospel message challenges the reality these military terms denote. They miss what might be called the gospel's *neo-political* and *neo-empire* contributions (the latter term denotes the worldwide permeation of the gospel and a church community-in-the-making). The appearance of empire terminology in the NT narratives does not fall on the negative side of the peace/violence ledger, but on the positive side, in my judgment. The gospel message and its

---

17. Wengst, *Pax Romana*, 7–51.

18. Ibid., 17–18.

19. Desjardins, *Peace, Violence*, 63–64.

20. Ibid., 64.

21. Desjardins does not consider the "spiritual warfare" of NT moral exhortation (e.g., the armor of God in Eph 6:10–17), in which military imagery is directed against Satan, not against "flesh and blood," i.e., humans. Even the cherished term *gospel of peace* (Mauser and Swartley) in its OT cradle (Isa 52:7) has *national* contextual origin. At issue is the principle of distinguishing between the cradle and the baby, born as Messiah, Christ the Lord, the prince of peace (Isa 9:6; Luke 2:10, 14).

reality penetrating the Roman Empire undermine and subvert the violence of the empire.[22] This is true because of the next factors to consider.

THE LARGER THEOLOGICAL-SEMANTIC FIELD OF PEACE AND VIOLENCE

Statistical analysis of the occurrences of nouns, verb, verbals, and compound word-forms constitutes a significant part of the study of violence and peace in the NT (Desjardins, Swartley, et al.). But the use of these terms, in order to assess their function in the NT, must be set within a larger theological-semantic field, such as this one:[23]

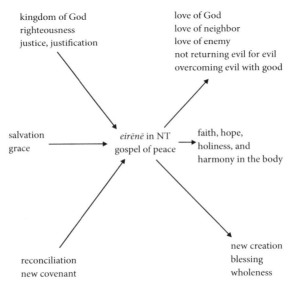

Fig. 13.1. Theological-semantic field of peace and violence

The semantic field on the left designates aspects of God's gift of peace; those on the right, the fruit of peace. The upper-right terms occur often in the NT as moral commands, as does *holiness* (Mark 9:50; 1 Pet 1:15–16) and *harmony* within the body (Eph 4:3, with theological warrant in vv. 4–6; Phil 2:2–4, et al.). New creation (Rom 5:1–11; 2 Cor 5:17), blessing (Eph 1:3–14; 2:13–22; Gal 3:6–9), and wholeness (1 Thess 5:23) in the lower-right

22. For a recent trenchant critique of imperial systems and their oppression, based on the teachings of Jesus, see Griffith, *God Is Subversive*.

23. This diagram appears in Swartley, *Covenant of Peace*, 41 and "Peace," *NIDB* 4:422, though here I added "new creation."

quadrant are gifts of peace, received personally and corporately, but with radiating impact on sisters and brothers within and beyond a given faith community to other believers and also to the world. The NT *peace* texts are deeply embedded in theological and christological expositions.

The same is true of many texts where *violent* imagery occurs, as Yoder Neufeld's book, *Killing Enmity*—and its exposition of Eph 2:13–18—demonstrates. Yoder Neufeld selects various NT Scriptures and episodes (most notably Jesus's *violent* death) to demonstrate this point: violent language functions frequently to "subvert and finally 'murder' violence."[24] The violent word, *killing* (*apokteinas*, Eph 2:16c), turns out to be, in this Pauline exposition, a *peacemaking* manifesto.

Statistical analysis is not enough for assessing *peace* and *violence* in the NT. The larger theological-semantic field must be considered: specifically, how violent imagery may function in relation to peace. The prolific apocalyptic violent imagery of *conquer*, *war*, and *destruction* in Revelation ends up with new heavens and a new earth (chaps. 21–22), in which the God of peace (Paul's contribution elsewhere in seven texts)[25] is all in all. Kings of the earth go in and out of the new city, whose light is the *slain* (violence!) Lamb. The river flowing out of the city, lined with the tree of life on either side, heals the nations. In 22:11–12, 15, however, judgment for evil deeds denies access to the city (the violence of exclusion?[26]).

Indeed, the reality of judgment in the NT (notably 2 Thess 1:4–10 and Jesus's numerous parables that contain violent imagery, which for the most part serves purposes of moral transformation, as Desjardins astutely observes[27]) and the violence it implies fall on the violence side of the ledger. But notice of God's judgment, like the parables of Jesus, is often, in the narrative, a 911 call: act quickly to save your life, for the sake of God, Christ, and your own *peace*, now and eternally. Consequently, God's actions (in judgment throughout salvation-history) are often asymmetrical in relation to God's expected moral conduct for humans (e.g., Exod 3:14), even though *imitation* also characterizes the relation of human moral action to God (Matt 5:48; Eph 5:1–2). This is a paradox not easily resolved, but one that NT moral instruction holds in tension.[28]

24. Yoder Neufeld, *Killing Enmity*, ix.

25. Swartley, *Covenant of Peace*, 208–12.

26. The question mark occurs here in light of the conclusions I draw elsewhere regarding the vocabulary for *violence* in the OT and NT (Swartley, *Covenant of Peace*, 393–95). See also Neville, *Peaceable Hope*, for an analysis of the violence/peace perspective of these parables.

27. Desjardins, *Peace, Violence*, 43–50.

28. See chaps. 13 and 14 in Swartley, *Covenant of Peace*, 356–78.

THE FORM OR MODES OF MORAL EXHORTATION

When seeking to understand peace and violence in the NT, we must consider the literary form of the narrative in which moral injunctions occur. Richard Hays has described the various literary modes of moral rhetoric: command, principle, paradigm, and symbolic world. One model, a "case" for authorizing pacifism,[29] illustrates these different modes:

1. Jesus's teachings (reflected in the apostles) are clearly pacifist.

   a. Jesus taught nonresistance or, better, nonviolent resistance:[30] overcome evil with good.

      "But I say to you. 'Do not resist an evildoer. But if any one strikes you on the right cheek, turn the other also; and if anyone wants to sue you and take your coat, give your cloak as well; and if anyone forces you to go one mile, go also the second mile' " (Matt 5:39–41). "Do not repay anyone evil for evil. . . . Never avenge yourselves. . . . If your enemies are hungry, feed them. . . . Do not be overcome by evil, but overcome evil with good" (Rom 12:17, 19–21). "Do not return evil for evil or abuse for abuse; but on the contrary, repay with a blessing" (1 Pet 3:9; cf. 1 Thess 5:15).

   b. Jesus taught love of neighbor and enemy.

      "You shall love your neighbor as yourself" (Matt 22:39; Mark 12:31; Luke 20:27; also Rom 12:9, 17–21; 13:8–10; Gal 5:14; Jas 2:8).
      "But I say to you, 'Love your enemies and pray for those who persecute you' " (Matt 5:44; Luke 6:27, 35; cf. Rom 12:20–21).

   c. Jesus taught against the use of the sword.

      Then Jesus said to him. "Put your sword back into its place; for all who take the sword will perish by the sword" (Matt 26:52).
      Jesus answered. "My kingdom is not from this world. If my kingdom were from this world, my followers would be fighting to keep me from being handed over to the Jews. But as it is, my kingdom is not from here" (John 18:36).
      "For the weapons of our warfare are not merely human, but they have divine power to destroy strongholds" (2 Cor 10:4).

2. The nature of God's kingdom and Jesus's messiahship support pacifism.

---

29. Swartley, *Slavery, Sabbath, War, and Women*, 118–37.

30. The imperative, *antistēnai*, likely means, according to Walter Wink's extensive research, "Do not resist violently": Wink, "Neither Passivity nor Violence," in *Love of Enemy*, ed. Swartley, 113–15. Or, the third inflection object, *tō ponērō*, can mean "by evil means." Either way, the command does not mean passivity when facing evil, but response that eschews and overcomes violence.

    a. Jesus's proclamation of the kingdom of God in the context of first-century politics shows Jesus's pacifist commitment.

    b. Jesus's temptations were political in nature; Jesus refused them.

    c. Peter's confession "You are the Messiah" (Mark 8:27–38), a political manifesto, prompted Jesus's teaching on the way of the cross, calling his disciples to "be at peace with one another" (9:50).

    d. The suffering servant—Son of man—Messiah introduced a bold new pacifist picture for messianic thought.

    e. Jesus as conquering lamb demonstrated the new way.

3. Christ's atonement calls for pacifist discipleship.

    a. Atonement means victory over the powers.

    b. Atonement means reconciling justification.

    c. Discipleship means identifying with/following/imitating Jesus Christ.

4. The nature and mission of the church leads to pacifism.

    a. The church is the body of Christ's peace.

    b. The church's mission is peace.

    c. The church is separate from the state, but subordinate to it, and called to witness to it.

5. Peace is the heart of the gospel.

    a. Peace permeates the NT.

    b. Peace is rooted in eschatology.

Many of these sanctions in support of pacifism appeal to either commands or principles, with imperative verbs (especially in number one). Some appeal to paradigms (mostly number two). The Good Samaritan story (Luke 10:25–37) and Jesus's passing through Samaria (John 4) are paradigms demonstrating love of enemy. Some appeal, such as topics in three and four and the assertion for number five, to the symbolic world of the new creation in Jesus Christ. For a fuller account of how the NT, using these modes of appeal, documents the peace-promoting ethos of the NT, see chapter fifteen in *Covenant of Peace*.[31]

But what about violence embedded in social structures that form the symbolic world of the biblical narrative as a whole? In cases such as slavery, war, and oppression of women, the matter of whether the text in its varied forms of moral address *prescribes* or *regulates* is a crucial consideration. In regard to slavery, NT texts regulate its practice but do not prescribe it. Statements such as Jesus's forecast, "There will be wars and rumors of wars," do not justify war but rather function to encourage the disciples to faithfully persevere until the end, despite many trials and "signs" that occur. Prescriptive statements may have a regulating more than a mandating function.[32] The NT nowhere mandates violence, though Desjardins considers the Pauline "silencing" of women (1 Cor 14:34–36) violent. But the warrant for the command in 14:33 is, "For God is not a God of confusion but of peace," thus contesting the point.

Rather, "the NT speaks univocally and pervasively of *peace/peacemaking* as one central feature of the gospel."[33] It is impossible, in my judgment, to hold that the NT promotes violence, when these methodological considerations are taken into account.

SANCTIONS FOR MORAL APPEALS

As Kelsey's book superbly demonstrates,[34] modern theologians appeal to different types of sanctions to warrant their theological or ethical perspectives. The same is true of NT moral exhortations. In some cases moral instruction is linked to eschatological urgency, as in Rom 13. A *time* factor is noted (vv. 11–12), but the paragraph is introduced with "Besides this . . . ," which indicates that eschatology is not the only warranting factor. In 13:1–2, *God's authority* warrants the moral appeals.

A slight appeal to the *time* factor (in 5:15–16) occurs in the diverse moral injunctions of Eph 5:1—6:19, but the overriding warrant for these admonitions is struck in 5:1–2, with its "Therefore . . . " (which by implication warrants also the moral imperatives in the last half of Eph 4). These two verses (5:1–2) specify God's and Christ's self-giving *agapē*-love as *the*

---

31. Swartley, *Covenant*, 399–414, together with the summary of this portion on 415–16.

32. Swartley, *Slavery, Sabbath, War, and Women*, 201–2.

33. Swartley, *Covenant*, 418.

34. Kelsey, *Proving Doctrine*.

pattern for imitation. God's and Christ's model segues to moral imperatives with the motif "as is fitting among the saints" (5:3c).[35]

Some NT scholars contend that Jesus and Paul expected an imminent end of history, and therefore the radical NT ethic of loving the enemy and nonretaliation does not merit consideration because Jesus's ethics were intended only for a short-term, an "interim ethic." This eschatological "escape" from Jesus's radical ethic overlooks, however, the more substantive warranting of NT ethics. Moral exhortation is fitting response to God's deeds of salvation and grace, and is grounded in God's nature revealed in Jesus Christ's life and teachings. In John's Gospel, the Father and Son give themselves in mutual donation for the life of the world (John 6:51). Jürgen Moltmann's and John H. Yoder's theological-ethical contributions[36] have done much to change this climate, so that eschatology, rather than justifying an escape from obedience, empowers the Christian moral life.

CONTEMPORARY CULTURAL SENSITIVITIES

Biblical interpretation involves three interacting worlds: the world behind the text (point one above); the world within the text (point three); and the world in front of the text, the world of the reader.[37] Readers bring interpretive eyes to the text, influenced by their life settings. Both Desjardins's and Tite's contributions reflect the reader-world of the interpretive-hermeneutic process—i.e., whether NT texts underwrite contemporary practices of violence. Tite reads 1 Peter through a sociological grid-lens of "insider" and "outsider" grouping. He regards the rhetoric of 1 Peter and John 1–12 as violent. After describing 1 Peter's encouragement of a persecuted, suffering ("insider") community, he says a "conceptual violence . . . emerges from this message; i.e., not only are those who oppose the recipients considered immoral and liable to God's damnation, they are also demonized as being actively in league with the forces of evil."[38] Such an indictment of 1 Peter is one-sided. In stressing 3:12b and glossing over 3:9, 11, 13, it sympathizes with the persecutors rather than the persecuted. His critique would be more appropriate of John 5 and 8 where the Johannine Jesus damns un-

35. "Fitting response" was one of H. Richard Niebuhr's ethical motifs in *The Responsible Self*, 60–61. Many Christian ethicists have employed this motif to describe the relation between the indicative (God's actions) and the imperative (human response).

36. Moltmann, *Theology of Hope,* and *Ethics of Hope;* Yoder, *Peace without Eschatology?* and *Politics of Jesus.*

37. Tate, *Biblical Interpretation.* Tate examines the hermeneutical process at work in these three tasks.

38. Tite, *Conceiving,* 107.

believing Jews in saying, "You are of your father the devil" (5:44 RSV). The *Wirkungsgeschichte* of this text has fueled the flame of anti-Semitism through the ages, even though these texts reflect intra-Jewish argument in language with parallels in other intra-Jewish disputes.[39]

How do we assess such charges against the NT? In the definitional section of this article it is clear that violent imagery is present in Scripture for intrinsic reasons. But Tite's charges do not exactly fit that intrinsic rationale. His critique is threefold. First, and most basic, is the inside/outside opposition as violence-promoting. With this construct he then charges Scripture with legitimating anti-Jewish violence and anti-GLBT violence. Each must be assessed separately.

First, the insider/outsider sociological construct is necessary in a faith community's identity, thus requiring boundaries. Since Abraham, the faith community necessarily lives with identity boundaries. Otherwise the "faith-ark" community ("church," for Cyprian) capsizes on the rocky shoals of the "world-sea." "Inclusion" is a foremost value of the gospel itself. The gospel welcomes all, but not all choose to follow Jesus. Hence an identity boundary necessarily marks the community of faith. Scripture bears overwhelming testimony to the faith community's inclusion of "outsiders" (evident even in Matthew's genealogy). The inclusion of "outcasts" and "outsiders," and even "the enemy" abounds in the Gospels and Pauline literature.[40] If inclusion, however, denies the gospel's particularity, it subverts the gospel. To regard identity boundaries as "violence" is problematic, for its alternative is a Constantinian-type conscription of all into the fold at the cost of personal decision and Christian nonconformity to the world.

The two specific issues Tite raises by selecting John 1–12 and 1 Peter are also of different substance. Adequate treatment of these is beyond the space and focus of this article; they are addressed prolifically in recent literature.[41]

CONCLUSION

This discussion of definition and five methodological considerations assists us in the endeavor to discern and assess the peacemaking character

39. See Swartley, *John*, the essay on "The Jews" and its web supplement.

40. A look at the many highlighted texts in *The Poverty and Justice Bible–CEV*, provides corroborative evidence for this point.

41. For the first, see Swartley, *John*, commentary on John 5 and 8, the essay on "The Jews," and the extended discussion in the web supplement to the commentary. For the second, see the helpful "conversation" in *Reasoning Together* by Grimsrud and Nation.

of Scripture. Richard Hays in his examination of NT Scripture says the NT consistently opposes violence: "There is not a syllable in the Pauline letters that can be cited in support of Christians employing violence."[42] Furthermore, "With regard to the issue of *violence,* the NT bears a powerful witness that is both univocal and pervasive, for it [renouncing violence] is integrally related to the heart of the kerygma and to God's fundamental elective purpose."[43]

Hays's definition of violence differs, however, from Desjardins' and Tite's, who include psychological violence (a *subjective* category in defining violence). Nevertheless, Tite's failure to assess John 8 in its historical-cultural setting, with its intra-Jewish debate conventions (point one above), is a limitation of his assessment. But it is true: John 8 in the context of our linguistic conventions sounds violent. Points one and five of these methodological considerations are thus in tensive relation and, as is often the case, necessarily so. By assessing this tension, the peace witness of John (note chap. 4; 14:27; 16:33; 20:19–26) can be affirmed.[44]

Only because of the dominant peace-promoting teaching of the NT are we able to withstand and transform violence, which the evil one foments in this world (in lies, hatreds, wars, and savage massacres). In the courageous words of Martin Luther King Jr., "We shall overcome" with God's help and receive *Strength to Love*[45] in the face of violence.

---

42. Hays, *The Moral Vision*, 331.

43. Ibid., 313–14.

44. Swartley, *Covenant*, 304–21.

45 A book of Martin Luther King Jr.'s sermons, first published in 1963. See the reprint by Fortress Press, 2010.

14

"Righteousness and Peace Will Kiss"

The Peaceableness of the "Super-righteous"

Thomas R. Yoder Neufeld

Steadfast love and faithfulness will meet; righteousness and peace will kiss each other. (Ps 85:10)[1]

Unless your righteousness exceeds that of the scribes and Pharisees, you will never enter the kingdom of heaven. Matt 5:20

Peace and *justice*[2] are commonly paired words in recent peace discourse. Indeed, *justice* has largely displaced *righteousness,* serving to distinguish peace as social justice and active peacemaking from a "spiritual rapprochement"[3] between the individual and God. Presumably the vocabulary of righteousness is more at home there. I will use the terms *righteousness* and *righteous* deliberately and somewhat mischievously in an attempt to transgress this heavily fortified border.[4]

The following essay is intended to probe and point more than settle the relationship between righteousness and peace. Overstatement and

1. All biblical quotations are taken from the NRSV unless otherwise indicated.
2. E.g., Isa 32:16–18.
3. Kraus, *Jesus Factor*, 39.
4. "*Super-righteousness*" is a playful take on Matt 5:20.

underdocumentation are thus unavoidable.[5] I begin by locating the meaning of the terminology in the OT and then bring together NT voices as diverse as Matthew, Paul, and James. Scholars are accustomed to treating biblical voices as distinct, even as opposed to each other. What we have then is less a choir than a series of soloists, performing for audiences that seldom go to the same concerts. I wish to put these distinct voices into one canonical choir, and relish unanticipated harmonies.

RIGHTEOUSNESS AND THE RIGHTEOUS

The essential biblical meaning of "righteousness" and "righteous" is hardly in dispute.[6] I need only sketch out the most relevant features.

In the Bible righteousness is given content by God's will and deed more than it is an abstract standard or virtue by which behavior, including God's, can be evaluated or judged. God's righteousness informs the order of creation, the liberation and defense of God's people, the covenant with Israel and its stipulations in Torah, and the realization of God's promises. Righteousness is thus intricately related to *shalom,* the Bible's word for salvation, justice, and peace (e.g., Ps 85:8–13).[7] To say that God is righteous is to claim that God is judge, vindicator and savior of victims, and punisher of the wicked.[8] Mercy and grace are intelligible precisely in relation to such righteous judgment (cf. Wis 11:15—12:2; Sir 18:1–14).[9] God's covenant partners are righteous when they walk in accord with the divine will, when they are holy as their divine covenant partner is holy (Lev 19:2). "The righteous shall live by *their* faith*fulness*" (Hab 2:4).

Such fidelity comes to expression most obviously in faithfulness to Torah (e.g., Pss 1, 119).[10] Among the many dimensions of such righteousness,

---

5. In addition to the many studies of peace (e.g., the SPS series), or on justice and righteousness, see especially Swartley, *Covenant of Peace* and its exhaustive bibliography. See also his "Relation of Justice/Righteousness."

6. "Righteousness": *tsedeq, tsedaqah* (Heb.), *dikaiosunē* (Gk.); "righteous": *tsaddiq* (Heb.), *dikaios* (Gk.). See, e.g., Leonhardt-Balzer, "Righteousness in Early Jewish Literature"; Soards, "Righteousness in the New Testament"; Scullion, "Righteousness (OT)"; Reumann, "Righteousness"; Kwakkel, "Righteousness"; Toews, *Romans,* 400–407.

7. Perry Yoder prefers "justice" to "righteousness" (*Shalom*). For "shalom," see Yoder and Swartley, eds., *The Meaning of Peace.*

8. *Tsedaqah* is paired with *mishpat* [LXX *krisis*], some eighty times, eighteen times in Isaiah alone (e.g., 32:16–18). While difficult to distinguish with precision, *mishpat* is related to giving judgment for and against, and *tsedaqah* more widely to "right-making."

9. See my "Power, Love, and Creation."

10. See, e.g., Creach, *Destiny of the Righteous.*

one of the most important is almsgiving, imitating the Creator's largesse in providing especially for the most vulnerable. Tellingly, *tsedaqah* becomes a virtual synonym for financial generosity in post-biblical Jewish writings.[11] While demanded of those who have been rewarded for their righteousness with material wellbeing,[12] all righteous persons, including the poor, are to emulate the generosity of God.[13]

Emerging from the same well of piety as obedience and imitation ("faith*fulness*") is radical trust ("faith") in God. "Abraham *trusted* God, and that counted as righteousness" (Gen 15:6). Such trust is tested most acutely when the righteous suffer unjustly, especially when it is their loyalty to God that gets them into trouble. Their meekness in the face of victimization, even if not always quiet,[14] can make them appear weak and passive. Such "passivity" is not stoic acceptance, however, but radical trust in and deference to the God who honors their faithfulness with vindication: "The righteous shall live by *my* faithfulness" (Hab 2:4 LXX).

We confront several tensions in this brief portrayal of righteousness. The first revolves around suffering and the elegantly simple axiom that righteousness is rewarded and wickedness punished.[15] The actual experience of the righteous, however, frequently does not reflect that quid pro quo. The wicked too often benefit from violence and greed while the righteous suffer.

For the truly righteous the default response to this conundrum is to view their suffering as a prod to repentance, to greater loyalty, with full confidence that God responds faithfully to pleas for clemency and forgiveness from those who truly turn from their ways.[16] They see their suffering as atoning for their own sins, but also for those of others (e.g., Isa 53; 4 Macc 6:26–29). At other times the righteous suffer because their righteous behavior offends the wicked (e.g., Wis 2:12–16). But often their suffering is enveloped in baffling mystery, as in the case of Job or in the psalmist's cry of abandonment in Ps 22:1. Even then, however, such depth of despair is in

---

11. See Przybylski, *Righteousness in Matthew*, 116, 119. For LXX examples of almsgiving and righteousness see also Prov 10:2; Sir 3:30; Tob 14:11; Dan 4:27.

12. See Wright, "Righteous Rich."

13. Levine cites Midrash Rabbah on Leviticus about a poor widow who has but a handful of flour; the rabbi's students are told not to mock her, since "it is as if she sacrificed her soul" (*Misunderstood Jew*, 150). See also, e.g., Bin Gorion, *Mimekor Yisrael*, 1178–99.

14. Laments and complaints are directed to God, to fellow worshipers, and to enemies listening in to the psalmist. See Suderman, "Prayers Heard and Overheard."

15. E.g., Prov 10–15; Pss 1, 14, 75, 92, etc.

16. E.g., Pss 6, 32, 51; Wis 11:23; Sir 18:1–14; Pr Man; *Pss. Sol.* 3:4; 10:1–3. The perfection of the righteous lies in their willingness to have their sins exposed and to respond to divine correction.

its own way a witness to the conviction that the righteous can demand vindication from their God. God is righteous, even if in ways beyond human comprehension.

The second point of tension is the relationship between the righteous and the unrighteous. On one hand, they are to disassociate themselves from the wicked (e.g., Pss 1:1; 37; 146:8–9). Such separatism is not so much a matter of staying at a safe distance from God's judgment as it is solidarity with the divine covenant partner (Ps 139:19–24). This standoffishness is reflected, for example, in Qumran's covenantal pledge, where pious hostility goes hand in hand with nonretaliation (1QS X, 17–23).[17]

On the other hand, there is a tradition of the righteous showing compassion toward those who are in trouble with the divine judge, interceding, even arguing, with God on their behalf. The list of such intercessors is long.[18] True, the ultimate fate of the wicked is premised on their repentance, but it is the desire of the righteous to create the space and opportunity for such repentance and to forestall the closure of judgment. Ironically, it is precisely in their arguing with God that their righteousness becomes evident, and thus also their imitation of the patience of a loving Creator with errant creatures (e.g., Wis 11:20—12:2; cf. Matt 5:45; 2 Pet 3:9).

One final somewhat puzzling aspect of this rough sketch is that the righteous inhabit the full spectrum of status. On one hand, they are the meek, the weak, the often humbled and the always humble,[19] living on the edge of survival by trust in divine care and vindication, willingly offering their cheeks to the beard pluckers (Isa 50:6; Lam 3:30). They are the vulnerable poor, the persecuted prophets and suffering servants of Yahweh. On the other, they are monarchs, and most astonishingly, divine "sons."[20] These diverse status levels often coexist, either in the same person[21] or as a reward for faithfulness extended to the very poor and grievously victimized.[22]

---

17. On whether Rom 12:17–21 should be interpreted in light of 1QS, see the exchange between Stendahl ("Hate, Nonretaliation, and Love," in *Meanings*, 137–61) and Klassen ("Coals of Fire").

18. E.g., 2 Esd/*4 Ezra* 7:106–111; 8:4–36. For the NT see the plea of Jesus on the cross (Luke 23:34), or Paul's wish that he might sacrifice himself for his own people (Rom 9:3). Does the Lord's Prayer (Matt 6:12) set an audacious example of forgiveness for God to emulate?

19. Humility of the righteous is well attested at Qumran, esp. in 1QS IV, 5; V, 3–4; see Kampen, *Wisdom Literature*, 278.

20. "Sons" rather than "children." Better to add "daughters," as does the author of Acts 2:17 quoting Joel 2:28, than to obscure the attribution of royal status (e.g., Ps 2:7; Wis 2:16–18; 5:1–5, 16).

21. Recall that the psalms of lament are attributed to King David.

22. Nickelsburg has shown—in relation to, e.g., Wis 2–5, 2 Macc 7, *1 En.* 94–104,

To summarize, the righteous are faithful to Torah, generous toward those in need, truthful and fair in adjudication, and determined not to collaborate with injustice. They are also humbly willing to extract from life's difficult and painful moments opportunities for correction and atonement, for themselves and others less righteous. This mix of special status, humility, poverty, generosity, peaceable patience, and confidence in divine attention and vindication continues to find expression in the traditions and legends of Judaism into the present.[23]

RIGHTEOUSNESS IN THE NEW TESTAMENT

We should thus have sensed the resonance of this portrait with what we find in the NT, especially if we read it less as "early Christian" and more as messianic Jewish literature.[24] Novel within NT treatment of righteousness is the eschatological conviction of NT writers—namely, that the *dikaiosunē* of God is bringing about a surfeit of righteousness most surprisingly among the *un*righteous through God's Messiah. Mercy, grace, love, and justification (or righteous-making) become the dominant even if not the only notes within the music of what is now called "gospel."

First, Jesus is the faithful righteous one par excellence.[25] He exhibits intimacy and confidence with God as a "son," entirely devoted to doing the will of his Abba. His practice of righteousness is that of an obedient supplicant, being baptized so as to "fulfill all righteousness" (Matt 3:15), of a prophet announcing and enacting God's reign, summoning to repentance, meeting human need, and finally, offering his own life not only for his friends and followers but for "sinners." While Jesus is supremely trusting of his Abba, at the moment of most intense suffering on the cross Mark and Matthew also depict him as sharing in the fathomless suffering of the righteous (Ps 22:1; Matt 27:46; Mark 15:34). By having Jesus plead for forgiveness for his torturers, Luke places him in the long line of the righteous who put themselves between sinners and the divine judge (23:34). It is the

and Qumran scrolls—that resurrection is the ultimate vindication of the "righteous poor" (*Resurrection, Immortality, and Eternal Life*).

23. See, for example, Kampen, *Wisdom Literature*, 274–79, 292–95, 326–28, or the post-Holocaust novelistic treatment in Schwarz-Bart's 1960 *The Last of the Just* [ET].

24. Levine rejects reading the NT as Jewish (*Misunderstood Jew*, 111), unlike messianic Jewish scholar Kinzer (*Post-Missionary Messianic Judaism*, 30–32). In my view Christians need to reread the NT as messianic Jewish literature, however much it might be viewed as Judaism's "prime heresy" (Boyarin, *Dying for God*, 17, 25). See also Sim, "Christian Judaism"; Yoder, *Jewish-Christian Schism Revisited*, 30–34.

25. Matt 27:19; Luke 23:47; Acts 3:14; 7:52; 22:14; Jas 5:6; 1 Pet 3:18; 1 John 2:1.

centurion who captures the significance of the moment: "Truly this one was a righteous one" (23:47).[26] His death becomes *the* example of the righteous atoning for the unrighteous. Finally, both narrative and veneration place Jesus at every point along the righteousness status spectrum, from poor and powerless to victimized prophet, servant of God, king, divine son, Wisdom's child, indeed, Wisdom herself, and finally to vindicated and exalted Lord.[27]

The writer of Hebrews claims that Jesus was "like us in every way," but without sin (4:15). That was obvious neither to Jesus's contemporaries nor to the detractors of the movement. Much of Jesus's activity is rehearsed as deliberately flouting the demands of righteousness, whether by eating and drinking with sinners, touching lepers, denigrating purity practices, or excoriating those devoted to righteousness. The evangelists and apostles nevertheless insist that in light of his vindication in the resurrection, Jesus truly was *the* Righteous One, *the* Servant and Son in whom God is well pleased (e.g., Acts 3:14; 7:52; 22:14).

Further, as much as Jesus's death by crucifixion came as a shock to his followers, threatening his status as righteous (Gal 3:13; Deut 21:23), and as much as its atoning function was only fully appreciated in light of his vindication in the resurrection, the meaningful suffering of the righteous as depicted in Scripture and tradition carries the seeds of such insight (e.g., Isa 53). The cross becomes a cipher for a righteous one dying for the unrighteous and thus the central symbol of the *dikaiosunē* of God at work in making peace (e.g., 1 Cor 1:17, 18; Eph 2:16; cf. Heb 7:26–28; 13:12).

RIGHTEOUSNESS IS NECESSARILY PERFORMED

The connection between Jesus's righteousness and his suffering and death is firmly entrenched in mainstream Christian theology. That theology is not nearly as insistent, however, that the beneficiaries of that righteousness are themselves to be *doers* of righteousness, let alone doers of *that kind* of righteousness. Put bluntly, it has not read the NT carefully, or taken its Jewish pedigree seriously.

For example, no one would have taken Jesus's announcement of the arrival of the reign of God and the urgent summons to repent in light of it as anything but a clarion call to *performed* righteousness. To be sure, such righteousness is premised on the grace and favor of God. Jesus first pronounces blessed those who hunger for righteousness (Matt 5:6). Only then

26. Usually (mis)translated as "innocent," it is a virtual synonym for Mark's "son of God" (Mark 15:39).

27. See my *Recovering Jesus*, 291–328.

does Matthew have Jesus introduce the unqualified demand for the super-righteous to turn the cheek, walk the second mile, give the remaining shirt, to be unreservedly generous, and, finally, to love their enemies, and thus for both a *deliberate* vulnerability befitting those who know their God is a vindicator (5:6, 9–12), and a *"defiant* vulnerability"[28] befitting those who *do* justice and *make* peace.

Even apart from the call to nonretaliation and love of enemies, Matthew's Sermon on the Mount is a virtual manual of practiced righteousness, including instruction in humble, repentant, and confident prayer to the one who judges and vindicates (6:5–18), in unselfconscious generosity (6:1–4; cf. 25:37), in unostentatious piety (6:19–20), and in seeking a righteousness that is premised on the care of the Creator for even the most vulnerable of creatures (6:25–34). The prayer Jesus teaches his followers is that of the righteous who address God as Father, just as he does, who speak with confidence and directness of their own need, and who pledge themselves to practice radical forgiveness (6:9–13). The end of the sermon should come as no surprise: any hearing without *doing* is building one's home on sand, only to have it swept away at the time of judgment (7:13–27; cf. 18:35; Rom 2:13; 6:15–19; Jas 2:12–13). In the view of the evangelists, Jesus did not come with a solution to unrealistic and destructive demands for righteous behavior, but rather to widen the circle of those of whom it can be expected—sinners, tax collectors, and Gentiles.

Matthew and the other evangelists are not alone. James provides something like a snapshot of the righteous (3:13–17): the wise and understanding are those who know the wisdom "from above." As companions of Sophia, their works emerge from the meekness of wisdom; they are resolutely opposed to the earthly wisdom reflected in greed, arrogance, and destructive zeal. Their walk is peaceable (*eirēnikē*), they are willing to yield and obey (*epiekēs, eupeithēs*), full of mercy and good fruit, nonjudgmental (*adiakritos*) and unhypocritical. James links righteousness and peace in the strongest possible terms: "The fruit of righteousness is sown in peace by those who make peace" (3:18; cf. Heb 12:11).

This stress on *lived* wisdom, *practiced* righteousness—good *works*—is present no less in Paul, in both undisputed letters and in those likely penned by his followers. Like some fellow Jews, Paul considers compliance with Torah to have been a dismal failure when looked at overall (e.g., Rom 3:9–20; 7:5–24; 2 Esd/4 *Ezra* 7), even if he sees himself to have been an exceptional athlete of righteousness (Phil 3:6). But Paul understands the righteousness of God to address precisely this failure, now *chōris nomou* ("apart from the

28. Wink, "Neither Passivity nor Violence," 115.

law"), in and through the faithfulness of Jesus,[29] justifying sinners while they are as yet weak, sinful enemies (Rom 3:21–26; 5:1, 6, 8, 10).

However, it simply cannot have occurred to Paul the Pharisee, now zealot of Messiah Jesus, that God's righteousness would stop at declaring sinners righteous without addressing their ability to *perform* righteousness. It is thus no overstatement to say that the very point of justification is to free recipients of God's righteousness to *perform* righteousness. Justification is the process of new creation, of making people able to walk in compliance with the Creator's will.[30] Justification might thus well be translated as "righteous-making."

To justification we add "spirit" (*pneuma*). Whatever else *pneuma* represents for Paul, it is the inscribing of God's will into the very decision-making core ("on the heart") of those who were once godless (2 Cor 3:1–6, playing on Jer 31:31–34). *Pneuma* is the eschatological intervention of God enabling righteousness in the disobedient (Rom 8:1–8; Gal 5:13–25).

The "reign of grace through the righteousness of God" (Rom 5:21) enables the "reign in life" of the righteous (5:17). Those who have been saved *by* grace have been saved *for* good works (Eph 2:5, 8, 10). By participating in the life, death, and resurrection of the righteous Messiah, and empowered by his spirit, they themselves become "slaves of righteousness" (Rom 6:18).[31] The echo of the *'ebed YHWH* (servant of the Lord) is clearly audible when these slaves are asked to present themselves to God as "weapons of righteousness" (Rom 6:13), thereby themselves becoming the righteousness of God (2 Cor 5:21).

Romans 12 provides an inventory of such "slavery," marked by the now expected mix of meekness and zealotry. The faithful are to be patient (v. 12) and peaceable (v. 18), all the while "pursuing (*diōkō*) the stranger with love" (v. 13), and blessing those who pursue (*diōkō*) them malevolently (v. 14; cf. Matt 5:44). They thereby do not so much "take it" as vanquish (*nikaō*) evil with good rather than with violence (vv. 20–21), confident, at the same time, in the certainty of divine vindication (v. 19, quoting Deut 32:35).[32]

29. With others I translate *pistis Iēsou Christou* thus rather than as "faith in Jesus." Also at Gal 2:16; see e.g., Hays, *Faith of Jesus Christ*; Toews, *Romans*, 108–10.

30. E.g., 2 Cor 5:21; Gal 5:22–24; 6:15–16; Eph 2:15; 4:20. Privileging the forensic aspect of justification has undercut justification as enablement. See also Gorman, "Justification and Justice in Paul."

31. Another way to characterize slavery to *dikaiosunē* is to speak of carrying the yoke of Wisdom/Torah/Christ (Matt 11:29; Sir 6:23–31; 51:25–26; 4Q420–421; Kampen, *Wisdom Literature*, 293–94).

32. See n19 above.

This view of righteousness pervades the whole of the Pauline corpus. What is often dismissed as moralizing in the pseudepigraphical letters was an increasingly necessary exhortation to performed righteousness. This is "Paul" fighting a misreading of Paul, in keeping with Paul's own exasperation as seen in Rom 6. Indeed, 2 Tim 3:16 is entirely Pauline in its emphasis that "all Scripture" (i.e., the Scriptures of the synagogue) is "useful for training in righteousness." When Paul urges his congregations to imitate him as he himself imitates the Messiah (1 Cor 11:1), he does so as a righteous one whose life imitates that of the Righteous One, the Messiah (e.g., 2 Cor 6:4–10; cf. Col 1:24). While Paul sees it as his calling to pry open the covenantal doors of hospitality to the unrighteous, sinners, and non-Jews, he never tires of exhorting them to holiness and righteousness (e.g., Rom 12:1–2; 1 Thess 4:1–8). Given the prominence of almsgiving in biblical righteousness, it is into this context that Paul's collecting of money for the Jerusalem believers needs to be placed, with Jesus as supreme model of a donor (2 Cor 8 and 9; Rom 15:25–29). Paul characterizes his apostolic mission as bringing about the "*obedience* of the Gentiles" (Rom 15:18), and dutifully warns them as a good *dikaios* that they will need to face the divine tribunal on "what they have done in the body" (2 Cor 5:10; cf. Rom 1:18; cf. Heb 12:14).[33]

PEACEMAKING AS PARTICIPATION IN THE RIGHTEOUSNESS OF GOD

The explicit link between peace and righteousness in the NT has already been noted (Rom 14:17; 2 Tim 2:22). NT authors learned that pairing from their scriptures (Pss 72:7; 85:10; Isa 32:17; 48:18; 60:17). The central question of this essay is this: if righteousness is *lived* conformity to the will of God, what does *practiced* righteousness look like for beneficiaries of God's surprising righteousness as exercised in and through the faithfulness of Jesus? How do the righteous mimic the righteousness of the "God of peace" as it comes to expression *in* Torah (Matt 5:17–20) and *apart from* Torah (Rom 3:21–26)? How do pursuers of righteousness act who have been dug from such a quarry (Isa 51:1), one in which righteousness is mined as grace and peace? Stated simply, they are to emulate and participate in the ingenuity, patience, mercy, love, and self-sacrifice of God in Jesus. Offering the other cheek and walking a second mile may on occasion be good

---

33. See also Rom 2:1–16; 14:10–12; 1 Cor 3:10–17; 6:9; 11:27–32; 2 Cor 5:9–10; Gal 6:7; 1 Thess 4:23–25; 2 Thess 1, 2. This is no more Pauline than how Jesus is remembered in, e.g., Matt 18:35.

subversive strategy (à la Walter Wink),[34] but such righteousness is finally the non-negotiable imitation of the God who gave his own son as an act of love for enemies.[35] Such generous and peaceable righteousness is "super-righteousness" (Matt 5:20); it is "perfection" (Matt 5:48; cf. Rom 12:2; Eph 4:13). This is how righteousness and peace kiss.

However much marked by meekness, patience, and suffering, such peaceable righteousness must never be severed from the repeated injunction to aggressively *pursue* (*diōkō*) peace (Ps 34:14; Rom 14:19; 2 Tim 2:22; Heb 12:14; 1 Pet 3:11). Notably, in every case but Rom 14, the pursuit of peace is part of the pursuit of righteousness, holiness, and good works. The pursuers have offered themselves (their "members") to God as "weapons of righteousness" (Rom 6:13), clad in "weapons of light" (Rom 13:12). The "breastplate of righteousness" (Eph 6:14) is only one part of a larger armor that includes the footwear for the pursuit of peace (6:15). This is aggressive love—love for God, neighbor, and enemy.

Some of this combative vocabulary emerges from the biblical tradition of God as warrior and judge (e.g., Isa 59 as taken up in 1 Thess 5 and Eph 6). Are the righteous to emulate this aspect of the righteousness of God? Is their pursuit of righteousness and peace violent?

As shown above, deference to a vindicating and judging God is very much part of the disposition of the righteous, suggesting the answer should be *no* (e.g., Rom 12:14–21). That is consistent, for example, with the repeated injunctions not to judge (e.g., Matt 7:1–5; Luke 6:37; Rom 14). At the same time, Jesus does call on his followers to "bind and loose" (Matt 18:15–20), in effect to participate now already in the judgment of God.[36] As well, Paul presents himself as a warrior enforcing righteousness (2 Cor 6:7; 2 Cor 10:3–5). In those instances, however, interventions are intra-communal, intended to forestall the judgment of God, to bring back the erring member into the sphere of righteousness (Matt 18:15–20; Gal 6:1). The rhetoric may be harsh, but it remains the exercise of neighborly love (Lev 19:17–18; cf. Eph 4:25–26).[37] As Ephesians illustrates, the imitation of God on the part of the righteous is focused principally on imitating the grace and kindness of God, and the self-offering of Jesus (4:32—5:2). Judging "the world" is left either to God or to the eschatological future.[38]

---

34. Wink, *Engaging the Powers*, 175–93; Wink, "Neither Passivity nor Violence," 102–25.

35. Connecting the dots of Matt 5; Rom 3, 5; Eph 5:1–2; Phil 2; 1 Pet 3–4; John 3.

36. Yoder Neufeld, *Killing Enmity*, 43–44.

37. Yoder Neufeld, *Ephesians*, 209–11, 221–22.

38. E.g., 1 Cor 5:12–13; 6:2; Matt 19:28.

It might surprise us then that Isaiah's divine warrior becomes the community clad in God's own armor, "wielding" faith, love, and hope (1 Thess 5:8), truth, righteousness, peace, faithfulness, salvation, and prayer (Eph 6:14–18).[39] "Pursuit" thus perfectly captures the persistence and aggressiveness with which the righteous go after peace, even if their zealotry is often indistinguishable from patient suffering. After all, they have in Jesus, who is "Peace," the supreme model for how one aggressively "murders hostility" (Eph 2:16).

The Bible frequently speaks of the righteous in individualistic terms as heroes of faithfulness.[40] For NT believers Jesus is then at the top of the list of heroes as *the* Righteous One, with apostles following in his wake. In the NT as in the OT, however, there is a presumption of *communal* righteousness, whether exercised in *ekklēsiai* as small as two or three (Matt 18:20), by Jesus's circle of friends (John 15:15), or by Paul's body of the Messiah made up of many diverse members (Rom 12; 1 Cor 12; Eph 1:23; 4:4, 16; Col 1:18). In this explosively growing *koinōnia* of righteousness and peace, drawn from the ranks of both the righteous and the unrighteous, Jews and Gentiles, the slaves of righteousness (Rom 6:18) are slaves of one another (Gal 5:13), prisoners bound to each other "in Christ" with chafing chains of peace (Eph 4:3). The walk of the righteous is gracefully ungainly, not least because they never walk alone. Hence the repeated stress on humility, deference, mercy, solidarity, truthfulness, and mutual assistance (Rom 12:3–13; Eph 4:2–3, 15, 25–32; Phil 2:2–4; Col 3:12–15). It is *together* that the righteous act in the world as the body of the Righteous One, and *together* that they live out their cruciform mission as the "new human." As John Toews has shown in his study of righteousness in Paul's letter to the Romans,[41] all these terms—peace, righteousness, slavery—were central to the imperial ideology and religion of Rome. When peace and righteousness are given content and meaning by the faithfulness of the Messiah Jesus, however, they forge a communal counterculture in direct opposition to imperial claimants to peace and justice, today no less than then.

---

39. See Yoder Neufeld, *Killing Enmity,* 135–43; for larger discussion of the divine armor, see my *Ephesians,* 290–316, and the earlier *"Put on the Armour of God."*

40. Recall 2 Esd/4 Ezra 7:106–11; cf. also Sir 44–50; Heb 11. Later Christian tradition refers to them as "saints."

41. Toews, "Righteousness in Romans."

CONCLUSIONS

First, I have not addressed the peaceable righteousness exercised by those outside the household of faith, by the "righteous Gentiles," as it were. The central burden of this essay, however, is to show how God's righteousness in and through Jesus impinges on those who claim that grace for themselves, and how it is inseparable from peacemaking, which is nothing less than the "super-righteousness" of sons and daughters of God.

Second, such peaceable righteousness is not a system of rules or strategies. True, it has produced a rich and profound body of wisdom, to be freely shared. But the necessarily unstable dialectic of meekness and aggressiveness, power and weakness, patience and pursuit, sovereignty and slavery, mercy and judgment, "kindness and severity" (Rom 11:22), does not lend itself to being reduced to an -ism, or an -ology, to mimic John Howard Yoder.[42] Righteousness is not compromised by mercy or forgiveness: they are its means of making righteous, even if it shows its harsh face when trivialized or taken for granted. It is justice without a blindfold, on the lookout for victims to be vindicated, for righteous ones to be rewarded, but also for the unrighteous to be sought out like lost sheep, sons, and precious coins (Luke 15; Matt 18:10–14). Super-righteousness emulates the ingenuity of the God of peace whose ways are beyond scrutiny or prediction (Rom 11:33–36). The practice of righteousness will thus by its very nature be inventive, potentially scandalous, occasionally rule defying, all the while moored in Torah, Wisdom, and Gospel.

Third, the contemporary peace movement's abandonment of "nonresistance" in favor of activism[43] runs the risk of ignoring an essential biblical thread in which peacemaking is participation in the profoundly vulnerable and unpredictably elastic patience of God with enemies (2 Pet 3:9). That said, any nonresistance practiced by those who do not resist by aggressively *pursuing* peace is a morally and spiritually moribund quietism.

Fourth, I have attempted to show that the taproot of righteousness in the NT is located in the long history of God's people, rooted in and witnessed to by Law and Prophets and extending forward into the history of Judaism and church. Not to do so relegates the OT to the status of problem and estranges Jesus and his witnesses from rootedness in Scriptures and synagogue, producing children orphaned from their parents in the faith. A canonically broad reading of righteousness, spanning both Testaments, provides a large arena for ecumenical and Jewish-Christian consideration

---

42. Yoder, *The Politics of Jesus*, 142–43.

43. See Driedger and Kraybill, *Mennonite Peacemaking*, and more recently Stutzman, *From Nonresistance to Justice*.

of peacemaking as fidelity to God's righteousness.[44] Inevitably, such shared consideration will often be in the form of contentious debate. Or perhaps, to return to the musical metaphor introduced at the outset, the harmonies may be startlingly novel but are no less to be welcomed.

Fifth, peacemaking is not the agenda of a sect, or the special charism of the historic peace churches. Nor is righteousness, whether as personal holiness or as justification by faith, owned by another tradition. Peace, in its full biblical circumference and depth, is the gift and goal of God's righteousness, and peacemaking is the necessary practice on the part of *all* who have tasted God's kindness.

---

44. For examples pointing the way, see Yoder's *Jewish-Christian Schism Revisited* and Lapide's *Sermon on the Mount.*

15

Jesus, the Peaceable Messiah of Israel

The Theology of Matthew in Light of Messianic Interpretation of Scriptures

Paul Yokota

INTRODUCTION

The purpose of this study is to understand more fully the significance of Matthew's presentation of Jesus the Messiah within its historical context, that is, early Jewish messianism. In order to accomplish this goal, I will focus on Matthew's interpretation in the light of early Jewish messianic interpretation of the Scriptures. A premise of this essay is that Matthew's theology significantly derives from the author's understanding of the Scriptures; as Richard Bauckham suggests, "We should remember that Hebrew Bible contains a range of texts that might be understood to refer to the Messiah, and what sort of Messiah one envisaged depended a lot on which texts one emphasized."[1]

Before analyzing the texts, we need to define "royal messiah" as it is used here. A royal messiah is a kingly figure who will play a critical role as part of God's decisive act in the future, so that a different state of affairs may ensue.[2] Three tables at the end of this chapter summarize my findings on the

---

1. Bauckham, *Jesus: A Very Short Introduction,* 88.
2. Cf. Nicklesburg, "Eschatology (Early Jewish)"; Aune, "Early Christian

messianic interpretation of the Scriptures within early Jewish documents and the Gospel of Matthew, and the comparison between them. On the basis of these data, I now turn to look at Matthew's presentation of Jesus the Messiah.[3]

MATTHEW'S INTERPRETATION OF THE ROYAL MESSIANIC TEXTS COMMON TO MATTHEW AND EARLY JUDAISM

The interpretation of some royal messianic texts common to Matthew and early Judaism (Isa 11:1; Num 24:17; Ps 2; Dan 7:13–14; 2 Sam 7:13–14) suggests that Matthew may depend on or at least be aware of some common exegetical traditions concerning the royal messiah (see Table 15.3). However, Matthew's interpretation of those royal messianic texts differs radically from that of early Judaism. It seems that Matthew carefully *redefines* them within the context of his narrative or through an exegetical link with other texts.

1. Numbers 24:17 was popularly interpreted in early Judaism to suggest a militant and nationalistic royal messiah who would destroy the enemies of Israel (4Q175; CD7; Ps 154; *Sib. Or.* 5; cf. Bar Kochba, "the son of the star"). However, in Matthew the Messiah to which Num 24:17 is applied is depicted as "a child" who suffers from the threat of Herod's violence. In the birth narrative "the king of the Jews" does not conquer Gentiles; he is worshiped by them (Matt 2:1–12).

2. Isaiah 11:1, a popular royal messianic text in early Judaism (4Q161; 4Q285; 1Q28b; *Pss. Sol.* 17; *4 Ezra* 13; *2 Bar.* 36–40), is also used in Matthew (2:23). However, Isa 11:4, often understood by other early Jewish literature to show the idea of judgment or conquering, is *not* referred to there. Rather, Isa 11:1 is connected with Nazareth, which may reflect its denigrated status at that time (Matt 26:71–73; cf. John 1:46; 7:41).

3. While Ps 2 was also interpreted in early Judaism as a portrait of a militant Messiah who will rule over the nations (Ps 2:1–2; 8–9. Cf. *Pss. Sol.* 17; *1 En.* 48:10; *4 Ezra* 13), in Matt 3:17 and 17:5, Ps 2:7 is alluded to *along with* Isa 42:1, which depicts the Servant of the Lord. This exegetical link may have been used to transform the kind of messianism that

Eschatology."

3. For exegetical discussions behind the tables, see my doctoral thesis, chaps. 2 and 4, where I give the arguments in detail. Yokota, "Jesus the Messiah of Israel."

Ps 2 suggested to many early Jewish interpreters. Although Matthew has the messianic interpretation of Ps 2:8–9 (along with Dan 7:14) of the idea of a Messiah ruling over the nations, the view is represented in his temptation narrative where it is placed on *the lips of Satan* (Matt 4:8–9). Furthermore, Matthew's messianic interpretation of Ps 2:6 in 3:17 and 17:5 may also be connected with Gen 22:2, 12, 16 (LXX). This exegetical link strengthens the *intimate* relationship between Father (God) and Son (the Messiah), an emphasis that may allow for the development of a high Christology (28:19–20), a dimension absent in early Jewish royal messianism.

4. Although 2 Sam 7 was used as the scriptural foundation *for expectation* of the coming Davidic Messiah in early Judaism (4Q174; *Pss. Sol.* 17; Sir 47), the theme of *the Messiah who will build the temple* is not common in the literature. In Matthew, however, the theme of the Messiah who will build the temple is prominent, likely deriving from a messianic interpretation of 2 Sam 7:13–14 (16:16, 18; cf. 26:61; 27:40). The temple that Jesus the Messiah will build is "my church," the community of the disciples following him (Matt 16:18; 18:17).

5. The human-like ruler of Dan 7, while not obviously a Davidic figure in that context, is identified with the Davidic Messiah in early Judaism (*4 Ezra* 11–13; *2 Bar.* 39–40; *Sib. Or.* 5:414–433; Similitudes of Enoch [*1 En.* 37–71]). The incorporation of the Danielic human-like figure in Davidic messianism leads to a more exalted description of the Messiah. The messianic interpretation of Dan 7 is attested in Matthew, but it is linked not so much with the earthly life of the Messiah as with his *post-resurrection* appearance, and with the Parousia when his rule will be established over all nations (24:30; 26:64; 28:18).[4]

MATTHEW'S INTERPRETATION OF ROYAL MESSIANIC TEXTS NOT IN COMMON WITH EARLY JUDAISM

There is also in Matthew use of apparently royal messianic texts *not* cited in early Judaism as far as our evidence goes (see Table 15.3). The choice of the texts may reveal features of Matthew's messianic theology that differ from that of early Judaism.

The first interpretive category of Matthew's messianic texts *not* common with early Judaism is of those that describe the *humble, compassionate,* and *nonmilitary* character of the Messiah. Whereas there is no unambiguous

4. See Riches' perceptive observations (*Conflicting Mythologies*, 289–90).

evidence of messianic interpretation of Ezek 34 in early Judaism, Matthew's interpretation of it is extensive, and it is a key text to describe the ministry of Jesus the Messiah (2:6; 9:36; 10:6, 16; 14:14; 15:24, 32; 18:12–14; 25:32).[5] Along with 2 Sam 5:2, it highlights the character of the Messiah as a good and compassionate shepherd who will care for God's flock, i.e., Israel. Furthermore, Matthew's extensive messianic interpretation of Ezek 34 focuses not on external warfare but on the gathering of Israel's dispersed sheep at her restoration. Finally, his interpretation of Ezek 34 implies that the current Jewish leaders are the false shepherds who fail to meet their responsibility to care for Israel.

While Zech 9:9 is easily understood as a royal messianic text, its messianic use is conspicuously absent in early Judaism.[6] Matthew's interpretation of Zech 9:9—which describes a *nonmilitary* ruler riding on (a) donkey(s),[7] not a war horse—highlights the nonmilitary nature of his messianic theology.

Matthew's messianic interpretation of Zech 11:12–13 and 13:7–9 makes a similar point. The former speaks of the rejection of the shepherd, the latter of the suffering of the shepherd. We do not have evidence to attest their messianic interpretation in early Judaism.

The second type of royal messianic texts is those open to interpretations that suggest *the inclusion of the Messiah in the unique divine identity*.[8] There is no unambiguous evidence to suggest the messianic interpretation of Ps 110:1 in early Judaism. The psalm's messianic interpretation has enormous theological potential, in that it can provide a scriptural basis for the Messiah's sitting on the heavenly throne with God.[9] This suggests, in a Jewish context, the inclusion of the Messiah in the unique divine identity. It is

---

5. See my dissertation, 4.13; Heil, "Ezekiel 34"; Swartley, *Covenant of Peace*, 80–81. Swartley's excellent contributions are in his penetrating study of the issue of peace and violence in the NT as a whole. Of interest here is his use of Ezek 34 as a key text to show God's vision of peace; that chapter is the source of the title of Swartley's book.

6. Although Black attempts to find a pre-Christian Jewish messianic interpretation of Zech 9:9–10, he fails to provide evidence for it, as he himself admits ("The Rejected and Slain Messiah," 95–112).

7. For the discussions of the two donkeys, see ibid., 171.

8. For the concept of "the unique divine identity" and the inclusion of Jesus Christ in NT Christology, see Bauckham, *Jesus and the God of Israel*, chaps. 1, 5–7.

9. Although 1 Chr 28:5 is sometimes cited as a biblical example to show the seating of a king on the throne of God without claiming divinity for him, Hengel argues that "1 Chr 28:5 offers no real parallel to the *later* messianic *transcendent* interpretation (of Ps 110:1). . . . Here it is not a question of the heavenly throne of God itself, but of the ideal kingdom of the house of David, that Yahweh as the true king of Israel established, a motif that can be traced to 2 Sam 7:14 in connection with 1 Sam 8:7 and 16:1" ("'Sit at My Right Hand!'" 179–80, Hengel's italics).

striking therefore that Matthew's Jesus applied Ps 110:1 to himself, claiming to sit on the heavenly throne with God. In doing so, he claimed to have a cosmic authority far beyond any earthly rule of the Davidic Messiah.[10]

While Isa 8:23—9:1 (MT) is cited at Matt 4:15–16 and since Isa 9:5 (MT) lies in the immediate context of Isa 8:23—9:1, Matt 4:15–16 may allude to the divine nature of the Messiah. The exegetical link of Isa 7:14 with Isa 8:8 in Matt 1:23 also creates a "new meaning," suggesting the identification between Jesus the Messiah and God.[11]

MATTHEW'S INTERPRETATION OF "NOT OBVIOUSLY ROYAL MESSIANIC" TEXTS

Matthew's choice of not obviously royal messianic texts further confirms the points we have made and suggests something further. The first type of text that Matthew chooses to apply to the Messiah is of the kind that speak of *the theological significance of the suffering and death of the Messiah*. While the Servant of the Lord in Isaiah is applied to the royal messiah in the Similitudes of Enoch, we find no clear evidence to suggest the application of the theme of the (vicarious) suffering of the servant in Isa 53 to the Messiah. On the other hand, in Matthew the identification of the Messiah with the Suffering Servant in Isa 53, as well as with the Passover lamb, plays a key role in explicating the redemptive significance of the suffering and death of Jesus the Messiah for Israel (20:28; 26:28).[12] Psalm 118:22–23 may also belong to this category, since the rejected stone becomes the cornerstone of the new temple (Matt 21:42).

The second type of text that Matthew uses is of those associated with *monotheism*. These texts whose immediate contexts speak of monotheism are applied to Jesus the Messiah. The immediate context of Isa 40:3 speaks of an eschatological monotheism (Matt 3:3), and Job 9:8 of creational monotheism (Matt 14:25). Similarly, Isa 43:1–13 clearly show creational monotheism (Matt 14:22–33). In applying these monotheistic texts to Jesus the Messiah, Matthew suggests his inclusion in the unique divine identity.[13]

10. Bauckham, "The Throne of God," 64.

11. For more detailed arguments, see my dissertation, 4:2.

12. Although Barrett and Hooker have attacked the traditional view of allusion to Isa 53:10–12 in Matt 20:28, they have been rightly criticized by France, Moo, and most thoroughly, Watts. See Barrett, "The Background of Mark 10:45," 7; Hooker, *Jesus and the Servant*, 74–75; France, *Jesus and the Old Testament*, 116–21; Moo, *The Old Testament*, 122–27; Watts, *Isaiah's New Exodus and Mark*, 125–51.

13. Cf. Bauckham, *Jesus and the God of Israel*, chap. 6.

The third type of text speaks of (the experience of) Israel. The genealogy of Jesus the Messiah summarizes the history of the people of Israel, in which the Messiah climactically appears (Matt 1:2–17). The "son" in Hos 11:1 that originally refers to Israel is applied to him (Matt 2:15). Furthermore, Jer 31:15 speaks of the tragic experience of the exile of Israel, an experience also implicitly applied to the Messiah (Matt 2:13–18). In this way, Jesus the Messiah is identified with (the experience of) Israel. Since this identification is placed in the early chapters of the Gospel (Matt 1:2–17; 2:15, 18; cf. 4:1–11), its significance must not be underestimated.

However, it is important to make clear that Jesus the Messiah is not to be subsumed under the category of corporate Israel. He is described as an individual figure standing over against Israel; he chose the twelve, representing the new Israel (cf. Matt 10:2–4; 19:28; 26:20–29). In my view, what Jesus the Messiah did—as *a new Israelite* and *the teacher of the new Israel*—was to bequeath a model for the new Israel to follow (Matt 10:24–25; 23:8–10; cf. 4:1–11).

Finally, the fourth type of text defines the *universal significance* of the Messiah. The Servant of the Lord in Isa 42:1–4 is illustrative (Matt 12:18–21). It speaks of the role of the servant in the salvation of all nations, including Israel (cf. Matt 24:14; 28:19–20). The inclusion of the Gentiles in the genealogy of the Messiah may make a similar point.[14] Finally, Ps 22 anticipates the establishment of God's universal kingdom after the suffering of the righteous (one) who is identified in Matthew with Jesus the Messiah (28:17–20).

CONCLUSION

This study has shown the following about Matthew's presentation of Jesus the Messiah:

1. Matthew accentuates Jesus the Messiah as the peaceable (nonviolent and humble) king. Early Jewish literature often envisages the royal messiah as destroying the enemies of Israel by force, a picture that derived mainly from Gen 49:9–10, Num 24:17, Isa 11:1–5, Ps 2:8–9, and Dan 7:13–14. Matthew, however, does not explicitly cite any of these texts in his portrayal of the pre-resurrection life of Jesus. Although we have identified allusions to some of those texts, indicating that Jesus is the expected Davidic Messiah, the way they are interpreted is carefully redefined in the narrative. While Jesus may be linked with Num 24:17 in Matt 2, the narrative portrays him as "a child" worshiped

14. Bauckham, *Gospel Women*, 41–46.

by the Gentiles, a picture far from that of the military conqueror of Israel's enemies. The messianic allusion to Ps 2:8–9, along with Dan 7:14,
is put on the lips of Satan rather than Jesus (4:8–9). While Isa 11:1 is
interpreted messianically in Matt 2:23, the way it is used is not only
implicit but also identified with an obscure place, Nazareth. Although
Dan 7:13–14 may be employed in a victorious manner in Matthew (as in
early Jewish literature), it depicts not so much Jesus's pre-resurrection
life as his appearance at the time of his Parousia (24:30; 26:43; 28:18).
Matthew also interprets "messianic" texts that are *not* used in early Judaism. Matthew's use of Zech 9:9 with a fulfillment formula is a case in
point (Matt 21:5). This choice reveals that in Matthew's messianic theology, Jesus the Messiah is a nonmilitary and humble king, markedly
different from the early Jewish royal messiah. We have also argued that
Jesus is described as the shepherding Messiah deriving primarily from
Ezek 34 (cf. Mic 4; 2 Sam 5:2). Matthew's extensive messianic interpretation of Ezek 34, not clearly evident in early Judaism, accentuates the
portrait of Jesus as the compassionate and caring Messiah.

2. An important contribution to Matthew's distinctive portrait of the
Messiah is his inclusion of the Isaianic Servant of the Lord. Matthew's
use of Isa 42:1–4 in 12:18–23, the longest citation in the Gospel, is a
case in point (cf. Matt 3:17; 17:5). Its messianic use suggests that Jesus
the Messiah is the compassionate, humble, and just ruler in whom the
nations will hope. However, the most distinctive contribution comes
from Matthew's inclusion of the Suffering Servant of Isa 53. Although
the Similitudes of Enoch may refer to the Isaianic servant in a messianic manner, the evidence suggesting the messianic use of the Suffering Servant is far from clear.[15] On the other hand, it is likely that
Matthew's Jesus identifies himself with the Suffering Servant (20:28;
26:28). It is the redemptive death of Jesus the Messiah that uniquely
defines his identity against the early Jewish royal messianism.

3. Jesus fulfills the expectation that the Messiah will build the temple,
but that temple is not a physical building but the community of the
disciples called "my church" (Matt 16:18; 2 Sam 7:13). This temple is
built by means of his death and resurrection (Matt 21:42; Ps 118:22).

4. Jesus the Messiah is included in the unique divine identity. The royal
messiah in early Judaism is a human figure, but Matthew's messianic
interpretation of the Scriptures suggests that Jesus is included in the
divine identity. The combination of Isa 7:14 with Isa 8:8 in its present

15. See my dissertation, 2.8.3.

form makes a subtle case for the identification of Jesus as God (1:23). Matthew also applies Isa 8:23—9:1 to Jesus, the immediate context of which speaks of the divine nature of the Messiah (Isa 9:5). Matthew's messianic use of Ps 110:1—not commonly done in early Judaism—makes a strong case for inclusion of Jesus in the divine identity. By applying Ps 110:1 to himself, Matthew's Jesus claims to sit on the heavenly throne with God, signifying Jesus's participation in the unique divine identity. The fact that Matthew applies monotheistic texts (e.g., Isa 40:3, 43:1–13; Job 9:8) to Jesus also strengthens the case for the inclusion of Jesus in the divine identity.[16]

16. I would like to state my appreciation to Prof. Willard Swartley not only for his excellent scholarship but also for his life as the embodiment of his theology. In addition, my thanks go to Prof. Richard Bauckham for reading my essay.

Table 15.1. Early Jewish messianic interpretation of key scriptural texts

	4 Ezra 11–12	4 Ezra 13	Sir 47	Sir 51	2 Bar 36–40	Ps 154	PsSol 17	Sib Or 5	Similitudes of Enoch	1Q28b	4Q161	4Q174	4Q175	4Q252	4Q285	CD VII	Josephus	Philo	BarKochba
Gen 49	C									C				C					
Num 24:7																	2C		
Num 24:17						C		C					C			C	L		C
2 Sam 7			P		C							C							
Ps 2	C						C	C				L							
Ps 132				P	C														
Isa 11:1–5	C			C			2C	2C	C	C	C								
Isa 11:10			P																
Isa Servant									3C										
Jer 23/33							C							C					
Dan 7	C	C			C			C	C										
Amos 9												C							
Mic 4										C									
Mic 5										L									

Note: The letters C (certain), L (likely), and P (possible) indicate the relative degree of certainty on messianic use of scriptural texts. The numbers attached to the letters indicates the frequency of the use of the scriptural texts in question.

Table 15.2. Matthew's messianic interpretation of key scriptural texts

OT Texts	Matthew	Use
Genealogy	1:2–17	A
Isa 7:14/Isa 8:8	1:23	C
Num 24:17	2:1–12	A
Mic 5:1/2 Sam 5:2	2:6	C
Hos 11:1	2:15	C
Jer 31:15	2:18	C
Isa 11:1	2:23	A
Isa 40:3	3:3	C
Ps 2:7/Isa 42:1	3:17	A
Ps 2:8/Dan 7:14	4:8–9	A
Isa 8:23—9:1	4:15–16	C
Isa 53:4	8:17	C
Ezek 34	9:36/10:6/14:14/15:24, 32	A
Isa 35:5–6/Isa 61:1	11:5	A
Mal 3:11 Ex 23:20	11:10	C
Isa 42:1–4	12:18–21	C
Job 9:8/Isa 43:1–13	14:22–33	A
2 Sam 7:12–14	16:16, 18	A
Ps 2:7/Isa 42:1	17:5	A
Isa 53:10–12	20:28	A
	26:28	A
Passover Lamb	26:28	
Jer 31:31, 34/Exod 24:8/Zech 9:11	26:28	A
Isa 62:11(Isa 40:10)/Zech 9:9	21:5	C
Zech 13:7–9	26:31–32	C
Zech 11:12–13	26:15/27:3–10	A
Ps 118:22–23	21:42	C
Ps 110:1	22:44	C
Ps 110:1/Dan 7:13	26:64	A
Dan 7:13–14	24:30	A
	26:64	A
	28:18	A
Ps 22	Passion Narrative/28:10/28:17–20	A

Note: C stands for citation. A stands for allusion.

Table 15.3. Matthew's messianic interpretation of key scriptural texts in the light of
Jewish messianic interpretation of key scriptural texts

Commonly used royal messianic texts	Matthew	Not commonly used royal messianic texts	Matthew	Not obviously royal messianic texts	Matthew
Isa 11:1	2:23	Ezek 34	9:36	Passover Lamb	26:28
Num 24:17	2:2		10:6	Isa 53:10–12	20:18
Ps 2:6	3:17		14:14		26:28
	17:5		15:24, 32	Ps 118:22–23	21:42
Ps 2:8–9/Dan 7:14	4:8–9	Mic 5:1/ 2 Sam 5:2	2:6	Ps 22	27:35
2 Sam 7:13–14	16:16, 18	Zech 9:9	21:5		27:39
Dan 7:13	24:30	Zech 11:12–13	26:15		27:43
	26:64		27:3–10		27:46
Dan 7:14	28:18	Zech 13:7–9	26:31–32		28:10
		Ps 110:1	22:44		28:17–20
			26:64	Isa 42:1	3:17
		Isa 7:14/8:8	1:23		17:5
		Isa 8:23–9:1	4:15–16	Isa 42:1–4	12:18–21
				Isa 40:3	3:3
				Isa 35:5–6	11:5
				Job 9:8/ Isa 43:1–13	14:22–33
				Genealogy	1:2–17
				Hos 11:1	2:15
				Jer 31:15	2:18
				Isa 61:1	11:5

16

Jesus's Action in the Temple

David Rensberger

Jesus's action in the temple in Jerusalem (the so-called cleansing of the temple) has had an interesting afterlife. Despite diverse portrayals in the NT Gospels, it later acquired a fairly uniform aspect, particularly in Western works of art. A physical element found only in John was imported into a scene drawn largely from Mark, and a factor not mentioned in any of the Gospels largely dominates the representation of the story: in visual media, in popular interpretation, and sometimes even in NT scholarship, an enraged Jesus is pictured furiously whipping a terrified mass of animal dealers and money changers out of the temple.[1]

In paintings, anywhere from two to two dozen merchants scramble after their coins, doves, and livestock, scurrying away from the dominating central figure of Jesus, his upraised whip clearly directed at them, not at the animals.[2] In print, one popular spiritual writer remarks, "No wonder Jesus was driven to rage at such a scene, and consciously made 'a whip out

---

1. An earlier form of some of this essay appeared as part of a series of studies of difficult sayings and actions of Jesus for nonviolence oriented toward a nontechnical readership, published by TheThoughtfulChristian.com: http://www.thethoughtfulchristian. com/Products/TC0359/did-jesus-ialwaysi-preach-nonviolence.aspx.

2. Of the collections of paintings on this subject online at this writing, the largest is at Biblical Art on the WWW (http://www.biblical-art.com/biblicalsubject.asp?id_ biblicalsubject=618&pagenum=1). Wikimedia Commons also has more than one hundred images (http://commons.wikimedia.org/wiki/Category:Temple_incident).

of cord' to drive it out (see John 2:15)."[3] A theologian, in an online essay, speaks of Jesus "incensed at the sacrilege of it all," engaged in a "dramatic outburst" and "violent act"; of "Jesus unhinged, throwing furniture, screaming at the top of his lungs, and flinging money into the air."[4] Commentaries and other scholarly works, though more sober, sometimes also present this typical picture. William L. Lane speaks of Jesus's "deep indignation," and calls this "the only act of violence recorded of the Lord,"[5] while George R. Beasley-Murray sees the event as "an act of wrath which the traders were powerless to resist."[6]

This widespread image of whip-cracking rage presents obvious problems for a shalom-centered understanding of Jesus. Supposing that Jesus did teach nonviolence and peacemaking, did he practice it consistently? If Jesus acted violently on his (justifiable) anger, what is to prevent Christians of any period from doing likewise when provoked by injustice or sacrilege? To argue that Jesus's teaching of nonviolence is *not* normative for Christians, and that his one violent outburst in the temple *is* normative, might seem implausible. Yet the presumed violence of the temple action seems, for many people, to provide the hermeneutical key needed to invalidate any effort to put Jesus's nonviolent teaching into practice.[7]

In NT scholarship, there is surprisingly little discussion of whether the temple action was violent. Klyne R. Snodgrass is a partial exception; in the context of his otherwise comprehensive study, he remarks only, "Jesus commits no physical violence on people in the temple, even though he does act forcefully."[8] Most others who mention the issue at all tend to *assume* without demonstration that the action was violent. Raymond E. Brown referred to the "sweeping violence" of John's account.[9] Richard A. Horsley describes the action in the temple as "a minimally violent prophetic demonstration. . . . It must have been an actual attack involving some violence against property if not against persons."[10] Those (such as Lane) who note its uniqueness

3. Rohr and Feister, *Hope against Darkness*, 7.

4. Clendenin, "Jesus Unhinged." See also Markquart's sermon, with six images of artwork (http://www.sermonsfromseattle.com/series_b_the_cleansing_of_the_temple_GA.htm): "A reader can feel the anger of Jesus in this scene, unlike almost any other scene from the gospels."

5. Lane, *Gospel according to Mark*, 404.

6. Beasley-Murray, *John*, 39.

7. Yoder Neufeld, *Killing Enmity*, 70–71.

8. "The Temple Incident," 439.

9. *Gospel According to John*, 1:122.

10. Horsley, *Jesus and the Spiral of Violence*, 299–300. Horsley's only justification for this is an *assumption* "that the gospel tradition would have softened rather than

as Jesus's *only* violent act seldom reflect on this inconsistency with the rest of his mission. S. G. F. Brandon at least had the merit of trying to make the temple action consistent with the rest of Jesus's work—by completely reinterpreting that work in light of this action![11]

It would seem at least equally reasonable to seek consistency by acknowledging the generally nonviolent character of Jesus's mission and then attempting to understand the temple action within that framework. Yet the depiction sketched above is so culturally pervasive that alternative readings may be greeted with skepticism, regarded as special pleading or at least denying the obvious. Proponents of a consistently nonviolent understanding of Jesus therefore need to be rather hardnosed in approaching this story, and to ask whether what seems "obvious" in the Gospels' narratives seems so only because of this widespread interpretive tradition. It is not special pleading, in my opinion, to ask, what does it say? and to resist importing more recent cultural artifacts into the interpretation. We cannot, of course, avoid bringing who we are and where we stand culturally to our reading of the biblical text, but we can at least be conscious of it when we do so, and recognize when a culturally predominant tradition is the source of an "obvious" reading.

The focus of this essay will be on the question of the violence or lack of violence in the stories of Jesus's action in the temple, which will mean that a range of other issues may be mentioned but cannot be given real consideration. I will be privileging textual details in an effort to avoid importing familiar visual and homiletic representations. I will assume the chronological priority of Mark; that Matthew and Luke depend on Mark (and other sources); and that John is not directly dependent on any of the Synoptics. On these assumptions, it is evident that Matthew and Luke basically abbreviate Mark's version, adding nothing original apart from the contexts in which they place the story; therefore, their versions will not figure significantly in my treatment. John's narrative differs in many respects. Most strikingly, it is placed near the beginning rather than toward the end of Jesus's mission, though it too is set at Passover time.[12] John also has several narrative details not found in Mark (cattle and sheep, the famous whip of cords, the coins that Jesus pours out), and a very different dialog following the action.

---

exaggerated the severity of the action" (ibid.).

11. Brandon, *Jesus and the Zealots*. Compare the appraisal of Brandon in Chilton, *Temple of Jesus*, 94–98.

12. The reasons for John's different placement of the event in the narrative are explored in the commentaries, which generally and rightly consider it as being due to modification of the tradition or of an existing Gospel text, rather than as representing a more accurate chronology or a different, earlier event in the temple.

Mark and John, then, present two noticeably different versions of what is surely the same event. The story, boiled down to the commonalities between these two versions, is simply this: just before Passover, Jesus went to Jerusalem, entered the temple, drove out people who were conducting business there, and spoke of how their activities violate the divine purpose or nature of the temple. In terms of "what actually happened," we are unlikely ever to be able to say anything more definite than that. To understand what it meant for Jesus, and might mean for us, however, we need to explore some of the details in Mark's and John's stories. I will discuss John before Mark, because it has most strongly affected impressions of the violent nature of Jesus's action. First, though, it is important to consider some particular aspects of the action.

THE DIMENSIONS AND PURPOSE OF JESUS'S ACTION IN THE TEMPLE

This event is commonly referred to as the "cleansing" of the temple, on the assumption that Jesus's motivation was to purify the temple of commercial or even dishonest activities that had corrupted the sacred precincts. None of the Gospels, however, uses the terminology of *cleansing* or *purification,* and it is questionable whether Jesus cleansed the temple in any large-scale or lasting way. Here too we need to undo some traditional understandings in order to have any hope of getting at what Jesus was doing.

The first requirement is an accurate picture of the incident, starting with scope. The temple in Jerusalem was an enormous compound, with a total area of more than thirty-five acres (about fifteen hectares).[13] The outer courtyard, the largest and most open area of the temple complex, was a busy place. Particularly in the days leading up to Passover, it would have been thronged with Jewish pilgrims. It was also the one area of the temple complex to which Gentiles were permitted access. The transformation of this outer court into a place of business was apparently a recent development in Jesus's day.[14] The outer court had become a place where people could purchase the animals necessary for sacrifice, and could exchange their Roman currency for the Tyrian coins that were acceptable for temple purposes.

Artistic representations of Jesus "cleansing" the temple often show him in a relatively confined space chasing away everyone in sight—a portrayal that may be understandable, given the limitations of canvas, but is

13. Snodgrass, "Temple Incident," 448. Scholars give varying precise figures, but all are in this general range.

14. See the commentaries, e.g., Lane, *Gospel,* 404; Collins, *Mark,* 527–28.

misleading. Rather, we need to envision him creating as much commotion as one man could manage in a few minutes' time in one portion of the open space in a complex encompassing about five or six city blocks, with hundreds of people coming and going.[15] *Most visitors to the temple that day would never have noticed it.*[16] We probably have to suppose that an hour or two later temple activities were largely back to business as usual.[17]

To make this point is not to minimize the importance of Jesus's action, for himself or for the temple authorities.[18] The latter would have taken notice of any sort of disturbance, however transitory—and Jesus surely meant his action to be noticed. The Romans also kept a vigilant eye out for any kind of disturbance among their Jewish and other subjects, and if Mark's chronology is correct, this incident may have been what spurred them to action against Jesus, leading to his crucifixion. Nevertheless, if we picture him compelling the businesspeople in the temple courtyards to change their ways by force, we are surely mistaken. It is not likely that Jesus himself would have imagined that he could do such a thing.[19]

It is more plausible, then, that Jesus intended his action in the temple to be *symbolic*, as a broad spectrum of scholars concludes.[20] We might compare it to symbolic actions performed by prophets in Jerusalem centuries earlier (see Isa 20; Ezek 12:1–7; Jer 19). Such actions were meant to dramatize what the prophets considered to be right values or behavior but

15. All the Gospels indicate that Jesus acted alone. Conceivably others who were present "supported" his action (Chilton, *Temple of Jesus*, 98; Snodgrass, "Temple Incident," 453), but that does not allow us to imagine a large-scale uprising. Horsley tries to support such an event by claiming "clear evidence that the gospel writers, for their particular concerns, would have reduced the scope of the event rather than have blown it up" (*Jesus*, 298), but he does not specify that evidence, and proceeds to "step back from the particulars" of what the Gospels actually do say (ibid., 298–99).

16. "He could not and did not bring temple traffic to a standstill. Most people in the precincts . . . that day would not have even noticed him" (Evans, *Mark 8:27—16:20*, 167).

17. Keener allows for a day (*The Gospel of John*, 1:522), but the point is the same.

18. Snodgrass deprecates a view of Jesus's action as "limited in scope, that is, *merely a symbolic gesture*" ("Temple Incident," 454; Snodgrass's italics). He successfully defends the historical plausibility of the action, particularly with regard to the restricted area occupied by the money changers, within which Jesus would have needed to operate. Yet this argument does not address the apparently brief *duration* of Jesus's action, and it unjustifiably minimizes the significance of even limited symbolic actions.

19. Compare Horsley, *Jesus*, 298, with reference to theories that Jesus's action was an actual attempted takeover of the temple.

20. Sanders: "Jesus' action is to be regarded as a symbolic demonstration . . . a gesture intended to make a point rather than to have a concrete result" (*Jesus and Judaism*, 69–70); see also Borg, *Conflict, Holiness, and Politics*, 182; Evans, *Mark 8:27—16:20*, 166–67; Keener, *Gospel of John*, 1:522; France, *Gospel of Mark*, 445.

not to *compel* their implementation. We should not think of such actions as "merely" symbolic; they can be dramatic and convincing. But they are not violently coercive, nor are they likely to be sudden angry outbursts.[21]

The question remains, what was it that Jesus intended to symbolize? On this there is no scholarly consensus. Interpretations largely track whether any particular scholar accepts or rejects Mark 11:17 as reflecting Jesus's own comment on his deeds.[22] It may be unwise, though, to insist that Jesus had just one intention in the temple event, and that all other interpretations are mistaken. Symbols generally have multiple possible meanings, and Jesus may have had more than one thing in view in undertaking this action. In any case, for our purposes it is not necessary to pin down his precise intention, even if that were possible, since nearly any intention could have been carried out with or without violence.

Therefore it may be enough to say that the action in the temple was in some way a symbolic criticism of the functioning of the central religious institution of the Judaism to which Jesus belonged. It may even have been a warning of that institution's coming demise. It was no doubt noisy and disruptive, on a small scale, and might well have been considered aggressive. It took place in a prominent public place and therefore probably drew negative official attention, but it could not have presented any sustained practical hindrance to the temple's operations. The question remains, however, whether it was a *violent* symbolic action. In seeking an answer to that question, we turn to the two fundamental Gospel narratives that relate it, those of John and Mark.

JOHN'S VERSION

Apart from its placement of the story so early in the narrative, the most distinctive feature of the Fourth Gospel's treatment is the whip of cords. A surprising number of artistic representations of the temple action, while showing Jesus flailing the whip over his head, omit another feature unique to John, the cattle and sheep. Yet these two features are inseparable from one

---

21. For more on this, see below on the nature of Jesus's action in Mark's version.

22. As a general sampling, far from comprehensive, see Keener, *Gospel of John*, 1:522–27 (a challenge to the temple authorities because of corruption; cf. Evans, *Mark 8:27—16:20*, 169–71); Donahue and Harrington, *The Gospel of Mark*, 332 (protest against excessive commercialization and secularization in the temple complex); Collins, *Mark*, 529 (placing God's honor above aristocratic pretensions and convenience); Borg, *Conflict*, 184–89 (critique of seeing the temple as guarantor of security against Rome, and of the ideology of holiness and separation from Gentiles); Sanders, *Jesus and Judaism*, 70–76 (imminent eschatological destruction and rebuilding of the temple).

another in the story as John tells it, and highlighting the whip while playing down the animals has seriously distorted the history of interpretation. In the Synoptic Gospels, Jesus interacts only with people (and furniture) and uses no implement; in John, he makes a whip and interacts with animals as well as people. The difference is crucial.

The joint appearance of whip and livestock only in John is no coincidence. The Greek word for whip here, *fragellion*, was a loanword from Latin *flagellum*. The object in question had a wide range of uses, and one of these was in handling livestock. The first-century Roman writer on agriculture Columella advises disciplining plow-animals verbally, using blows only as a last resort, and even then never using a goad, which would only irritate the animal; instead one should use a *flagellum* (*Rust.* 2.2.26).[23] This counsel suits John's version of the temple action perfectly. Jesus desires to get the livestock moving, needs more than words to do so, and uses the least harmful instrument for the purpose. A few slaps, not a beating, would be all that was needed. John pictures Jesus braiding whatever light rope was available[24] into a whip with multiple thongs at the end in order to bestir the sheep and cattle.

Despite the clear connection between whip and livestock, many commentators and English translations (as well as artists down through the ages) have envisioned Jesus whipping the *merchants*. The question turns on careful interpretation of the Greek grammar in John 2:15. The "all" (*pantas*) that Jesus expelled may refer only or primarily to the *people* mentioned in verse 14, so that the following "both . . . and" (*te . . . kai*) clause concerning the sheep and cattle is additional to it; or "all" may mean "all the *animals*," so that the reference to sheep and cattle serves to specify this fact. As examples of the former interpretation, the ESV reads, "He drove them all out of the temple, with the sheep and oxen"; and the CEB, "[He] chased them all out of the temple, including the cattle and the sheep."[25] Exemplifying the latter, the NRSV renders the text, "He drove all of them out of the temple, both the sheep and the cattle"; and the NIV, "[He] drove all from the temple courts, both sheep and cattle."[26]

---

23. Columella, *On Agriculture*, LCL 361, 124–27.

24. Brown suggested that he used the rushes employed for the animals' bedding (*Gospel*, 1.115).

25. Commentators supporting this reading of the grammar include Brown, *Gospel*, 1:115; Michaels, *Gospel of John*, 159 with n8; Schnackenburg, *The Gospel According to St John*, 1.346 with n15; Barrett, *Gospel according to St. John*, 197–98; and Moloney, *Gospel of John*, 77.

26. Commentators supporting this reading include Keener, *Gospel of John*, 1:522; and Haenchen, *Gospel of John*, 183.

In a recent study, N. Clayton Croy has confirmed the second of these interpretations. He finds that the common way of using the *te . . . kai* construction employed here is indeed to identify the members of a previously mentioned group: the phrase "both the sheep and the cattle" specifies what is meant by "all." He also finds that the grammatically masculine *pantas* can cover the sheep (neuter) and cattle (masculine) without including the people. Croy points out in addition that, as the story flows, Jesus cannot have driven out all the *people* with the whip, since the money changers are still present and he must still tell the dove sellers to leave.[27] Croy's analysis is persuasive: John shows Jesus using the *flagellum* on animals, not on people.[28]

This may still not be wholly unproblematic as an image of Jesus, but it eliminates the image of Jesus whipping the merchants and money changers out of the temple. The vocabulary, the grammar, and the whole construction of the story all point quite conclusively to Jesus using the whip to generate a stampede of the livestock, which would be consistent with a symbolic disruption of commercial activities, without suggesting that any of the people were harmed or even threatened with the whip. It is certainly not a passive exercise, not exactly "meek and mild," but it is not truly violent either.[29] Once we have rid our minds of the fallacious artistic tradition of Jesus brandishing a whip at the merchants (and given the pervasiveness of the tradition, this is an extraordinarily difficult thing to do), the presence of violence in the story ceases to be "obvious" at all.

MARK'S VERSION

Mark's narrative presents a different set of issues regarding violence in the temple. There is no whip or other weapon. The possibility of violence is seen primarily in the suggestions that Jesus imposed his will on people: he "began expelling" the merchants and their customers, overturning tables and chairs; and he "did not permit" anyone to carry anything through the temple.[30] The latter is unique to Mark; even Matthew and Luke do not mention it. The expulsion and overturning of furniture, of course, are in John as well, but it will be convenient to address them here. It will also be convenient

---

27. Croy, "Messianic Whippersnapper," 533–66.

28. In agreement also with Yoder Neufeld, *Killing Enmity*, 60–61.

29. Horsley speaks of Jesus's action as "involving some violence against property if not against persons" (*Jesus*, 300), but "violence against property" seems a questionable concept in the context of this discussion.

30. My translations.

to treat another issue that comes up in discussions of all versions of the story—namely, Jesus's anger.

The verb *ekballō*, used by all four NT Gospels to depict Jesus's action (whether toward people, as in the Synoptics, or livestock, as in John) is etymologically "throw out," but has a broad range of connotation. It is used seventy-two times in the Gospels, very frequently (in the Synoptics; compare John 12:31) for the exorcism of demons. Concerning people, it can be used for "throwing them out" of a vineyard (Mark 12:8//Matt 21:39//Luke 20:12, 15), a town (Luke 4:29), or a courtroom (John 9:34–35); or sending them into the "outer darkness" (Matt 8:12 [cf. Luke 13:28]; 22:13; 25:30); or (not) driving them away from Jesus (John 6:37). But it also describes simply sending people outside a room (Mark 5:40//Matt 9:25); sending someone away after a healing (Mark 1:43); the Spirit "driving" Jesus into the wilderness after his baptism (Mark 1:12); and even sending laborers into a harvest (Matt 9:38//Luke 10:2). With reference to objects, it describes taking coins out of a purse (Luke 10:35); leading sheep out of a fold (John 10:4); and even a procedure as delicate as removing something from an eye (Matt 7:4–5// Luke 6:42).[31] There is thus nothing inherently violent about the word itself. Where it refers to sending people (or demons) away against their will, this is virtually always done through words alone. The clear exception is the vineyard parable (Mark 12:8 and parallels, referred to above), and perhaps Luke 4:29, where Jesus is hustled out of Nazareth and nearly thrown off a cliff.

Thus the statement that Jesus "expelled" merchants and their customers from the temple does not imply a use of force; (indeed, in Mark and Matthew he only "*began* expelling" them). No weapon is mentioned; Jesus simply assumes an authority to direct people's actions. The overturning of tables and chairs (and the pouring out of coins in John) is more clearly forcible. Yet on the whole, Jesus's action in Mark has a quality something like that of a modern-day protester who chains himself to a door to prevent people from entering a building. It is obstructive and aggravating, but nobody suffers bodily injury.[32] In Jesus's own time, we might think of the young Torah scholars who, instigated by their teachers, scaled the outside of the temple around 4 BCE and chopped down the golden eagle that Herod the Great had hung above the main gate (Josephus, *J.W.* 1.648–655; *Ant.* 17.149–167).[33]

31. Metaphorically, it can be used for throwing out someone's name (Luke 6:22) and for ripping out one's eye (Mark 9:47), but also for bringing things out of a treasury (Matt 12:35; 13:52).

32. From just such a perspective, peace activist John Dear describes Jesus's action as "a classic example of symbolic, nonviolent direct action" ("Didn't Jesus Overturn Tables?" 186; see also 187, 190–91).

33. For further examples and discussion, see pt. 2, "Popular Jewish Nonviolent

Though this was more practical than symbolic, it was, like Jesus's action, a sudden move against objects, but not persons, at the temple in broad daylight. In Jesus's case, we might imagine that the merchants would not have yielded control of their furniture (let alone their coins) without a fight. Or we might imagine that Jesus's maneuver was so quick and unexpected that it took them by surprise. In either case, we are simply imagining. The texts themselves say nothing about resistance by the merchants or force on the part of Jesus, and it seems unhelpful to appeal to what *must* have happened in the absence of evidence that it *did* happen.

Then what about Mark's assertion that Jesus "did not permit anyone to carry any object through the temple" (11:16)?[34] How could that be accomplished without violence, or at least intimidation? It is noteworthy that, in the other three places where Mark uses this language to speak of Jesus "not permitting" something (1:34; 5:19, 37), the only force involved is his personal authority. Such language could also describe a teacher issuing an edict or ruling, and indeed Jesus's interdiction has often been compared with the ban on using the temple as a shortcut in *m. Ber.* 9:5. Of course, the mere statement that Jesus "did not permit" people to do something does not prove that they actually stopped doing it![35] All in all, Mark's statement suggests a prohibition by a teacher or charismatic (whether efficacious or not) that need not have involved physical coercion.

Finally, it is often assumed that in this incident Jesus must have been acting in anger. While anger and violence are not necessarily connected, it is probably easier to imagine an angry Jesus as a violent Jesus, so a few words on this topic will be apropos.

The fact is that the Gospels give no description of Jesus's emotions here. In the one incident in which readers are most inclined to see an angry Jesus, the Gospels themselves say nothing of the kind. They simply narrate a series of actions without mentioning emotion. The actions may give us an impression of anger, but that says more about our psychologies than Jesus's. Even more than with the whip, the impression of Jesus's wrath is rooted in cultural assumptions, and centuries of artwork, not in the texts. Once again it is necessary to be hardheaded and to insist that whatever emotions we

---

Resistance," in Horsley, *Jesus*, 59–145.

34. My translation. *Skeuos* is literally "a vessel," but with no article or further specification it commonly means "any object, anything" in general (France, *Gospel*, 444).

35. Snodgrass makes a plausible case that Jesus could have prevented people from carrying things through the temple, given the confined spaces involved ("Temple Incident," 454), but does not address whether coercion might be needed. And again there is the question of the *duration* of Jesus's activity.

perceive in these stories we read into them ourselves, based on our own presuppositions.

It is not as if the Gospel writers were unwilling to ascribe emotion to Jesus. Mark, for instance, does speak of Jesus's anger elsewhere (3:5; 10:14). Both Luke (10:21; 19:41) and John (11:15, 35) show him both rejoicing and weeping. John, in that same context and elsewhere, uses the verbs *tarassō* and *embrimaomai*, representing deep emotions perhaps of disturbance and indignation, respectively (11:33, 38; 12:27; 13:21). The latter verb in Mark 1:43 and Matt 9:30 seems to mean a stern warning or scolding. Of course, the Synoptics often speak of Jesus's compassion, too (Mark 1:41; 6:34//Matt 14:14; 8:2//Matt 15:32; Matt 9:36; 20:34; Luke 7:13).

Thus the Gospel writers thought of Jesus as having a full range of emotions, and surely would have portrayed him as angry during the temple action, had they found reason to do so. In fact, their complete silence about Jesus's emotions is itself suggestive. To quote Marcus Borg, "It is inadequate to refer to it as his 'temple tantrum,' as if he were suddenly filled with anger at what he saw there. . . . Rather, the act looks very intentional. . . . It was deliberate, thought out in advance."[36] As a *symbolic* deed, the temple action would not have been a crazed outburst but coolly calculated and methodically executed. Instead of an enraged Jesus, I suggest we envision a determined Jesus, going about the business of being a prophet and knowing the cost full well.

CONCLUSIONS

The traditional understanding of Jesus's action in the temple as an act of violent fury cannot be sustained on a careful reading of the Gospels. Neither Mark nor John shows Jesus angrily projecting force or using violence against other people. Instead, they portray a symbolic action (whatever it may have been meant to symbolize) of the kind that requires forethought. The "violent, angry outburst" reading, perhaps influenced by artistic depictions, simply does not hold water.

Nevertheless, the narratives of the temple incident seem likely to remain contested. For one thing, precisely because they are so spare, it is easy to fill them with details that the interpreter wishes to find. For another, they present one of the few entry points in the Gospels for portraying Jesus as less countercultural, less counterintuitive, less alien than most people find him when they take him seriously. In the traditional portrayal, Jesus enters the temple, sees an aggravating set of circumstances, and responds *just as we*

36. *Jesus*, 233–34.

would: he flies into a rage and starts swinging at people and throwing things around. Or rather, he responds just as our cultural ideal of the masculine hero would. He is the New Sheriff in Town—or perhaps the Incredible Hulk. Here, at last, is Jesus with hair on his chest! The violent Jesus in the temple who appears in so many works of art, homiletics, and even scholarship says more about our need for violent, enraged saviors than it does about Jesus or the earliest stories of him.

Of course, even those who read the temple incident in this way acknowledge that it is the *most* violent act of Jesus's life. The very impossibility of fitting such a violent incident into the rest of what is knowable about him should suggest that something is wrong with this reading. Rather than considering it the "obvious" or "commonsense" interpretation, exegetes may need to call our common sense itself into question, and ask what should be obvious about a man who counseled an occupied people to love their enemies and yet ended up on the enemies' cross.

17

Swords and Prayer

Luke 22:31–62

Mary H. Schertz

There are few texts interpreted in more diverse ways than Luke 22:35–38, the scene at the farewell table where Jesus commands his disciples to go out and buy swords if they do not have them. The passage is a genuine enigma that has been used, for instance, to support the two swords of state and church as well as the claim that Jesus prohibited any use of the sword whatsoever by Christians.[1] Since the middle of the last century, however, most interpreters have recognized the connection between this passage and the arrest scene (22:47–53) where one of the disciples attacks the servant of the high priest with one of the two swords produced at the table. There, Jesus heals the wound struck by the unknown sword wielder and also says, *eate heōs toutou* ("No more of this!" Luke 22:51 NRSV).[2] Jesus's reactions to the swordplay reduce the likelihood that his telling the disciples to go buy swords is a straightforward call to arms.

Recognition of the connection between the "swords at table" and the "sword in the night" scenes has turned the weight of scholarly consensus toward metaphorical interpretation of the two swords in 22:35–38. But the

---

1. Tiede, *Luke,* 388.

2. The translation of the idiom is difficult. In its most literal form, it might be rendered "Allow up to this," according to Johnson, *Gospel of Luke,* 353. "Let them be, even this far!" is the suggestion of Fitzmyer, *Gospel according to Luke,* 2:1451. All biblical translations are mine unless otherwise indicated.

191

metaphorical scope has been wide indeed. Recently, scholars have tended to see Jesus's injunction as a test for his disciples. Many efforts to unravel the passage rest on the use of irony—either by Jesus or by Luke as author.[3] In these interpretations, Jesus emerges with greater coherence in his message than in some of the earlier interpretations, and the disciples appear to be even more morally deficient—misunderstanding Jesus and exposing their own seditious natures.[4]

André Trocmé and John Howard Yoder provide an alternative view that places the puzzling ambiguities of the passage more squarely at the feet of the main character, Jesus.[5] This suggestion has not received much serious notice from Luke commentators. Apart from Trocmé and Yoder, only recently has the issue of whether Luke might be portraying Jesus as ambivalent about the use of violence in these passages been raised. In a 1997 article, H. A. J. Kruger[6] suggests that Jesus, in the last hours before his arrest, may have been struggling with the issue of divine warfare. Might he not need to drink the cup, after all?[7]

In this essay, I suggest that the reading guide that Luke offers with his chiastic arrangement of the five scenes in Luke 22:31–62 provides a reason to look again at the two swords passage. The arrangement of this passage is:

A   Jesus predicts Peter's denial (vv. 31–34).

 B Jesus tells the disciples to buy swords (vv. 35–38).

  C Jesus prays: Take this cup (vv. 39–46).

 B´ Jesus: Have you come out with swords? (vv. 47–54).

A´   Peter denies that he knows Jesus (vv. 55–62).

The narrative flow pulls the reader inward from both ends to focus attention on Jesus's prayer to the Father in verses 39–46. This guide that Luke gives us raises the question of how the prayer functions in the story. Does what happens on Olivet change the direction of the unfolding events, and if so, what is that transformation?

---

3. Unless indicated otherwise, when I say "Jesus" I mean Jesus as Luke has portrayed him.

4. Tannehill is arguably the scholar who most convincingly describes the passage as ironic (*Narrative Unity of Luke-Acts*, 1:265–68).

5. See Trocmé, *Jesus and the Nonviolent Revolution*; Yoder, *Politics of Jesus*.

6. Kruger, "A Sword over His Head or in His Hand?" 597–604.

7. Trocmé, Yoder, and Kruger nuance the language and imagery of holy war differently. What these views have in common is a willingness to consider that Jesus, at this point in the narrative, is not entirely certain about God's will. Most other scholars seem to dismiss this possibility out of hand.

This particular sequence of five smaller stories begins with the penultimate discussion around the last table that Jesus shares with his disciples before the crucifixion.[8] In verses 31–34 Jesus predicts that three times Peter will deny that he knows him. Peter protests that he is loyal to the end, but over his protests, Jesus reiterates and specifies the prediction. That story is followed in verses 35–38 with the puzzling discussion in which Jesus rescinds his earlier instructions and tells the disciples to take up the bags, wallets, and swords that he had earlier told them to abandon. After that, at the heart, or turn, of the chiasm in verses 39–46, Jesus takes his disciples and moves from the table to a familiar place on Olivet, where he not only prays but also tells the disciples to pray. Then the chiasm heads back to its beginning point with the arrest scene in verses 47–53. In this scene, one of the two swords revealed at the table comes into play and leads to Jesus's last healing before his death. Finally, in verses 54–62, Peter denies three times that he knows Jesus, and then the cock crows. Thus the arrangement of the scenes looks like this: Denial + Sword + Prayer + Sword + Denial.

This arrangement raises some interesting questions. One is whether the stories sandwiching the scene at Olivet yield any insight into the content of Jesus's prayer to the Father. Was the cup that Jesus dreaded (22:42) and his *agōnia* (struggle), 22:44, a natural revulsion at contemplating the ordeal to come, a fear of pain and death, as most commentators have concluded?[9] Or was it, in addition, a struggle to understand and accept the nonviolent and so much more costly means by which God willed the establishment of the kingdom? Without denying Jesus's natural foreboding about what is about to happen, is that explanation sufficient in light of the literary context in which the prayer is embedded in Luke's Gospel? As Luke portrays him, Jesus has had to make difficult hermeneutical decisions in the course of his teaching. He has dealt with issues of the law: What constitutes the heart of the law? How does it apply to real life? He has dealt with a variety of

8. Virtually no commentator divides the larger literary context in the manner I suggest here. Most use the geographic marker in v. 39, where the group moves from the table to the mountain, as the boundary of the unit. Luke's literary style is predominantly episodic, however, and one literary unit loops into another. This is analogous to *anastrophe,* a Greek rhetorical figure in which the last word of a clause becomes the first word of the next clause. These last two discussions at the table—the prediction of Peter's denial and the sword talk—have a dual narrative role. They function with respect both to the farewell dialog that precedes them and to the trials of Jesus in the passion narrative that follows them.

9. Fitzmyer suggests that "nowhere else in the gospel tradition is the humanity of Jesus so evident as here. His reaction refers not only to the physical suffering and psychic anguish that are coming, but probably includes as well inner distress and doubt about the meaning of it all" (*Gospel according to Luke,* 2:1442).

theological and ethical questions, including ones about resurrection and the payment of taxes. Does he here, in his last moments alone with God before the chaos of the passion, likewise struggle to sort through the biblical expressions of God's will as God's violence, in order to discern what is required of him in this moment?

Other interesting questions are raised by the relationship between the issues of denial, righteous violence, and the will of God, but this consideration will necessarily be limited to the conjunction of the sword passages—both the discussion at the table and the swordplay at the arrest—and the prayer passage. The two denial passages are included because they clarify the chiastic structure, which, incidentally, may extend beyond the denial scenes. If so, the next concentric circle surrounding denial would have to do with power.[10] But adequate exploration of those questions will need another effort.

Here I will first lay out the text in clauses, highlighting notable features of the text and making observations. Then I will look more closely at the two swords passage, with its well-known conundrums, as well as at the prayer passage, and then consider how the two may relate. Finally, I will make suggestions about the importance these questions may have for Luke's theology of the cross and its relationship to issues of nonviolence.

THE NARRATIVE STRUCTURE OF 22:31–62

Scene A: Jesus predicts a disciple's failure

v. 31		"*Simon, Simon,*
		Look, Satan has requisitioned you, to sift (you) like grain:
v. 32		But I have prayed about you,
		that your faithfulness not desert;
		that you, when you have come to yourself, settle down your brothers."
v. 33	Then he said to him:	"*Lord,* I am prepared to walk after you
		—even into prison,
		—even into death."
v. 34	But he said:	"I tell you, *Peter,*
		the cock will not crow today,
		before you deny you know me three times."

---

10. The dispute about greatness and service (vv. 24–30) and the interrogation of Jesus as prophet, anointed one, and Son of God (vv. 63–71).

Scene B: Jesus, the disciples and two swords

v. 35	He said to them:	"When I sent you out without a bag, or a wallet, or shoes,
		did you lack anything?"
	They said:	"Nothing."
v. 36	Then he said to them:	"But now, let the one who has a bag take it up, and likewise a wallet—
		and the one who does not have [——]
		let him sell his cloak
		and let him buy a sword.
v. 37		For I say to you:
		This Scripture must be fulfilled by me:[11]
		'He was counted among the lawless ones.'
		For all that concerns me has a fulfillment."
v. 38	They said:	"*Lord*, look, here are two swords."
	And he said to them:	"It is sufficient."

Scene C: Jesus, the disciples and a prayer

v. 39	And he went, as was his custom, to the mountain of olives.
	The disciples followed him.
v. 40	When he came to the place,
	He said to them:	"Pray that you do not enter into temptation."
v. 41	He went away from them about a stone's throw
	and falling to his knees he prayed:
v. 42		"*Father*, if you will,
		Take away this cup from me:
		Nevertheless, not my will but yours be done."
v. 43	Then there appeared before him an angel from heaven, who strengthened him.

11. *En*—the preposition in question here—is usually spatial. Use of it in an instrumental sense, including personal agency, became common in the LXX, influenced by Hebrew. See *EDNT*, 1:448. Here the instrumental and spatial meanings may overlap (whether Scripture is fulfilled in Jesus or by Jesus may be a moot point). Still, the instrumental sense may have more coherence with the moral and spiritual athleticism of the struggle in the prayer scene.

v. 44   And because he was praying in intense struggle,

his sweat was like drops of blood falling on the ground.

v. 45   When he rose from prayer,

he went to the disciples

and found them sleeping from grief.

v. 46   And he said to them: "Why are you lying down?

Get up and pray that you not enter into temptation."

Scene B´: Jesus, the disciples, a sword and a crowd

v. 47   While he was speaking,

Look, there was a crowd

and the one called Judas, one of the twelve, was leading them,

and he drew near Jesus to kiss him.

v. 48   And Jesus said to him: "*Judas*, are you betraying the Son of Man with a kiss?"

v. 49   And when the ones around him saw what was going to happen, they said:

"*Lord*, shall we strike with a sword?"

v. 50   And one of them struck the slave of the high priest

and severed his right ear.

v. 51   But Jesus said: "Enough of this."

and touching the bit of ear,

he healed him.

v. 52   And Jesus said to those who had come out against him,

the high priests and officers of the temple and elders,

"As for a thief you have come out with swords and clubs?

v. 53   Every day I was with you in the temple,

but you did not stretch out your hands against me.

However, this is your hour and the power of darkness."

v. 54   Arresting him, they led him away

and they brought him into the house of the high priest:

A´: The disciple fails

Peter was following from a distance.

v. 55   When they lit a fire in the middle of the courtyard,

and sat down around it, Peter was in the middle of them.

v. 56   A female servant saw him sitting by the fire,

and looking intently at him, she said:

"This one also was with him."

v. 57   But he denied, saying: "I do not know him, *woman*."

v. 58   After a short time, another, seeing him, said:

"You also are one of them."

But Peter said: "*Man*, I am not."

v. 59   An hour later, another person insisted, saying:

"Truly, this one was with him,

for he is also a Galilean."

v. 60   But Peter said: "*Man*, I do not know what you are saying."

Immediately, while he was still speaking, the cock crowed.

v. 61   Turning, the Lord looked intently at Peter

and Peter remembered the word of the Lord,

how he said to him that   "Before the cock crows today

you will deny me three times."

v. 62   He went out and wept bitterly.

COMMENTS

A number of features are striking about this group of texts. They are dia-logical. In all five scenes, the narrative moves forward through conversa-tion that, in every case except the last episode, is initiated and controlled by Jesus. These conversations are short and to the point, even if the point is hard to determine.

There is also frequent use of the vocative (shown in italics). Jesus ad-dresses Peter and Judas as well as the Father directly. Peter he names by his other name, Simon, which has not been used since 6:14, when the twelve were called out from among the disciples. The disciples also use direct ad-dress. Peter pledges his loyalty: "*Lord*, I am prepared to walk after you even into prison, even into death." A well-meant, but unfulfilled vow. The other two direct addresses of Jesus as Lord have to do with the sword—when the disciples produce the two swords in verse 38 and when they ask if they should use them in verse 49. Finally, there is a frequency of the vocative in the last story. When Peter denies that he knows Jesus, he peppers these denials with the vocative, addressing each of his questioners generically— *Woman! Man! Man!*

The movement of the five scenes has to do with the tensions and struggle of relationship. The entire passage begins and ends with the relationship between Jesus and Peter, and it climaxes in the center with the relationship between Jesus and the Father. Along the way, Judas is involved, as are the disciples as a group. At this narrative juncture, just before the trials of Jesus begin, the struggles are internal and intimate: the conflicts take place within the inner circle of disciples and between Jesus and his God.

Thus, as the chiastic structure reveals, the unit has its own coherence as a literary unit. Additionally, it loops into the units before and after: verses 31–34 and 35–38 end the table discussion as well as begin the Olivet unit, and the arrest scene and Peter's denial move into the trials passages and end the Olivet unit.

"Here are two swords"

Likely there are no completely satisfying answers to the puzzle of the so-called two swords passage.[12] The tensions within the text are such that any interpretive solution has its weak points. Nevertheless, interpretations of this passage may be categorized generally according to where the spotlight shines. Some interpreters emphasize the time and place: the changed circumstance of Jesus and the disciples is the issue. This time between the ministry and the passion calls for different preparations and different responses. Other interpreters in the recent trajectory of scholarship emphasize the disciples and their perfidy. The closer the crisis looms, the weaker and more obtuse the disciples become. The intent of Jesus's instruction is to test them, to expose their disloyalty. A few interpreters emphasize the character of Jesus himself. This transitional point between the ministry and the passion not only tests the mettle of the disciples but also proves to be Jesus's last temptation. Here he must decide once more the questions of power and the place of violence in holiness—and the stakes will never be higher.

---

12. Nolland takes issue with the traditional title for this pericope, saying that the central concern of the conversation is not swords at all but what the disciples need coping with the looming difficulties (Nolland, *Luke*, 1077).

Times and Circumstances Change

Although many of the major commentators take issue with Hans Conzel-mann's overemphasis on the clear division between the time of Jesus and the time of the church as a reason for the "but now" in 22:36,[13] some of them nevertheless offer a modified and more nuanced rendition of this basic con-cept. Of these, Joseph Fitzmyer is representative. He defines "but now" as a reference primarily in its immediate literary context to the crisis looming before Jesus and the disciples. Secondarily, however, it also refers to the time of the church, since the Lukan author also has his readers in mind at this point.[14] This crisis means several reassessments for the disciples and Jesus. The disciples must be newly "armed" in a certain way, and that Jesus must understand how alone he is in this hour.

With respect to the disciples, Fitzmyer writes, "Whoever sets out in Jesus' name must be fully equipped—not with material armor, but with armor in his sense." This metaphorical sense of gearing up for an ordeal is preferable to any literal interpretation of the swords, which he rejects along with any perception of a zealot tendency in the text. Furthermore, Fitzmyer sees no warrant in this text to support modern armament, since Jesus's re-action to the disciples' production of two swords in verse 38 is negative.[15] This symbolic sense of the armor the disciples are enjoined to put on has its counterpart in the mental readiness required of Jesus. Luke's use of the servant motif, the reference to LXX Isa 53:12 in the phrase "counted among the lawless" (22:37), is part of the evangelist's "humiliation-exaltation" theme. That servant mentality denotes the essential aloneness in which Je-sus faces the coming ordeal. It does not, however, designate the disciples as the lawless among whom Jesus is to be numbered. That interpretive move Fitzmyer finds "strange" and uncalled for—even taking the drawn sword in verses 49–52 into account.[16] For God's plan to find fulfillment calls for mental adjustments on the part of both the disciples and Jesus. The disciples disappoint Jesus with their lack of understanding about his metaphorical use of sword imagery, but that does not render them "lawless."

The strength of this interpretation is that those who express it tend to deal more straightforwardly with the stark, plain-sense meaning of Je-sus's command to buy swords. The command is what it is—a command that stands in contradiction to former commands in chapters 9 and 10.

---

13. Conzelmann, *Theology of St. Luke*, 81.

14. Fitzmyer, *Gospel according to Luke*, 2:1431.

15. Ibid., 2:1432.

16. Ibid., 2:1433.

The swords are what they are. They do not need to be explained as kitchen knives or some other less nocuous utensil.

Still, interpreters using this reasoning tend to read Luke's narrative of the Galilean ministry and the journey to Jerusalem as more idyllic than depicted. In so doing they do disservice to Luke's theology. It is true that Satan departs after the wilderness temptation in Luke 4:13 and does not reappear in the narrative until 22:3, when he enters Judas. But it is not true that Jesus and the disciples have found a welcome everywhere, and it is certainly not true that there have been no hints of approaching disaster and hardship. Mob violence threatens Jesus in 4:29, at the very inauguration of his ministry. The opposition of the religious rulers and the charges of blasphemy begin in 6:21 and continue periodically throughout the account. Herod emerges as a menace in chapter 9 and again in chapter 13. Just as there have been portents of hard times, so Jesus has attempted to teach of these realities. He warns his disciples about the coming passion on a number of occasions, starting right after the mountaintop experience in chapter 9. He weeps over the city of Jerusalem when he enters in chapter 19. Although the disciples may have been in denial about these dangers and potential dangers, perhaps especially in chapter 22, it is not that either the narrative itself or Jesus as the hero of the narrative has presented the so-called Satan-free era as all that wonderful. That Jesus would rescind earlier instructions—instructions that have been in character and in keeping with his overall ministry and teaching—because these new times are so radically different from the old days in Galilee and on the way to Jerusalem, seems doubtful. Furthermore, not only is the earlier time not depicted as all *that* rosy, it skews Jesus's (and Luke's) theology to imagine that trust in divine providence is only operative in the good, carefree, Satan-free times. To think that the Lord's Prayer, the Sermon on the Plain, the calming of the sea storm, the feeding of the crowds, and so much more, are not instructive for life after Jesus's departure, but only illustrative of the time when Jesus lived on earth, is incongruous with the general tenor and ethos of the Gospel.

The Disciples: Disobedient and Intending Violence

In 1964, Paul S. Minear wrote an article in which he suggested that the passage does not focus on the changed reality of Jesus and his disciples but on the treachery of the disciples.[17] He suggested that Jesus's command to buy a sword does not countermand his earlier commands. Rather, Jesus's point in the instruction is to expose the condition of the disciples' hearts at this point

17. Minear, "A Note on Luke xxii 36," 128–34.

in the narrative. That faithlessness, he claims, is in line with the other critical pieces of the farewell address—the vying for greatness, Judas's betrayal,
Peter's denial—and now this failure on the part of the entire group.[18]

Robert Tannehill is by no means the only exegete who has picked up
Minear's proposal, but he has done so most comprehensively and thus best
represents this second line of interpretation. Tannehill, like other interpreters who espouse this approach, uses a narrative analytical model—one of
the strengths of his work. He looks at verses 31–38 as a unit—the conversation in which Jesus first brings up Peter's weakness of loyalty and then raises
the issue of bag, wallet, shoes, and swords. Tannehill contends that Jesus's
intention in both conversations is to expose the apostles' faithlessness in
facing their own danger and death.[19]

Tannehill first rejects any literal, or straightforward, understanding of
the injunction to buy swords. He says that because of the outcome in the arrest scene, the command cannot have been intended to prepare the disciples
to fight against Jesus's enemies. Besides, he adds somewhat parenthetically,
two swords would obviously have been insufficient—rather than "sufficient," as pronounced in 22.38. Not only that, he adds, it also contradicts
earlier instructions, denies God's providence, puts the lie to all the rescue
stories in Acts, and counters Jesus's own attitude of trust in God when he
dies in 23:46.[20] For all these reasons, he understands the Isaiah quotation of
verse 37, "counted among the lawless," as a reference to the disciples themselves. The new instructions from Jesus are part of their faithlessness.

The strength of this interpretation is the tendency to take the literary
context more seriously. There is more effort to understand the command
to buy swords in light of Jesus's earlier teachings about nonviolence and
in his subsequent rebuke of the use of the sword in the arrest scene. But
there are also some problems. The most obvious is that Jesus becomes something of a trickster. Jesus has in this Gospel shown himself to be clever with
opponents. But he is more apt to be seeing his way through traps rather
than setting them; moreover, with his disciples he has been consistently
straightforward. In the immediate context, the last table fellowship and the
arrest scene, he verges on bluntness. He handles all the problems of the inner circle—Judas's betrayal, the competition for the places of honor, Peter's
disloyalty, the disciples' collective lack of discipline in prayer, and finally the
sword attack—with completely forthright confrontation. If the command to
buy swords is an elaborate ruse to tease out the disciples' disobedience, then

---

18. Ibid., 133.

19. Tannehill, *Narrative Unity of Luke-Acts*, 1:263.

20. Ibid., 1:266.

it is an anomaly not only here but also in the Gospel of Luke. Generally, as is illustrated so well in the two Peter stories that surround these texts, Jesus sees through his disciples' various pretensions and addresses the heart of the matter directly rather than setting traps to expose them.

A Succession of Day-to-Day Decisions

As noted above, Trocmé and Yoder both suggest that Jesus was struggling here at the end of his time with his disciples over the place holy violence might have in the project of God. Neither of them develops the idea in a comprehensive way, and neither tests it exegetically. Nevertheless, both are provocative in their suggestions. Trocmé suggests that Jesus's commitment to nonviolence was not a given but rather a hard-won determination accumulated from "a succession of day to day decisions."[21] Yoder sees the temptation to take hold of a Zealot-like kingship, first put forth by the tempter in the wilderness, returning in force for Jesus's consideration three discrete times: first in his opportunity to capitalize on his popularity after the feeding of the multitude; then as he came with triumph into Jerusalem and its temple; and here, just before the arrest.[22]

Kruger posits that the reference to the two swords in 22:35–38 is an evocation of the OT divine warrior imagery. He suggests, "Although Jesus adhered to a non-violent standpoint before and after the sword incident of Lk 22:35–38, at that particular point in time, he looked beyond the mundane, recognized God the Father in the image of the Divine Warrior, considered the sword, and thus extending the role of Yahweh the Divine Warrior, the God of Israel, to his own time and situation."[23]

The evocation of OT holy war tradition does not, however, stand alone in the text. Jesus's Bible is not univocal on the issue of divine violence; he also has the Suffering Servant motif with which to contend. This theme is present in the citation from the Servant Song of Isa 53, the notion of Jesus being counted among the lawless.[24]

Kruger, as Trocmé and Yoder before him, lodges the inherent and seemingly insoluble tension in the text not with changing times and circumstances or with the disciples' unfaithfulness in crisis but in the mind

---

21. Trocmé, *Jesus and the Nonviolent Revolution*, 132.

22. Yoder, *Politics of Jesus*, 47–48.

23. Kruger, "A Sword over His Head or in His Hand?," 602.

24. Ibid.

and heart of Jesus himself—or at least in the mind and heart of Jesus as Luke portrays him.[25]

"TAKE AWAY THIS CUP FROM ME"

Apart from Trocmé and Yoder, Kruger is virtually the only scholar surveyed here that interprets the two swords passage in light of the prayer passage. He says that the prayer at Olivet (vv. 39–46) "highlights the tension between the idea of the Warrior and the Servant, and provides a key to the understanding of the command to buy swords (vv. 35–38) and its outcome, namely Jesus's subsequent disapproval of such action (vv. 47–53)."[26] Citing such texts as Num 10:35, Jdg 5:12, and Zech 13:7, he finds resonance of holy war terminology in Jesus's admonition of the disciples to stay awake, rise, and pray.[27] Since those admonitions to the disciples come after the surrender of Jesus's will to the Father's will, Kruger surmises that "Jesus, even when he was moving to a final decision to resign himself to God's will, still considered the way of the Divine Warrior as a means to establish his Kingdom."[28]

The command to buy swords is an indication that Jesus was struggling to discern the Father's will regarding the means of establishing the kingdom of God. The notion that Jesus was genuinely ambivalent about holy war is at least as convincing as the notion either that Jesus was countermanding earlier teachings or that he was engaging in an elaborate ruse to manipulate the disciples into showing him their swords.

The commitment to nonviolent power as the foundation of the kingdom of God, a commitment that Jesus brought out of the wilderness in Luke 4—a commitment that he has been preaching, teaching and practicing ever since—wavers at the end of the farewell meal. When that happens, Jesus himself is in crisis. We must take the first part of his prayer seriously. When Jesus prays, "Take this cup away from me," he is asking for just that. It is no mere example; it is not *pro forma*. Kruger is correct in his assessment of the intensity and the content of that struggle: Jesus is trying to discern the will of the Father through the lens of the biblical strands of holy war and the Suffering Servant. Contrary to Kruger, however, what happened in that

---

25. Most scholars agree that this text is either a Lukan composition or has a pre-Lukan source, since none of the other Gospels has a parallel (see Fitzmyer, *Gospel according to Luke*, 2:1492). Yet it is so difficult to reconcile with the rest of Luke's Gospel that Lukan composition seems unlikely.

26. Kruger, "A Sword over His Head or in His Hand?" 603.

27. Ibid.

28. Ibid.

prayer was not the rejection of holy war in favor of the Suffering Servant but the integration of these two biblical strands into one. The struggle is not so much between the two approaches but for integration. It is not just Jesus who undergoes a radical change of convictions in the prayer;[29] it is the convictions themselves that undergo a radical change. From this point on, Jesus will suffer and die on the cross as God's holy warrior. He will be the ultimate divine warrior, but one who is paradoxically not violent.

29. Ibid.

18

Restoring the Concepts of Friendship and Reciprocity to Christian Discourse

Jo-Ann A. Brant

Scholarship on the theme of peace in the Bible has typically focused on the tradition of *shalom* in Hebrew Scriptures and treated the Greco-Roman notion of peace as a foil. Compared to the robust capacity of shalom, the concepts of *eirēnē* and *pax* have been seen as thin reeds to bear the weight of social justice and nonviolence.[1] In the last few decades, NT scholars have given increased attention to the discourse of Greek and Latin writers during the early Roman imperial era. Rather than seeing the writings of NT authors as homiletics based on Hebrew Scripture, they have increasingly seen early Christian literature as contributions to conversations and speeches that occurred in public settings throughout the Mediterranean world. This paper seeks to show how the early church drew from Greek and Roman discourse on the nature of true friendship to inform its understanding of salvation and reconciliation. True friendships stood at the heart of the Greco-Roman understanding of what it meant to have an abundant life. This paper will

---

1. Dinkler contends that when one sees the word *eirēnē* in the NT, one should make the mental translation to the Hebrew *shalom* and understand it as it is used in the OT ("Eirene," 176). Mauser writes, "Beyond those formal agreements [in usage], however, the New Testament employs *eirene* with a wideness of connotations that indicate the decisive influence of Old Testament statements about *shalom*," in *A Gospel of Peace*, 31. See also Swartley, *Covenant of Peace*, 35–40.

demonstrate that the concept of reciprocity motivated by friendship has a place within a discussion of how to work for shalom.[2]

Throughout much of the twentieth century, Protestant discussion of the understanding of love in the NT was influenced by Anders Nygren's *Den kristna karlekstanken genom tiderna: Eros och Agape* (1930, 1936).[3] Nygren gave minimal attention to *philia* (friendship) and devoted his attention to the difference between his construction of Greek love, *eros,* and Christian love, *agapē.* Nygren defined *agapē* as unconditional and without motive, self-sacrificial and expressed only by God. Christians participate in this love by being conduits channeling to others the love that they received. Nygren dismissed the possibility of friendship with God on two grounds: *philia* is an acquisitive love that treats God as the means by which human desires are satisfied and *philia* "presupposes an equality between Divine and human love that does not exist."[4] Nygren's conclusions became extremely influential in popular twentieth-century Christian thought and preaching, even though NT word studies have not been able to substantiate his definition of *agapē.*[5] Moreover, a reading of Greco-Roman literature on friendship cannot sustain a sharp dichotomy between Christian and Hellenistic thought.

Although the words *philos* and *philia* appear infrequently in the NT, scholars who have read the Greco-Roman literature on friendship have found that most, if not all, of the authors of the NT draw on the *topos* in significant ways. As John T. Fitzgerald points out, the language of *philos* and *philia* is absent from the Septuagint's description of David and Jonathan's relationship, but nevertheless we treat it as a friendship.[6] The words used to describe friendship in Greco-Roman literature—hospitality (*xenia*), equality (*isotēs*), frankness (*parrhēsia*), unity (*henotēs*), like-mindedness or harmony (*homonoia*), faithfulness or trust (*pistis*), constancy (*hypomonē*), goodwill or kindness (*eunoia*), and fellowship (*koinōnia*)—appear with frequency in NT writings. Such observations have led to a rich discussion of the significance of the concept of friendship to NT thought.

The *topos* of friendship comprehends such things as equality, reciprocity, trust, help in time of need, self-sacrifice, fidelity, worthiness, and frank

---

2. I am indebted to my colleagues Joe C. Liechty and Paul Keim for allowing me to join in their discussion of the concept of *lex talionis* and the importance of restoring its place in the discussion of forgiveness and justice. Their work in this area led to any insights to which I have come.

3. Nygren, *Agape and Eros* [ET].

4. Ibid., 92.

5. Barr, "Words for Love," 3–18; Joly, *Le vocabulaire chrétien de l'amour.*

6. Fitzgerald, "Christian Friendship," 286.

or truthful speech.[7] Aristotle sees friendship as both good and necessary: "Without friends no one would choose to live, though he had all other goods" (trans. W. D. Ross, *Eth. nic.* 1155a5–6; see also 1155a6–16, 26–27). While the language of friendship could be used to describe the utilitarian relationship of a patron to a client, discussions about friendship reveal a concept bound by mutual affection and commitment rather than obligatory reciprocity.[8] Abraham J. Malherbe provides a selection of frequently cited norms that illustrate the intimacy and solidarity sought in friendship:

1. Friendship obtains when souls are drawn together by identical inclinations into an alliance of honorable desires.

2. Equality knits friends together.

3. Friends share one soul.

4. Friends have all things in common.[9]

The last of these maxims appears with frequency in Plato's and Aristotle's works (Plato, *Lysis* 207c; *Leg.* 739c; Aristotle, *Eth. eud.* 1137b, 1240b; *Eth. nic.* 1159b31–32, 1168b8; *Pol.* 2.1263a). That friends share all things in common seems to be echoed in Acts 4:32.

The following discussion will examine two concerns in the Greco-Roman discussion related directly to the theme of reciprocity: how does friendship transcend the utility of other reciprocal relationships, and how is friendship between people of unequal social standing possible? The discussion will then move to issues at the center of Christian theology and the concept of peace: forgiveness, atonement, and reconciliation. I will demonstrate how these actions, informed by an understanding of friendship, can challenge the notion that they must be altruistic and disinterested in order to be effective or genuine.

THE TOPOS OF FRIENDSHIP AND RECIPROCITY

One of the prevailing concerns in Greco-Roman discourse on friendship is how to distinguish friendship from utilitarian reciprocal relationships (see Cicero, *Amic.* 6.20; Aristotle, *Eth. nic.* 1157b29–38). Aristotle characterizes relationships of utility as the friendship of the "commercially minded" and distinguishes them from "perfect friendship" (*Eth. nic.* 1158a), the friendship of those who are good. Cicero presents reciprocity as a property of

---

7. See Aune, *New Testament*, 173.

8. For a thorough argument supporting this assertion, see Konstan, *Friendship*.

9. Malherbe, *Moral Exhortation*, 144.

friendship and not its cause: one reciprocates the benefits of friendship out of love (*Amic.* 8). He explains that beneficence and generosity arise from love inspired by a friend's good qualities rather than from a desire to exact kindness in return (*Amic.* 9). Seneca follows a similar line of reasoning when contending with Epicurus's notion that a wise man is self-sufficient and needs no friends. Seneca points out that a wise man wants to make use of his noble qualities by sitting by someone's sick-bed or setting someone free who is in hostile hands (*Ep.* 9; see also *Ben.* 2.17).

The understanding that friends confer benefits on each other seems to be an implicit assumption at the heart of Paul's writing in several contexts. Peter Marshall makes sense of the Corinthian correspondence by revealing how Paul's refusal to accept financial assistance from the Corinthians while accepting aid from the Philippians was taken by the Corinthians as a rejection of their former friendship.[10] Paul's language of reciprocal boasting (2 Cor 1:14); his claim that he needs no letter of recommendation from the Corinthians because they are his letter written on the heart (2 Cor 3:1–2); his assertion that his frank speech is a sign of his open heart and unbridled affection (2 Cor 6:11–12); the emphasis on a ministry of reconciliation (2 Cor 5:11–21); and his apology, in which he concedes nothing but affirms that friends share of themselves by stating that he does not want their possessions but their very selves (2 Cor 12:13–14)—all these elements point to Paul's attempts to undo the damage he has done and to reconcile himself to the Corinthians. Stephen Fowl makes sense of Paul's awkward acknowledgment of the Philippians' gift toward the end of his letter (Phil 4:10–13) in terms of the norms of friendship.[11] While the purpose of the letter is to acknowledge the gift, he waits until the end to address the topic and then never explicitly offers thanks. Instead he expresses his gratitude by describing his affection and concern for them (1:3–11), thanking God for their partnership (1:4–5) and expressing his joy in their relationship (2:16–18). Paul's insistence that he has no needs and that he is content avoids placing the Philippians, as friends, under the obligation to seek to alter his circumstances.[12]

Greco-Roman discussions also deal with the possible tension between equality inherent within friendship and inequality of social rank. For Cicero, what is most remarkable in friendship is that superior and inferior can stand on an equal footing (*Amic.* 19.69). For Aristotle, friendship of utility tends to demand similar social station, whereas the friendship of those

10. Marshall, *Enmity in Corinth*, 132–33.

11. Fowl, *Philippians*, 189–203.

12. Ibid., 194.

who are virtuous allows inequality of means but demands equality of virtue (*Eth. nic.* 1158b). The Greco-Roman conversation seems to return again and again to the question of whether it is possible for slave and master to be friends. Seneca argues that such friendship is not only possible but desirable: a master should seek friendship with his slaves so that his household is like a commonwealth (*Ep.* 47). According to Seneca, when a slave serves his master out of affection, that service becomes a benefit and the slave becomes a friend (*Ben.* 3.12). As a result, the master ought to feel gratitude toward his slave and discharge the debt of goodwill by a return of goodwill (*Ben.* 2.35). Such friendships may be rare or restricted in their expressions, but within the realm of discourse the possibility exists that friendship would allow individuals to transcend the social restrictions of their culture.

At the heart of the early Christian community stood the understanding that baptism erases former social distinctions that prevent participation in the life and rituals of the community (cf. Rom 12:16; 1:7; Gal 3:28). Alan C. Mitchell concludes from an examination of the use of the friendship *topos* in Luke-Acts that Luke intended "to challenge his community to extend friendship to one another across status divisions."[13] Luke uses two friendship maxims—*hapanta koina* (Acts 2:44, 4:32) and *psychē mia* (Acts 4:32)—in his appeal to "encourage upper status people in the community to benefit those beneath them."[14] Mitchell argues that Luke describes not an early Christian utopian society but rather something more conventional in which individuals hold private property according to the laws of the state and practice a friendship ethic of "all things in common" within some reasonable limits.

Paul in his letter to Philemon relies on both fictive familial ties (Phlm 1, 7, 10, 16) and the bonds of friendship (Phlm 1) and *agapē* (Phlm 7, 9) to make his point that Philemon should welcome Onesimus as Philemon would welcome Paul (Phlm 17; see also Phil 4:1; 1 John 3:2). Exchanging the language of brother for that of friend is typical to Greco-Roman discourse. Friends enjoy the freedom to enter into the private realm of the household, into a degree of intimacy with the expectation of solidarity shared among family members. In return, friendship demands loyalty (*pistis* or *fides*) and constancy (*asphaleia* or *constantia*) (see for example, Epictetus, *Diatr.* 2.22.29–30; Cicero, *Amic.* 19.65; Plutarch, *Frat. amor.* 479–84.) Friendship is, perhaps, an essential piece of the conceptual framework within which the early church was able to help converts from the Greco-Roman world make the transition from the old economy based largely on the family to the

13. Mitchell, "Greet the Friends," 237.
14. Ibid., 237–39.

Christian economy that ignored ancestry and familial loyalty. Equity within the early Christian community is based not on social position but on divine gift giving, shared virtues, partnership, joy and sorrow: themes germane to the friendship *topos* (see Acts 11:17; Rom 12:3; 1 Cor 12; 2 Pet 1:1; Jude 3; 1 John 3:2–3, 21–24).

FRIENDSHIP, FORGIVENESS, AND ATONEMENT

Christian discussions of friendship frequently get entangled in the knot of whether grace can be a free gift and at the same time engender an obligation of gratitude and obedience to God's will. Christian notions of forgiveness also come under challenge for setting aside the demand of justice that includes penance on the part of the offender and restitution on the part of the offended. I propose looking at divine grace within the economy of friendship in order to make sense of how reciprocity or obligation can become part of the equation of grace without reestablishing a debt economy.

When one party does harm to or offends another party, the latter loses honor, property, and livelihood or life itself, and a debt is created. Justice calls for the restoration of order. First, the offender must suffer punishment or retribution in order to feel the gravity of the offense. Second, the debt needs to be repaid. The covenantal law seeks to make both punishment and recompense equitable through the use of the scales of talionic justice (Exod 21:22–25; Lev 24:19–21; Deut 19:16–21) and to prevent unbridled vengeance (Deut 25:1–3). Biblical teachings add two elements to the equation. The first is nonretaliation. Suspension of retribution leaves justice to God and allows the offender time to acknowledge the harm done. In the language of the HB, the offender returns to God (*šwb*) and, in the language of the NT, experiences a reversal (*metanoia*), voluntarily offering recompense (e.g., the story of Zacchaeus in Luke 19:1–10). The second addition is forgiveness, whereby the debt is converted into a gift. This gift can be placed within two frameworks in the ancient world. In a client-patron relationship, the offender incurs a new sort of debt, that of gratitude, and reciprocates in ways that signify a hierarchical relationship. The obligation of the gift of benefaction persists until the gift is repaid (e.g., Horace, *Ep.* 1.13). In a friendship, the gift is made as an act of goodwill that establishes equality between the two parties. The need for reciprocity arises not out of obligation but out of a sense of virtue or mutual goodwill. Feelings of gratitude are characterized by joy in having such a friend rather than by feelings of obligation. As part of the shared property of friendship, the gift itself should be honored because of the value instilled in it by friendship. The client-patron relationship is dissolved when the client performs an act of reciprocation, whereas reciprocation within friendship serves only to strengthen its bonds.

Throughout the NT, the motivation for God's forgiveness is grounded in divine love or goodwill for humanity (e.g., John 3:16; Rom 5:8). This presupposition is especially evident in the Gospel of Luke. Zechariah sings in celebration of his son's birth that the Baptist will "give knowledge of salvation to his people by the forgiveness of their sins. By the tender mercy of our God, the dawn from on high will break upon us" (Luke 1:76–79).[15] The story of the woman anointing Jesus's feet (Luke 7:41–43; John 12:1–3) illustrates that the appropriate response to forgiveness or divine gift is the outpouring of affection through an act of friendship. Paul refers to his vision of Christ as a gift (*charis*; Gal 1:15; 1 Cor 3:10) that obligates him to proclaim the gospel (1 Cor 3:11; 9:16). Zeba A. Crook describes this obligation as a debt of gratitude and reciprocity owed to a patron, but toward the end of 1 Corinthians, Paul sets his gift within the context of other divine benefactions that make possible membership in one body (1 Cor 12:1–31), and he grounds the actions of reciprocation within love (1 Cor 13:1–13).[16]

Rather than teaching that a debt does not need to be repaid, various NT authors suggest that the nature of that debt is transformed by the love of the community. Paul captures the concept that reciprocity perpetuates rather than terminates a relationship when he writes, "Owe no one anything, except to love one another; for the one who loves another has fulfilled the law" (Rom 13:8). In 2 Cor 2:5–10, Paul describes the aftermath of forgiveness as acts of friendship. The community is called to comfort the offender and to reaffirm its love for him. In Jesus's teaching about forgiveness, that the offender will fail to acknowledge the gift and repeat the offense remains a possibility (Matt 18:21–23). Matthew follows the command to be generous in one's forgiveness with a story that illustrates the need to reciprocate the forgiveness of a debt by imitating the goodness of the one who has forgiven (Matt 18:23–34). The notion that divine forgiveness of debts requires an act of reciprocal imitation stands at the center of the Lord's Prayer (Matt 6:12; Luke 11:4; see also Eph 4:32; Col 3:13).

To say that God's forgiveness is unconditional ignores the reality that God's forgiveness aims at *metanoia*, a change of heart.[17] Unlike the act of admission of guilt within the judicial model that leads to payment of a debt, the act of repentance is an expression of remorse that leads to the

15. All biblical quotations are taken from the NRSV unless otherwise indicated.

16. Crook, "Grace as Benefaction," 37.

17. Jones calls God's gift of forgiveness unconditional but states that we must engage in practices of repentance in order to appropriate that forgiveness; *Embodying Forgiveness*, 146.

reestablishment of the relationship. The description of how one goes about drawing attention to an offense in Matt 18:15–17 is similar to the advice that Plutarch gives on how to rebuke a friend. He contends that a friend alerts a friend to failures or vices in private, and he warns that a public reproof leads to recalcitrance rather than reform (*Adul. amic.* 32). Using language characteristic of the description of friendship, Paul describes his rebuke of the Corinthian community as an act motivated by his affection for them: "You are in our hearts, to die together and to live together" (2 Cor 7:2–4).[18]

The act of forgiveness is central to the broader action of reconciliation. The principal meaning of reconciliation (*katallassein* and *diallassen*) is to change from enmity to friendship. Fitzgerald demonstrates that reconciliation and friendship are used synonymously in Jewish Greek literature (e.g., Sir 22:20; 22; Philo, *Somn.* 2.108).[19] The relationship between friendship and reconciliation invites a reexamination of much of the language of salvation in the NT, revealing that the concept of friendship should temper our understanding of how Jesus's death brings reconciliation.

In recent years an accusation has been made against the language of sacrifice used to describe the significance of Jesus's death. The allegation runs along the following lines: if God demands that a life be given to satisfy a debt or to demonstrate repentance, then at the heart of the Christian doctrine of salvation lies a theology in which God demands violence.[20] Contemporary concerns about the violence at the heart of a sacrificial Christology might be turned in the direction of affirmation of self-sacrifice if we recognize that NT writers contextualize that sacrifice within friendship. Within the *topos* of friendship, offering one's life or dying for a friend is held up as the ultimate gift of friendship (Aristotle, *Eth. nic.* 1169a; Plato, *Symp.* 179b; Diodorus Siculus, *Bibl. hist.* 10.4.4–6; Epictetus, *Ench.* 31.1). Seneca makes self-sacrifice the *telos* of friendship: "For what purpose, then, do I make a man my friend? In order to have someone for whom I may die, whom I may follow into exile, against whose death I may stake my own life, and pay the pledge, too" (trans. Richard M. Gummere, *Ep.* 9.10). The Gospel of John characterizes Jesus's death as such an act of friendship and encourages Jesus's followers to be willing to demonstrate their love for each other through a comparable willingness to die (John 15:9–17). Suffering in itself is not redemptive.[21]

18. Fredrickson, "Paul, Hardships, and Suffering," 182. See also Fiore, "Friendship," 96–97.

19. Fitzgerald, "Christian Friendship," 289; "Paul and Friendship," 334–36.

20. E.g., Weaver, "Violence in Christian Theology," 150–76.

21. Paul characterizes Jesus's death as an act of service to others and the actions of Jesus's followers that lead to suffering as acts of imitation of Christ (Phil 2:6–11; Eph

John's pointed claim that Jesus's death demonstrates the love that he shares with his father, for his followers in particular (15:9–17) and with the world in general (3:16), gains significance when one recognizes that these verses are a summary of the story that John tells of Jesus's death. John makes clear that Jesus dies as a result of giving life to a specific friend, Lazarus, and that he hands himself over to prevent the death of his followers, whom he raises to the status of friends by disclosing his identity and intentions. His death is then linked inextricably with the divine gift of abundant life (10:10) and is extricated from the necessity of saving the lives of friends through the sorts of violence that fill the heroic narratives of antiquity and our own contemporary culture.

In many ways, the Johannine story of Jesus seems to explore one of the classical questions about of friendship in that it shows how Jesus navigates the competing demands of his status as Son of God and his love for his friends. When Jesus receives word that Lazarus is dying, the message comes to him in the form of an implicit appeal to friendship, "Lord, he whom you love (*phileis*) is ill" (John 11:3). Jesus responds to the news from the vantage point of his relationship to God. Lazarus's illness will serve the purpose of divine glory (11:4). The narrator, however, underscores that Jesus's delay in responding to the news is a violation of the demands of friendship: "Jesus loved (*ēgapa*) Martha and her sister and Lazarus. Nevertheless, when he heard that Lazarus was ill, he remained where he was two days" (11:5–6).[22] When Jesus finally states his intention to go to Bethany, his disciples warn him that his life will be in danger (11:8), and Thomas states that following Jesus to Judea will mean that all of them will die (11:16). The disciples are correct. When Jesus is moved to resurrect Lazarus, after witnessing the grief of his sisters and hearing them lament that Lazarus would not have died if Jesus had been there, his fate is sealed. He in fact dies so that Lazarus may live. But Thomas is wrong. Jesus protects his disciples from dying with him by making his identity known to the arrest party and saying, "If you seek me, let these retreat" (18:8).[23] If Jesus were to resist the authorities as Peter seeks to do, the outcome would be the violent death of all the disciples. The claim that Jesus dies as a friend ought to be treated within the larger framework of the story of reconciliation, in which God creates humanity with the intent of fellowship, humanity abandons that friendship, and God gives the Son to restore the friendship. The concept of friendship with God

5:1) or of Paul as a model of Christ (Phil 2:17; 3:17).

22. My translation.

23. My translation.

is therefore at the heart of the concept of salvation and also central to the notion of shalom or the peace of Christ.[24]

In a two part article entitled "The Soul of Reciprocity"—"Part One: Reciprocity Refused" and "Part Two: Reciprocity Granted"—John Milbank challenges the idea of pure gift as a "one-way gift utterly indifferent to return" and points out the misstep of constructing a theology predicated on communion with God limited to revelation.[25] As a result of this misstep, we have come to conceive of divine gift as a unilateral action, "a one-way self sacrificial charity construed as the ultimate gesture."[26] We have come to see true Christian charity and forgiveness as selfless acts in which we are called to deny the being of the giver, to act as though we are not only anonymous but even irrelevant to the act. Moreover, the giver must in a sense treat the recipient as anonymous. Milbank constructs a phenomenology of giving that respects the recipient's gesture of constructing or speculating on the subjectivity of the donor and the recognition of the alterity of the other, that the other is more than the identity that we construct for him or her.[27] Admitting friendship into the goal of forgiveness and reconciliation restores to the one who forgives the expectation or hope of gratitude and reciprocation and compensates the giver for what was lost. Forgiveness admits justice. We need no longer demand of ourselves indifferent acts of love; we can satisfy our desires insofar as we desire what is good and seek to form friendships based on mutual affection and commitment.

CONCLUSION

Readers who resist reconsidering the centrality of friendship and reciprocity to NT thought will no doubt turn to the command to love one's enemies (Matt 5:43–48). The point of this passage is not to dismiss the goodness of friendship with its reciprocal goodwill but rather to generate that sort of goodwill toward one's enemies. Those who resist my conclusions might also point to the admonition to change the guest list for a luncheon from friends and relatives or rich patrons, those from whom one expects reciprocity, to

24. The concept of a friendship with God informed Second Temple Jewish discourse and found a place in early Christian discourse (see 2 Chr 20:7; Isa 41:8; Exod 33:11; Job 29:4; Wis 7:7–14; *Jub.* 30:20–22; Philo, *Contempl.* 90; *Virt.* 179). Paul's descriptions of God's love also point to a concept of friendship with God (see Rom 5:5–11, 15–17; 8:37–39; 1 Cor 13).

25. Milbank, "Soul of Reciprocity Part One," 335–39, see in particular 344; "The Soul of Reciprocity Part Two," 485–507.

26. Milbank, "Soul of Reciprocity Part One," 350.

27. Ibid., 349.

"the poor, the crippled, the lame, and the blind," who cannot repay the hospitality (Luke 14:12–14a). This passage does not deny friendship but rather extends it beyond the confines of a lifetime into the eschatological age. Jesus ends his admonition with the assurance that those who are generous to the destitute "will be repaid at the resurrection of the righteous" (Luke 14:14b). NT authors envision the possibility of ever-expanding circles of friendship made possible by a shared communion with God mediated through Jesus and a shared sense of purpose or common commitments.

When one looks at the biblical material at the center of classical articulations of salvation through the lens of the friendship, the importance of relational language becomes much clearer. Gestures of generosity and compassion for those whose lives lie beyond our normal social obligations become expressions of our interest in the lives of others as participants within a larger reality described by Jesus as the reign of God. Reciprocity—indebtedness to those who love us and obligation to honor gifts—should be a vital part of discourse about what it means to be redeemed. God is not simply our benefactor to whom we owe gratitude. While NT authors recognize that the gifts that God bestows on us are beyond the capacity of human beings to confer and thus to return in kind, the gifts do not submit us to the state of indebtedness beyond our capacity to repay. Instead they call for a disposition, the reciprocation of relationship, the constancy and reliability of friendship. The rewards of the activities of friendship lie not in the benefits we receive in kind but in the satisfaction that we gain, the joy that we feel through being part of the lives of others. That joy is made complete when it is reciprocated by others who return the friendship and, as Paul puts it, are "like-minded, having the same love, being one in spirit and purpose" (Phil 2:2).

19

The Political Is Personal

Anabaptist-Mennonite Appropriation of the Book of Acts in the Sixteenth and Twentieth Centuries

Joshua Yoder

The book of Acts is a treasure trove for the politically minded NT scholar. The relationship between Christians and political authorities frequently becomes an issue in the narrative, whether those authorities are Judean political leaders (4:1–22; 5:17–22; 6:8–15; 12:1–19), municipal officers of the Roman colony of Philippi (16:19–40), Roman provincial governors (13:4–12; 18:12–17; 23:31—26:32), or the Roman emperor himself (25:10–12; 27:24; 28:30–31). Thus Acts has proved fruitful ground for Mennonites and their Anabaptist forebears, for whom the relationship between the church and the state has been of vital concern. This essay examines how sixteenth-century Anabaptists and some influential contributors to twentieth-century Mennonite peace theology—Guy F. Hershberger, John Howard Yoder, and finally the dedicatees of this volume, Perry Yoder and Willard Swartley—have used Acts to support their positions on the relation of church, state, and society.

EARLY ANABAPTISTS

The sixteenth-century Anabaptists frequently turned to Acts to justify their conflictive relationship with political authorities. Acts 5:29—in which the

216

disciples tell the Judean council, "We must obey God rather than people"[1]—was a favorite text.[2] Anabaptists also employed the similar expression in Acts 4:19.[3] In "The Cross of the Saints," Menno Simons argues that this principle justifies disobeying political authorities if they seek to extend their authority beyond the matters ordained to them and to "rule and lord it above Christ Jesus."[4] It is the Anabaptists' willingness to "regard and honor God more than man," he claims, that earns them the hatred of their neighbors.[5]

The Anabaptists appealed to Acts for evidence that political opposition and accusations of subversion are normal and even inevitable for Christians. Hans Schlaffer writes, "It is no wonder or odd, nor is it new that they call us a heretical insurrectionist sect. For God's sake, look only at the accusation against Christ before Pilate and of Paul before Felix."[6] His inclusion of the accusation "insurrectionist" alludes to the political overtones that accusers of Jesus and Paul opportunistically give their charges in both Luke (23:1–5) and Acts (24:5–6).[7] Dirk Philips concurs: "The apostle Paul had to be regarded by the Jews as an agitator and by Festus as mad, Acts 21:38; 26:24. Thus the world has always been perverted like it still is and deals in a perverted manner with the Christians."[8]

Given such political opposition, suffering was to be expected. Paul's words to new churches, "It is through many persecutions that we must enter

---

1. This rendering of the Greek, while lacking the euphony of the NRSV "rather than any human authority," is closer to the German version that many Anabaptists would have read (e.g., Luther's translation, "*Man muss Gott mehr gehorchen denn den Menschen*" [1545]). Other NT quotations in this essay follow the NRSV.

2. In a letter to a colleague, Zwingli refers to the verse as a characteristic saying of the Anabaptists (*Sources of Swiss Anabaptism*, ed. Harder, 375).

3. E.g., Dirk Philips, "Apology," in *Writings of Dirk Philips*, 195. All other quotations of Philips are from this volume. Cf. Hans Umlauft, "Letter to Stephan Rauchenecker," in *Sources of South German/Austrian Anabaptism*, ed. Snyder, 285; and the account of the martyrdom of Hans Krüsi and the "Appeal of the Prisoners," in *Sources of Swiss Anabaptism*, ed. Harder, 424, 514.

4. *Complete Writings of Menno Simons*, 604. All other quotations of Simons are from this volume. Cf. "Foundation of Christian Doctrine," 177; "Brief Defense to All Theologians," 536; "Epistle to Martin Micron," 923.

5. Simons, "Cross," 586. Cf. "Reply to False Accusations," 574.

6. "A Brief Instruction for the Beginning of a Truly Christian Life and Confession and Defense," in *Sources of South German/Austrian Anabaptism*, ed. Snyder, 102.

7. Jesus's opponents accuse him of forbidding the payment of taxes, though he has studiously avoided taking a clear stance on the issue in public (see Luke 20:26). They specify for Pilate's benefit that "Messiah" means "king" (Luke 23:2). Paul is called a "plague" (*loimos*), a term long used of one who represents a threat to public peace and welfare (see, e.g., Demosthenes, *Or.* 25.80), and an "agitator" (Acts 24:5).

8. "The Sending of Preachers," from the *Enchiridion*, 227.

the kingdom of God" (Acts 14:22), reassured persecuted Anabaptists that their suffering was normal and necessary.[9] Anabaptists found a model in Stephen, whose martyrdom is described in Acts 7:54–60. Simons writes, "All those who believe the Word of the Lord with true hearts . . . must with Stephen be cast out of the city and get a taste of flying stones."[10] Paul's tribulations likewise testified to the necessity of suffering.[11]

Acts served not only to legitimate resistance, opposition, and suffering, but also to legitimate particular Anabaptist missionary tactics, especially covert preaching and evasion of the authorities. Philips argues that reluctance to preach in public when arrest and imprisonment were certain does not entail lack of faith in God's power; Christians should not presume on miraculous rescues of the sort described in Acts 5:18; 12:7; and 16:25: "The disciples at Damascus also knew and believed that God is almighty, but nevertheless they helped Paul over the wall at night. . . . The Christians at Ephesus also knew and indeed believed that God is almighty. . . . Nevertheless they would not permit Paul to go among the people and give them a reply."[12]

Simons likewise cited Paul's escape from Damascus (Acts 9:25) to justify strategic flexibility, concluding, "Thus great men of God have feared death, and did not usually go where they feared violence until they were admonished to do so by an oracle or by a revelation from angels," as in Acts 5:20–21 or Acts 18:9.[13] Simons and Philips also found justification for meeting under cover of darkness in examples from Acts (12:7; 20:7).[14]

9. See, e.g., Simons, "Cross," 583 (without indicating his source); Philips, "Three Admonitions," *Enchiridion*, 423. In a letter to an imprisoned Anabaptist, Philips reprises Paul's role as comforter by repeating Paul's words (620–21). Schlaffer cites the text among scriptural testimonies that Christians must suffer ("Brief Instruction," in *Sources of South German/Austrian Anabaptism*, ed. Snyder, 88–89; cf. Umlauft, "Letter to Rauchenecker," in *Sources of South German/Austrian Anabaptism*, ed. Snyder, 280; Paul Glock, "Letter to Leonhard Lanzenstiel," in *Sources of South German/Austrian Anabaptism*, ed. Snyder, 328).

10. "Cross," 593–94.

11. See "Reply," 741, on the stoning of Paul in Lystra (Acts 14:19). In "Cross," Simons adduces Paul's tribulations described in Acts 21–28 (595). Simons's summary goes beyond (and against) the evidence of Acts: he reports that Paul was scourged in Jerusalem (according to Acts 22:24–29, he narrowly avoided it), was captured in Caesarea (according to Acts 23:31–33, he was brought there under guard), and was executed by Nero, "the most bloodthirsty of tyrants." Acts ends with Paul's arrival at Rome.

12. "Sending," *Enchiridion*, 228–29, citing Acts 9:25, 19:30; cf. ibid., 232–33. Indeed, Philips cites Acts 16:6 as evidence that in some times and places God commands disciples *not* to preach.

13. "Reply," 573.

14. Ibid., 635; cf. "Accusations," 567; Philips, "Sending," *Enchiridion*, 230.

To Philips, it was the circumstances of the time that necessitated a strategy of evasion: "We also see . . . how perilous the times now are, much more than at the time of the apostles. . . . Then the heathen government was so reasonable and proper that they did not wish to oppose strongly the faith and affairs of the Christian religion, Acts 17:9; 18:14[−15]; 23:22. But now almost everyone wants to be a lord over the conscience [of others] and a judge of faith."[15]

Not all agreed with Philips in seeing the Roman government portrayed in Acts as "reasonable and proper." Hans Umlauft speaks of "grim force and tyranny": "With Paul, I ask nothing except examination, judgment, and justice, and by it I will let myself be treated well or ill. But where there is nothing but grim force and tyranny through the instigation of some individuals, there I shall make use of the example of Paul at Damascus and not await the conspiracy of the forty (Acts 9:23ff, 23:13)."[16] Though Umlauft does not cite the text, he clearly alludes to Paul's appeal to the emperor (Acts 25:10−11), in which Paul declares himself willing to be subject to true justice but strongly implies that because of the undue influence of his opponents he is not getting a fair trial from the Roman governor of Judea.

As the preceding excerpt suggests, the Anabaptists frequently likened their own political situation to that of the early church: a Christian minority in the midst of an un-Christian society. The rulers of sixteenth-century Europe may have viewed themselves as Christian leaders of Christian nations, but the Anabaptists saw them reprising the role of those authorities who cooperated in the persecution of the early Christians at the instigation of rival religious leaders.[17] Because their struggles were analogous to those of the early church, the Anabaptists could expect the experiences and example of the Christians in Acts to be directly relevant to themselves.[18]

15. "Sending," 234.

16. "Letter to Rauchenecker," in *Sources of South German/Austrian Anabaptism*, ed. Snyder, 284. Umlauft combines a reference to Paul's escape from Damascus with an allusion to the conspiracy against Paul following his arrest in Jerusalem.

17. Simons, "Cross," 582; Umlauft, "Letter to Rauchenecker," in *Sources of South German/Austrian Anabaptism*, ed. Snyder, 285.

18. On the Anabaptists' sense of continuity between their congregations' "life situation and perspectives" and those of the first-century church, see further Murray, *Biblical Interpretation*, 176.

GUY F. HERSHBERGER

Guy F. Hershberger's *War, Peace, and Nonresistance*, first published in 1944, followed the example of Harold Bender[19] in attempting to recapture the sixteenth-century Anabaptist vision for modern Mennonites.[20] Hershberger examined some of the contemporary implications of this theology in *The Way of the Cross in Human Relations.*

Though Hershberger's appropriation of Acts reflects some new issues in twentieth-century Anabaptist discourse (he cites Acts in discussions of race relations and women's roles),[21] many of the earlier themes continue: the sovereignty of God over secular authority, acceptance of confrontation and persecution, and a clear distinction between the Christian church and the surrounding society. Like the early Anabaptists, Hershberger turns to Acts 5:29, "We must obey God rather than people," as a guiding principle: "This must certainly be the Christian's answer when the state requests him to violate God's moral law and the principle of nonviolence."[22] Like the Anabaptists, Hershberger points to Stephen and Paul as examples of suffering for Christ.[23] Acts' depiction of Paul also serves Hershberger as a model of "prophetic" Christian witness before government officials.[24] Nor does Hershberger's view of Western society differ fundamentally from the Anabaptists' view of European Christendom: he refers to "the transparent veneer of Christianity with which the nominal Christian world so often attempts to cover its deeds which are anything but Christian."[25]

However, Hershberger's writing introduces a new note: a critique of his own people. Instead of acting as a "colony of heaven" serving as the conscience of a "sub-Christian society," Mennonites had all too often uncritically accepted the prevailing culture and "fallen under spell of materialism."[26] However laudable their continuing allegiance to pacifism, in contexts where

19. See Bender, *The Anabaptist Vision*, 3–24.

20. Citations are from the 5th ed. (2009). For an assessment of the book's contribution and subsequent developments in Mennonite peace theology, see Ervin Stutzman, introduction to the 5th ed., and J. R. Burkholder, introduction to the 4th ed. (1991).

21. God has made "no distinction between us" is applied to modern race-based divides: see Acts 10:34, 35; 15:8, 9 (*Way of the Cross*, 338); on the prominence of women in the early church, see Acts 1:12; 5:14; 8:3, 12; 9:2, 36; 16:13–15; 17:4, 34 (ibid., 351).

22. *War, Peace, and Nonresistance*, 55. Hershberger cites Acts 4:19–20 (ibid., 295). Cf. Hershberger, *Way of the Cross*, 11; Hershberger, *Christian Relationships to the State and Community*, 56.

23. *War, Peace, and Nonresistance*, 52.

24. See his use of Acts 24:25 in "Our Citizenship is in Heaven," 277.

25. *Way of the Cross*, 2.

26. Ibid., 283–85.

nonconformity might prove more socially costly (such as in race relations) Mennonites had been timid. "We have failed to see that mere nonparticipation in violence . . . is not an adequate expression of the doctrine of love."[27]

Hershberger's writing reflects an Anabaptist movement that had ceased to be marginalized and persecuted and become established and acculturated. The use of Acts to justify fleeing arrest and meeting in secret has disappeared. Civil disobedience has gone from being a fact of life that must be biblically justified to a possibility that should be borne in mind in case of a military draft. Hershberger promotes Anabaptist ideals in a manner that is prescriptive, not descriptive: he writes not to explain and defend Anabaptist beliefs and behavior but to encourage the Anabaptists themselves to behave as their spiritual ancestors once did.

JOHN HOWARD YODER

John Howard Yoder and his generation inherited the renewal of the Anabaptist vision, and Yoder made it his life's work to articulate that vision in a form that would be compelling to an ecumenical audience. Acts does not have a dominant presence in Yoder's writing; indeed, in *The Politics of Jesus* he felt obliged to explain his preference for the letters of Paul as a source of evidence for the belief and practice of the early church.[28]

Like Hershberger, Yoder finds in Paul a model of prophetic witness: his appearances before Roman officers show the church putting its view of the state into action.[29] "We may, indeed we should, demand of the state, even the non-Christian state, that it be just," Yoder remarks. "The apostle Paul did not just tell the state authority he was dealing with, 'As a Christian I would not be able to be in your position'; he also told him that as an official he should deal correctly, in accordance with the law."[30] Yoder also holds up the church of Acts as a model of witness in the face of opposition, as evoked by Acts 4:27–29: "Look at their threats, and grant to your servants to speak your word with all boldness." For Yoder, like Menno Simons, such

27. Ibid., 338–39, quoting "The Way of Christian Love in Race Relations," a statement adopted by the General Conference in 1955.

28. *Politics of Jesus*, 2nd ed., 94n1. Yoder's desire to avoid potential distortions connected to Luke's "particular concerns" and to seek corroboration of Luke's narrative from an independent source betrays a fundamental orientation toward the historical.

29. *Christian Witness to the State*, 13.

30. *Discipleship as Political Responsibility*, 24–25. The book originated from talks given in 1957, later published as *Nachfolge Christi als Gestalt politischer Verantwortung*. Yoder is evidently thinking of Acts 24:25; 25:10–11. Also relevant are Acts 16:37; 22:25.

witness is an essential mark of the true church.[31] The church of Acts also models suffering; the early church's experiences described in Acts 2:36; 4:10; 7:52 confirm what Jesus's death had also attested: "Death is the fate of the prophets."[32]

Yoder upholds his predecessors' distinction between church and society. Church and society have changed much since the first century, but not so fundamentally that the NT teaching concerning their relation is no longer valid.[33] Nor does the fact that most Christians no longer endure state-sponsored persecution mean that their situation has fundamentally changed. Thinking evidently of texts such as Acts 2:47 and 9:31, Yoder argues, "Even the church in the New Testament experienced times of peace, but that did not mean that the state was evaluated differently or that Christians started moving into governmental positions."[34] Like his predecessors, Yoder affirms the principle of Acts 5:29, warning in a 1979 lecture presented to the South Africa Council of Churches that "in segments of the Christian church, the idea that Christians should 'obey God rather than men' is only theoretically imaginable (Acts 5:29). From that perspective, it is not possible to think further about the prerequisites of nonviolent resistance."[35]

However, it is not Acts 5:29 but Rom 13 that dominates Yoder's discourse on the relationship between church and state. Indeed, there are few examples in Acts of the sort of voluntary submission to the state counseled in Rom 13 and championed by Yoder. Acts mostly shows its heroes either defying the political authorities or being unjustly coerced by them.[36] Even so, Yoder does attempt to harness Acts to his agenda: in the course of his exposition of Rom 13 in *The Politics of Jesus,* he notes that in Acts "Paul's experiences with the authorities were that they had protected his missionary freedom against hostile Gentiles (19:35–41), and his life in the face of hostile Jews (23:12–24) and soldiers (27:42–43)."[37] Many contemporary

---

31. "A People in the World," 83; Yoder refers to Menno Simons on this point: to Menno "what is central is that the witness be proclaimed without compromise in the face of opposition" (ibid., 84).

32. *Politics of Jesus*, 126.

33. *Discipleship as Political Responsibility*, 35–36. Cf. *Christian Witness to the State,* 14.

34. *Discipleship as Political Responsibility*, 38. Cf. "A People in the World," 66–68, against the notion that the Anabaptist critique is no longer relevant now that the state does not interfere in "religious" matters.

35. "The Church and Change," 158.

36. In Acts 25:11 Paul volunteers to submit to a just application of the law—underscoring the injustice he is actually experiencing.

37. *Politics of Jesus*, 207n18.

biblical scholars would see this as a rather rosy picture of Paul's experiences with Roman authorities.[38] Similarly, Yoder's depiction of the state's role in the divine dispensation will seem to some a rather rosy view of how the state can be expected to behave. Acts 5:29 may need to counter-balance Rom 13 more often than the limited exposure Yoder gives it would suggest.

Much of Yoder's work aims at explaining and commending Anabaptist perspectives and ideals within a wider conversation. When it comes to actual fidelity to those ideals, however, he appears to see little difference between contemporary Mennonites and other Christians, asking at one point, "Could it not be that the cause of the current crisis in Christendom and the Christian West is that we today, just as in the Middle Ages, as heirs of the Anabaptist tradition, just as in the territorial churches, have not believed this saving offensive Gospel?"[39] Like Hershberger, Yoder's use of Acts is prescriptive, not descriptive. The principle of Acts 5:29 serves not to justify the church's present resistance to secular authorities but to evoke the possibility of such practice. The centrality of suffering and the way of the cross are ideals, not sources of comfort and strength for people who are presently experiencing them. Yoder is primarily occupied with explaining and defending Anabaptist theology and ethics to a wider world, not explaining and defending actual Anabaptists.

PERRY YODER

Though a Hebrew Bible scholar, Perry Yoder extends his investigations into the NT in *Shalom: The Bible's Word for Salvation, Justice and Peace*. Yoder turns to Acts along with other NT texts to illuminate the meaning of salvation and peace in the Bible. In Acts salvation can refer to healing from disease (4:9; 14:9) or rescue from the peril of death by shipwreck (27:20, 31), and it often involves becoming a member of the Christian community (4:12; 11:14; 15:1, 11; 16:30, 31). Thus, as in other biblical contexts, in Acts

38. Paul leaves town immediately after the incident described in Acts 19. In Acts 23 he is arrested by the Romans (incidentally saving him from lynching) and is threatened with interrogation under the lash; he escapes by claiming the prerogatives of Roman citizenship. In Acts 27 a centurion protects Paul and his fellow prisoners from summary execution by the soldiers under the centurion's command.

39. *Discipleship as Political Responsibility*, 46–47. On Yoder's critique of his fellow Mennonites, see Craig Carter, *Politics of the Cross*, 31–59, esp. 56–59. Particularly noteworthy are his words to Mennonite seminarians in May 1970, inspired by Isa 49: "It is too slight a task for you, my servants, to regroup and reassure the children of church people, to keep communities alive through the last stages of acculturation. . . . I want to make you a light to the nations" ("Your Hope is Too Small," in *He Came Preaching*, 129–30).

salvation has a physical as well as a spiritual and theological dimension.[40] Similarly, Acts contributes to the NT evidence that *eirēnē* is about positive relationships (cf. 24:2), not just the absence of conflict or war (7:26), and is a central part of the gospel (10:36).[41] The data from Acts reinforces Yoder's argument that salvation and peace are inextricably connected with this-worldly justice.

Yoder also turns to Acts as a witness to the importance of the concept "the kingdom of God" in the mission and message of the early church, for it depicts the expansion of the message of the kingdom from the first disciples (1:3) all the way to Rome (28:1), with many stops in between (8:12; 14:22; 19:8; 20:25).[42] To Yoder, Acts demonstrates that the early church sustained Jesus's concern for the kingdom not only in its preaching but also by modeling the "kingdom way of life," including the practice of an "economics of justice," as attested in the portraits in Acts 2:42–47 and 4:32–35.[43]

This understanding of the church's vocation leads Yoder to consider the relationship between church and state. Yoder echoes earlier Anabaptist thinkers in privileging the church over the state as the bearer of God's agenda in history: "The state . . . does not know God's wisdom or purpose in history. . . . [I]t is within the church that God's purposes ought to be seen most clearly."[44] However, Yoder immediately raises two caveats. First, work for liberation, justice, and *shalom* is also going on outside the church; should not Christians "be discerning to see where in history God's liberation and justice is developing and seek ways of entering into that struggle?"[45] Second, the church itself often fails to work for justice and liberation and simply "mirrors the society around it."[46] Thus "shalom makers may find the church not only lonely, but even an adversary."[47]

Yoder's view of the church is the most pessimistic of any of the Anabaptist-Mennonite thinkers surveyed here. In promoting the ideal of shalom, Yoder appeals not to "the church" or even "churches" but to "shalom makers," who are as likely to find partners in God's work outside the church as within it and are as likely to meet opposition to their peacemaking work

---

40. *Shalom*, 47, 127; cf. 138.

41. Ibid., 20.

42. Ibid., 136–37.

43. Ibid., 137–38.

44. Ibid., 138. Yoder does not deny that the state *can* serve God's purposes.

45. Ibid., 139.

46. Ibid.

47. Ibid.

from their own churches as from the state.[48] By speaking of "shalom makers"
he is able to refer to real people engaged in real struggles for shalom (particularly Christian peacemakers he had learned to know in the Philippines),
thus regaining the early Anabaptists' rootedness in actual experiences and
practice. However, it comes at a price: the church no longer seems essential
to the establishment of the kingdom. It is only through the transformation
of social structures that the poor and oppressed will experience shalom.

WILLARD SWARTLEY

Swartley's work has focused on the Gospels more than on Acts.[49] However,
A Covenant of Peace includes a chapter-length study, "Acts: God's Strategies
for Peace in the Church."[50] Swartley notes that in Acts *eirēnē* is used in two
different contexts, that of the life of the church, and that of the *Pax Romana*.
Peace as a characteristic of the life of the church receives particular emphasis
when incorporation of outsiders is at issue (Acts 9:31; 10:36; 15:33).[51] Some
of the uses of *eirēnē* in the Roman contexts, on the other hand, point to the
hypocrisy involved in Roman claims to bring "peace." Roman magistrates in
Philippi offer peace to Paul, but he rejects it and insists on an apology for the
injustice they have done to him and Silas (Acts 16:36–37). At Paul's trial the
lawyer for the prosecution elaborately compliments the corrupt governor
Felix on, among other things, the peace he has brought to the province.
These uses of *eirēnē* show the "limited nature and insubstantiality" of the
Pax Romana compared to the true peace brought by Christ and lived by the
church.[52] The Cornelius story demonstrates Christ's lordship over the state
(10:36): "Cornelius's conversion symbolizes Rome, with the *Pax Romana* it
sought to achieve, kneeling before the lordship of Jesus Christ."[53]

The exploration of the peace theme leads Swartley into consideration
of the divergent scholarly views on Luke's approach to the Roman Empire.
Swartley sides with Richard Cassidy in emphasizing that Acts's appeal to
the kingdom of God and the lordship of Christ is "not framed to win favor

---

48. Yoder's pessimism reflects experience of the church's indifference or opposition
in the course of work as a Christian peace activist and advocate for those in the third
world struggling for liberation. The development of his view of the church since the
1980s is beyond the scope of this essay.

49. Note especially "Politics and Peace (Eirene) in Luke's Gospel," 18–37; and "Luke's
Transforming of Tradition," in *Love of Enemy and Nonretaliation*, ed. Swartley, 157–76.

50. *Covenant of Peace*, 152–76.

51. Ibid., 155–64.

52. Ibid., 168–70.

53. Ibid., 162.

with Rome," and that Paul's interactions with Roman officials show neither deference on his side nor admirable conduct on theirs. With Cassidy, he concludes that the numerous trial narratives in Acts are primarily designed to prepare Christians to undergo similar experiences, not to demonstrate compatibility between the church and Rome.[54]

Nevertheless, Swartley also argues that "the positive portrait of Rome cannot be denied," adducing the conversion of Roman officials Cornelius and Sergius Paulus, the tolerant attitude toward Christianity adopted by Roman judges such as Gallio and Festus—which commends Paul's evident faith in Rome's "due process of law"—and the witness to that due process in Paul's trial under Festus.[55] While the present writer would not wish to deny that Luke's portrait of Rome has its positive aspects, not all of Swartley's examples demonstrate his point, and some actually undermine it. For example, Festus's remark that it is senseless to send a man to Caesar without an indication of the charges against him (Acts 25:27) is not a witness to Roman due process so much as an indictment of Festus's failure to observe it, for this is exactly what the governor's refusal to release a man he knows is innocent will eventually compel him to do.

Swartley's analysis touches on many themes familiar from previous Anabaptist-Mennonite discourse. The church, as the true bearer of peace and justice, is sharply differentiated from the state, with its pretensions to the same. Acts insists that Jesus is Lord of the state, and prepares its readers for the possibility of conflict with it. At the same time, such oppositional relations seem to be a possibility, not an expectation. There is no mention of the Acts 5:29 principle (or of 4:19), and suffering and the cross do not receive strong emphasis. The emphases of Swartley's study are in part occasioned by the focus on peace and the selective reading of Acts that such a focus requires. This in itself is worthy of comment, however. In the twentieth century, peace has become a (if not the) defining characteristic of Anabaptism, such that a study looking at Acts through the lens of peace language seems natural. However, Acts is also full of conflict and tension, a fact every bit as significant to an Anabaptist reading. The sixteenth-century Anabaptists seem to have recognized this more readily than the modern interpreters do.

In his work on Acts (as well as on Luke), Swartley goes where John Yoder declined to tread—to a study of Luke as a redactor. Whereas Yoder aimed at recapturing the historical Jesus and his earliest followers, Swartley is willing to talk about Luke's *representation* of Jesus and the early church. Whereas Yoder attempted to illuminate the history behind the texts,

---

54. Ibid., 167. See Cassidy, *Society and Politics*.

55. *Covenant of Peace*, 167.

Swartley's work acknowledges the necessity of reckoning with the ideology embodied in the texts' presentation of that history. Just as Yoder represented an advance in Anabaptist apologetics over the crude proof-texting and imperfectly remembered paraphrases of the sixteenth-century writers, so Swartley's work reflects the greater sophistication of a succeeding generation of Anabaptist scholars. The next generation's *Politics of Jesus* must be a *Politics of Luke*.

CONCLUSION

This is a fruitful time for Mennonites to be in conversation with other biblical scholars about Acts. Currently there is much interest in Acts's view of politics and church-state relations. Previous Anabaptist-Mennonite use of Acts has shown that Acts holds much that supports an Anabaptist view of politics: the assertion of the primacy of Christian vocation over loyalty to the state, models of confronting political and social hostility and accepting suffering, the precedent of a persecuted church, and appeals to the state to meet its own professed standards of justice. Clearly, Anabaptist-inspired biblical scholarship has something to contribute to the current conversation.

Present-day Anabaptists are more ready to enter that conversation than ever before. Anabaptist-Mennonite appropriation of Acts has become more sophisticated. Recognition of the ideologically freighted nature of Acts's representation of history marks another step forward. However, if Mennonites are to make a meaningful contribution to the understanding of Acts in the twenty-first century, our efforts at methodological sophistication must be matched by our efforts to learn what it means to embody Acts in our own day as we confront state and society in witness to an offensive gospel.

20

"Be(a)ware of the Dogs, Evildoers and Butchery"

Text and Theory in the Discourse on Peace and Violence in Paul

Gordon Zerbe

Some time ago, when engaged in a conversation with my colleague Gordon Matties, who was then in the midst of writing his commentary on Joshua and agonizing over how abiding theological value might be found in that book,[1] I teasingly quipped: "Just call it genocidal and be done with it." It might have seemed like I was saying this from the safe haven of the peace-loving, violence-free NT. But I have come to realize that the challenge that both Gordons (representing both Testaments) have is one that differs in degree, not in kind. In fact, the problem of violence and war in the NT is in some respects more profoundly challenging, since that part of our Bibles is supposed to represent the authoritatively final and pure form of divine revelation, even if we do not chop off the OT.

---

1. Matties, *Joshua*.

SHIFTING CONTEXTS, CHANGING AUDIENCES, VARYING THEORY

There was once a time when biblical discourse on violence and peace, at least in North America, operated within a setting of relative cultural coherence (late Christendom), where partisans played by largely agreed-on rules of the game. The protagonists mainly played out the options of Christian pacifism in response to Christian just war—or just revolution—theory, and violence was commonly understood to pertain to some form of overt physical harm. The significant contribution of Perry Yoder was to put the social and political justice question squarely into the center of biblical peace discussion,[2] even though it was not entirely absent in earlier studies, including that of Willard Swartley.[3]

In recent discourse, however, not only has the definition of violence been exploded,[4] but so also the rules (theory, premises, methods) by which biblical scholars interpret texts in the context of their chosen communities or audiences have multiplied.[5] In accordance with a growing trend that sees religion in general as complicit in violence, a significant contributing factor to violence, or inherently violent,[6] recent biblical scholarship has been finding violence to be endemic also to Scripture, including the NT and Paul.[7]

2. Yoder, *Shalom*.

3. Swartley, *Slavery, Sabbath, War, and Women*, 96–149.

4. E.g., Brown, *Religion and Violence*; Scheper-Hughes and Bourgois, eds., *Violence in War and Peace*; Žižek, *Violence*. Even when *violence* signified primarily some kind of overt physical harm to person or property, its use was certainly complicated in that it was not so much a descriptive term as an evaluative one, denoting not so much something that is immediately injurious (physically) but something that is judged to be wrong, inherently harmful, or illegal. Thus, surgery, policing, or (just) war, for instance, could be excluded from its purview. It is certainly proper that violence is now seen in institutional, latent, verbal, psychological, systemic, covert, and social forms. But the term *violence* is now becoming a blunt, catch-all pejorative, replacing (or absorbing) words such as oppression, domination, harm, exclusion, marginalization, and discrimination.

5. The explicit reference to some aspect of theory or location in the very organization of scholarly communities in the SBL has multiplied immensely in the last twenty-five or so years.

6. Juergensmeyer, *Terror in the Mind of God*; Ellens, ed., *Destructive Power of Religion*; Hoffman, ed., *Just War and Jihad*; Eller, *Cruel Creeds, Virtuous Violence*; Teeham, *In the Name of God*; Murphy, ed., *Blackwell Companion to Religion and Violence*; Kimball, *When Religion Becomes Lethal*; Ross, *Religion and Violence*; Juergensmeyer and Kitts, eds., *Princeton Readings in Religion and Violence*. For one rejoinder, see Cavanaugh, *Myth of Religious Violence*.

7. Sherwood and Bekkenkamp, eds., *Sanctified Aggression*; Mathews and Gibson, eds., *Violence in the New Testament*; Bernat and Klawans, eds., *Religion and Violence*;

As the scope and understanding of violence have expanded, it has become more manifest even within the Bible. Accordingly, many studies aligned with some sort of nonviolence theory may well find the NT to be deficient in a variety of ways precisely on this question.

As a result, biblical peace scholarship, especially as allied with nonviolent theory in some form,[8] now operates on many fronts (or with various dialogue partners), complicating its discourse and making it more challenging. My own view is that biblical peace scholarship will need to use rhetorical flexibility (of the sort perhaps also demonstrated by Paul himself, "for the sake of the gospel") in varied contexts to remain viable and relevant.[9]

I proceed, then, by giving attention to a particular text as a way to situate the discussion of violence in Paul's writings and to raise problems pertaining to that issue. This will lead to a review of texts and texture where Paul's writings generally are considered in recent discussion to be violent, dangerous, or deficient in some respect. And I will close by returning to the problem of theoretical variation and broader cultural (and theoretical) multiplicity as crucial aspects and contexts of future biblical peace discourse.

THE CASE OF PHILIPPIANS 3:2—SLANDEROUS, ANTI-JUDAIC INVECTIVE OR REBELLIOUS ASSAULT ON EMPIRE?

Following a brief pause in Phil 3:1b, Paul unloads with a sharp rhetorical flourish of paronomasia (3:2–3a), exhibiting what some recent scholars suggest is a good bit of violence:[10]

Boustan, Jassen and Roetzel, eds., *Violence, Scripture, and Textual Practices*; Villiers and van Henten, eds., *Coping with Violence in the New Testament*. Also noteworthy is the continued work of the SBL section on Violence and Representations of Violence among Jews and Christians.

8. There are many strands of "nonviolence theory," one of which is enshrined in Mennonite confessions of faith (e.g., *Confession of Faith in a Mennonite Perspective*, Articles 20–24). Swartley is to be applauded for seeking to keep peacemaking biblical and tracing peace themes throughout the Bible; Swartley, *Covenant of Peace*, 1–10. At the same time, those who embrace that confessional commitment will make alliances and correlations in the broader nonviolence movement, not all of which will make the same kind of confessional commitments, and not all will have the same regard for Paul as an apostle of peace. Indeed, some of the attacks on Paul for his violence come from precisely those who espouse a theory of nonviolence.

9. See, for instance, the concluding words in my "Politics of Paul," 73.

10. E.g., Gager, with Gibson, "Violent Acts," 18; Marchal, "Imperial Intersections," 155.

v. 2 *blepete tous kynas*	Be(a)ware[A] of the dogs.[B]
blepete tous kakous ergatas	Be(a)ware of the evil workers.
blepete tēn katatomēn	Be(a)ware of the butchery [the cutting up].
v. 3a *hēmeis gar esmen hē peritomē*	For we are the circumcision [the cutting around]

A. *Blepete* here has the dual sense of "observe" and "danger," as in the French "Attention!"

B. All biblical translations are mine unless otherwise indicated.

If this is indeed a violent text, we must immediately inquire, in what sense is it violent?

1. Is it violent simply because Paul uses a word that can denote physical injury (*katatomē*), and a word that is socially derogatory (dogs)? That is, is the violence simply in the texture and imagery that Paul employs?

2. Is it violent in intent? That is, does Paul intend to harm in some specific sense? Is it violent because it engages in slanderous or retaliatory invective against some kind of adversary or rival, even though these adversaries are not directly addressed?

3. Or is it violent in its potential or in its effect? That is, does it have either the potential to or the inevitable effect of inciting social binaries that are exclusive, and thus of promoting or facilitating identitarian conflict and violence?

4. Does it manifest a "violent personality,"[11] or does it display endemic and patterned cultural violence, and not the idiosyncrasy of an individual?

5. Does it matter what group is being referenced (with the "dogs, evildoers, and butchery"), whether an (imperial) oppressor or a similarly marginalized socio-religious rival (below)? That is, does the text read differently if Paul is engaging in an act of resistance and naming imperial violence, as opposed to slanderously attacking sibling rivals? Do differing assumed referents of the verbal invective make the text more or less violent, whether in intent, potential, or effect?

6. Does it matter if the referents actually engaged in physical and/or socio-psychological violence?[12]

7. Does it matter that the verbal outburst comes from someone experiencing physical and psychological torture and abuse, as is likely?

11. Gager, with Gibson, "Violent Acts," 16–19.

12. For Roman violence, see for instance Wistrand, *Entertainment and Violence*; Lintott, *Violence*; Wengst, *Pax Romana*.

8. Does the text's canonical status give the text a greater moral burden to bear (on the side of espousing or facilitating nonviolence), or make it more susceptible to facilitating physical and/or social violence?

9. Is the text more or less violent (in character and/or effect) when interpreted or claimed from a location of marginality, or from a position of power?

All this is to suggest at the outset that flat, simplistic depictions of the text as violent (or even as not violent) cannot explain its complexity and multivalent character and potentiality.

When it comes to interpreting this text according to the traditional rules of historical interpretation, a good case can be made that the referent of Paul's verbal outburst and warning is the (violent) Roman imperium and elite Roman culture in general, not "judaizing" nor "Judaic" rivals. Space does not permit a full discussion of this reading here,[13] but the main lines of evidence and argument are as follows:

1. *Katatomē* does not lexically signify "mutilation" in particular (though that translation has become the unquestioned rendering in the last hundred years), but more generally denotes "cutting down/against," "cutting in two," or "intensively cutting," and can apply to

    (a) the cutting or chopping of flesh, whether in the butcher shop, medicine, personal assault, or war,

    (b) leather working, or

    (c) earthen excavation or rock inscriptions. This same range of meaning is more or less characteristic of the Latin translation, *concisio*.

2. The threefold imagistic combination of "dogs," "evil-doers," and "cutting" derives from the lament of Ps 22:16 (following the textual tradition of the DSS and LXX, "gouging hands and feet"),[14] where the combined referent is unmistakably to oppressors and persecutors. Paul's language in Phil 1:18–20 makes it clear that he is indeed recalling and resonating with lament psalms during his ordeal, both in terms of the imagery of persecution and suffering, and also in terms of the ultimate deliverance and universal supremacy that comes through Messiah.

---

13. See forthcoming Zerbe, *Philippians*.

14. The MT of Ps 22:16 [Heb 22:17] is garbled. The verbs used in the DSS (*krh*) and the LXX (*orussō*) overlap in meaning with *katatemnō*, referring usually to gouging or digging in the ground, but sometimes also to the incision or chopping of flesh. Paul's choice of *katatomē* is occasioned not first by the required contrast with *peritomē* but by the paronomasia of Phil 3:2, in its correlation with Ps 22:16.

3. The function of Phil 3:2 within the evident circumstance, main argument, and rhetorical agenda of Phil 3:2—4:1, and the entire letter more generally,[15] specifically suggests that it is a coded reference to the Roman *imperium* and its powerful allies. For instance, the adversaries referred to throughout Philippians, directly and indirectly, are those representing the persecuting elite of Philippi and the Roman imperial authorities holding Paul (probably in Ephesus). Meanwhile, Paul positively appropriates his Judaic citizenship markers, while also contextualizing them in reference to Messiah (3:2–11), as a way to set up his prime target: the preoccupation with the status, the questing for, or the practice of Roman citizenship and its values (3:17–21).[16]

4. Recent scholarship has increasingly recognized that there are no "judaizing" elements in the vicinity of Philippi,[17] and that 3:2–11 is hortatory and paradigmatic, not polemical or apologetic.[18]

5. Later texts show Paul's retrospective reflection on terror, torture, and suffering at the hands of the Roman authorities, conjuring up his ordeal in Ephesus from which he writes Philippians.[19]

6. The history of interpretation shows that the "judaizing" interpretation is not attested until the anti-Judaic rhetoric of Augustine and John Chrysostom[20] in the emerging Christian imperial situation, when attacks on the synagogue from the church were mounting.[21] Moreover, the traditional rendering assumes Galatians as the paradigmatic Paul, importing that agenda and context into the reading of Philippians, and thereby assumes that if there was opposition to Paul (and warning from him) it must have been primarily from a Jewish (or judaizing) source. Within the context of Christendom, it becomes unimaginable

15. When this focus of Paul's rhetoric is recognized (the close correlation of 1:27—2:16 and 3:1—4:1), all the reasons to postulate multiple letter fragments collapse.

16. For this general line of interpretation (but still assuming that Phil 3:2 refers to judaizers or Jews in some way), see Wright, "Paul's Gospel and Caesar's Empire," 173–81; Zerbe, "Citizenship and Politics," 201–4.

17. For instance, Fee, *Philippians*, 293–96.

18. Hellerman, *Reconstructing Honor*, 121–28. "No confidence in the flesh" (Phil 3:3) does not refer to a negation of circumcision in particular but anticipates the question of worldly privilege and status more generally (Phil 3:4–21; cf. 1:27–2:11; similarly 2 Cor 11:18).

19. 2 Cor 1:8–11; 2:14–16; 4:7–12; 6:2–10; 11:23—12:10; Rom 5:3–5; 8:17–27, 31–37.

20. Augustine, *A Treatise against Two Letters of the Pelagians* 22; John Chrysostom, *Homily on the Epistle of St. Paul to the Philippians* 10.

21. Gafni, "World of the Talmud," 240–51.

that Paul would have attacked the Roman imperium so directly and embraced so unequivocally his Judaic heritage.

7. Even the first translations of Phil 3:2 into English indicate that the text is understood to refer to schismatics in general (Wycliffe, *dyuysioun* [division]; Tyndale, Coverdale, *dissencion*; based on the possible sense of *katatomē* as "cutting in two"), in accordance with the pre-Christendom interpretive tradition, not judaizers in particular (the latter reading made explicit in the KJV's heading of Phil 3,[22] and following the translation "concision" of the Geneva and Bishops Bibles).

On the other hand, what is astonishing is the glee with which the anti-Judaic or anti-judaizing interpretation is often propounded in mainstream Christian commentaries, with hardly a nod to how this might affect contemporary social dynamics, and no thought for what kind of apologizing might be appropriate as a result of this and other outbursts, in terms of their eventual effects.[23] Commonly and uncritically repeated is the notion that Paul is simply throwing back the cursing invective of "dogs" from its (supposed Judaic) source,[24] thereby somehow exonerating its use, but not admitting that this very retaliatory verbal assault would not measure up against Paul's own ethical standards (Rom 12:14; 1 Cor 4:13).

But what about the counter-imperial reading?

1. Does it make this text any less violent in its presumed original setting?

2. Does it mitigate the violent potential or effect of this text in particular?

3. Does it make Paul in general any less violent in character or potential?

4. Might this historical reading be articulated with the interest of making Paul less violent (a case of special pleading)?

5. Did it or might it perhaps facilitate (either then or now) some form of "seditious resistance"?[25]

While this last query must be taken seriously, it seems to me crucial that the potential for a theory of resistance also be recognized in Paul[26]—not just a theory of nonretaliation (or nonviolence)—in accordance with Paul's interest in the justice question, expressed in various ways. Peace and justice are a biblical hendiadys, in Paul and elsewhere.[27] At the same time, this is

22. "Hee warneth them to beware of the false teachers of the Circumcision."

23. For instance, Fee, *Philippians*, 294–96.

24. Nanos, "Paul's Reversal of Jews Calling Gentiles 'Dogs.'"

25. Marchal, "Imperial Intersections," 159.

26. For instance, Wink, *Engaging the Powers*; Elliott, *Arrogance of Nations*, 143–66.

27. See Zerbe, "Peace and Justice in the Bible."

not to say that Paul can be easily exonerated of all forms of violence or violent potential, and to this issue we must now turn.

PRESUMED VIOLENCE AND ETHICAL-THEOLOGICAL
DEFICIENCIES IN PAUL

Violent elements can be (or have been) found in

1. Paul's direct ethical-social teaching,

2. his exercise of power and authority in his assemblies,

3. his ecclesial social construction,

4. his language and thought structure, and

5. his personality.

We will look at each of these areas in turn, acknowledging that these are
overlapping areas and that they are used here only for analytical purposes.

Nonretaliation and peace, along with justice, are central features of
Paul's direct ethical teaching and theological vision.[28] While interpreters
generally agree that Paul did not endorse overt physical or lethal violence
of any sort (including against the Roman Empire),[29] questions have been
raised about the character of his very ethic of nonretaliation, peace-making,
and love. Kent Yinger, for instance, has argued that this ethic applies only to
relations within the assembly and not to persecuting outsiders or outsiders
in general.[30] This reading could presumably be spun in more than one way:
nonretaliation and love are wrongly restricted only to the elect, or absolute
pacifism is properly not within Paul's purview. Another question pertains
to the obviously apocalyptic framework in which this ethic is propounded, as deference to God's exclusive prerogative for executive vindication
("wrath").[31] While some interpreters continue to minimize this aspect of
Paul's ethic, others point to its deficiency (it is motivated by eschatological
revenge, or enhances a view of God as ultimately violent), and still others
highlight that it can only be properly understood in reference to the final
justice question. Nonretaliation, peace, and love operate within a scheme

28. See Klassen, "Love of Enemies," 110–32; Zerbe, "Paul's Ethic" in *Love of Enemy*,
ed. Swartley; Hays, *Moral Vision*, 16–59, 317–46; Swartley, *Covenant of Peace*, 189–253;
Gorman, *Inhabiting the Cruciform God*, 129–60.

29. E.g., Elliott, *Arrogance of Nations*, 12: "Paul issued no call to arms against Rome;
he rallied no rebel garrison," even though "inescapably in conflict with the empire's
absolutizing claims on allegiance."

30. Yinger, "Romans 12:14–21 and Nonretaliation."

31. Zerbe, "Paul's Ethic."

that also embraces the matter of justice (whether retributive or restorative), and forgiveness and reconciliation are never blind to the necessities of accountability and consequences (thus the complementarity of "kindness" and "severity" even in the divine character, in, for example, Rom 11:22–24). A god devoid of concerns of justice is an anemic god who merely assists in self-actualization or adapts to the status quo.

Violence or the potential for violence has also been found in (or experienced through!) Paul's teaching or pronouncements in the dynamics of a presumed hierarchy of being[32] in which one party naturally submits or is subordinate to the other (masters and slaves, rulers and subjects, men and women). While a good bit of ambiguity rests within these very texts, it cannot be doubted that for the greater part of Christian history these texts were interpreted "sympathetically" (at the literal level), favoring men over women,[33] masters over slaves, and rulers over subjects.[34] In recent years, however, as social mores and ideological premises have shifted, these texts have received a critical look, either explained as categorically irreparable and dangerous (so flawed that they can only be deconstructed or else avoided), or explained (relative to their inherent ambiguity or ambivalence) as not quite as bad as they seem, or indeed as offering an emancipatory ethic.[35] And more recently, the obviously less ambiguous texts of heterosexism have become the subject of scrutiny,[36] as their complicity in the ongoing violence against homosexuality has become patently clear.

In recent years, Paul has also been found to be deficient (or violent) in his exercise of apostolic power and authority within his assemblies. Some interpreters explain this strictly and negatively as "power over," and as a pressure toward "sameness" that rejects "difference."[37] Others explain this matter with greater nuance, while not blind to the negative potentiality of Paul's texts.[38] It is certainly to be noted that the more authoritarian or threatening side of Paul emerges in the Corinthian and Galatian correspondence, and some sense of those dynamics must be entertained in the assessment of these texts. In the Corinthian case, Paul warns that his coming may be either "with a rod" or "in love in a spirit of gentleness," depending on

---

32. See below on the "kyriarchic" character of Paul's worldview.

33. See, for instance, Bird, "To What End?"

34. Elliott, *Liberating Paul*, 1–90.

35. Yoder Neufeld, *Killing Enmity*, 98–121.

36. Tite, *Conceiving Peace and Violence*, 135–91.

37. Castelli, *Imitating Paul*; Polaski, *Paul and the Discourse of Power*.

38. Kittredge, *Community and Authority*; Ehrensperger, *Paul and the Dynamics of Power*; Still, "Organizational Structures."

their response (1 Cor 4:21); and later he admits that he is angrily "on fire" (2 Cor 11:29), cautioning that he may need to be "courageous" (as if in a battle, 2 Cor 10:1–8) and "severe" (2 Cor 13:10) and "to punish" residual disobedience (10:6). Still, Paul claims that his apostolic authority is ultimately for the building up of the community, not its tearing down (2 Cor 10:8; 13:10), even as his work may involve the demolishing of intellectual strongholds (2 Cor 10:3–8). At the very least, Paul's exercise of authority and power needs to be entertained in the context of ancient conventions,[39] but also in relation to the exigencies of discipline and leadership in radical movements more generally.[40]

Paul believes that the judgment of (legal action against) outsiders should be left to God, whereas the community, under the direction of its apostolic leader, is to engage in judgment in its midst (1 Cor 5:12–13; within a set of judicial rules and procedures, 2 Cor 13:1–2). Accordingly, Paul pronounces judgment and utters curses on some of his theological rivals, for the sake of the gospel (against a "different gospel," Gal 1:6, 8; 2 Cor 11:4). He does this despite (or in contrast to) an irenic disposition toward rival apostles elsewhere, where judgment is left to God (1 Cor 3–4; Phil 1).[41] In Galatians, for instance, Paul offers an explicit curse on anyone promoting a different gospel (Gal 1:8–9), pronounces that the troublemaker will bear his judgment (Gal 5:10), and expresses this as a wish for the castration of those unsettling the community (Gal 5:12). His attack on Peter is somewhat subdued by comparison: he is "self-condemned" (Gal 2:11; even though it would appear that Peter seemed more keen to preserve the overall global unity of the church, not wanting to alienate his side of the emerging movement). In Rom 3 Paul notes that some theological rivals are making "slanderous charges" against him, and he responds with a reciprocal derogation, "their judgment is just" (Rom 3:8). In 2 Corinthians, Paul also engages in retaliatory invective, painting his fellow messianist rivals as "ministers of Satan" and "doers of evil," and pronouncing that "their judgment is sure" (11:12–15; cf. 10:12–18; 11:4–6, 22–23; 12:11). While most interpreters avoid the evident tension between this invective and Paul's own promoted

39. For the imagery of warfare in ancient moral discourse, see Malherbe, "Antisthenes and Odysseus."

40. The notion of leaderless movements is a fairly recent innovation. On the issue of discipline and hegemony within (arguably analogous) radical movements, see Day, *Gramsci Is Dead*. See also Zerbe, "Exigency of a Messianic Ecclesia."

41. Cf. Rom 14:10–12, where [personal] judgment against fellow members is censured, in favor of deferring to God's judgment.

ethic of nonretaliation (even in cursing), George Shillington has faced this problem head on.[42]

A third general area in which Paul has been found to be deficient is in his "violently dualistic" social and ecclesial construction, with "violently enforced boundaries." Paul, according to Joseph Marchal, engages in a thoroughgoing in/out, we/they, right/wrong, saved/perishing binary construction that is absolutist, exclusive, and inherently violent, even in the apparently harmless letter to the Philippians. Paul's attitude fosters a position that is diametrically opposed to the (ultimate) virtues of "dialogue and interdependence."[43] Whether the label of violence is the most apt here could be challenged, but Paul's categorical reference to all outsiders as the "perishing" (1 Cor 1:18; 2 Cor 2:15; 4:3; cf. 2 Thess 2:10) and as facing the prospect of "wrath, anger, trouble, and distress" (Rom 2:8–9) does need to be faced, albeit placed alongside the contrary direction of the universal inclusion and reconciliation of all humanity and creation in the final drama, a drama in which for Paul even the binary of "believer" and "unbeliever" will be overcome (e.g., Rom 11:11–36).[44] Still, whether this latter is necessarily a coercive universalism, or an embrace of diversity and the overcoming of dividing binaries, needs to be vigorously addressed.

Closely related to this ecclesial construction is the matter of violence in Paul's language and thought structure. Some interpreters have found Paul's use of military imagery violent in and of itself, insofar as it might promote taking a posture of engagement in a cosmic battle or in a literal one in the immediate social surrounding of the faithful who are being addressed.[45] Alternatively, it is suggested that the use of military imagery shows that Paul was supportive of the military in general, and the Roman military in particular, as mediating the will of God in the world.[46] More likely, Paul employs military and soldiering imagery ultimately to subvert worldly combat.[47]

The assessment of Paul's overall thought structure as "kyriarchic" (from the term *kyrios*, "lord," a category in which, for instance, patriarchy can also be included), in connection with Paul's underlying apocalyptic-millenarian framework,[48] is also open to multiple readings. Admittedly, in Paul's eschato-

42. Shillington, *2 Corinthians*, 237–38.

43. Marchal, "Imperial Intersections," 154–59; Marchal, "Boundaries, Binaries, and Belonging." Compared to other scholars, Marchal may use the word *violent* to depict Paul's ideology and texts more frequently.

44. Zerbe, "Paul's Eschatological Ecclesiology."

45. Marchal, "Military Images in Philippians 1–2."

46. Desjardins, *Violence and the New Testament*, 82.

47. Zerbe, "Politics of Paul," 66–68; Zerbe, "Soldiering and Battling."

48. Schüssler-Fiorenza, *Power of the Word*, 13–29, 82–109, 149–93.

logical drama, God out-empires empire (1 Cor 2:6; 15:24–28; Rom 8:31–39), whether imaged as world-subjection[49] or as world-reconciliation,[50] and to that extent never fully transcends imperial conceptuality (except perhaps in the sense of God being "all in all," 1 Cor 15:28; cf. Rom 11:36; Col 3:11; Eph 1:10; 4:6). In connection with his eschatological drama, we should also locate Paul's pronouncements of doom on the present world order, including that of Rome and its allies (1 Cor 2:6; 1 Thess 5:3; Phil 3:19–21).[51] These pronouncements put God in the role of military actor (replete with divine warfare imagery),[52] and to that extent cast God as a violent actor (since it would be inconsistent to label all human military activity as inherently violent but not also divine military activity).[53] On the positive side, this imagery can be appropriated as offering a theory of resistance,[54] even if it comes with a deficient theory of ecclesial agency.[55] Moreover, its function to pacify and democratize the divine warrior tradition needs to be recognized.[56] Others, however, suppose that it may foster "seditious resistance,"[57] or emanate from a revengeful resentment.[58] But there is no question that for Paul, final cosmic peace is always an embattled peace, even as—arguably—justice for Paul is ultimately a form of restorative justice.[59]

Paul's "violent Christology of the cross" has also been targeted for special criticism. The use of the cross as central symbol—along with solidarity in suffering as a pattern for Messiah, himself, and the adhering

49. Phil 2:9–11; 3:20–21; Rom 15:8–12; 1 Cor 2:6–8; 15:24–28.

50. Rom 8:18–25; 11:15; cf. Col 1:19–20; Eph 1:10, 22–23; 2:1—3:21.

51. I take the final statement on the final judgment of the Jews in 1 Thess 2:16 (at the least) to be a later gloss; but the heightened rhetoric against persecutors and non-believers in 2 Thess 1:5–9; 2:8–12 cannot be so confidently discarded as non-Pauline in character or source.

52. Yoder Neufeld, *Put on the Armour of God*, 73–156; Yoder Neufeld, *Killing Enmity*, 122–49; Swartley, *Covenant of Peace*, 222–53.

53. It is perhaps ironic that this is the one area where for biblical pacifists (including Mennonites) warfare is not always by definition labeled as violent. Still, this selectivity would be consistent with common usage of the word *violence,* according to which it is not so much a descriptive word as an evaluative one: certain "violent" acts are deemed to be proper, and thus not named as violent. See above n4.

54. E.g., Taubes, *Political Theology of Paul*; Swartley, *Covenant of Peace*, 222–53; Zerbe, "Exigency of a Messianic Ecclesia."

55. Elliott, *Arrogance of Nations*, 152–66.

56. Yoder Neufeld, *Put on the Armour of God*, 84–93; Zerbe, "'Pacifism' and 'Passive Resistance.'"

57. Marchal, "Imperial Intersections," 159.

58. E.g., F. Nietzsche. For excerpts, see Meeks, *Writings of St. Paul*, 288–302.

59. Zerbe, "Soldiering and Battling."

community[60]—is thought to represent a personal predilection for violence.[61] Paul is not to be understood "as a typical Jew, but rather, in his own words, as eccentric precisely in his attraction to violence."[62] Even within the early Jesus movement, "Paul's commitment to the crucified Christ was highly eccentric . . . both before and after his time."[63] Indeed, analyzing "like good amateur psychologists," Gager and Gibson suggest that Paul's persecution of early Jesus followers and his later embrace of the crucified Christ are of one piece, best explained in terms of Paul's persistent "violent personality," his "excessive zeal." This rendering of Paul as suffering from a particular violent psychological malady is indeed amateurish,[64] and seems unable to understand the liberating power of remembering martyrs in their labors for justice, as still experienced by oppressed groups today.[65] Michael Gorman has offered a helpful rejoinder.[66]

THEORY IN THE ENGAGEMENT WITH TEXTS

Textual interpretation is inevitably bound up in some theory, so it is appropriate to review some basic postures in the discourse on peace and violence in Paul. Here is one possible typology (or continuum) of approaches.[67]

60. Citing texts such as Rom 6:6; 8:36; 1 Cor 2:2; 4:9; 2 Cor 6:5; 11:23–29; Gal 2:19.

61. Gager, with Gibson, "Violent Acts," 16–19.

62. Ibid., 16.

63. Ibid., 19. Since Paul had other Christological options before him—Jesus the prophet, teacher, healer, gloriously resurrected Son of God in heaven, and others—his unique cruciform Christology requires special explanation. That Paul's Christology was eccentric in this sense is historically doubtful.

64. At the very least, there is no discussion of Paul's supposed personality dysfunction in reference to current psychological, social-psychological, or socio-cultural theory.

65. See Schottroff, *Feminist Interpretation*, 218–23, esp. her discussion titled "Cross—Sacrifice—The Concept of God—Christology." Schottroff identifies two reasons for her "support of a feminist theology of the cross." First, she points to the crucial and revitalizing human experience of "the remembrance of the dead and their labors for justice," whether from the distant or the recent past. Second, drawing attention to the Jewish martyr tradition (4 Macc 17:20–22), she argues that "the remembrance of those martyrs and the liberating power of their death apparent in this text must not be confused with interpretations of the reconciling death of Jesus that are tools of oppression" (220–21).

66. Gorman, *Inhabiting the Cruciform God*, 129–60.

67. Other factors could be laid over it, for instance, questions of social and cultural location and function of interpretation.

One approach operates on the premise of a singular, authoritative, and normative voice of Paul (and other NT texts), and seeks to minimize diversity, ambiguity, multivalence, and multipotential in Paul's texts (decrying diversity as a concession to interpretive license, in which meaning is to be found simply in the transaction between reader and text, with priority to the reader). While this approach usually denies any reliance on (presuppositional) "theory," it practically operates according to the theory of a confessional stance[68] and takes up some modest use of historical critical methods. Troublesome texts are either exonerated or rescued, or their violent potential is minimized, and violent use is explained as stemming from misreading.

On the other side of the spectrum, some interpreters are convinced that Paul's personality and texts are so flawed that they are inherently dangerous, not merely potentially so. These interpreters point to the canonical status of these texts as increasing their violent potential; thus the necessity of emphasizing their violent dimensions and of undermining their status, privilege, and canonical authority. An additional charge, as with any religious texts, is that the aura of certitude that surrounds the reading of the texts is dangerous and potentially violent. In these circumstances, the interpretive posture is usually (but not always) admitted up front, often with the designations feminist, postcolonial, or queer.[69]

Somewhere in a middle[70] position are those who are unwilling to relinquish the voice of Paul in constructive theo-political inquiry, while acknowledging the ambiguous potential and multivalent character of Paul's texts, and their violent effects in various settings. This general stance of sympathetic appropriation may be characteristic, on the one hand, of those who seek to be robustly Christian (using such texts in normative articulation for faith and life), or, on the other hand, of those who seek to be informed by Paul's theory apart from any specific commitment to Christian practice or belief.[71] In both cases, readers assume that the positive core and potential of Paul's texts are not entirely negated by the deficient, dangerous, or violent

68. For instance, in the preamble to *Confession of Faith in a Mennonite Perspective*, 8, the first stated function of confessions of faith is to "provide guidelines for the interpretation of Scripture."

69. E.g., Bird, "To What End?"; Mathews and Gibson, "Introduction"; Marchal, "Imperial Intersections."

70. One might call this a "mediating" position, except that such mediation might certainly be rejected (as with many attempts at mediation) by either of the two ends of the continuum already noted, even when there is agreement on core values of nonviolence.

71. E.g., Taubes, *The Political Theology of Paul*; Agamben, *Time That Remains*; Boyarin, "Paul among the Antiphilosophers."

aspects of his rhetoric. In effect, this approach allows the reader to read Paul as he read his own sacred texts: from the perspective of their emancipatory, inclusive center and direction.[72]

72. Paul, too, was aware of both the limits and the revelatory potentiality of the sacred written text (Rom 3:21–31; 2 Cor 3:4—4:6).

21

"Not Peace But a Sword"

Class Conflict In Paul's Corinthian Churches

Reta Halteman Finger

Many students in my Bible classes at Messiah College came from inter-denominational or Baptist churches that do not emphasize the practice of nonviolence as a Christian value. So those with some Bible knowledge would not uncommonly argue that Jesus's words in Matt 10:34—"Do not think that I have come to bring peace to the earth; I have not come to bring peace, but a sword"[1]—mean that Jesus does not oppose killing enemies when the need arises.

But context matters. The "sword" in this saying refers to the hostility an extended family directs toward a relative who chooses to follow Jesus above all else. In a subsistence economy where a tightly knit kin group was an individual's only social security, such radical outside loyalty could churn up a family system and tear huge holes in its members' safety net.

For those wounded by the sword of rejection by family or society, Jesus's answer was to create what sociologists call a "fictive-kin group" centered around his life, teachings, and practices. We see the results in Acts 2–6 as the Jerusalem believers organize into an intentional community. Here unrelated believers eat together and share goods and livelihoods—Hebrews and Hellenists, unattached women (Acts 6:1), wealthy people such as

---

1. All biblical quotations are taken from the NRSV unless otherwise indicated.

Barnabas (4:36), beggars with disabilities and those who had been healed (i.e., 3:1–10), and even former enemies (2:23, 37, 38).[2]

Literal weapons of sword, cross, and stones were indeed prominent in this cultural shift, as we see in the executions of Jesus, Stephen, and James (Acts 2:23; 7:54–60; 12:1–2). Swords of resistance pervade the book of Acts as the church penetrates new Jewish and Gentile communities and lifestyles. Passing the "peace of Christ" in the Roman Empire was risky business!

What tensions arise when Jesus's gospel meets the constructs of culture the NT calls "this world" or "this age"? By bringing together people from different ethnic, religious, and socioeconomic backgrounds, Jesus's apostles confronted many internal conflicts. New converts from "this age" brought a lot of baggage into the little house assemblies scattered around the empire. Yes, Jesus promises peace that the world cannot give (John 14:27). Yes, Paul begins every letter to his churches with "grace and peace." But the domestic sword of Matt 10 remains.

Nothing highlights the clash of old-age/new-age cultures in the Jesus movement more vividly than the apostle Paul's Corinthian correspondence. This is primary literature discussing strife as it happens! In this essay I will explore a few of the problems and conflicts this passionate missionary encountered as he hurled an upside-down gospel into a culture far more foreign and pagan than that of Palestine.

We have at least three letters in our canon[3] that Paul wrote to house churches he had earlier planted in Corinth, a major trading city in Achaia. Several years after he left, one leader, Chloe, paid for two men from her household, Acaicus and Fortunatas, to sail across the Aegean Sea to Ephesus to bring Paul the news that their assemblies were falling apart (1 Cor 1:10–13; 16:17–18). Around the same time, Stephanas, another household head, brought Paul a letter full of questions about how to live as Jesus people (16:17–18). That letter is lost, but when Paul quotes from it we get a sense of how far off the mark some of their theology was. What attitudes and behaviors were tearing apart the house churches of Corinth? What advice, scolding, and encouragement did Paul give? Did he bring peace—or a sword?

---

2. Finger, *Widows and Meals*, 134–36.

3. This assumes that 2 Cor is a compilation of several letters written by Paul to the Corinthians at different times and under various circumstances, as many scholars suggest.

THE BACKSTORY

The region of Achaia (now the Greek Peloponnesus) was connected to Macedonia by a slender land bridge called the Isthmus of Corinth. Since 1889, a canal has sheared the isthmus in two, but in Paul's day Corinth's economy thrived as mules hauled ships' cargo from one body of water to the other. Commentators often paint Corinth as especially immoral because of sailors passing through or because of the Greek temple to Aphrodite that in earlier centuries had crowned the Acrocorinth, the massive rock formation that dominated the Corinthia. But first-century Roman Corinth was probably little more degenerate than other cities of the empire.

According to Acts 17 and 18, Paul arrives here after a lukewarm reception in Athens. He spends eighteen months in Corinth (50–51 CE)[4] evangelizing and building a community of believers in Messiah Jesus—a gospel radically opposed to the gospel of the imperial religion. He probably rents a room in a densely populated tenement, making tents and awnings with fellow Jew, Aquila, and Aquila's wife, Priscilla, in their shop (Acts 18:1–3). Interacting with customers, bystanders, and synagogue contacts, Rabbi Paul introduces the crucified and risen Messiah.

After several house assemblies are established, Paul sails to Ephesus with Priscilla and Aquila. He leaves them there while he continues eastward to visit Jerusalem, Antioch, and previous church plants (Acts 18:18–23). During Paul's absence in Ephesus, a Jew named Apollos arrives from Alexandria, Egypt, and impresses everyone with his eloquence. After Priscilla and Aquila patch the holes in his theology, they encourage Apollos to visit Corinth and they include a letter of recommendation for him (Acts 18:24–28).

Apollos is a smash hit in Corinth as well, "powerfully refuting Jews in public" and "showing by the Scriptures that the Messiah is Jesus" (Acts 18:28). More converts are added to the little house assemblies that meet in various places around the city and its environs. While Apollos is in Corinth, Paul returns to Ephesus (19:1). By the time 1 Corinthians is written, Apollos is back in Ephesus or the surrounding region (1 Cor 16:12).

But after several years, the house assemblies are riven with factions and quarrels. Some support Paul, but others prefer the teaching of Apollos, and still others say they are "of Cephas," which may refer to Jewish influence in the group. A fourth group, in true nondenominational form, insists that they are followers of Christ alone! (1 Cor 1:10–13) Paul's visitors also

---

4. Paul's time in Corinth can be dated precisely because he is taken before Gallio, the proconsul (governor) of Achaia. An inscription confirms that Gallio governed there only for parts of the years 51–52. Horsley, *1 Corinthians*, 28–29.

mention sexual indiscretions by some men in the churches. It all sounds like serious backsliding into what we might call a worldly way of life. Reading between the lines, it looks like the Paul faction would really like him to come back, clean house, and rescue them!

CORINTHIAN LIFE IN THE EMPIRE OF DOMINATION

For this essay, I owe much to the research that biblical and classical scholars and archeologists are doing on life and power relations in the Roman Empire.[5] I primarily use an "empire-critical" method to examine the sociological, political, religious, and economic structures that underpin the Roman Empire of the first century. This method highlights the contrast not only with our American democratic ideals but also—especially—with the "kingdom of God" proclaimed by Jesus.

First, the empire is an empire and not a democracy. The Roman elite assume they are superior to other ethnic groups and thus have the right to rule those beneath them in the hierarchy. Gradations of hierarchy exist everywhere, from the emperor to senators to equestrians to the lesser aristocracy to ordinary free citizens to freeborn noncitizens to freed persons and finally to the backbone of empire, slaves—with layers and gradations among the slaves themselves. There is little upward social mobility; stability and hierarchy are valued above all else. Democracy means chaos.

Second, such stability and hierarchy are best maintained through a system of inequality called *patronage*. No one can survive in their present status in the empire without a patron of a slightly higher class to provide what is needed to maintain one's status—whether social connections, economic opportunities, or legal counsel. In return, the client is required to publicly honor his or her patron in any way possible. Clients themselves are patrons to people below them. Throughout the empire, many of these pyramids operate to maintain both inequality and social stability. This hierarchy is buttressed by civil religion promoted by priests and emperor. The emperor is either worshiped as divine or regarded as the chosen earthly representative of the Roman gods.

Because of patronage, there is little "class warfare." People of a similar underclass cannot easily organize, for their first loyalty must be to a higher-class patron who helps them survive, even if only at subsistence level.[6] As a result, there are few slave revolts in Roman history.

5. For example, Crossan and Reed, *In Search of Paul;* Elliott, *Arrogance of Nations;* Martin, *Corinthian Body;* Meeks, *First Urban Christians.*

6. Carney, *Shape of the Past*, 63, 90, 94, 171; noted in Crossan and Reed, 292.

The Corinthians of Paul's day seem obsessed with rank and status, from the wealthy elite who scramble for public honor in their city, down to minor officials, skilled and unskilled freeborn laborers, freed persons, and slaves. This obsession leads to ruthless competition among the aristocrats. Richard Horsley notes that first-century Corinth was developing "a reputation as the most competitive of all cities. Even in economic matters, [it was] a city of unprincipled profit takers who would stop at nothing to outdo their rivals."[7]

Such intense competition no doubt harks back to Corinth's recent history. Greek Corinth had been destroyed by the Romans in 146 BCE and mostly lay in ruins until 46 BCE, when Julius Caesar resettled some of his retired soldiers there, along with freedmen and women sent from the overcrowded city of Rome.[8] These nonelite people struggled upward socially, so that by the time of Paul, their grandchildren were competing with each other to become the leading aristocrats of Corinth.

PAUL AND PATRONAGE

Compare the above to the inclusiveness and self-giving that characterize Jesus's gospel, and one can easily see what Paul is up against as he travels to major cities in this powerful empire and plants small Jesus assemblies. For patrons of any level with clients below them on the social ladder, how is this call to self-emptying "good news"?

Robert Jewett has noted that patronage is not a major issue in the Thessalonian church of Macedonia. Although Paul encourages believers to "respect those who labor among you, and have charge of you in the Lord" (1 Thess 5:12), no leader is named. In both Thessalonian letters, the authors—Paul, Silvanus, and Timothy—speak of toiling night and day so they will not burden the church (1 Thess 2:9; 2 Thess 3:7–8). These words likely mean that the body of believers there is very poor. The church does not have a patron to host the daily *agapē* meal in his or her villa, so each person must work in order to earn enough bread for the potluck (2 Thess 3:10). Jewett concludes that such assemblies must meet in crowded spaces in tenement buildings.[9]

In contrast, 1 Corinthians names several persons who appear to be leaders: Chloe, Crispus, Gaius, and Stephanas (1:11, 14, 16). Most likely, groups of believers meet in their homes or in a rented ground-floor shop

7. Horsley, *1 Corinthians*, 31.
8. Ibid., 22–23.
9. Jewett, *Paul*, 73–86.

in a tenement. Such a house church automatically becomes assimilated into the hierarchical social structure of the Roman world.[10] We do not know how Paul dealt with this dynamic when he was living in Corinth. As we will see later, he does not cooperate in patronage himself. Perhaps the hierarchical structure has strengthened since he left, or during or after the time Apollos was there.

I will use selected texts from 1 Corinthians as evidence that Paul's overarching concern is the problem of patronage and one-upmanship. Wealthier, more privileged people assume they have the right to pull rank in relation to those socially beneath them. How does Paul show them the "self-emptying," downwardly mobile example of Jesus? (Phil 2:5–8) Will his advice create more or less peace within the believing community?

1 Corinthians 1:18—3:23: Crazy, Upside-Down Logic

This first theological section immediately challenges the "not many" among the believers who are "wise by human standards, powerful, and of noble birth" (1:26). It encourages those who are less educated and "weak, low, and despised in the world" (1:27–28). Waving a cross, the ancient instrument of torture, Paul insists that "we proclaim Christ crucified, a stumbling block to Jews and foolishness to Gentiles" (1:23). This is not atonement theology; this is the upside-down logic of God's reign—that Yahweh's human representative should be so dishonored and shamed by the empire, by the "rulers of this age," that he was executed as a criminal or terrorist. And these rulers are like the very ones some of the "noble" members are sucking up to!

Apollos may have preached the same message. But he was a gifted orator from Alexandria, where Philo's wisdom had influenced the Jewish community. Perhaps Apollos' education had attracted some lower-level officials who were household heads hanging onto upper-class privileges by their fingertips. Here was a good opportunity to become patrons to believers with less status who could provide them additional public honor.

But Paul insists that he and Apollos have the same theology. He planted; Apollos watered (3:5–6). They are not rivals. Therefore it is essential that the factions of Paul and Apollos unite. But the believers are still such spiritual babies, still "of the flesh," quarreling and jealous of each other (3:1–4).

10. Meeks, *First Urban Christians*, ix.

1 Corinthians 5:1—6:20: Sex, Lawsuits, and Banquets

Next Paul tackles a report from Chloe's people that one of the men in the church is in a sexual relationship with his stepmother—his father's wife (5:1). Paul is shocked because this behavior conflicts with Roman practice as well as Hebrew law (Lev 18:8). Why does the assembly tolerate and even express pride in this behavior? Put this man out of the church until he repents! (1 Cor 5:3–5) There can be no peace while such blatant sin remains.

This issue puzzles readers today. It is usually explained that the father's first wife has died, leaving a (perhaps teenage) son. The father marries a younger woman around the age of the son. Then the father dies, so the son establishes a relationship with her. However, it is hard to see how this violates Roman law. Bruce Winter argues that the father is alive—in which case the son *is* transgressing the law of honor. But the family is wealthy, and the father does not want to call public attention to this shame, for it would hurt his reputation and he would lose both wife and heir to exile or death. For the same reasons of wealth and prestige, the Corinthian assemblies do not excommunicate the son. He is their patron and benefactor.[11] Note that Paul connects greed and robbery to sexual immorality twice in this section (5:10; 6:9–10).

Paul probably discusses lawsuits next (6:1–8) because of the legal mess described above. But in any case, only elite patrons of the church could file a grievance in a Roman court. The scales of Roman justice are not blind, and people of lower rank may not sue a person of higher rank. Court proceedings are notorious for unbridled language, defamation of character, public shaming, and bitter wrangling.[12]

Paul insists that internal problems be brought before "the saints" (6:1–6). "Can it be that there is no one among you wise enough to decide between one believer and another?" (v. 5) This approach is risky for those with power and privilege. What if the wisest person in a house church is a slave, perhaps a slave of the patron? What if she herself has a grievance against her master, who beats or rapes her? One can only imagine the sword of controversy that would tear apart such a Jesus assembly if slaves think they deserve as much status and respect as their owners!

Paul goes on to curtail the privileges of all elite men in 6:12–20. They have misunderstood his law-free gospel and now say, "All things are lawful." More specifically, their ethical guidelines stipulate that "food is meant for the stomach and the stomach for food" (6:13); therefore, "sex is for the body

11. Winter, *After Paul Left Corinth*, 49–52.
12. Ibid., 58–67.

and the body is for sex."[13] The context for this passage is elite banquets, the "intimate and unholy trinity" of eating and drinking and, in our parlance, hook-ups. Winter argues that "gluttony and drunkenness were an accepted part of social life in Corinth, as were the promiscuous 'after-dinners.'"[14] But how would those patrons of noble birth react to a client or slave challenging them about attending these banquets? Probably not with peaceful acquiescence!

Gender inequality is also evident here: even upper-class Roman women are expected to remain faithful to their husbands. Paul uses two arguments to shame male sexual behavior and to call free men to the same standards as those in place for women: sexual intercourse implies a spiritual bond between one man and one woman (6:16); and the physical body must be a spiritual temple for the Lord because God has bodily "raised the Lord and will raise our bodies by his power" (6:13b–20). In fact, those who are greedy, drunkards, or sexually immoral should not even come to the community's daily agape meals! (5:11)

1 Corinthians 7:1–40: Slavery, Sex, and Family Systems

Now Paul's tone shifts to become less emotional and more nuanced. He has hurled his righteous anger at the bad behavior reported orally to him; now he must respond to the letter he has received from others, to tell them about how to live as Jesus believers in a pagan world.

First, Paul corrects an ascetic, male-oriented attitude opposite from that of the libertines of chapter 6 who think "all things are lawful." Some men think it is a good thing for them to have no sexual contact with any woman (7:1), presumably even their wives. But Paul's solution for married couples is completely egalitarian. Corinthian culture assumed that the wife's body belonged to the husband, but *not* the reverse. The wife can freely ask the husband for affection and sex—imagine that! (7:3–5)

Second, Paul encourages those presently unmarried to consider the single, celibate life. This is highly countercultural, since marriage and children were expected of every normal freeborn person. Yet marriage for women was risky (many died in childbirth) and, for nonelite women, full of the drudgery of unending housework and food production. Paul encourages both unmarried women and men to consider remaining single so they can be more concerned "about the affairs of the Lord" (7:34). One of Paul's reasons is apocalyptic: Jesus is soon returning, so concentrate on spiritual

13. Ibid., 72.
14. Ibid., 88.

issues. Reflecting a shift from his former Pharisaic assumptions, he offers the same option—time spent in prayer and Scripture study—for women as for men. (Were fathers of virgin daughters happy to hear this?)

A third issue concerns slavery, and here Paul's advice sounds tame to our ears. The NRSV makes it sound like slaves should be content in their present condition. But the Greek literally reads: "A slave were you when called? Do not let it matter to you. But if you are able to become free, rather use [it]" (7:21).[15] On one hand, we must cut Paul some slack here, since slavery was the economic underpinning of the empire, and he had no power to abolish it. Nevertheless, Paul says little about the plight of slaves. They were neither single nor married. They were "bodies" without honor, sexually available to their owner or to whomever he gave permission to rape them. Legally, they could not marry—and even if freed, their previous owner retained certain rights over them. Some slaves did establish a liaison with a partner, but any children were usually taken from them to break up family bonds. We might wish that Paul had forbidden Christian slave owners to rape their slaves. But perhaps that probihition is implied by Paul's insistence on no extramarital sex. Many prostitutes of both genders visited by upper-class men were slaves of pimps—just as with the sex slavery that thrives today. Perhaps Paul's statement above relieved slaves of the shame or guilt they felt in their trapped condition.

1 Corinthians 8–10: The Risk of Eating Idol Food

Eating food previously dedicated to a Greco-Roman deity was a theologically charged issue. Every formal meal began with a bread-breaking ritual to honor one god or another. However, since Paul refers to the "meat market" (10:25), no doubt the major question of conscience arose around animals that had been slaughtered for some pagan sacrifice, after which the meat was sold in the market. (Greco-Romans believed the gods only liked the smoke and inedible parts of a sacrifice.) Was it okay for believers to eat such meat at private meals or at public banquets sponsored by aristocrats?

If idol *meat* is indeed the point of reference, Paul is once again addressing elite men in the house churches. Then as now, eating meat means eating from the top of the food chain. The only time the poor ate meat was at citywide celebrations where bulls were sacrificed and the meat distributed to the people. But Paul issues two instructions that specifically curtail privileges of elite, upwardly mobile men.

15. In this case, the NIV has a better reading: "Were you a slave when you were called? Don't let it trouble you—although if you can gain your freedom, do so."

First, since "no idol in the world really exists" (8:4), Paul agrees with the libertines that it is okay to eat whatever food is offered at a private dinner—unless someone there tells you it was offered in sacrifice. Then, for the sake of that person's conscience, do not eat it (10:27–29). Such information would most likely come from a Christian slave serving the meal, who knows where the meat came from.

Second, Paul absolutely forbids public banquets. Temple banquets play a central role in the life of elite Corinthians. They reinforce the hierarchical structures of life in the empire. The host seats diners according to their rank, sometimes offering better food to the higher-ups. Besides the dessert course mentioned above, these meals are times of networking; strengthening business, political, and personal ties; and reinforcing patronage relations. It's the "good old boys' club" where things are really decided. For Paul, to participate in such meals is to sit down at the table of demons (10:14–22), the table of the domination system of this world that God opposes.

This is one touchy issue. Paul realizes he is asking a lot. By not attending these banquets, these elite patrons are literally putting themselves outside their class, off their rung on the ladder of hierarchy. It will not make them happy!

For this reason, Paul includes chapter 9—a long section in the middle of this topic—about a privilege he himself has given up for the sake of the gospel: he has refused to receive any financial support from the Corinthians. He has a right to it, but he will not make use of that right (9:1–7, 12, 15). Paul knows his support would come from the patrons at the top of the house church pyramid. He would be beholden to them rather than to the majority of believers, who are poor, less educated laborers and slaves. He would be co-opted into the patronal system that stands in opposition to the good news of equal inclusion offered through Christ (9:16–18).

Instead, Paul becomes a lower-class handworker in his rented tent-making shop (Acts 18:1–3). He sees this self-emptying of privilege as the very core of Jesus's gospel. But by offering himself as an example of what Jesus did, he knows he will anger his would-be patrons. It would be a public honor to have Teacher Paul as a house philosopher whom they support financially. In response, some reject his apostleship outright (a painful situation Paul addresses in 2 Cor 10–13).

1 Corinthians 11:17–34: Not a Supper of the Lord!

The context of chapters 11–14 is a worship service. Though Paul first discusses what men and women should or should not wear on their heads, he assumes women will pray and teach or prophesy publicly as do men. Paul may seem somewhat confused about gender relations in this section, but he is clear about what it means to partake of a "supper of the Lord"!

Since wealthier members do not have to work for a living, they arrive at a patron's house for supper in the late afternoon and probably recline in the dining room on couches. Slaves and other laborers cannot arrive until after sunset. By that time, the food is gone, and the early diners are drunk (11:20–21). This is eating and drinking in an unworthy manner, says Paul. It is not "discerning the body" (11:29). It is why some—who do not get enough food—"are weak and ill and some have died" (v. 30).

This entire text presupposes a full meal that begins with a bread-breaking ritual and ends with a ritual of the cup—in honor of the Lord Jesus.[16] The confusing words "homes" and "at home" in verses 22 and 34 literally say "house," meaning, in this case, the "house church."[17]

Paul uses the example of Jesus's Last Supper to play on the word *body*. Jesus shared bread as a symbol both of his own physical body and of the group gathered around him (vv. 23–25). The elite members of the house church are to remember the "death of the Lord" (v. 26) when they are asked to die to their privilege of an early supper in order that all may eat together.

This is far more intrusive than it sounds. People of higher social classes do not eat with those beneath them. Even small social gradations mean that some get food inferior to what others at a meal receive. But Paul is adamant. If you are not eating together, it is not a Supper of the Lord. You are eating your own suppers, and you humiliate those who have nothing (vv. 20–22). Alas, the community cannot even eat together in peace!

1 Corinthians 12–13: Spiritual Gifts for the One Body

Paul continues his "church-as-one-body" theme in chapter 12. Verse 1 should not read, "now concerning spiritual *gifts*," but rather "now concerning spiritual *things* or *people*." Upper-class members, probably from the Apollos faction, see themselves as *innately* wise and spiritual. But Paul insists that they are all equal *gifts* from God (vv. 4–11) and are all given for the "common good" (v. 7), not personal one-upmanship.

Then follows a long passage comparing the church body to the physical body, making the case that even the weaker or less honorable parts of the body are as important as the ones "we clothe with greater honor and

16. Pagan meals had a similar ritual in which they invoked a particular deity into their midst.

17. Henderson, "If Anyone Hungers," 195–208.

respect" (12:22–26). Greco-Roman authors and politicians also use the body image, but in the opposite way: because some parts of the physical body are more honorable or valuable than others, in Roman society some are more important and of higher value than others.[18] Thus Paul is challenging aristocratic writers of the empire.

By now, chapter 13 on *agapē* love can be read in its context as a description of self-emptying of privileges for the sake of equality in the whole body of Christ. It is far more than a text for a wedding sermon!

1 Corinthians 15—Resurrection of the Body

Even in the dramatic climax of his letter, Paul identifies with lower status believers. The idea of bodily resurrection would have struck educated people as ridiculous or as a superstition of the masses. They are more likely not to expect an afterlife at all, or to assume that only the soul is eternal.[19] But Paul's drumbeat of the spiritual importance of the physical body throughout this letter rests on his bedrock conviction that God will bodily raise those in Christ at the end of the age. The less educated more easily embrace such hope.

No doubt many elite members of Paul's house churches are skeptical. Much of their energies revolve around getting ahead in "this age." They do not see how Paul's theology might pose a political threat to the "powers of this world," the system of domination that the Lord Caesar so successfully presides over. But a Lord Jesus coming down bodily from heaven to destroy "every ruler and every authority and power" (15:24–25) poses an ultimate political threat to the powerful aristocrats—and a living hope for the underclasses and for those who have already died (15:18–19).

CONCLUSION

Does Paul's letter bring peace and unity to his house churches? Not at all! But Paul does not give up. From the patchwork evidence of 2 Corinthians, we know that Paul does visit Corinth later and is insulted by at least one person (2:5; 7:12). He writes an angry, sarcastic letter (chaps. 10–13)[20] contrasting himself to "super-apostles" (11:5) who probably *are* accepting patronage. Not until Titus checks on affairs and returns with a good report can

18. Martin, *Corinthian Body*, 94–96.

19. Ibid., 114–15.

20. See n3 above.

Paul relax (2:13; 7:5–6; 12:17) and write a letter of reconciliation (1:1—2:13; 7:5–16).

Nothing creates more resistance than a call to give up privileges for the common good. Whether we have privileges of whiteness, maleness, class, education, wealth, or heterosexual orientation, we will fight to maintain our rights. Jesus's pattern of self-emptying, named in the Christ hymn (Phil 2:6–8) and detailed in 1 Corinthians, is not popular. The privileged Corinthians do not want to give up anything either. No wonder Jesus said, "I have not come to bring peace on the earth, but a sword."

22

"Making Every Effort"

Peacemaking and Ecclesiology in Ephesians 4:1–6

Christopher Marshall

In his comprehensive analysis of the theme of peace in the NT, Willard Swartley observes that there are almost as many explicit references to peace in the letter to the Ephesians as there are in the epistle to the Romans (eight and ten respectively, which together constitute some 40 percent of the occurrences of the term in the Pauline corpus). This notable similarity, he suggests, "strengthens the case for Pauline authorship of Ephesians," though not the Pastorals, where peace terminology also occurs a few times but carries little theological weight.[1] Later in the book, Swartley suggests that the striking parallel between the thought logic of 1 Cor 12–14 and Eph 4:1–6 lends further credence to Paul being the author of Ephesians. In both of these passages, a commitment to peace-building is a necessary corollary of the church being the body of Christ.[2]

Like Swartley, I too incline toward accepting Pauline authorship of Ephesians, at least in the sense of Paul's distinctive thought and theological vocabulary being the genesis of and controlling influence on the penning of the letter, even if a close follower may have wielded the pen. In this chapter, I want to probe further the profound link Paul draws between peace practice and ecclesiology in Eph 4:1–6, as a modest supplement to Professor

---

1 Swartley, *Covenant of Peace*, 192n6.

2. Ibid., 218–19n75.

Swartley's splendid study and as a mark of deep appreciation for his example of humble, godly scholarship in the service of peace over many years.[3]

> I therefore, the prisoner in the Lord, beg you to lead a life worthy of the calling to which you have been called, with all humility and gentleness, with patience, bearing with one another in love, making every effort to maintain the unity of the Spirit in the bond of peace. There is one body and one Spirit, just as you were called to the one hope of your calling, one Lord, one faith, one baptism, one God and Father of all, who is above all and through all and in all. (Eph 4:1–6)[4]

The letter to the Ephesians opens with Paul's customary greeting: "To the saints who are faithful in Christ Jesus: Grace to you and peace from God our Father and the Lord Jesus Christ" (1:2). It closes on a virtually identical note: "Peace to the whole community, and love with faith, from God the Father and the Lord Jesus Christ; grace be with all who have an undying love for our Lord Jesus Christ" (6:23–24). The words "grace," "peace," and "faith" are singled out for mention at both the beginning and the end of the letter. This is significant, for the "bookends" of an epistle—how it begins and ends—often give an important clue about the author's main intention in the work. In the case of Ephesians, the bookends signal that Paul's overriding concern in this letter is to expound the gospel as a demonstration of God's boundless grace, love, faithfulness, and peacemaking, concepts that recur over and over again throughout the document.

In the first half of the epistle (chaps. 1–3), Paul recounts the "glorious grace" (1:6; cf. 2:4, 7–8) that God has shown in sending Jesus to secure the healing of the broken universe and to "make peace" (2:14–15) between hostile peoples. He reminds his readers of the transforming impact that God's gracious initiative has already had on their moral and spiritual experience. Once they were alienated from God, devoid of all hope in the world (which for Paul was particularly indicative of pagan lifestyle),[5] and subject to the

3 This chapter is a revised version of an address to the MWC 14 in Asunción, Paraguay, originally titled, "Together in the Way of Christ (Eph 4:1–6)," delivered 16 July 2009. The German translation appeared in Paraguay as "Gemeinsam auf dem Weg Jesu Christi."

4. All biblical quotations are taken from the NRSV unless otherwise indicated.

5. For Paul, the absence of hope was a telling characteristic of pagan society (Eph 2:12; cf. 1 Thess 4:13; 1 Cor 15:19), and stands in contrast to the hope engendered by the gospel (Eph 1:18; cf. Col 1:5; 1 Pet 1:13). Such Christian hope is not simply a matter of acquiring a sunny disposition; it is inseparable from faith in the "God of hope" (Rom 15:13) who has secured universal salvation by God's own power. As such, hope is a fundamental element of Christian character and is frequently mentioned as part of the

rule of malevolent spiritual forces that held them in a state of living death, puppets to their own sinful passions (2:2–3, 11–12; cf. 5:10). But now, as a result of God's "immeasurably rich grace" (2:7–8; cf. 1:6–8) and "immense love" (2:4; cf. 1:5, 15; 3:17, 19), they have been set free from spiritual oppression, pardoned of their sins, adopted as God's children, filled with the Holy Spirit, incorporated into the commonwealth of God's people, and infused with expectancy for the future (1:3–10; 2:11–21). "For by grace you have been saved through faith," Paul exults, "and this is not your own doing; it is the gift of God, not the result of works, so that no one may boast" (2:8–9). It is pure, unadulterated, life-giving, freedom-creating, salvation-effecting grace.

In the second half of the letter (chaps. 4–6), which commences with our passage in 4:1–6, Paul spells out the implications of God's gracious salvation for how his readers should live their current Christian lives. The passage begins with the significant little word "therefore" (*oun*). "I *therefore*, the prisoner in the Lord, beg you to lead a life worthy of the calling to which you have been called" (4:1). This "therefore" is incredibly important. It is intended, most likely, to refer back to everything covered in the first half of the letter. In light of all that has been said so far about God's sovereign saving grace, Paul now issues an ethical challenge to his readers to live in a manner commensurate with this reality.

In Paul's writings, theology and ethics are always held together inseparably, nowhere more clearly so than in Ephesians. On the one hand, good theology—right belief or true knowledge of God—*must* issue in transformed ethical living; otherwise it is mere speculative theory. The final test of truth is not philosophical or logical or even theological coherence, important though these are, but moral transformation. At the same time, good ethics depends ultimately on good theology. Sound ethical behavior is enriched and empowered by being grounded on true insight into divine truth. Christian ethical conduct is never mere external conformity to a set of objective moral rules; it is an entire way of life consistent with the full, experiential knowledge of God disclosed in Jesus Christ and infused with his Spirit.

Paul's "therefore" in verse 1 is intended to recall, I suggest, two particular themes from his previous discussion as the basis for his ethical injunction. One relates to Paul's own apostolic role and experience; the other to his readers' past and present experience of God's liberating power and love.

---

triad "faith, love, and hope" (1 Cor 13:13; 1 Thess 1:3; 5:8).

PAUL'S APOSTOLIC EXAMPLE

Paul frames his ethical appeal in strikingly personal terms, using an emphatic personal pronoun (*egō*): "I therefore, the prisoner in the Lord, beg you . . ." (4:1). It's *I* who am imploring you! Paul speaks not as one believer among many but as the apostle to the Gentiles, as one possessed of unique insight into the "mysterious thing" (1:9; 3:3, 9) that God has done through the Messiah to unify Jew and Gentile. "Although I am the very least of all the saints, this grace was given to me to bring to the Gentiles the news of the boundless riches of Christ, and to make everyone see what is the plan of the mystery hidden for ages in God who created all things" (3:8–9).

Paul considers himself to be a reliable mediator of "the word of truth, the gospel of your salvation" (1:13; cf. 4:21), so his appeal to his readers in chapter 4 is intended to carry distinctive weight. But significantly, it is not his unique revelatory role that Paul draws his readers' attention to here (cf. 3:2). Rather it is his patient, suffering witness as "the prisoner in the Lord," as one who, at the very time of writing, is suffering "for you," which is "your glory" (3:13). Paul mentions his imprisonment not to elicit sympathy from his readers but to attest to his faithful embodiment of the inescapable paradox that lies at the heart of the gospel.

What is this paradox? It is the fact that, to borrow the language of 2 Cor 4, "this extraordinary power from God" in the gospel is experienced in weak, fragile, defenseless, "jars of clay," in mortal bodies that still suffer, weaken, and die. In referring to himself as "the prisoner in the Lord," or later as "an ambassador in chains" (6:20; cf. 3:1, 13; 4:1), Paul highlights the suffering and affliction that have characterized his apostolic ministry. Yet in this self-same letter, he speaks simultaneously of "the immeasurable greatness of his *power* in us who believe, according to the working of his great might" (1:19), a power demonstrated in Christ's exaltation from death to the place of universal lordship (1:19–23; 4:8–10), an overwhelming power that prevails against every spiritual evil (6:10–20), a power that strengthens the inner being (3:16) and enables believers to know and be filled "with all the fullness of God" (3:19), "the power at work within us [that] is able to accomplish abundantly far more than all we can ask or imagine" (3:20).

The power of the gospel, then, is clearly not the power of coercion or control or command. It is not the power of violence that seeks exemption from suffering by ensuring that one possesses the necessary means to make others suffer instead. Paul has no power to avoid the chains of imprisonment! The power of the gospel, rather, is a peaceful power. It is a power in weakness. It is greater than the power of external coercion for it is the power of moral transformation and spiritual freedom "at work *within us* . . . to accomplish abundantly far more than all we can ask or imagine" (3.20). So the first thing the "therefore" in verse 1 recalls is Paul's paradigmatic experience of nonretributive, apostolic suffering in fidelity to the gospel of divine power. The second thing it recalls is his previous description of his readers' past experience of this liberating power of grace.

THE READERS' PREVIOUS EXPERIENCE

It is in view of what God has already done for you, Paul says, that you must now commit yourselves to a new way of living (literally, to a new way of "walking") in the world.[6] You must strive to "lead a life worthy of the calling to which you have been called." This is the central command—indeed, the only direct imperative—in our passage: Paul pleads with his readers to fashion lives that are consistent with the grace and love and peace they have received from God. In short, he calls on them to practice what they preach. Yes, they have been "saved by grace and not by works." But the purpose of having been showered in such grace is that that now, recreated in Christ Jesus, they should do good works and walk in them (2:8–10).

This is a feature of Paul's theology that Protestant interpreters have often not appreciated. Faith and works cannot be separated. It is not enough to know the truth of God's saving grace in our heads and hearts alone; it must be lived out in daily moral experience. Otherwise it counts for nothing. Or, as we might put it today, our ethics must match our theology. And since our theology is all about God's transforming grace, peace, and love, so too must be our ethics.

How does this work? What does it mean, in practice, to "lead a life worthy of the calling to which we have been called"? In Eph 4, it means one thing above all others: *it means being committed to reconciliation and peacemaking,* especially within the family of the church. It means "making every effort to maintain the unity of the Spirit in the bond of peace" (v. 3). Anabaptist Christians have tried to take this obligation seriously. They have rightly insisted that a dedication to peacemaking and reconciliation is not

---

6. In keeping with Jewish usage, Paul uses "walk" to designate one's whole manner of life. Faith in Christ means a changed walk (1 Cor 7:17; Eph 4:17). Baptism ends the walk in sin (Col 3:7) or walking according to the flesh (Rom 8:4), with all its indulgences (1 Thess 4:1–12). Instead believers are to walk in the Spirit (Gal 5:16), to walk worthy of God (1 Thess 2:12) or the Lord (Col 1:10) or their calling (Eph. 4:1), to walk as children of light (Eph 5:8). They still walk *in* the flesh (2 Cor 10:3), but not *according to* the flesh, not according to sinful dictates. The flesh is no longer in control; they now walk by faith (2 Cor 5:7) and in newness of life (Rom 6:4). Believers who do not walk as required are to be avoided (2 Thess 3:6, 11).

an optional extra for disciples of Jesus Christ. It is an indispensable ingredient of Christian faith. It lies at the very heart of discipleship. Without a commitment to peace, we deny the very "gospel of peace" (6:15) we proclaim. Without peacemaking, our Christian lives are, simply, *unworthy* of the calling to which we have been called. Our theology becomes mere theory, and our ethics is severely truncated. For that reason, Mennonites have often been at the forefront of peacemaking and conflict resolution initiatives in hostile environments all around the world, which is something to be justly proud of.

But the point that needs to be underscored here from Eph 4 is that the call to Christian peacemaking relates, first and foremost, to relationships within the community of faith. Certainly Christians must be agents for making peace in the wider world as well. But we will never be credible as peacemakers in a violent world unless we "make every effort to maintain the unity of the Spirit in the bond of peace" (v. 3) within our own congregations and between our great denominations.

Of course, as we know all too well, Christian churches often appear to be as bitterly divided and painfully crippled with conflict as is the surrounding world. Within local congregations, there are often broken relationships and unhealed hurts that alienate believers from one another. And between larger Christian denominations and theological traditions, there has been a shameful history of rancorous discord, competitive rivalry, and even violent bloodshed. Nothing has done more damage to the cause of Christ in the world, and nothing has more deeply stained the reputation of Christ's followers, than our involvement in violent or hated-filled conflict with one another. Nothing is more detrimental to the interests of the gospel than unwillingness by those who claim the name of Christ "to maintain the unity of the Spirit in the bond of peace."

Yet Paul calls on his readers to make "every effort" (*spoudazontes*) to do so. The verb *spoudazō* means to "make haste," hence to show diligence or make a determined effort. The present indicative participle is imperatival and suggests an eagerness of such intensity that one expends every ounce of energy one possesses in order to achieve it. But how is this to be done? What does striving tirelessly and zealously to maintain the unity of the Spirit in the bond of peace involve? According to our passage, it requires three things in particular.

The Content of Christian Calling

First of all, it requires Christians to be absolutely clear on the content of their Christian calling. Paul implores his readers to "lead a life worthy of the *calling* to which you have been *called*" (v. 1), and later speaks of the "one hope of your *calling*" (v. 4). To understand precisely what this calling is, we need to turn once again to the first half of the epistle. There Paul explains that believers are called to participate in and reap the initial benefits of God's great work of healing the universe through Jesus Christ. God's ultimate intention in salvation, Paul states at the very outset of the letter, is to *unite* "all things in him, things in heaven and things on earth" (1:10)—that is, to heal every rupture in the universe, to bring violence and antagonism to a definitive end, and to restore universal harmony to all creation. And Christians are called to be part of it! We are called to know the "mystery" of salvation (1:9, 18; 3:8–9; 5:32; 6:19) and make it known to others. We are called to tell and retell the story of God's reconciling love and healing grace in Jesus Christ, to proclaim to the whole world the one who "came and proclaimed peace to you who were far off and peace to those who are near" (2:17), who brought hostility to an end through his body on the cross, "thus making peace" (2:15–16).

The "calling to which you have been called," then, is the call to be involved in God's unifying, reconciling, peacemaking program in Jesus. Or as Paul puts it simply in 1 Cor 7:15, we are "called to peace." This means that to "lead a life worthy of our calling" is to lead a life of peacemaking, a life in which we practice unifying, restoring, reconciling grace in all our relationships, and especially in the body of Christ.

The Qualities of Christian Character

This leads to the second thing that must be done to "maintain the unity of the Spirit in the bond of peace": believers must intentionally cultivate in themselves, as individuals, those qualities of Christian character that are consistent with their calling. We must work diligently at developing those personal attributes and graces that are most essential to achieving reconciliation and peace in situations of tension and turmoil.

In our passage Paul mentions four virtues in particular: humility, gentleness, patience, and loving tolerance. These are not radically distinct qualities but different ways of expressing the same essential reality, though each term can be described separately. "With all humility" or lowliness (*pasēs tapeinofrosynēs*) means having the appropriate view of one's own weaknesses, faults, and limitations. "All lowliness" presumably means humility with respect to every kind of circumstance and every type of person.[7] "Gentleness" or meekness (*praytēs*) means doing nothing deliberately to hurt or humiliate another person. It includes both an inward attitude of humbleness and outward actions of kindness; it is the polar opposite of self-assertion, rudeness, and harshness. It is supremely defined by Jesus himself (2 Cor 10:1; cf. Matt 11:29) and should characterize those who follow him (Gal 5:23; 6:1; Col 3:12; 2 Tim 2:25; cf. Matt 5:5; 1 Pet 3:15). "Patience" or long-suffering (*makrothymia*) means a readiness to endure the discomfort of conflict without lashing out in revenge. It requires self-restraint to withstand adversity and absorb hurts without hastening to retaliate (cf. Gal 5:22; Col 1:11; 3:12; 2 Tim 4:2; Jas 5:10). "Tolerance" or "forbearing one another in love" (*anechromenoi allēlōn en agapē*) means making room for those whom we may disagree with, and may not even like very much, but to whom we are eternally bound by our common calling in the love of Christ. When these four interrelated virtues are present, when these moral disciplines are individually and collectively cultivated, it is possible for believers to overcome any conflict or injury that threatens the unity of the Spirit in the bond of peace.

The Meaning of the Church

This brings us to the third crucial requirement for sustaining Christian unity and peace. Paul summons his readers—in addition to being clear on the content of their Christian calling, and on the Christ-like qualities of character they must cultivate—to be crystal clear on what the church actually is, on what it really means to be members of the body of Christ. A commitment to peace flows from a clear-sighted ecclesiology.

It is hugely significant that Paul tells his readers in verse 3 not to *create* the unity of the Spirit in the bond of peace but to *maintain* it (*tēreō*). The unity of the church is not something its members manufacture by being unusually nice to one another. It is something that already exists. It is an objective reality, effected by the Spirit of God. Notwithstanding the church's

---

7. Outside the Judeo-Christian tradition, humility was regarded as a vice, typical of slaves. It designated an abject lack (or loss) of power and prestige, a condition of servile weakness and lowliness. In biblical tradition, however, humility is esteemed. It denotes grateful awareness that life is a gift, i.e., human beings are finally and utterly dependent on the grace and power of one who is greater than they. Such awareness, a consciousness of the universal contingency and equality of all people before God, should be reflected in all their relationships. Jesus exemplified such humility (Phil 2:6–8; Matt 11:29; Mark 10:45).

immense diversity and frequently fractious history, the truth is that there is only "*one* body" and "*one* Spirit" (4:4), just as there is "*one* Lord" (4:5) and "*one* God and Father of us all" (4:6). The word "one" recurs no fewer than eight times in three verses. It is desperately important to Paul. The oneness of the church is every bit as fundamental to Christian orthodoxy as the oneness of God and the lordship of Christ.[8] It is a truth of profound consequence.

There are, I suggest, two reasons why, as far as Paul is concerned, there is one church and can only ever be but one church. The first is because the church belongs to Jesus Christ, and there is only one Jesus Christ. The church is not just a human institution or a social organization or a voluntary club or an association of like-minded individuals or even a global communion of co-religionists. It is the "body of Christ"—the very embodiment of Jesus Christ on earth, the visible expression of Christ's personal presence in the world. It comprises all those who have been united personally with Christ through "one faith and one baptism" (v. 5), and who are therefore inextricably united to one another.[9] Paul never tires of stressing the oneness of the church simply because it is the church of Christ, and there is only one Christ, and Christ has only one body, and that body is his one church.

The second reason why the oneness of the church is so critical is because of what the church itself represents in the saving purposes of God. We have seen that God's ultimate intention in salvation is to heal every wound in the universe, to bring tribal violence and antagonism to an end forever, and to restore universal concord to all creation—to unite "all things in him, things in heaven and things on earth" (1:10). This is the "one hope of your calling" mentioned in 4:4—the hope of witnessing creation's ultimate healing and restoration in Christ. But this great hope of cosmic reconciliation

8. Trinitarian implications are clearly present here: one Spirit, one Lord, and one Father. Whether there is any intended pattern in the ordering of elements here is unclear. But it is perhaps significant that Paul moves from the empirical community of faith ("one body"), energized and infused with hope by the "one Spirit," to the "one Lord," whose personal body it is and with whom believers are united through "one faith and one baptism," to the ultimacy of "one God and Father" who rules invisibly over all things. The visible church bears witness to God's invisible universal sovereignty.

9. Some interpreters take "one faith" to refer to the Christian faith as a settled body of doctrinal truth (cf. Eph 4:15; Acts 6:7; Jude 3; 2 Tim 2:2); others take it to denote the subjective act of believing in God (cf. Col 2:7). Similarly "one baptism" is seen by some as a reference to water baptism, and by others to Spirit baptism (cf. 1 Cor 12:13). It seems best to take "one faith . . . one baptism" as a unified reference to Christian initiation in general, the total means by which the Spirit makes a living union between believers and the person and work of Christ. "One faith—one baptism" designates the sole and singular way of joining the church, which is through willing surrender to the work of God's Spirit.

is not a hazy dream for the far-distant future. The good news of the gospel is that it has already commenced. Cosmic restoration is already underway. It has already started to impinge directly on human experience, bringing dramatic and powerful change, even now.

But where is this eschatological healing to be seen? Where is this cosmic change already occurring? In the church! God's ultimate, saving purposes are made transparent, Paul believes, in the existence and character of the church. For the church is a new kind of human society, one that is held together not by the bonds of race, class, language, religion, nationality, or culture but by "the bond of peace" (4:3)—that is, by the unique bond of fellowship forged by the peacemaking work of Jesus Christ on the cross (2:14–22).[10]

The church is the only kind of human community that is not racially defined, or class defined, or gender defined, or law defined, or culture defined, or occupation defined, or even religion defined. It is *Christ* defined. It derives its identity solely from its living union with the singular person of Jesus Christ, an identity that transcends all other human distinctions of race, class, gender, or culture, and thus provides a unique basis for human solidarity. The multiracial, multicultural, and transtemporal church represents and prefigures the final unifying of all things in creation. The church is the fellowship of all those who share the common experience of being reconciled to their creator God through Jesus Christ, and who discover, in that common experience, a new basis of kinship with one another. That is why there can be only one church, for the church is, by definition, a community of the reconciled, and a divided community of the reconciled is a contradiction in terms. The church of the reconciled must, of theological necessity, be a single, unified, peacemaking body—a community of the reconciled and of reconcilers.

Paul insists, then, that there is only one church, there is only one body of Christ, there is only one Holy Spirit who indwells that body, just as there is only one Lord and one God and Father of us all, for it can be no other way.

---

10. "Bond of peace" is usually construed either as a genitive of result ("the bond that results in or maintains peace," the bond itself being mutual love; see Col 3:14–15) or as a genitive of description (the "bond that is itself peace"; see Eph 2:14). Perhaps it is most helpfully described as a genitive of means: peace is the means by which the bond of unity is achieved. Peace is not some generic kind of harmony but a specific reference to the messianic peacemaking work of Christ on the cross ("for he is our peace," 2:14). It is by their co-participation in his peace work that believers are unified in the one body of Christ (2:11–21). Christian unity is not, therefore, something to be achieved by coercion or forced uniformity; it is something gifted from beyond by the peacemaking work and Spirit of Christ.

The unity of the church is a divine fact, for Christ is not, and can never be, divided (1 Cor 1:13).

But this objective unity of the church is also something that must be maintained or kept or preserved. The spiritual oneness of the church must be lived out at a practical or ethical level. Our common union in Christ must become visible in a steadfast commitment by every believer, in every congregation, and every Christian denomination, in every place and at every time, to confront the strife and discord that inevitably arise in human relationships in a way that "makes for peace" (Rom 14:19), to deal with our conflicts and differences in a manner that refuses hatred or malice or bitterness, but instead practices humility, gentleness, patience, and tolerance.

Of course, this is not easy, and it is never cheap. Maintaining the unity of the Spirit in the bond of peace is difficult—so difficult that it requires us to make "every effort" to achieve it. Christian unity is costly because the peace that Christ demands is always a *just* peace. It is not simply the cessation of conflict but the positive attainment of relations of equality, justice, mutual respect, dignity, and freedom (cf. 2:17–19). To attain to the unity of the Spirit in the bond of Christian peace obliges us to speak "the truth in love" to one another (4:15)—to speak truthfully of the hurts and wrongs and sins that divide us, but always to do so only in a spirit of love, and with the intention of building the body up in love (4:16), not of winning our corner.

We have seen how in the opening pericope of Eph 4, which commences the second half of Paul's majestic epistle, the apostle summons his readers to "live a life worthy of the calling to which they have been called" in Christ. In practice this means a steadfast determination to honor the unity of Christ's body, which is a foretaste of universal reconciliation, by cultivating relationships of humility, gentleness, patience, and forbearance. Christian peacemaking is grounded in, and a vital expression of, ecclesiology.

23

Paul, Peace, and Apocalyptic

Jacob W. Elias

An exploration of how Paul's theology informs his understanding of peace needs to be undertaken from within an articulation of his core faith affirmations. Does Paul's understanding of the righteousness of God and justification by faith relate in any way to his convictions about the ethical and political implications of the gospel? This study begins with a survey of scholarship on this broad question, but it also considers how social world analyses have contributed to our understandings.

To bring specificity to this discussion, this paper continues by focusing on 2 Thessalonians. The apocalyptic cast of this letter has made it a fertile source for some preachers in their articulation of scenarios of the end times. Interpreters not disposed toward this kind of hermeneutic have tended to relegate this letter to the sidelines. Does the author of this letter urge individuals to prepare themselves to escape the evil world when the Day of the Lord comes? Or might it be the case that this epistle actually seeks to promote communal resilience and faithfulness to God within a hostile environment?

THE GOSPEL OF SALVATION

Salvation has often been viewed as an individualized spiritual experience. However, there have also been voices urging that salvation be understood within a broader theological framework: God's saving activity takes place on a cosmic stage and leads to potential social and political transformation. The work of Perry Yoder[1] and Willard Swartley[2] demonstrates that salvation as portrayed in both OT and NT writings encompasses dimensions of human experience beyond the appropriation of its personal benefits. The challenge before us here is to ascertain the extent to which current scholarship demonstrates the conviction that Paul's view of salvation includes social transformation and peacemaking.

In his search for the essence of Paul's thought, J. Christiaan Beker argues that the coherent center of Paul's thought is the triumph of God. Building on the work of Albert Schweitzer and Ernst Käsemann, Beker sees an apocalyptic framework in Paul's theology: "Paul's coherent center is marked not only by an apocalyptic matrix and pattern but also by a future orientation which gives his thought its driving thrust. The pulsating quality of his thought does not find a respite until it climaxes in the arrival of the triumph of God which will turn all present approximations and ambiguities into the joy of everlasting peace."[3] Such peace, though personal, is not individualistic; though future oriented, is not escapist; though confident of God's ultimate triumph over evil, is not triumphalistic. Again, Beker: "And so we must continue to be agitators for the kingdom, joyful that in Christ we may detect and erect some signs of its dawning, and yet burdened because God's triumph has not yet defeated the awful powers of injustice, suffering, and death in our world."[4] From this central conviction, Beker argues, Paul articulates the contingent consequences within each congregation in his care.

This apocalyptic matrix characterizing Paul's pastoral counsel for congregations has been widely recognized. J. Louis Martyn identifies what he calls Paul's "bi-focal vision of apocalyptic" within which the gospel of Jesus Christ is recognized as an invasion of God's grace into the orbit of evil and sin. Martyn describes the consequences of this powerful "new creation" invasion through Christ into the "Old Age": "The basic characteristic of the present time is given in the fact that it is the juncture of the Old Age and the new creation. To use a spatial image, it is the arena made what it is by the fact that God's new creation is invading the Old Age in a kind of jungle warfare. The 'now' about which Paul speaks as the now of salvation is the

---

1. Yoder, *Shalom*; Yoder and Swartley, *The Meaning of Peace*.
2. Swartley, *Covenant of Peace*.
3. Beker, *Triumph of God*, xii.
4. Beker, *Paul's Apocalyptic Gospel*, 120.

redemptive now because it is the now of God's apocalyptic war of liberation, not the now of a retreat from the real world."[5]

In advocating for this view of how God's salvation through Christ breaks into the social and political realities of the day, Martyn argues that Paul espouses "cosmological apocalyptic eschatology," whereas other Jewish teachers advocate "forensic apocalyptic eschatology." The cosmological view sees redemption as liberation from the powers; within the forensic view the emphasis is on the individual's acceptance of God's law, receiving forgiveness for sins of disobedience, and thereby being assured of eternal life.[6]

It is the forensic view that gained dominance within Christian theology, with justification by faith replacing reliance on the Law and its ritual provisions for atonement. Such sidelining of the Law and its rituals has often led to the view that Paul regards Judaism as a failed effort to gain salvation through legalistic observance of the Law. E. P. Sanders in his groundbreaking analysis of patterns of religion contemporary with Paul confronts such dismissal of Judaism. Sanders argues that Paul's insight was that "the believer becomes one with Christ Jesus and that this effects a transfer of lordship and the beginning of a transformation that will be completed with the coming of the Lord."[7]

Other scholars within the so-called New Perspective have recognized that, as Jewish apostle to the Gentiles, Paul sees God's creative and restorative work through Jesus the Messiah as both continuing and fulfilling the earlier divine narrative. Of particular relevance in our pursuit of the ethical relevance of Paul's gospel is the work of Douglas A. Campbell, who in one book lays out a strategy for rescuing Paul from "Lutheran" understandings of the gospel[8] and in another painstakingly pursues this strategy.[9] Vigorously refuting scholars who see justification by faith as the coherent core of Paul's theology, Campbell argues for an apocalyptic framework within which Paul understands salvation; he calls this the "pneumatically participatory martyrological eschatology" model.[10]

In Paul's soteriology, Campbell insists, God rescues and transforms.[11] Jesus refused to respond violently to the unjust crucifixion that led to his

5. Martyn, *Theological Issues*, 283.

6. Ibid., 298–99.

7. Sanders, *Paul and Palestinian Judaism*, 549.

8. Campbell, *Quest for Paul's Gospel*.

9. Campbell, *Deliverance of God*.

10. Campbell, *Quest for Paul's Gospel*, 29–68.

11. This paragraph offers a précis of Campbell, *Deliverance of God*, 89–94, an excursus "The Case—Briefly—against Coercive Violence in Paul."

death; he submitted, endured the shame, and died as a martyr. Those who follow Jesus participate in his death, steadfastly suffering violence without retaliating, thereby receiving assurance of resurrection life, experienced already although its consummation is still future. In anticipation of this eschatological victory, believers abandon vengeful retaliation and entrust themselves to God, whose warfare against oppressive powers continues to seek to rescue those enslaved by these powers. Campbell defines God's righteousness as "the deliverance of God."[12] God's wrath is not the anger of affronted justice requiring satisfaction through divine violence against the Son; it is God's aggrieved love working to eliminate evil by defeating the power of sin.

In addition to the contributions of scholars whose primary effort has been to identify afresh the center of Pauline theology, there have been lively discussions about how Paul's strategy of planting churches intersected with the Roman imperial context. Especially pertinent has been the work of scholars engaging in analyses of the social and political world within which Paul circulated. Topics include "the gospel of imperial salvation" and "Paul's counter-imperial Gospel."[13] These scholars not only pursue a faithful understanding of Paul in his context but are also intent on dismantling what has frequently been a reading of Paul's theology that promotes unquestioned obedience to the state, acceptance of slavery, suppression of women, and dismissive attitudes toward ethnic and other minorities.[14]

As can be expected, traditional readings of Paul's gospel continue to be defended.[15] However, our brief survey has shown that persistent voices among NT scholars have promoted socially and politically relevant understandings of the gospel proclaimed by Paul. This gospel has clear implications for ethics generally and more specifically for the church's role in peacemaking.

In an effort to move beyond a general overview we turn now to a specific epistle: 2 Thessalonians. This study provides an opportunity both to test whether the new paradigm in Pauline studies might open fruitful

---

12. Ibid., 699–702.

13. These are subheadings in Horsley, *Paul and Empire*. Scholars contributing essays in Horsley, *Paul and Politics* and *Paul and the Roman Imperial Order* ground this discussion further both through exegesis of particular texts and through the application of rhetorical and social world analytical methodologies.

14. A contribution that pre-dates the volumes edited by Horsley is that of Elliott, *Liberating Paul*, which seeks both to elucidate Paul's liberative message and to liberate Paul from being co-opted by readings that oppress. See also Harink, *Paul among the Postliberals*, especially chapter 3, "Politics."

15. For example, Westerholm, *Perspectives Old and New on Paul.*

understandings into this apocalyptic treatise and to cast some new light on an obscure and (in some circles, at least) hotly contested text.

REASSURED BY GOD'S RIGHTEOUS JUDGMENT

In 2 Thess 2:6–7, Paul[16] alludes to an enigmatic force (*to katechon*) and a personality (*ho katechōn*) with dramatic roles in an eschatological drama. The verses immediately preceding portray a situation which Paul characterizes as "the rebellion"[17] (*hē apostasia*, literally "the apostasy"): an antagonist[18] takes his seat in the temple of God and there proclaims "I am God" (2:3–4). The verses that follow first depict a holy war in which the Lord Jesus slays the antagonist with the breath of his mouth (2:8). As backdrop for this dramatic scene Paul next enlarges on the role of Satan, who acts through the antagonist with power, signs, and lying wonders, and whose deceptive antics threaten to sidetrack the believers from the way of truth and righteousness (2:9–12).

This apocalyptic drama, viewed within the rhetoric and argument of 2 Thessalonians as a whole, becomes an intriguing case study in our pursuit of an understanding of how Paul's theology relates to the theme of peace. We proceed in several stages. First, we examine the literary framework and the historical and political circumstances in first-century Thessalonica in light of which Paul's apocalyptic drama in 2 Thess 2:1–12, and specifically 2:6–7, can be understood. Next we sketch the theological framework within which Paul interprets the life and witness of the Thessalonian believers. Finally, we outline several proposals for understanding the relationship between apocalyptic and peace.

Paul's overarching theological framework becomes apparent when one examines how 2 Thess 2:1–12 fits within its literary context. The opening

16. The authorship of 2 Thess continues to be contested among Pauline scholars. Vigorous arguments have been made for pseudonymous authorship toward the end of the first century (Richards, *1 and 2 Thessalonians*, 19–29). However, some scholars argue that one of the co-authors named in the epistolary prescript (Timothy or Silvanus) or an amanuensis might have drafted the letter in about 50 or 51 CE, shortly after the writing of 1 Thess (Holmes, *1 & 2 Thessalonians*, 25–27; Fee, *The First and Second Letters*, 237–41; cf. also Elias, *1 and 2 Thessalonians*, 24–28, 374–77). In the discussion that follows, the presumption is that Paul or a partner or an amanuensis wrote this letter shortly after writing the first letter to the Thessalonians.

17. Unless otherwise noted, all translations are my own.

18. For the sake of brevity and convenience I suggest the label "antagonist" for the eschatological tyrant who is described in a variety of ways: *ho anthōpos tēs anomias* and *ho hios tēs apōleias* (2:3), *ho antikeimenos kai huperairomenos* (2:4), and *ho anomos* (2:8). Similarly Holland, *Tradition*, 46.

thanksgiving in this letter already sounds the dissonant chords of suffering, affliction, vengeance, and eternal destruction (1:3–10). However, it concludes with an upbeat intercessory prayer report (1:11) and a doxological announcement of the assured outcome: "So that the name of our Lord Jesus may be glorified in you, and you in him, according to the grace of our God and the Lord Jesus Christ" (1:12). In short, themes of prayer and worship precede Paul's apocalyptic diagnosis in 2:1–12. Strikingly similar themes surface in the paragraph immediately following. The graphic language about the demise of the antagonist and the believers' risk of being deceived by Satanic signs and wonders in 2:9–12 gives way to a renewed call to thanksgiving (2:13). Why give thanks? "God chose you as first fruits for salvation"! A reminder concerning the outcome of God's call again follows: "So that you may obtain the glory of our Lord Jesus Christ" (2:14). God's grace and glory provide the big picture within which the Christian community in its worship and daily life is reminded to view itself, even when (or perhaps especially when) it experiences adversity and affliction.

Second Thessalonians was written to a suffering church. Indeed, both letters to the church at Thessalonica provide glimpses into their experiences of affliction: 1 Thess 1:6; 2:14; 3:3, 4; 2 Thess 1:4, 6. Judging from the mood and content of 2 Thess 1:3–4, the suffering of the Thessalonian believers had intensified by the time the second letter was written. The theme of the righteous judgment of God in 1:5–10 points clearly to a question of special concern when the faith community suffers adversity—namely, where is God's justice?

What was the nature of their suffering? On the basis of Stoic and Cynic parallels, Abraham Malherbe argues that the affliction experienced by the Thessalonian believers was "the distress and anguish of heart experienced by persons who broke with their past as they received the gospel."[19] However, the references to suffering in the Thessalonian Christian community are more plausible when their affliction is recognized as the result of social opposition and physical persecution. The fact that the new believers in Thessalonica dealt with grief at the death of some of their members (1 Thess 4:13) also suggests the possibility that these persons had died as the result of persecution.[20]

If the community experienced some form of persecution, what factors might have provoked it? The political dynamics that shaped first-century Thessalonica contain clues.[21] In 146 BCE, Thessalonica was named capital of

19. Malherbe, *Paul and the Thessalonians*, 48.
20. Donfried, "The Imperial Cults of Thessalonica," 220–23.
21. Horsley, *Paul and Empire*, 10–24; cf. also Donfried, "The Imperial Cults"; and

the Roman province of Macedonia. Because of well placed political support for what turned out to be the winning side in a major battle during the Roman Civil War, Thessalonica in 42 BCE had been granted considerable freedom to run its own civic affairs. However, the city officials in Thessalonica also found it politically and economically expedient to continue to actively cultivate the goodwill of the Roman emperors and the support of Roman benefactors. Through games, monuments, a temple of Caesar, the minting of coins, and various civic rituals, the city politicians endeavored to cultivate and maintain the enthusiastic allegiance of the population toward the Roman imperial power.[22] Local officials wanted to keep the population in harmony with the aims of the empire. The empire in turn conferred benefits, not the least of which was the promise of peace and security (see 1 Thess 5:3). To help flush out dissenters, the city and provincial officials administered an oath of allegiance to Caesar. For those residents of Thessalonica who for political or religious reasons could not pledge such loyalty, the consequences could be severe, even fatal. In confessing Christ rather than Caesar as Lord, and in refusing to participate in the rituals designed to exalt and honor Caesar, the believers in Thessalonica came under suspicion. As Luke later puts it, while the city officials sought to administer "the decrees of the emperor," the missionaries proclaimed the subversive message of "another king named Jesus" (Acts 17:6–7).[23] The church in its worship and its public life therefore came to be viewed officially as potentially seditious, and oppression and sporadic persecution emerged as a result.

In this political climate the meaning of *to katechon* and *ho katechōn* in 2 Thess 2:6, 7 comes more clearly into view. The prevailing understanding of *katechon/katechōn* continues to be that Paul here refers to the Roman Empire as restraining force and the emperor as restrainer keeping the end time antagonist at bay until the Day of the Lord, thereby assuring the church of a measure of stability during the interim period.[24] However, the

---

"Religions in the Greco-Roman World," in Elias, *1 and 2 Thessalonians*, 366–68.

22. For archeological and epigraphic evidence regarding the emperor cult in Thessalonica: Hendrix, "Archeology and Eschatology," 107–18.

23. Judge, "Decrees," 1–7.

24. The traditional view, which dates back to Tertullian (*ca.* 145–220 CE), suggests that through the imperial structures of law and order the empire and the emperor respectively impose limits on the antagonist. Other proposals have also been put forward: the apostolic preaching of the gospel and the apostle Paul himself exert such a restraining influence, since the gospel first needs to be preached to all the nations before the end comes (cf. Mark 13:10); *to katechon* and *ho katechōn* both point to God who through an angel or the Holy Spirit delays the final revelation of the antagonist. For representatives of these views, and discussion: Elias, *1 and 2 Thessalonians*, 282–83. Giblin, *Threat to Faith,* 167–242 identifies *to katechon* as the misleading prophecy that

imagery employed in the description of the eschatological drama in 2 Thess 2:1–12 suggests instead that the emperor and the empire (*to katechon* and *ho katechōn*) are experienced by the church as hostile and oppressive.[25] The underlying verb *katechō* has a range of meanings, including "to lay legal claim, take possession, seize, oppress, hinder, restrain, or prevail."[26] Employing secretive language, Paul depicts the religious, political, and cultural power of the Roman empire as *to katechon,* and he portrays the emperor and those who administer his policies as *ho katechōn.* The hearers of the letter will have heard a veiled reference to the imperial structures that laid legal claim on them by imposing an ideology foreign to their commitment to Christ as Lord. Paul alludes to the fact that "the mystery of lawlessness is already at work" (2:7), an oblique reference to the imperial cult that increasingly became integrated into the rituals of the mystery religions. Paul will have longed for the Thessalonian congregation to understand that their affliction came as a consequence of their rejection of the ultimate claims the imperial ideology made on their allegiance. One dimension of this pervasive ideological structure of the empire was the pressure on the citizens and subject peoples to join in the public rites showing homage to the emperor.

In light of this reconstruction of the historical and political circumstances facing the Christians in Thessalonica, Paul's enigmatic language in 2 Thess 2:6–7 can be restated as follows: "And now the oppression (the imperial ideological structures) you know so that he (the antagonist) may be revealed in his time. For the mystery of lawlessness works already; only the oppressor (the emperor through the administrators of the imperial ideology) [works] already until he is taken from the midst."

Reference to the removal of the oppressor in 2:7 anticipates the graphic portrayal of the climactic holy war in 2:8–12. As precursor to the later antagonist, the oppressor whom the Thessalonians know now will be dislodged. The divine passive points clearly to God as the active agent. The demise of the oppressor anticipates the downfall of the future antagonist, who as Satan's deputy seeks to deceive the believers through imperial signs and wonders, but he will ultimately face defeat himself. Paul deploys holy war rhetoric to encourage his hearers to stand firm against the claims of the Roman establishment. The God whom they worship and serve will ultimately win the victory! This God deserves their ongoing worship. God is faithful, and can be trusted to bring deliverance.

"the day of the Lord is already here" (2:2) and *ho katechōn* as the frenzied false prophet who exerts a spellbinding influence in the Christian community.

25. Wanamaker, *Epistles to the Thessalonians,* 252–57 proposes that the writer here cryptically names a rebellious force and its human agent.

26. Krodel, "The 'Religious Power of Lawlessness,'" 440–46.

In Paul's apocalyptic vision, the triumph of Christ's resurrection anticipates and foreshadows God's ultimate triumph over all the powers.[27] In the community shaped and empowered by this vision, this future triumph invades the present.[28] For the Christian community the eschatological future is already present, the end-time has already come. As Elisabeth Schüssler Fiorenza puts it, "Since early Christian apocalyptic does not just hope for eschatological salvation in the near future but also knows that the end-time is already inaugurated through the exaltation and resurrection of Jesus Christ, it no longer thinks in terms of two succeeding aeons and worlds but maintains the contemporaneity of this world and the world to come with respect to Jesus Christ and to the Christian community. There is only one time, the end-time."[29]

Given the political ethos of the Roman Empire, even the congregation's worship of God as made known in Jesus Christ came readily to be viewed by the imperial powers as defiant and subversive. Leaders in the cities and provinces of the empire responded by strengthening their insistence that all citizens and subject peoples participate in the imperial cult. Harassment and persecution of dissidents therefore came as a result.

Yet, as the opening thanksgiving section of Paul's second letter to the church at Thessalonica shows, even this official oppression ("all your persecutions and afflictions that you are enduring" [1:4]) comes to be pictured by Paul as "evidence of the righteous judgment of God" (1:5). Within the framework of thanksgiving and worship, even their affliction can be understood as evidence that God will (and does) judge justly. Persecution itself does not elicit thanksgiving; the Thessalonians' steadfastness and faithfulness in the midst of such persecution provides occasion for boasting and thanksgiving.[30] When suffering for their witness to the lordship of Christ and the ultimate triumph of God, the Thessalonian believers in their weakness give powerful proof that God's justice will finally prevail. As Paul goes on to say, God will repay with affliction those who persecute others, and will grant relief to those who are afflicted (1:6–7). Such a dramatic reversal

---

27. The assurance of God's triumph over the powers, and the ethical stance in harmony with it, is one of the major themes of Wink's trilogy on the powers: *Naming the Powers*; *Unmasking the Powers*; and esp., *Engaging the Powers*.

28. Peters, "Eschatological Sanctions," speaks of "the proleptic presence of God's eschatological future" (130), which sanctions the life of Christian faithfulness. Wink, *Engaging the Powers*, 323, puts it this way: "Faith does not wait for God's sovereignty to be established on earth; it behaves as if that sovereignty already holds full sway."

29. Schüssler Fiorenza, "Early Christian Apocalyptic," 312.

30. For an elaboration of this understanding of the "evidence of the righteous judgment of God," see Elias, *1 and 2 Thessalonians*, 256–58.

of fortunes still lies in the future ("when the Lord Jesus is revealed from heaven" [1:7]), but the awareness of God's ultimate vindication inspires those who are suffering to remain faithful even while they endure their present distress. In short, God's deliverance of the faithful from their affliction, definitely assured in the future, also pertains to their circumstances in the present.

Clearly Paul urges communal resilience and faithfulness to God within a hostile environment. The message that comforts the afflicted afflicts the comfortable. God's judgment both reassures the victims and threatens those who wield their power unjustly. Paul employs picturesque language and graphic images reminiscent of prophetic and apocalyptic in the Hebrew Bible to portray the execution of God's justice (1:7–9). The Lord Jesus as holy warrior annihilates the antagonist with the breath of his mouth (2:8).

GOD'S SAVING JUSTICE

Paul's apocalyptic scenarios depicting the deliverance of God in violent terms urge reflection on whether holy war imagery can inform peacemaking.

Biblical apocalyptic literature generally asks to be understood through the experiences of the suffering and the disadvantaged. Through a constitutive reading of apocalyptic texts,[31] the poor and the oppressed receive assurance that, contrary to what their present circumstances may suggest, the faithful and just God will ultimately prevail over the powers that lay claim to their allegiance and seek to create conformity to imperial ideology. Graphic judgment imagery may provide a measure of catharsis[32] or a sense of social power[33] for those who suffer persecution. However, this literature does not invite gloating anticipation of the time when God will destroy the enemies, nor does it endorse passive waiting for the time when judgment will fall. Ultimately judgment and vengeance can and must be left to God. In short, the notion of divine justice removes revenge from the human realm and leaves judgment where it belongs—with God.

But how can this understanding of God as judge be harmonized with the picture of God as loving and compassionate to all? Miroslav Volf reflects on the ironic fact that Jesus suffers violence on the cross but as exalted

---

31. Sanders, *Canon and Community*, 53, distinguishes between two hermeneutic axioms: "That of prophetic critique when God as God of *all* is stressed; and that of a constitutive mode when God as particular Redeemer of Israel or church is stressed."

32. Collins, *Crisis and Catharsis.*

33. Meeks, "Social Functions of Apocalyptic Language."

Christ acts violently.[34] How are we to understand the violence that Jesus Christ as the crucified Messiah suffered and the violence he inflicts with the breath of his mouth (2 Thess 2:8)? Volf points out that the Gospels portray Jesus as one who sought to overcome violence by refusing to participate in it. As for the violence inflicted by the fire-breathing cosmic Christ, Volf suggests that this kind of imagery is "the symbolic portrayal of the final exclusion of everything that refuses to be redeemed by God's suffering love."[35] He continues, "For the sake of the peace of God's good creation, we can and must affirm *this* divine anger and *this* divine violence, while at the same time holding on to the hope that in the end, even the flag bearer will desert the army that desires to make war against the Lamb."[36] Indeed, "Without entrusting oneself to the God who judges justly, it will hardly be possible to follow the crucified Messiah and refuse to retaliate when abused. The certainty of God's just judgment at the end of history is the presupposition for the renunciation of violence in the middle of it. The divine system of judgment is not the flip side of the human reign of terror, but a necessary correlate of human non-violence."[37]

In a word, judgment calls for divine violence, the violence of removing and excluding those whose choices and actions put themselves outside the realm of God's new creation. The *katechon/katechōn* will be taken from the midst; the antagonist will be destroyed. The key question is, "Who exercises such violent judgment?" And the reply is clear: vengeance belongs to God. With grieved compassion and constantly renewed call to repentance, God judges with righteousness and truth and will exercise final judgment.

What, then, is the consequent ethic? God judges justly, even to the point of excluding those who persist in perpetuating injustice through oppression and deceit. The community of faith is invited to exercise revolutionary trust in the God who judges justly. Such trust involves neither passive waiting for God to act nor violent activism. The God who acts justly is the holy warrior, who enters into conflict with the forces of evil in the world. The faith community's response to God's promise of deliverance is to testify and to act. However, such activity in response to injustice, oppression, and violence is neither "redemptive violence" (fight) nor "pacifism" (flight) but Jesus's "third way" of nonviolent engagement.[38] Ted Peters talks about the "transformatory power in proleptic ethics": "We begin with an

---

34. Volf, *Exclusion and Embrace*, chap. 7.

35. Ibid., 299.

36. Ibid.; italics original.

37. Ibid., 302.

38. See Wink, *Engaging the Powers*, pt. 3: "Engaging the Powers Nonviolently."

eschatological vision of God's new creation and then seek transformation of the present world in light of it. Rather than a sedative, the promise of heaven is a stimulus to earthly action."[39]

God as holy warrior works for justice and fights against evil. God's people are called to be fully engaged in this warfare, but participation in God's liberating agenda does not include the use of violence. The church as God's warriors does not engage in a Zealot-like militant fight for personal or national liberation. Nor does this stance permit passivity, simply trusting God to deliver without human cooperation. As spiritual warriors, the Christian community joins the Divine Warrior in working toward wholeness, peace, and justice. The weapons for the believers' participation in this battle are faith and love and the hope of salvation (see 1 Thess 5:8). In the end, God will triumph. The community of faith, even while suffering, lives already in the joyous reality of this final victory.

---

39. Peters, "Eschatological Sanctions," 150.

24

Shalom in the Book of Revelation

God, Church, Judgment, New Creation

Michael J. Gorman

The title of this essay is counterintuitive, if not oxymoronic. One is tempted to look at it and cry, "'Peace, peace' when there is no peace" (Jer 6:14; 8:11). The Greek word *eirēnē* only appears twice in Revelation (1:4; 6:4). Moreover, the book's unpeaceful, even violent character has led some to criticize its content sharply and even question its presence in the Christian canon, as Willard Swartley and others have noted.[1]

Despite such concerns, there is more to Revelation than scenes of violence. As even the sharpest critics must recognize, there are beautiful, peaceful scenes in the book's conclusion—which is also, of course, the conclusion to the Christian canon. Furthermore, a careful reading of Revelation unveils several dimensions of *shalom* within its pages. We will briefly explore four of these dimensions—God, church, judgment, and new creation—and consider their theological significance both for the book itself and for those who receive it as Scripture.[2]

---

1. Swartley, *Covenant of Peace*, 324; cf. Gorman, *Reading Revelation*, 1–4.

2. This is a huge subject that can be touched on only lightly in this essay. For recent work stressing peace and/or nonviolence in Rev, see Swartley, *Covenant of Peace*, 324–55; my *Reading Revelation*; Bredin, *Jesus*; Hays and Alkier, eds., *Revelation and Politics of Interpretation*; Neville, *Peaceable Hope*, 217–45; and Yoder Neufeld, *Killing Enmity*, 123–35.

SHALOM

There has been significant recent work on shalom/*eirēnē*/peace in the Bible, not least in the writings of the two scholars honored in this book, and in the ripple effects of their work.[3] For our purposes, we will define shalom rather generally. First, negatively, shalom is the cessation—and henceforth the absence—of chaos, conflict, broken relations, and the evil powers that cause these things. Second, positively, shalom is the establishment, and henceforth the presence, of wholeness, reconciliation, goodness, justice, and the flourishing of creation.

Shalom, therefore, is clearly a thick theological term (and reality), a kind of semantic magnet that draws other terms (and realities) into its orb. Swartley contends that shalom in the Christian OT is semantically and theologically related to righteousness and justice, salvation, eschatology, the kingdom of God, covenant, and grace. *Eirēnē*, in the NT, is related to love of God, neighbor, and enemy, including nonretaliation; faith, hope, holiness, and harmony in the corporate body; blessing and wholeness; reconciliation and new covenant; salvation and grace; and kingdom of God, righteousness, justice, and justification.[4]

Shalom, then, is relational and specifically covenantal, a situation in which humans are in proper relation to one another, God, and the whole creation. This is a situation for which God's people long, experiencing it only partially and proleptically in the present, having an eschatological hope for shalom in its fullness. At the same time, a distinguishing mark of NT theology, even in Revelation, is that the eschatological reality of peace has broken into the present through God's gifts of the Son and the Spirit.

GOD'S GIFT OF SHALOM AND THE SOCIOPOLITICAL CONTEXT OF REVELATION (REVELATION 1)

The first of the two occurrences of the word *peace* in Revelation seems, at first glance, innocuous, part of a standard epistolary greeting:

> John to the seven churches that are in Asia: Grace to you and
> peace from him who is and who was and who is to come, and

---

3. I am honored to make this small contribution to a subject so important to these scholars. In addition to this book, see, e.g., Swartley, *Covenant of Peace*; Swartley, "Peace in the NT"; Yoder, *Shalom*; Smith-Christopher, "Peace in the OT"; plus the bibliographies therein.

4. See 147 of this volume and *Covenant of Peace*, 30, 41, where he supplies helpful graphics to illustrate these semantic connections.

from the seven spirits who are before his throne, and from Jesus
Christ, the faithful witness, the firstborn of the dead, and the
ruler of the kings of the earth. To him who loves us and freed us
from our sins by his blood, and made us to be a kingdom, priests
serving his God and Father, to him be glory and dominion forever and ever. Amen. (1:4–6)[5]

Much like a Pauline letter, Revelation begins (after a preliminary word
in 1:1–3 identifying the letter as containing an apocalypse-prophecy) with
a greeting of grace and peace. The source of these twin gifts is triadic: the
eternal God on the heavenly throne (cf. chap. 4), the seven spirits before the
throne,[6] and Jesus the Messiah, about whom much is said. He is identified
with three noun-phrases (faithful witness, firstborn of the dead, ruler of the
kings of the earth) and three verb-phrases (loves us, freed us from our sins
by his blood, made us to be a priestly kingdom[7]), all part of an acclamation
of Christ's eternal glory and dominion.

This Christological doxology anticipates various aspects of the graphic
narrative that is about to unfold, but it also provides commentary on the
words *grace* and *peace*. Jesus's liberating, loving, kingdom-and-priesthood-
forming death was an act of grace and of peacemaking, the benefits of
which continue to flow to John's addressees. And because in that death—by
crucifixion at the hands of Rome, as John's audience knows—Jesus was a
faithful witness, God has raised him from the dead and made him "ruler
of the kings of the earth"—i.e., Lord of the nations. These are not narrowly
religious claims and gifts but also political ones.

The political ideology of imperial Rome—*Roma aeterna*—was theological. Its emperors and their various propagandists claimed that Rome
was the gods' agent of peace and harmony in the world.[8] Military conquest,
or victory (*victoria*), and peace went hand in hand, from Rome's perspective. But for John the Seer, the *pax Romana* is a pseudo-peace, even an anti-
pax. It is such because Rome is (or at least is animated by) an anti-Christ,
opposed to the person and the community of the slaughtered Lamb. Imperial Rome is not a divine agent but a satanic one (chaps. 12–13). It does
not practice the things that make for peace, but just the opposite (chaps.
17–18). We will not appreciate the intensity of John's imagery and narrative,
or of his seemingly violent brand of peacemaking through horrific divine

5. All biblical quotations are taken from the NRSV unless otherwise indicated.

6. Bauckham (*Theology*, 109–15) persuasively interprets this image as a reference
to the divine Spirit (and not, e.g., angels).

7. Cf. Exod 19:6.

8. Carter, *Roman Empire*, 83–99; Wengst, *Pax Romana*, 46–51.

judgments, until we understand the gravity of the Roman anti-*pax* from his perspective, which he holds to be God's perspective. As Marianne Meye Thompson has put it, "The exaggerated images of the book . . . are all enlisted to make the point: the world is not as you see it, and in order to see it as God does, all its features must be exaggerated. Rome is not *Dea* (Goddess) sitting on seven hills offering the benefits of the *Pax Romana*, but a whore seated on a seven-headed monster, beguiling and corrupting the inhabitants of the earth."[9] The claim that the crucified-by-Rome Jesus brings peace, and the acclamation that he deserves glory and dominion forever over his royal priesthood and over all earthly rulers, both echo and subvert the Roman imperial claims of *pax Romana* and *Roma aeterna*.

Thus the entire opening of Revelation is an "epistolary shot across Caesar's imperial bow."[10] Jesus has created a people by shedding his own blood rather than by shedding their blood. God's resurrection of the crucified Jesus means that Roman power amounts to nothing in the face of God's power. The universal lordship of the resurrected Jesus means that the messianic age of shalom has been inaugurated, and will soon be brought to completion. Rome, however, is not the agent of this peace. Indeed, despite claims like those of Rome, no empire offers the shalom of God inaugurated in Jesus and now brought to his followers by the power of the Spirit.

Already, therefore, in the midst of temptation and tribulation, the churches addressed in Revelation, both then and now, are part of Jesus's messianic kingdom of priests. Thus they can know the peace of the Messiah's reign even in their times of trouble, even in the midst of the anti-*pax* of Rome and its imperial heirs throughout the centuries.

THE CHURCH: COMMUNITY OF THE LAMB, COMMUNITY OF SHALOM (REVELATION 2–5 AND OTHER TEXTS)

In the opening of Revelation, its recipients are reminded of the peace that has come, and continues to come, from the divine triad of God, the Spirit, and Jesus. Throughout Revelation, the church is a community of shalom in two respects. First, its constituency is international, an assembly of the nations. Second, it is a community of shalom in its "uncivil" practices of

9. Thompson, "Reading," 166.
10. Blount, *Revelation*, 34.

worship and witness—including prophetic, nonviolent resistance, even to the point of suffering and death.[11]

One of the most significant aspects of the age of shalom in the "holy city Jerusalem coming down out of heaven from God" (21:10) is its international character: "The nations will walk by its light, and the kings of the earth will bring their glory into it. . . . People will bring into it the glory and the honor of the nations. . . . On either side of the river is the tree of life with its twelve kinds of fruit, producing its fruit each month; and the leaves of the tree are for the healing of the nations" (21:24, 26; 22:2b).

This vision of a community of nations is anticipated already in the throne room vision of chapter 5, with echoes in the vision of God's people in chapter 7: "They [the four living creatures and the twenty-four elders] sing a new song: 'You are worthy to take the scroll and to open its seals, for you were slaughtered and by your blood you ransomed for God saints from every tribe and language and people and nation; you have made them to be a kingdom and priests serving our God, and they will reign on earth'" (5:9–10). And, "[T]here was a great multitude that no one could count, from every nation, from all tribes and peoples and languages, standing before the throne and before the Lamb, robed in white, with palm branches in their hands. They cried out in a loud voice, saying, 'Salvation belongs to our God who is seated on the throne, and to the Lamb!'" (7:9–10). This multitude is identified as those who "have come out of the great ordeal; they have washed their robes and made them white in the blood of the Lamb" (7:14b). Because these people from every nation have been victorious through the great ordeal, they enjoy the worship of God forever, without any future threat of harm, under the protection of God and the Lamb (7:15–17, with language that reappears in chaps. 21–22).

This passage depicts an international body of faithful disciples of Jesus. By reverse extrapolation, we can—indeed we must—conclude that John understands the kingdom of priests created by Jesus's death (1:5b–6; cf. 7:10) to be a universal body, a global church, a reality much bigger than the network of seven communities to which Revelation is addressed.[12] Moreover, this body will continue to expand, even in tribulation, as the eternal gospel is proclaimed to "every nation and tribe and language and people" (14:6), rescuing people from those groups who are currently in the grip of the beast.[13]

---

11. By *uncivil* I mean in contrast to civil religion (e.g., the imperial cult); see my *Reading Revelation*. On the importance of worship and especially witness in Rev, see also Peters, *Mandate*.

12. Seven represents fullness: all followers of the Lamb in all places are addressed.

13. E.g., 13:7; 14:8; 17:15. The Lamb's disciples "have been redeemed from humankind as first fruits for God and the Lamb" (14:4b).

Although Revelation attributes this evangelistic work to an angel, the angel also announces what the church proclaims: "Fear God and give him glory, for the hour of his judgment has come; and worship him who made heaven and earth, the sea and the springs of water" (Rev 14:7).

These followers of the Lamb (14:4), worshipers of God from every people and place, constitute a body that anticipates the constituency of the new Jerusalem, in which the nations worship God and the Lamb together and are healed (21:24, 26; 22:2b, quoted above). Furthermore, they constitute the truly "ecumenical" reality (cf. Gk. *oikoumenē*, often used of the Roman Empire), brought into being by the life-giving, liberating blood of the Lamb, as the divine counterpoint to Rome's oppressive and bloody subjugation of the nations. The true divinely peace-endowed community, then, is the church, not the empire created by military conquest and pacification.

As the recipients of this divine peace, brokered by the one who is called the Faithful Witness (1:5; 3:14), the church in Revelation is commissioned to embody this faithful, peaceful, missional, prophetic witness. John makes this vocation clear in several ways. For one thing, the theme of victory, or conquering—which ends each message to the seven churches and runs throughout the book—is ultimately a sharing in the victory or conquest of the slaughtered Lamb (5:5)—a "clear contrast to the Roman *victoria*."[14] The story of Jesus is the "hermeneutical key" to the churches' life.[15] This comes to its most poignant expression in the description of those pursued and accused by Satan (chap. 12). Their victory is won not by violence but by their identification with the slaughtered Lamb and by their corollary, even participatory, resistance and faithful witness: "But they have conquered him by the blood of the Lamb and by the word of their testimony, for they did not cling to life even in the face of death" (12:11).[16] Jesus, the martyrs/witnesses, and John himself (1:9) all embody this peaceful, missional, prophetic paradigm. As Swartley says, "[t]he Lamb Christology combined with the faithful word-witness is the heartbeat of Revelation's distinctive contribution to peace theology."[17]

The church's prophetic task, symbolized also by the two witnesses (11:3–13), may, then, lead to opposition and even martyrdom. The witnesses' only weapon against opponents is their message (portrayed as a

---

14. Wengst, *Pax Romana*, 134.

15. Alkier, "Witness or Warrior?" 136.

16. Swartley (*Covenant of Peace*, 343) rightly notes that the church is to exhibit both passive and active resistance, the former in noncooperation, the latter in worship and witness.

17. Ibid., 333. See also Pattemore, *People of God*.

consuming fire from their mouth; 11:5).[18] Furthermore, even when martyrs cry out for God to avenge their deaths (6:10), there is not a single word suggesting that those still living on earth should take up arms. Indeed, the opposite is the case, even when violence is directed at the still living: "If you are to be taken captive, into captivity you go; if you kill with the sword, with the sword you must be killed. Here is . . . the endurance and faith of the saints" (13:10).[19]

This is not to say that the church on earth already fully embodies this reality, as even a superficial reading of Rev 2–3 quickly proves. But if one of the main purposes of Revelation is to unveil reality from a transcendent perspective, and thus to "counter the Roman imperial view of the world,"[20] then the visions of the church triumphant speak directly both *about* and *to* the church on earth. The individual churches must see themselves as one ecumenical body, created and defined by the peacemaking God, not by Rome. And they do so most fully and most imaginatively when they join with one another, the elders, the martyrs, and all creation in the uncivil worship of God and the Lamb (chaps. 4–5). With an imagination refurbished in worship, the church can be what it is called to be in the world.

The church (i.e., the body of Jesus's faithful disciples), then, as a global, peace-graced, worshiping community, is both a foretaste of the eschatological healing of the nations and a sign of how that healing has been inaugurated—by the faithful death of the Lamb. In its lifestyle, the church bears faithful witness to the Faithful Witness, while in its very constitution as an international community it bears witness to God's ultimate plan for humanity. As such, it is a contrast-society or alter-culture drawn from the nations.[21] Canonically speaking, the visions in Rev 5, 7, and 14 re-present—and augment—the ecclesial reality described by Pauline texts such as Gal 3:28, Rom 9–11 and 14–15, and especially Eph 2–3. In Christ the dividing wall of hostility has been broken down, and reconciliation has taken place; the healing of the nations has begun.

18. See, e.g., Aune, *Revelation 6–16*, 613–14.

19. I have deleted the NRSV's phrase "a call for," which is not in the Greek text. For similar conclusions, see (inter alia) Hays, *Moral Vision*, 169–85, esp. 175–79; Bauckham, *Theology*, 77–79; Boxall, *Revelation*, 125; as well as Bauckham (*Climax*, 210–13) and Massyngbaerde Ford ("Shalom," 71), who contrast Revelation with the Qumran *War Scroll*, in which God enlists humans to fight. For Bauckham, Revelation is a (nonviolent) Christian war scroll enlisting Christians to "fight" by witnessing and suffering (*Climax*, 210–37).

20. Bauckham, *Theology*, 6. He adds, "The visual power of the book effects a kind of purging of the Christian imagination, refurbishing it with alternative visions of how the world is and will be" (ibid., 17).

21. So also McNicol, *Conversion*, 21–24.

SHALOM AND THE JUDGMENTS IN REVELATION (REVELATION 6–20)

The shalom anticipated in the constituency and practices of the church is realized fully in the new Jerusalem (chaps. 21–22). But there is a long road between Rev 1–5 and Rev 21–22, and it passes though many visions of judgment. At the very first stop on this road, the vision of the four horsemen (6:1–9), we encounter the second and last occurrence of *eirēnē* in Revelation (6:4)—referring to the removal of peace, perhaps the (pseudo) *Pax Romana*. What can the ensuing scenes, most quite violent, have to do with peace?

Visions of shalom in the Christian OT often possess two closely related features that reappear in Revelation. The first feature is that shalom is a kind of "tough love" requiring the removal of evil. Shalom does not come naturally to the human community by means of an ethical glissando from the present state into a future utopia. The second, related feature is that the Bible often portrays this removal of evil in terms of royal or divine warfare. Both of these features find a happy home in an apocalyptic document like Revelation, even though they are also transformed in that document. Neither of these two biblical/apocalyptic emphases is particularly welcome, however, in contemporary culture (and perhaps not in contemporary theology either), but there they are, unavoidable in the texts.

The narrative of Revelation appears to follow a pattern established by expectations of royal figures in the ancient Near East, and particularly in Israel. An ideal king was expected to bring about justice, peace, and human flourishing (shalom), but to do so he (or God) was expected not only to execute justice for the people, especially the vulnerable, but also to remove evil from the land by subjugating, punishing, banishing, or even destroying enemies (e.g., Ps 72).[22] Only then would there be true shalom. Stress is often placed on the order of these elements: first, the removal of evil; then, the arrival of justice and peace: "When the oppressor is no more, and destruction has ceased, and marauders have vanished from the land, then a throne shall be established in steadfast love in the tent of David, and on it shall sit in faithfulness a ruler who seeks justice and is swift to do what is right" (Isa 16:4b–5; cf. 9:2–7).

This expectation sometimes comes to expression in ways that are so idealistic that it is couched in mythic, imaginative language pointing to a future reality beyond normal human hopes. In Isa 11, for instance, the hope is for a Davidic king, filled with God's Spirit, who will judge righteously for

---

22. Allan McNicol (*Conversion*) has independently argued that Revelation follows an OT pattern about the conquest and conversion of the nations. If he is correct, my proposal supplements his, which does not focus on removing evil and establishing shalom.

the poor and slay the wicked: "He shall not judge by what his eyes see, or
decide by what his ears hear; but with righteousness he shall judge the poor,
and decide with equity for the meek of the earth; he shall strike the earth
with the rod of his mouth, and with the breath of his lips he shall kill the
wicked" (Isa 11:3b–4). The consequence of this divine beneficent invasion,
through a human agent, is a paradisiacal peace: "The wolf shall live with the
lamb, the leopard shall lie down with the kid, the calf and the lion and the
fatling together, and a little child shall lead them. . . . They will not hurt or
destroy on all my holy mountain; for the earth will be full of the knowledge
of the Lord as the waters cover the sea" (Isa 11:6–9; cf. Isa 65:25). Although,
surprisingly, the second part of this text from Isa 11 is not echoed with any
volume in Revelation,[23] the earlier part (Isa 11:3b–4) is:

> He is clothed in a robe dipped in blood, and his name is called
> The Word of God. And the armies of heaven, wearing fine linen,
> white and pure, were following him on white horses. From his
> mouth comes a sharp sword with which to strike down the na-
> tions, and he will rule them with a rod of iron; he will tread the
> wine press of the fury of the wrath of God the Almighty. . . . And
> the rest [the kings of the earth with their armies] were killed by
> the sword of the rider on the horse, the sword that came from
> his mouth; and all the birds were gorged with their flesh. (Rev
> 19:13–15, 21; cf. 1:16; 2:16)

As in Isa 11 and elsewhere, in Rev 21–22 the vision of shalom is the
conclusion of a larger narrative in which evil is first removed, and that
by means of a royal word, a royal pronouncement—a performative utterance. This pronouncement is, in fact, the means of warfare in both Isa 11
and Rev 19. In the case of Revelation, at least, we should not imagine this
speech-as-war as a reference to any form of literal warfare. This unique performative utterance is the word not of a human king but of the divine Word
of God, who is also the Lamb of God and thus the slaughtered faithful and
true witness.[24] The sword signifies the ability of the Word of God, Jesus, to
speak evil out of existence in preparation for the permanent presence of
peace. It signifies the ultimate victory of the slaughtered Lamb over evil.
Whether this powerful speech should be understood as the unfolding of the
consequences of Jesus's death, the testimony of the martyrs, the spread of

23. But see the reference to "a great, high mountain" in Rev 21:10.

24. The epithet "Faithful and True" (19:11; cf. 1:5; 3:14), together with the blood
on his robe before the battle is even announced, identifies the Word of God with the
slaughtered Lamb. See, e.g., Johns, *Lamb Christology*, 184; Aune, *Revelation 17–22*,
1057, 1069. On Revelation's inclusion of Jesus in the divine identity, see Bauckham,
Theology, 54–65; Hays, "Faithful Witness, Alpha and Omega."

the gospel, and/or a final word of judgment, it is clearly not a literal military campaign any more than its aftermath is a literal ornithological feasting on the war-dead (19:17, 21).

That is, despite the use of violent imagery and language to express the divine eradication of evil as part of the process of bringing shalom and salvation, *we would be wrong to imagine John imagining a God or a Messiah who literally uses violence to terminate evil.* Rather, this is symbolic language about a divine mystery, and John, I am convinced, was completely aware that he (or the Spirit) was reworking the holy-war tradition in light of the slaughtered Lamb.[25] As I have written elsewhere:

> The language and images of death and destruction symbolize—in comprehensible, if disturbing, idiom—the *universality* and *finality* of God's ultimate eradication of evil *rather than the means by which God brings about that eradication.* As the omnipotent One who spoke creation into existence, God hardly needs to resort to literal violence to effect the cessation of evil. . . . Instead, Revelation should be understood as portraying *symbolically* what God does *actually* with a divine performative utterance, an effective word not unlike the word that spoke creation into existence. It is a word of *new* creation. Revelation's symbolic language uses the only kinds of realities known to humans to approximate the universality and finality of God's eschatological dealing with evil. What, after all, is more comprehensive and permanent in human experience than total destruction?[26]

Where do these observations lead us? *We should describe Rev 6–20 as an extended narrative interpretation of the prophetic pattern of the conquest and removal of evil prior to the establishment of* shalom. At the same time, however, we must note a transformation of this prophetic pattern. If part of the pattern includes the defeat of Israel's enemies and their subsequent obeisance to YHWH (see also Ps 2; 110; Rev 15:4), in Revelation the nations are not merely judged and defeated (e.g., 16:19; 19:15); they are healed. Their final fate is found in the last chapters of Revelation.

THE FULLNESS OF SHALOM (REVELATION 21–22)

Revelation ends where Genesis began: in a garden of peace. It is a spectacular conclusion to the biblical narrative, and to both the human hope for and the divine promise of peace.

25. So also Barr, "Lamb," esp. 213.

26. Gorman, *Reading Revelation*, 152, emphasis original.

Revelation's culminating vision of shalom is noteworthy for what is absent—the antitheses of peace:

- the sea (21:1), associated with chaos in the biblical tradition;
- pain and death (21:4; cf. 1 Cor 15:26);
- tears, mourning, and crying (21:4);
- perpetrators of evil (21:8, 27; 22:3);
- night (21:25); and
- closed gates (21:25).[27]

These absences, as indicators of new creation and peace,[28] were anticipated in Isaiah (25:7–8; 35:10; 52:1; 60:11, 18–20; 65:19). God has taken the entire creation "beyond the threat of evil."[29] Also significant is the location of the garden—in a city; it is an urban garden. The normal city, which is often thought of as a dangerous place that needs constant security, has been transformed into a place of absolute security without its gates ever closing.

This grand and beautiful vision is also noteworthy for what—actually, who—is present. The nations that have been the target of divine judgment are present in the new Jerusalem (21:24–26), and not merely as defeated enemies but as participants in the healing—the shalom—of God: "Then the angel showed me the river of the water of life, bright as crystal, flowing from the throne of God and of the Lamb through the middle of the street of the city. On either side of the river is the tree of life with its twelve kinds of fruit, producing its fruit each month; and the leaves of the tree are for the healing of the nations" (Rev 22:1–2; cf. Ezek 47:12).

How has this happened? Through the preaching of the eternal gospel? Through repentance in the face of God's judgments? John is not explicit. But the presence of the nations means that whatever else we say about the judgments in chapters 6–20, we must conclude that such divine judgment is coherent with an overall divine goal of restoration and healing, which in turn is coherent with an understanding of the Lamb's death as that which nonviolently overcomes evil and sin, and creates thereby a people of every nation, tribe, people, and language.[30] The healing of the nations portrayed

27. In addition, there is no temple, because the city's temple "is the Lord God the Almighty and the Lamb" (21:22), and there is no sun, moon, or other luminaries, and yet no night (21:23, 25; 22:5; cf. Isa 60:19–20).

28. Cf. Isa 60:17; 65:17; 66:22.

29. Bauckham, *Theology*, 53.

30. "We do not and cannot know how God might judge ultimately, but a christologically conditioned religious epistemology leads to the view that divine judgment is more likely to be restorative than strictly retributive" (Neville, *Peaceable Hope*, 240).

in Revelation's final, glorious vision of shalom is the divine *telos* to which
the church has borne peaceful and prophetic witness, sometimes by martyrdom, throughout the pages of Revelation—and of history.

CONCLUSION

We must of course acknowledge that the Christian church has struggled
not only with this book but with the very meaning of discipleship as an
adventure in shalom. The church has not always been the faithful, peaceful,
prophetic, missional, multinational community of the Lamb's followers that
God through John the Seer has called it to be. Some would blame the book
of Revelation, in part, for this problem. If read rightly, however, as Christian Scripture bearing witness to the divine peace initiative displayed in the
gifts of Jesus and the Spirit, Revelation has the potential to help restore the
church as a community of shalom in anticipation of the new creation God
has promised.[31]

---

31. I am grateful to my research assistant Daniel Jackson for his assistance in pre-
paring this essay.

25

Peace and Scripture

Mennonite Perspectives from the Global South

Nancy R. Heisey

In *Covenant of Peace*, NT scholar Willard Swartley seeks to redress a significant lacuna that he has observed in modern scholarship on NT theology and ethics—the lack of attention to peace and reconciliation themes throughout the NT.[1] This masterful survey concludes by naming particular NT phrases and images that reveal these themes: "Jesus' seventh Beatitude, 'blessed are the peacemakers'; Paul's unique title for God 'God of Peace'; NT imitation [of Christ] and discipleship texts; Paul's bold claim that 'Christ is our peace'; and the Lamb's War in Revelation." Swartley suggests that "perhaps we should consider also a sixth: the shape and structure of the Synoptic Gospels' narrative portrait of Jesus' life, death, and resurrection . . . [the] 'master narrative' [that] forms identity for the early Christians."[2]

One of Swartley's appendices analyzes the work of twenty-five NT theologians and ethicists published between 1951 and 2004, examining their indices for mentions of the terms *peace, reconciliation,* or *love of enemies.*[3] All these works are written by North American or European scholars (only one by a woman).

This essay pursues a contemporary question emerging from Swartley's survey: what can be said about the way that scholars and students of the

1. Swartley, *Covenant of Peace.*
2. Ibid., 400.
3. Ibid., 433.

Bible from other parts of the world have noticed and used (or not used) peace-related themes in the Bible? Beginning with a brief note about biblical scholarship from the global South[4] within the past twenty years, I will next turn to a reading of sources from within the Anabaptist-related family of churches. In this section I examine articles published in the official MWC periodical *Courier*,[5] then consider the work of three individual Mennonites who comment extensively on biblical peace-related themes in their work. This survey will show that articles in *Courier* reflect a consistent concern for peace teaching and peace and justice engagement within the MWC family, with a broad-ranging biblical grounding. The three authors from outside North America and Europe—a pastor, a mediator/consultant, and a poet— also draw on biblical materials in ways that stretch and enrich traditional northern Anabaptist biblical readings. Our overview thus invites all who seek to deepen conversations about peace in Scripture to create space for the perspectives and questions raised by the discernment of biblical peace themes in many contexts around the world.

GLOBALIZING BIBLICAL STUDIES

Forty years ago biblical scholars of African, Asian, or Latin American origin who were in conversation with North Atlantic biblical scholars were few in number. In theological circles, Latin American liberation theologians, with work rooted in biblical themes, were recognized, and the intersecting concerns of black and feminist theologians hinted at the presence of many others outside the guild who might demand to be taken into account in future biblical studies conversations. At the end of the first decade of the twenty-first century, the conversation has dramatically expanded. Many northern academic biblical studies journals and book publishers list titles by scholars from around the world.[6] Going beyond traditional explorations of military-related violence, these scholars address the use of Scripture for both liberation and oppression, and experiences such as immigration, mi-

---

4. The term *global South* covers a broad range of meanings. It may refer to geography (the U.S. is north of Brazil), economic difference (Germany is wealthy while Zambia is economically poor), or cultural contrast (Canada is "western," while Korea is "eastern"). In many settings this term replaces previously used labels such as "third world" or "developing nations."

5. In MWC circles, this periodical is known as C/C/C, for *Courier/Correo/Courrier,* its title in MWC's three official languages.

6. See Heisey, "'Reading With' and Related Biblical Conversations," for a bibliographic essay covering more than forty titles. Available at http://www.ubs-translations. org/tt/.

grant labor, and domestic violence. Central to almost all these writers is the challenge of contesting biblical readings based on northern norms. The gap between scholarly and "ordinary" readers has also been a concern among southern biblical scholars. Several one-volume biblical commentaries have brought together the interpretive work of an impressive guild of southern scholars who address these concerns.[7]

Mennonite-related voices have not been strongly present in these conversations. Within the Spanish speaking Mennonite world, the extensive oeuvre of John (Juan) Driver, spanning more than thirty years, would be worthy of its own essay. While Driver's work is primarily missiological, his interaction with liberation theologians has brought biblical peace questions into the heart of that missiology.[8] Recently, Elizabeth Soto Albrecht has articulated important pastoral concerns related to nonviolence within families.[9] Other Spanish-language theological and biblical titles published in Anabaptist settings in Latin America could also be studied.[10] Daniel Schipani participated in an extensive three-year ecumenical global Bible study and dialogue process, and co-edited the volume reporting on this study, published by IMS.[11] But for a geographically broader Anabaptist perspective, we next turn to articles published in the official MWC periodical.

PEACE REPORTING AND REFLECTION IN COURIER

From its inception in 1986, *Courier* built peace themes into its reporting on the work of Anabaptist-related groups around the world. This survey takes into account only those articles written by southerners or reporting on events and statements from southern bodies. Most of the articles are short, written with an eye to the ordinary reader. Several kinds of material are included—news accounts, reflections/teachings/sermons, and personal stories. In news reporting from churches and regions, direct biblical references are few, while broad Anabaptist commitments are frequently named. The periodical's first volume includes a report on a peace seminar led by

7. E.g., Adeyemo, ed., *Africa Bible Commentary*; Patte, ed., *Global Bible Commentary*.

8. Selected works of Driver in English include: *Community and Commitment*; *Kingdom Citizens*; *Becoming God's Community*; *Understanding the Atonement*; *How Christians Made Peace With War*; *Images of the Church in Mission*; *Radical Faith*; and (with Escobar) *Christian Mission and Social Justice*.

9. Albrecht, *Family Violence*; and *Seek Peace and Pursue It*.

10. Ediciones SEMILLA (Guatemala) and Ediciones CLARA (Colombia)—merged in 2012—provide Anabaptist-themed biblical and theological literature in Spanish. Lists of titles can be located through publisher searches in WorldCat.

11. De Wit et al., eds., *Through the Eyes of Another*.

a Japanese Mennonite pastor in the city of the first atomic bomb.[12] Peace-related news items throughout the decades additionally come from Central America, Colombia, India, the Southern Cone of South America, Zaire (now Democratic Republic of the Congo [DRC]), Zambia, and Zimbabwe. Of particular interest are official statements made by regional Anabaptist bodies. An inter-Mennonite gathering in Zaire in 1987 issued a call for "re-newing and strengthening the Anabaptist vision of the church in relation to peace, justice work, and forgiveness," and urged "that our biblical and theological training centers integrate into their programs teaching on the Anabaptist vision of church and society."[13] In a context of regional civil war, the fourteenth Anabaptist-Mennonite Consultation of Central America and Panama asserted "that we are in solidarity with all those initiatives that, following the teachings and example of our Lord Jesus Christ, foster the way of peaceful coexistence," concluding with the Beatitude "Blessed are the peacemakers"(Matt 5:9).[14] The Africa Mennonite and Brethren in Christ Fellowship, meeting in Kenya in 1994, stated: "We understand peace is not a technique but a style of life. 'Christ is our Peace.'"[15] Mennonite Christian Service Fellowship of India responded to continuing unease on the India-Pakistan border with the claim: "We affirm our allegiance to Lord Jesus Christ, the Prince of Peace, by recommitting ourselves to follow his example and teachings, as recorded in the New Testament"; the response also made reference to "the rich nonviolence traditions of Indian heritage."[16]

Reflections and sermons with peace themes make up well over half of the more than fifty surveyed peace-related *Courier* articles by southern authors. Readers could luxuriate in the richness of the authors' names themselves; Mesach Krisetya, Leonor de Mendez, Mario Higueros, Paulus Widjaja, Jenny Neme, Nzuzi Mukawa, Elfriede Véron, and Dietrich Pana are among Anabaptist leaders whose voices call out the biblical message of peace.[17] Likewise, the texts from which these teachers draw represent a vivid cross section of the Bible: from the OT, Gen 1, Exod 20, Ps 85, Isa 52 and 58, and Micah; from the NT, Matt 6–7, Mark 8 and 10, Luke 10, Rom 12, 1 Cor 3, 2 Cor 1 and 12, Phil 2, 1 Pet 2, and Rev 9.[18] Throughout these

12. "Japanese Share Peace Message," 16.

13. "Declaration by Participants," 7.

14. "CAMCA Declaration," 3.

15. "Statement of AMBCF," 3.

16. "MCSFI Issues Statement," 3.

17. Due to limited space, the entire article list surveyed is not included here, but is available from the author on request.

18. The theme text for the 2003 MWC assembly in Zimbabwe was 1 Cor 12; the theme text for the 2009 assembly in Paraguay was Phil 2.

teachings, writers consistently assert that the biblical message addresses the particular contexts of the writers. Hiroshi Yanada answered the question of how the Christian message can speak to Asian people, by presenting Jesus Christ as the Prince of Peace, underlining "his identification with people . . . [and] his servant stance."[19] As new president of MWC in 1990, Argentine pastor Raul Garcia referred to Jesus's ministry of teaching and healing as the way the churches face "ignorance, hunger, sickness, mental and physical disabilities, social discrimination."[20] In a setting of civil war, Leonor de Mendez, MWC executive committee member from Guatemala, interpreted the "intense supplication" of Ps 85 as "an appropriate prayer request for today." "God's work is to fulfill in his people the promise of messianic peace. . . . However, it is the responsibility of humankind to radically renounce attitudes of social insensitivity, violence, division and discrimination."[21] Current MWC President Danisa Ndlovu, reflecting on his Zimbabwean government's use of election violence against the people, claimed: "I find Christ's words (from Matt 5:38–41) to be incredibly empowering. In these verses, Jesus suggests that no one should be given the right to be in charge of another person's destiny. . . . By turning the other cheek, by walking the second mile, we disempower the one who tried to assume power over us."[22]

Gentle exhortation from southern sisters and brothers to act out our peace convictions is also present. In 1986, as the struggle against apartheid in South Africa threatened to engulf the entire region, and Anabaptist-related leaders in the north deliberated about their response to the crisis, a Zambian Brethren in Christ leader proclaimed: "If the church will tell the world this message [of *lived* Christianity] peace in Southern Africa will come; otherwise the judgment which will come upon the church for her wrong emphasis will be unbearable."[23] A persistent advocate that northern Anabaptist-related churches accept their southern kin as full partners, Indonesian Mesach Krisetya (MWC president from 1997–2003) repeatedly tied this justice awareness to the broad peace commitment of the global family. Drawing from 1 Cor 12 and Phil 2, Krisetya asked "members of the body" not to "compete with one another." Later, his counsel was even stronger: "Communion is more than sentimental fellowship. . . . It assumes confessing that division is a sin and that it is wrong to be at war with one another as it

---

19. Yanada, "What Kind of Christianity?" 4–5.
20. Roth, "President Raul Garcia," 2–3.
21. Mendez, "Restore Us, O God!," 16.
22. Ndlovu, "The Other Cheek," 16.
23. Mudenda, "Churches Face Critical Task," 16.

is to be at war with another country."[24] From Colombia, Mennonites have frequently pointed out the role of the United States government in perpetuating ongoing violence in their country. After the 2001 terrorist attacks on the United States, peace advocate Ricardo Esquivia reminded northerners of the Pauline instructions "not to take revenge into our own hands." He continued: "This is a direct message to all the church of Christ that finds itself in the center of world political power, and that is where you are."[25]

While these *Courier* texts do not represent the pattern of scholarly biblical exegesis that occasioned our question, they do reveal the importance of the biblical peace witness as the global Anabaptist family seeks to embody Christ's way in their varied settings. This survey also suggests that a richer array of language is needed to capture those commitments to the peace witness. Turning next to a specific scholarly work rooted in scholarly exegesis, we find that the understandings referred to in the *Courier* survey are present in a specific contextualized biblical reading.

A CONGOLESE EXEGESIS OF EPHESIANS 6:10-17

Invisible to northern Mennonites, members of our faith family are carrying out biblical and theological scholarly work in many other places. One country survey alone shows that more than 140 bachelors, masters and doctoral theses have been prepared by Congolese (DRC) Mennonites.[26] Among these studies, titles suggest at least thirteen that cover peace-related themes or material (four in this group are by women). While the majority of these theses cannot be accessed through channels available to northern scholars, some are held in the Kinshasa office of MCC. One such manuscript is a thesis for a bachelor's degree in theology granted by the Christian University of Kinshasa to Crispin Muhenya Guwamba, a Mennonite pastor. The thesis is divided into three chapters: an exegesis of Eph 6:10–17, a broader discussion of NT teachings on war, and a historical, economic and social overview of wars in the DRC.[27] The introduction raises the question whether the war in the Congo is evidence of the near return of Christ. "We do not accept the idea that the disasters that accompany the return of Christ should take place in third world countries alone. Rather, that will be a cosmic event,"

24. Krisetya, "Living Together in Mission," 12–13; Krisetya, "A Vision of Global Communion," 11.

25. Esquivia, "To the Anabaptist-Mennonite Churches," 8.

26. Tim Lind, e-mail message to author, 21 December 2011.

27. Muhenya, "Enseignement du Nouveau Testament"; manuscript in possession of the author. All French translations are mine unless otherwise indicated.

Muhenya asserts. He notes further that "the weapons of Eph 6:10–17 never destroy the ecosystem or human life," opening the spiritual warfare theme that is woven throughout his exegesis. "A close reading of this pericope . . . demonstrates that the New Testament takes us down to the basics, warns us against false doctrines, and exhorts Christians to practice love (John 13:34; 1 Cor 13:1–13)."[28]

Muhenya situates his choice of Eph 6 in the context of how the entire NT addresses the war in the DRC. He acknowledges the vast scope of biblical teaching on war and peace, and then proclaims his passage as the "hinge" or "turning point" of the NT.[29] Muhenya's exegesis chapter follows the rubrics in which northern students of the biblical text have long been trained and it raises the issues that one would expect to find in any such study. The conclusion of chapter 1 underlines his understanding that peacemaking Christians are indeed called to conflict rooted in the spiritual realm. This claim shapes the rest of his thesis:

> In Eph 6:10–17, the Apostle Paul clears away the claims of Roman weaponry, for which he substitutes spiritual weapons. . . . These weapons do not destroy the ecosystem and do not provoke economic and cosmic disasters such as those we are currently experiencing in the DRC during this war. Rather, these weapons guarantee the life eternal of Christ, and they must be used daily without respite. . . . This victory is not the prerogative of the personal strength of Christians but the victory gained through faith in the death and resurrection of Christ.[30]

Chapter 2 discusses NT texts that underpin the idea of nonresistance, acknowledges Jesus's sayings that predict coming war, and notes a variety of terms that the author labels Jesus's "code language" for war (tied to the idea that the NT sees only spiritual battles as appropriate for Christians): taking up the cross (Matt 16:24), bringing fire to earth (Luke 12:49), causing division (Luke 12:51), renouncing the self (Luke 9:23), controversy (Luke 12:41–44), treason (Luke 22:1–6), denial (Luke 22:31–34), new birth (as "internal war") (John 3:3, 5), and opposition (Luke 9:53–56). This discussion is followed by an extensive review of the NT texts using the word "peace" (*eirēnē*).

In chapter 3, Muhenya provides a historical overview of the conflicts that have ravaged the Congo since its independence from Belgium in 1960, culminating in what he calls the "war of aggression" which began with the

28. Ibid., 2.
29. Ibid., 4.
30. Ibid., 26–27.

Rwandan genocide in 1994.[31] He denounces the national players—Rwanda, Uganda, and Burundi—as "puppets of the West."[32] Eventually he returns to the theme of spiritual struggle, which for him is carried out against and within the church community. He describes the ways the war has ravaged the churches, cites names of religious leaders who were killed, and lists church buildings that were destroyed.[33] He comments on attempted peace processes, whose supporters have included the Church of Christ in the Congo (the Congolese Protestant umbrella body), as well as governmental, nongovernmental and international bodies.[34] Yet of equal significance for him, "within local churches, many prayer vigils, fasts, morning and Sunday services" have been held to pray for peace. The church, whose mission is described in Matt 28, needs the fruits of the Spirit (Gal 5:22–23) to succeed in her efforts, to carry out her role as "the voice of the voiceless."[35] He repeats that the specific actions he has described come from the understanding that Eph 6 calls for spiritual battle, concluding, "We must march in obedience and faithfulness to God . . . only warring against the devil, arming ourselves with the weapons of Eph 6:10–17, walking hand in hand in love."[36]

Muhenya's reading, clearly in tune with the Ephesian letter's focus on "the spiritual forces of evil in the heavenly places" (6:12 NRSV), also sees those forces in social terms that are physically visible in the eastern Congo. Further, he insists that the churches' responses likewise encompass both spiritual and material dimensions of human existence. This understanding is shared in the work to which we next turn.

A MEDIATION TRAINING MANUAL FOR FRANCOPHONE AFRICANS

Pascal Kulungu is a Congolese Mennonite Brethren conflict mediation practitioner and trainer. His recently published manual is designed to train French-speaking Africans mediating conflicts in family, church, school,

---

31. It is interesting that Muhenya does not discuss the tragic and violent history of the Congo's occupation by its Belgian colonizers. What Muhenya refers to as the "war of aggression," also called the "Second Congo War," formally ended in 2002; however, violence continues to wreak havoc in eastern Congo.

32. Ibid., 43.

33. Ibid., 65.

34. Ibid., 70.

35. Ibid., 71.

36. Ibid., 75.

and political settings.[37] The work's preface observes that Kulungu's manual is based in the intersection between the Christian tradition, "founded on the words of Jesus Christ: 'Blessed are the peacemakers' (Matt 5:9)," and the burgeoning academic field of peace and conflict studies.[38] Kulungu's forward provides a biblical overview, noting first the broad semantic field of the terms on which the practice of mediation is based, then offering four broad biblical definitions of "peace":

1. Well-being and material prosperity evidenced by physical health and the absence of war, illness and famine (Jer 33:6, 9)

2. Just relationships between peoples, nations and social groups (Isa 54:13–14)

3. The moral integrity of a person (Ps 34:13–14)

4. Godliness and the Good News coming from God [found in the phrase] "God of Peace" (Rom 15:13; 16:20; 2 Cor 13:11; 1 Thess 5:23; 2 Thess 3:16; Heb 13:20)[39]

He then lays out the theological foundation for the practices described in the manual: grounded in peace with God, those who work for peace are able to construct peace with neighbors and even eventually with enemies. He assumes that most if not all his readers are Christians, and he calls for two disciplines in their work: "the discipline of discernment," and a "radical Christocentric life." Discernment leads Christians to acknowledge that all spheres of life call for their engagement, since "everything in this world is under [Christ's] lordship." The "Christocentric life" is an understanding that "faith is not a gnosis (knowledge) but rather a way of living in faithfulness to God."[40] The introduction concludes with a biblical text: "We must envision a situation where 'steadfast love and faithfulness will meet; righteousness and peace will kiss each other' (Ps 85:10)."[41]

In chapter 1, Kulungu covers a broad array of topics, including descriptions of the work of several nonviolent world leaders: Martin Luther King Jr., Nelson Mandela, Mother Teresa, and Simon Kimbangu, a Congolese prophet (1887–1951). He asserts that Jesus was the source of inspiration for these historical peacemakers, adding, "Our goal is not to compare Jesus

---

37. Kulungu, *Manuel de Formation*.

38. Dalton Reimer, "Preface," in Kulungu, *Manuel de Formation*, viii.

39. Kulungu, *Manuel de Formation*, xiv.

40. Ibid., xvi–xvii.

41. Ibid., xviii.

Christ to humans such as we are but to present him as Prince of Peace and model to follow."[42]

When Kulungu turns to a history of conflict, the importance of its origins in the spiritual realm appears. Kulungu claims, "In our time, many people recognize that our world is just a battlefield where spiritual forces of good and evil confront one another." The parable of the wheat and the weeds (Matt 13:24–29) offers an even more specific identification of the problem: "An enemy has done this."[43] After an extensive discussion of the rebellion of Lucifer, based on extra biblical sources,[44] Kulungu returns to Scripture to declare that this "cosmic conflict," of "mysterious" origin, will also end by "God's orders." This section on the cosmic conflict (Kulungu insists that "the history of humanity is much more than the theater of human actions") refers to texts from both the OT and NT (Gen 3; Isa 14; Ezek 28; Rom 1; 5; 8; 1 Cor 4; Heb 1; and 2 Pet 3). He concludes, "The Bible teaches that sin and sinners will finally be destroyed, and the universe will be restored to its perfection and original harmony" (John 14:30; 19:30; Rev 1:18).[45]

Kulungu's professional work represents a significant development among both southern and northern leaders of the global Anabaptist community.[46] Yet biblical understanding and active peace work predate the emergence of the professional peacebuilding field. Japanese Mennonite professor/pastor Yorifumi Yaguchi, whose life has also been shaped by personal experience with war, is one of the most consistent lifelong peace activists in the global Anabaptist communion. He has articulated his commitments to this lifework in internationally acclaimed poetry with congruent yet also questioning biblical reflections.

POETRY FROM JAPAN

A thorough reading of Yorifumi Yaguchi's work would require a broader survey than this essay allows, but consideration of several specific poems reveals a deep biblical stream.[47] Within that stream, the theme of peace is

42. Ibid., 88.

43. Ibid, 91.

44. Kulungu provides the following citation: franc.bravehost.com, material that seems to draw entirely from the Urantia Book, www.urantia.org.

45. Kulungu, *Manuel de Formation*, 91–94.

46. Key players include the Center for Justice and Peacebuilding at EMU, the Peace and Conflict Studies Program at Fresno Pacific University (of which Pascal Kulungu is a graduate), and the many local and regional trainings around the world offered by graduates of these programs.

47. See Birky, "Introduction," in *Poetry of Yorifumi Yaguchi*, 7–9, for a survey of

frequently evoked, often as a puzzle. His 1987 volume *Jesus*, written first in Japanese for the Protestant churches in Japan, included a section of poems in the voices of those who lived and walked with Jesus.[48] Among these voices are witnesses to the crucifixion, haunted by the unexpected behavior of this man. One of the crucifying soldiers remembers:

> I hadn't expected
> he would give
> no resistence
>
> And there was no attack,
> As I had feared, from heavenly armies
> He just hung there, and died
>
> But suddenly a panic gripped me and shook my body
> so that I reeled and staggered
>
> My strength drained out with cold sweat
> my body limp, I collapsed,
> unable to rise[49]

Toward the end of this collection, Yaguchi directly addresses the questions that face a Japanese Christian, especially a pacifist:

> There are Christians who in their later years
> return to ancestral religion . . .
>
> I too in recent days have been momentarily charmed
> by the Buddha's serene face
> rather than the suffering Christ's
>
> But it was the gods and buddhas who
> once stirred up
> militarist passions in me
>
> It is the Christ, the Prince of Peace
> whom I continue to follow
> who was killed, but did not kill.[50]

Yaguchi's published work in English.

48. Yaguchi, *Jesus*.

49. "First Soldier's Account," in ibid., 27.

50. "To Follow Christ," in ibid., 78.

Yaguchi's autobiography recounts his childhood and youth in a devout Buddhist family, the devastation of World War II and the ensuing American occupation of Japan, his conversion to pacifist Christianity, and his deeply principled and longstanding public resistance to ongoing threats of Japanese militarism. This account offers deeper perspective on what he hints at in the poems in *Jesus*.[51] Readers meet a Korean forcibly conscripted into the Japanese army, family members who became soldiers, a Japanese soldier who threatened the young Yaguchi for speaking English, the American GIs who swore "Jesus Christ," his observations of American soldiers worshiping the baby Jesus at Christmas, and his dream-haunting encounter with a deer-hunting American Mennonite seminary friend.[52]

Yaguchi comments on his later work, "One of my main concerns has been to write on biblical themes about our contemporary social problems."[53] Three poems in the epilogue reveal how central to his vision is both the puzzle and the call of the biblical peace message. The prophetic book of Jonah, "one of the greatest anti-war messages in the Bible," is encapsulated in thirty-two lines, concluding with Jonah's protest: "Oh God! Don't let them repent! / Exterminate the whole city, our enemy city!"[54] Two verses from one of Isaiah's Servant Songs (42:1–2) give rise to the prophet's midrashic question:

> "If this incomprehensible voice
> Came indeed from God,
> Then where did the promise of a strong messiah
> Spoken by my predecessors
> Come from?"
> The doubt spreads on his face like a spider's nest.[55]

Returning again to the crucifixion, "the climax of Jesus' life as a servant," Yaguchi offers this final image:

> The soldiers, the crucified robbers, and the spectators
> Looked at crucified Jesus and
> Reviled him, "Come down from the cross
> That we may see and believe."
> He did not come down.[56]

51. Yaguchi, *Wing-Beaten Air*.

52. Yaguchi, "Chou-san," "Who," "A Muzzle," "I sometimes liked GIs," "The child and the soldiers," and "A Deer," in *Wing-Beaten Air*, 51–53, 59, 72, 75, 77, 114.

53 Ibid., 207.

54. Ibid., 209.

55. Ibid., 210–11.

56. Ibid., 212–13.

CONCLUSION

This brief survey suggests that Anabaptist sisters and brothers in the global South have long engaged NT peace themes that Willard Swartley has articulated so carefully; they cannot be included in his critique of many northern theologians and biblical scholars who have failed to give those themes attention. Their writings show strong congruence with Swartley's search for the peace, reconciliation, and love-of-enemies themes central to his analysis. Southern biblical readers have also pushed more broadly throughout the biblical witness to connect that witness to their own experiences. Of particular note, especially in the Congolese writings, is attention to the spiritual forces implicated in the Christian struggle for peace. While Swartley is also widely recognized for his work with persons affected by the powers of evil, and refers to the NT record on this question in *Covenant of Peace*, he does not list his published writing in that area in its bibliography.[57] Further, his and other northern Mennonite writing on combat with the powers of evil is more focused on the personal than the social, in contrast to some of the material considered in this survey.[58] That the NT peace witness, especially its embodiment in Jesus, can be held in question throughout a life of commitment to following Jesus, is a further challenge to northern scholars who have learned from the certainty which Swartley has presented to us throughout his career. Our gratitude to him is only deepened by the opportunity to read those who love the Jesus and the Bible that he loves, and whose lives and encounters with the challenges of peacemaking are amazingly complex and different from our own.

57. Swartley, *Covenant of Peace,* 98–100, 224–26.
58. See Swartley and others in Johns and Kraybill, eds., *Even the Demons Submit.*

Bibliography

Abegg, Martin G. "Qumran, Non-biblical Manuscripts." In *Accordance Bible Software*. Altamonte Springs, FL: Oaktree Software Specialists, 2006.

Adeyemo, Tokunboh, editor. *Africa Bible Commentary: A One-Volume Commentary Written by 70 African Scholars*. 2nd ed. Grand Rapids: Zondervan, 2010.

Agamben, G. *The Time That Remains: A Commentary on the Letter to the Romans*. Translated by Patricia Dailey. Stanford: Stanford University Press, 2005.

Albrecht, Elizabeth Soto. *Family Violence: Reclaiming a Theology of Nonviolence*. Maryknoll, NY: Orbis, 2008.

————. *Seek Peace and Pursue It: Women, Faith and Family Care*. Scottdale, PA: Faith & Life Resources, 2010.

Albrektson, Bertil. "On the Syntax of 'hyh 'šr 'hyh in Exodus 3:14." In *Words and Meanings: Essays Presented to David Winton Thomas on His Retirement from the Regius Professorship of Hebrew in the University of Cambridge, 1968*, edited by Peter R. Ackroyd and Barnabas Lindars, 15–28. Cambridge: Cambridge University Press, 1968.

Alkier, Stefan. "Witness or Warrior? How the Book of Revelation Can Help Christians Live Their Political Lives." In *Revelation and the Politics of Interpretation*, edited by Richard B. Hays and Stefan Alkier, 125–42. Waco, TX: Baylor University Press, 2012.

Ames, William. *The Marrow of Theology*. Translated by John Dykstra Eusden. Durham, NC: Labyrinth, 1983.

Aune, David E. "Early Christian Eschatology." In *ABD* 2:594–609.

————. *The New Testament and Its Literary Environment*. LEC 8. Philadelphia: Westminster, 1987.

————. *Revelation 6–16*. WBC 52B. Nashville: Nelson, 1998.

————. *Revelation 17–22*. WBC 52C. Nashville: Nelson, 1998.

Baker, David. "Pathros." In *ABD* 5:178.

Barr, David L. "The Lamb Who Looks Like a Dragon? Characterizing Jesus in John's Apocalypse." In *The Reality of Apocalypse: Rhetoric and Politics in the Book of Revelation*, edited by David L. Barr, 205–20. SBL Symposium Series 39. Atlanta: Society of Biblical Literature, 2006.

Barr, James. *Biblical Words for Time*. Studies in Biblical Theology 1/33. 2nd ed. Naperville, IL: Allenson, 1969.

———. "Words for Love in Biblical Greek." In *The Glory of Christ in the New Testament: Studies in Christology in Memory of George Bradford Caird*, edited by L. D. Hurst and N. T. Wright, 3–18. Oxford: Oxford University Press, 1987.

Barrett, C. K. "The Background of Mark 10:45." In *New Testament Essays: Studies in Memory of Thomas Walter Manson, 1893–1958*, edited by A. J. B. Higgins, 1–18. Manchester: Manchester University Press, 1959.

———. *The Gospel according to St. John*. 2nd ed. Philadelphia: Westminster, 1978.

Barth, Karl. *Church Dogmatics*, Vol. 2/1: *The Doctrine of God*. Translated by G. W. Bromiley et al. Edited by G. W. Bromiley and T. F. Torrance. New York: T. & T. Clark, 2009.

Barton, George Aaron. *The Book of Ecclesiastes*. ICC. Edinburgh: T. & T. Clark, 1908.

Baruch, Elaine, and Lucienne Serrano, editors. "Interview with Julia Kristeva." In *Women Analyze Women*, 135–36. New York: New York University Press, 1988.

Bauckham, Richard. *The Climax of Prophecy: Studies on the Book of Revelation*. London: T. & T. Clark, 1993.

———. *Gospel Women: Studies of the Named Women in the Gospels*. Edinburgh: T. & T. Clark, 2002.

———. *Jesus and the God of Israel: God Crucified and Other Studies on the New Testament's Christology of Divine Identity*. Milton Keynes, UK: Paternoster, 2008.

———. *Jesus: A Very Short Introduction*. Oxford: Oxford University Press, 2011.

———. *The Theology of the Book of Revelation*. NTT. Cambridge: Cambridge University Press, 1993.

———. "The Throne of God and the Worship of Jesus." In *The Jewish Roots of Christological Monotheism: Papers from the St. Andrews Conference on the Historical Origins of the Worship of Jesus*, edited by Carey C. Newman, James R. Davila, and Gladys S. Lewis, 43–69. Leiden: Brill, 1999.

Bauman, Zygmunt. *Postmodernity and Its Discontents*. New York: New York University Press, 1997.

———. "What Prospects of Morality in Times of Uncertainty?" *Theory, Culture and Society* 15 (1998) 11–22.

Beasley-Murray, George R. *John*. WBC 36. Waco, TX: Word, 1987.

Begg, Christopher T. "'Seeking Yahweh' and the Purpose of Chronicles." *LS* 9 (1982) 128–41.

Beitzel, B. J. "Exodus 3:14 and the Divine Name: A Case of Biblical Paronomasia." *TJ* 1 (1980) 5–20.

Beker, J. Christiaan. *Paul the Apostle: The Triumph of God in Life and Thought*. 2nd ed. Philadelphia: Fortress, 1984.

———. *Paul's Apocalyptic Gospel: The Coming Triumph of God*. Philadelphia: Fortress, 1982.

———. *The Triumph of God: The Essence of Paul's Thought*. Minneapolis: Fortress, 1990.

Bender, Harold. *The Anabaptist Vision*. Rev. ed. Scottdale, PA: Herald, 1944.

Ben Zvi, Ehud. "The Book of Chronicles: Another Look." *SR* 31 (2002) 261–81.

Bernat, David A., and Jonathan Klawans, editors. *Religion and Violence: The Biblical Heritage*. Recent Research in Biblical Studies 2. Sheffield: Sheffield Phoenix, 2007.

Biesecker-Mast, Gerald. *Separation and the Sword in Anabaptist Persuasion*. Telford, PA: Cascadia, 2006.

Bin Gorion, Misha Joseph, editor. *Mimekor Yisrael: Classical Jewish Folktales*. Vol. 3. Bloomington: Indiana University Press, 1976.

Bird, Jennifer. "To What End? Revisiting the Gendered Space of 1 Corinthians 11:2–16 from a Feminist Postcolonial Perspective." In *The Colonized Apostle: Paul through Postcolonial Eyes*, edited by Christopher D. Stanley, 175–85. Paul in Critical Contexts. Minneapolis: Fortress, 2011.

Birky, Wilbur J. "Introduction." In *The Poetry of Yorifumi Yaguchi: A Japanese Voice in English*, 7–9. Intercourse, PA: Good Books, 2006.

Black, Mark C. "The Rejected and Slain Messiah Who Is Coming with His Angels: The Messianic Exegesis of Zechariah 9–14 in the Passion Narratives." PhD diss., Emory University, 1990.

Blenkinsopp, Joseph. "The Cosmological and Protological Language of Deutero-Isaiah." *CBQ* 73 (2011) 493–510.

———. "Ecclesiastes 3.1–15: Another Interpretation." *JSOT* 66 (1995) 55–64.

———. *Isaiah 1–39: A New Translation with Introduction and Commentary*. AB 19. New York: Doubleday, 2000.

Block, Daniel I. *The Book of Ezekiel: Chapters 25–48*. NICOT. Grand Rapids: Eerdmans, 1998.

Blount, Brian K. *Revelation: A Commentary*. NTL. Louisville: Westminster John Knox, 2009.

Bodi, Daniel. "Les gillûlîm chez Ézéchiel et dans l'Ancient Testament, et les différentes partiques cultuelles associées à ce terme." *RB* 100 (1993) 481–510.

Borg, Marcus. *Conflict, Holiness, and Politics in the Teachings of Jesus*. Harrisburg, PA: Trinity, 1998.

———. *Jesus, a New Vision: Spirit, Culture and the Life of Discipleship*. San Francisco: Harper & Row, 1988.

———. *Jesus: Uncovering the Life, Teachings, and Relevance of a Religious Revolutionary*. San Francisco: HarperSanFrancisco, 2006.

Boustan, Ra'anan S., Alex Jassen, and Calvin Roetzel, editors. *Violence, Scripture, and Textual Practice in Early Judaism and Christianity*. Leiden: Brill, 2010.

Boxall, Ian. *Revelation: Vision and Insight*. London: SPCK, 2002.

Boyarin, Daniel. *Dying for God: Martyrdom and the Making of Christianity and Judaism*. Stanford, CA: Stanford University Press, 1999.

———. "Paul among the Antiphilosophers; or, Saul among the Sophists." In *St. Paul among the Philosophers*, edited by John Caputo and Linda Martin, 109–40. Indiana Series in the Philosophy of Religion. Bloomington: Indiana University Press, 2009.

Boyd, Gregory A. *God at War: The Bible and Spiritual Conflict*. Downers Grove, IL: InterVarsity, 1997.

———. *Satan and the Problem of Evil: Constructing a Trinitarian Warfare Theodicy*. Downers Grove, IL: InterVarsity, 2001.

Bradley, K. R. "On the Roman Slave Supply and Slavebreeding." In *Classical Slavery*, edited by M. I. Finley, 42–64. London: Cass, 1987.

Brandon, S. G. F. *Jesus and the Zealots: A Study of the Political Factor in Primitive Christianity*. New York: Scribner, 1967.

Bratcher, Robert G., and Barclay M. Newman. *A Translator's Handbook on the Book of Joshua*. Helps for Translators. New York: United Bible Societies, 1983.

Bredin, Mark. *Jesus: Revolutionary of Peace: A Nonviolent Christology in the Book of Revelation*. Paternoster Biblical and Theological Monographs. Carlisle, UK: Paternoster, 2003.

Brenneman, James E. "Sequencing Allegiances: Idolatry and the One God." *Vision* 12/1 (2011) 5–13.

Brenner, Athalya. "M Text Authority in Biblical Love Lyrics: The Case of Qoheleth 3:1–9 and Its Textual Relatives." In *On Gendering Texts: Female and Male Voices in the Hebrew Bible*, edited by A. Brenner and Fokkelien van Dijk-Hemmes, 133–63. Biblical Interpretation Series 1. Leiden: Brill, 1993.

Brimlow, Robert W. *What about Hitler? Wrestling with Jesus's Call to Nonviolence in an Evil World*. Christian Practice of Everyday Life. Grand Rapids: Brazos, 2006.

Brin, Gershon. *The Concept of Time in the Bible and the Dead Sea Scrolls*. Studies on the Texts of the Desert of Judah 39. Leiden: Brill, 2001.

Brown, Raymond E. *The Gospel according to John*. 2 vols. AB 29–29A. Garden City, NY: Doubleday, 1966–1970.

Brown, Robert McAffee. *Religion and Violence*. 2nd ed. Philadelphia: Westminster, 1987.

Cahill, Lisa Sowle. *Love Your Enemies: Discipleship, Pacifism, and Just War Theory*. Minneapolis: Fortress, 1994.

"CAMCA Declaration." *Courier* 3/1 (1988) 3.

Campbell, Douglas. *The Deliverance of God: An Apocalyptic Rereading of Justification in Paul*. Grand Rapids: Eerdmans, 2009.

———. *The Quest for Paul's Gospel: A Suggested Strategy*. JSNTSup 274. London: T. & T. Clark, 2005.

Carney, Thomas Francis. *The Shape of the Past: Models and Antiquity*. Lawrence, KS: Coronado, 1975.

Carter, Craig. *He Came Preaching Peace*. Eugene, OR: Wipf & Stock, 1998.

———. *The Politics of the Cross: The Theology and Social Ethics of John Howard Yoder*. Grand Rapids: Brazos, 2001.

Carter, Warren. *The Roman Empire and the New Testament: An Essential Guide*. Abingdon Essential Guides. Nashville: Abingdon, 2006.

Cassidy, Richard. *Society and Politics in the Acts of the Apostles*. Maryknoll, NY: Orbis, 1987.

Cassuto, Umberto. *A Commentary on the Book of Exodus*. Translated by Israel Abrahams. Publications of the Perry Foundation for Biblical Research in the Hebrew University of Jerusalem. Jerusalem: Magnes, 1967.

Castelli, Elizabeth A. *Imitating Paul: A Discourse of Power*. LCBI. Louisville: Westminster John Knox, 1991.

Cavanaugh, William. *The Myth of Religious Violence: Secular Ideology and the Roots of Modern Conflict*. Oxford: Oxford University Press, 2009.

Childs, Brevard S. *The Book of Exodus: A Critical, Theological Commentary*. OTL. Louisville: Westminster, 1974.

Chilton, Bruce. *The Temple of Jesus: His Sacrificial Program within a Cultural History of Sacrifice*. University Park: Pennsylvania State University Press, 1992.

Clauson, Kevin L. "Environmentalism: A Modern Idolatry." Covenant Community Church of Orange County, Center for Reformed Theology and Apologetics, 1990. Online: http://www.reformed.org/webfiles/antithesis/index.html?mainframe=/webfiles/antithesis/v1n2/ant_v1n2_environ.html.

Clendenin, Daniel B. "Jesus Unhinged: The Cleansing of the Temple; Third Sunday in Lent 2009." The Journey with Jesus: Notes to Myself, March 9, 2009. Online: http://www.journeywithjesus.net/Essays/20090309JJ.shtml.

Cohen, A. *Midrash Rabbah: Ecclesiastes.* 3rd ed. London: Soncino [electronic], 1983.

Collins, Adela Yarbro. *Crisis and Catharsis: The Power of the Apocalypse.* Philadelphia: Westminster, 1984.

———. *Mark: A Commentary.* Hermeneia. Minneapolis: Fortress, 2007.

Collins, John J. *Beyond the Qumran Community: The Sectarian Movement of the Dead Sea Scrolls.* Grand Rapids: Eerdmans, 2010.

Collins, Matthew A. *The Use of Sobriquets in the Qumran Dead Sea Scrolls.* Library of Second Temple Studies 67. London: T. & T. Clark, 2009.

Columella (Lucius Junius Moderatus). *On Agriculture (De Re Rustica) Books 1–4.* Edited and translated by Harrison Boyd Ash. Vol. 1. LCL 361. Cambridge, MA: Harvard University Press, 1941.

Conzelmann, Hans. *The Theology of St. Luke.* Translated by Geoffrey Buswell. Philadelphia: Fortress, 1961.

Cooke, G. A. *A Critical and Exegetical Commentary on the Book of Ezekiel.* ICC. Edinburgh: T. & T. Clark, 1936.

Craigie, Peter C. *The Problem of War in the Old Testament.* Grand Rapids: Eerdmans, 1978.

Creach, Jerome F. D. *The Destiny of the Righteous in the Psalms.* St. Louis: Chalice, 2008.

———. *Joshua.* Interpretation. Louisville: John Knox, 2003.

Creed, Barbara. *The Monstrous Feminine: Film, Feminism, Psychoanalysis.* London: Routledge, 1993.

Crenshaw, James L. *Ecclesiastes, A Commentary.* OTL. Philadelphia: Westminster, 1987.

Crook, Zeba A. "Grace as Benefaction in Galatians 2:9, 1 Corinthians 3:10, and Romans 12:3; 15:15." In *The Social Sciences and Biblical Translation*, edited by Dietmar Neufeld, 25–38. SBL Symposium Series 41. Leiden: Brill, 2008.

Crossan, John Dominic, and Jonathan L. Reed. *In Search of Paul: How Jesus's Apostle Opposed Rome's Empire with God's Kingdom.* San Francisco: HarperSanFrancisco, 2004.

Croy, N. Clayton. "The Messianic Whippersnapper: Did Jesus Use a Whip on People in the Temple (John 2:15)?" *JBL* 128 (2009) 553–66.

Curtis, Edward M. "Idol, Idolatry." In *ABD* 3:376–81.

Davidson, Jo Ann. "'Even if Noah, Daniel, and Job' (Ezekiel 14:14, 20)—Why these Three?" *JATS* 12 (2001) 132–44.

Davies, Philip R. "Defending the Boundaries of Israel in the Second Temple Period: 2 Chronicles 20 and the 'Salvation Army.'" In *Priests, Prophets and Scribes: Essays on the Formation and Heritage of Second Temple Judaism in Honour of Joseph Blenkinsopp*, edited by E. Ulrich et al., 43–54. JSOTSup 149. Sheffield: Sheffield Academic, 1992.

Davies, Philip R., George J. Brooke, and Phillip R. Callaway. *The Complete World of the Dead Sea Scrolls.* New York: Thames & Hudson, 2002.

Davis, Ellen F. "'And Pharaoh Will Change His Mind . . .' (Ezekiel 32:31): Dismantling Mythical Discourse." In *Theological Exegesis: Essays in Honor of Brevard S. Childs*, edited by Christopher Seitz and Kathryn Greene-McCreight, 224–39. Grand Rapids: Eerdmans, 1999.

Day, John. *God's Conflict with the Dragon and the Sea: Echoes of a Canaanite Myth in the Old Testament.* UCOP 35. Cambridge: Cambridge University Press, 1985.

Day, Richard J. F. *Gramsci Is Dead: Anarchist Currents in the Newest Social Movements.* Toronto: Between the Lines, 2005.

Dear, John. "Didn't Jesus Overturn Tables and Chase People Out of the Temple with a Whip?" In *A Faith Not Worth Fighting For: Addressing Commonly Asked Questions about Christian Nonviolence,* edited by Tripp York and Justin Bronson Barringer, 184–91. Peaceable Kingdom 1. Eugene, OR: Cascade, 2012.

"Declaration by Participants at Peace Seminar in Zaire." *Courier* 2/1 (1987) 7.

Delitzsch, Franz. *Proverbs, Ecclesiastes, Song of Solomon.* Grand Rapids: Eerdmans, 1975.

Dentan, Robert C. "The Literary Affinities of Exodus 34:6f." *VT* 13 (1963) 34–51.

Desjardins, Michel. *Peace, Violence and the New Testament.* Biblical Seminar 46. Sheffield: Sheffield Academic, 1997.

De Wit, Hans, et al., editors. *Through the Eyes of Another: Intercultural Reading of the Bible.* Elkhart, IN: IMS, 2004.

Dinkler, Erich. "*Eirēnē*—the Early Christian Concept of Peace." In *The Meaning of Peace: Biblical Studies,* edited by Perry B. Yoder and Willard M. Swartley, 71–120. 2nd ed. SPS 2. Elkhart, IN: IMS, 2001.

Donahue, John R., and Daniel J. Harrington. *The Gospel of Mark.* SP 2. Collegeville, MN: Liturgical, 2002.

Donfried, Karl P. "The Imperial Cults of Thessalonica and Political Conflict in 1 Thessalonians." In *Paul and Empire: Religion and Power in Roman Imperial Society,* edited by Richard Horsley, 215–23. Harrisburg, PA: Trinity, 1997.

Dozeman, Thomas B. *Commentary on Exodus.* Grand Rapids: Eerdmans, 2009.

Dressler, Harold H. P. "The Identification of the Ugaritic Dnil with the Daniel of Ezekiel." *VT* 29 (1979) 152–61.

———. "Reading and Interpreting the Aqht Text: A Rejoinder to Drs. J. Day and B. Margalit." *VT* 34 (1984) 78–82.

Driedger, Leo, and Donald B. Kraybill. *Mennonite Peacemaking: From Quietism to Activism.* Scottdale, PA: Herald, 1994.

Driver, John. *Becoming God's Community.* Elgin, IL: Brethren, 1981.

———. *Christian Mission and Social Justice.* With Samuel Escobar. Scottdale, PA: Herald, 1978.

———. *Community and Commitment.* Scottdale, PA: Herald, 1976.

———. *How Christians Made Peace with War: Early Christian Understandings of War.* Scottdale, PA: Herald, 1988.

———. *Images of the Church in Mission.* Scottdale, PA: Herald, 1997.

———. *Kingdom Citizens.* Scottdale, PA: Herald, 1980.

———. *Radical Faith: An Alternative History of the Christian Church.* Kitchener, ON: Pandora, 1999.

———. *Understanding the Atonement for the Mission of the Church.* Scottdale, PA: Herald, 1986.

Driver, S. R. *Notes on the Hebrew Text of the Books of Samuel.* 2nd ed. 1913. Reprint, Eugene, OR: Wipf & Stock, 2004.

Durham, John I. *Exodus.* WBC 3. Nashville: Nelson, 1987.

Durnbaugh, Donald F. *On Earth Peace: Discussions on War/Peace Issues between Friends, Mennonites, Brethren, and European Churches, 1935–75.* Elgin, IL: Brethren, 1978.

Eaton, Michael A. *Ecclesiastes: An Introduction and Commentary*. Tyndale Old Testament Commentaries 18. Leicester, UK: Inter-Varsity, 1983.

Edwards, George R. *Jesus and the Politics of Violence*. New York: Harper & Row, 1972.

Ehrensperger, Kathy. *Paul and the Dynamics of Power: Communication and Interaction in the Early-Christ Movement*. LNTS 325. London: T. & T. Clark, 2007.

Ehrlich, Carl S. "'Make Yourself No Graven Image': The Second Commandment and Judaism." In *Textures and Meaning: Thirty Years of Judaic Studies at the University of Massachusetts Amherst*, edited by Leonard H. Ehrlich et al., 254–71. Amherst: Dept. of Judaic and Near Eastern Studies, University of Massachusetts Amherst, 2004. Online: http://www.umass.edu/judaic/anniversaryvolume/articles/18-D1-CEhrlich.pdf.

Eichrodt, Walther. *Ezekiel: A Commentary*. Translated by Cosslett Quin. OTL. Philadelphia: Westminster, 1970.

Elias, Jacob W. *1 and 2 Thessalonians*. BCBC. Scottdale, PA: Herald, 1995.

———. *Remember the Future: The Pastoral Theology of Paul the Apostle*. Scottdale, PA: Herald, 2006.

Ellens, J. Harold, editor. *The Destructive Power of Religion: Violence in Judaism, Christianity, and Islam*. 4 vols. Westport, CT: Praeger, 2004.

Eller, Jack David. *Cruel Creeds, Virtuous Violence: Religious Violence across Culture and History*. New York: Prometheus, 2010.

Eller, Vernard. *War and Peace from Genesis to Revelation*. Scottdale, PA: Herald, 1981.

Elliott, Neil. *The Arrogance of Nations: Reading Romans in the Shadow of Empire*. Paul in Critical Contexts. Minneapolis: Fortress, 2008.

———. *Liberating Paul: The Justice of God and the Politics of the Apostle*. 1994. Reprint, Minneapolis: Fortress, 2005.

Endres, John C. "Theology of Worship in Chronicles." In *The Chronicler as Theologian: Essays in Honor of Ralph W. Klein*, edited by M. P. Graham et al., 165–88. JSOTSup 371. London: T. & T. Clark, 2003.

Esquivia Ballestas, Ricardo. "To the Anabaptist-Mennonite Churches of the United States of America: A Message of Gratitude, Condolence, and Hope." *Courier* 16/3–4 (2001) 8.

Evans, Craig A. *Mark 8:27—16:20*. WBC 34B. Nashville: Nelson, 2001.

Exegetical Dictionary of the New Testament. 3 vols. Edited by Horst Balz and Gerhard Schneider. Grand Rapids: Eerdmans, 1990–1993.

Farmer, Kathleen A. *Who Knows What Is Good? A Commentary on the Books of Proverbs and Ecclesiastes*. ITC. Grand Rapids: Eerdmans, 1991.

Fee, Gordon. *The First and Second Letters to the Thessalonians*. NICNT. Grand Rapids: Eerdmans, 2009.

———. *Paul's Letter to the Philippians*. NICNT. Grand Rapids: Eerdmans, 1995.

Finger, Reta Halteman. *Of Widows and Meals: Communal Meals in the Book of Acts*. Grand Rapids: Eerdmans, 2007.

Fiore, Benjamin. "Friendship in the Exhortation of Romans 15:14–33." In *Proceedings of the Eastern Great Lakes and Midwest Biblical Societies* 7 (1987) 95–103.

Fitzgerald, John T. "Christian Friendship: John, Paul and the Philippians." *Int* 61 (2007) 284–96.

———. "Paul and Friendship." In *Paul in the Greco-Roman World: A Handbook*, edited by J. Paul Sampley, 319–43. Harrisburg, PA: Trinity, 2003.

Fitzmyer, Joseph A. *The Gospel according to Luke X–XXIV*. AB 28A. New York: Doubleday, 1985.

Flusser, David. "The Hatred through the Love." In *The Spiritual History of the Dead Sea Sect*, 76–82. Woodstock, VT: Jewish Lights, 1989.

Foerster, W. "*Eirēnē*." In *TDNT* 2:400–402.

Ford, Josephine Massyngbaerde. "Shalom in the Johannine Corpus." *HBT* 6/2 (1984) 67–90.

Fowl, Stephen E. *Philippians*. THNTC. Grand Rapids: Eerdmans, 2005.

Fox, Michael V. *Qohelet and His Contradictions*. Bible and Literature Series. Sheffield: Almond, 1989.

———. "The Rhetoric of Ezekiel's Vision of the Valley of the Bones." *HUCA* 51 (1980) 1–15.

———. *A Time to Tear Down and a Time to Build Up: A Rereading of Ecclesiastes*. Grand Rapids: Eerdmans, 1999.

———. "The Uses of Indeterminacy." *Semeia* 71 (1995) 173–92.

France, R. T. *The Gospel of Mark: A Commentary on the Greek Text*. NIGTC. Grand Rapids: Eerdmans 2002.

———. *Jesus and the Old Testament: His Application of Old Testament Passages to Himself and His Mission*. Vancouver: Regent College Publishing, 1998.

Frankemölle, Hubert. *Friede und Schwert: Frieden schaffen nach dem Neuen Testament*. Mainz: Matthias-Grünewald, 1983.

Frankfort, H. *Kingship and the Gods*. Chicago: University of Chicago Press, 1948.

Fredericks, Daniel C. "Ecclesiastes." In *Ecclesiastes and the Song of Songs*, by Daniel C. Fredericks and Daniel J. Estes. Apollos Old Testament Commentary. Downers Grove, IL: InterVarsity, 2010.

Fredrickson, David E. "Paul, Hardships, and Suffering." In *Paul in the Greco-Roman World: A Handbook*, edited by J. Paul Sampley, 172–97. Harrisburg, PA: Trinity, 2003.

Freedman, David Noel, editor. *The Anchor Bible Dictionary*. 6 vols. New York: Doubleday, 1992.

———. "The Name of the God of Moses." *JBL* 79 (1960) 151–56.

Frydrych, Tomáš. *Living under the Sun: Examination of Proverbs and Qoheleth*. VTSup 90. Leiden: Brill, 2002.

Gafni, Isaiah M. "The World of the Talmud: From the Mishnah to the Arab Conquest." In *Christianity and Rabbinic Judaism: A Parallel History of Their Origins and Development*, edited by Hershel Shanks, 225–65. Washington, DC: Biblical Archaeological Society, 1992.

Gager, John G. "Violent Acts and Violent Language in the Apostle Paul." In *Violence in the New Testament*, edited by Shelly Matthews and E. Leigh Gibson, 13–21. New York: T. & T. Clark, 2005.

Galtung, Johan. "Violence, Peace, and Peace Research." *Journal of Peace Research* 6 (1969) 167–91.

The General Board of the General Conference Mennonite Church and the Mennonite Church General Board. *Confession of Faith in a Mennonite Perspective*. Scottdale, PA: Herald, 1995.

General Conference Mennonite Church. "The Way of Christian Love in Race Relations" (24 August 1955). *Global Anabaptist Mennonite Encyclopedia Online*. Online:

http://www.anabaptistwiki.org/mediawiki/index.php/The_Way_of_Christian_Love_in_Race_Relations_%28Mennonite_Church,_1955%29.

Giblin, Charles H. *The Threat to Faith: An Exegetical and Theological Re-examination of 2 Thessalonians 2*. AnBib 31. Rome: Pontificio Istituto Biblio, 1967.

Gingerich, Ray C., and Ted Grimsrud, editors. *Transforming the Powers: Peace, Justice, and the Domination System*. Minneapolis: Fortress, 2006.

Glancy, Jennifer A. *Slavery in Early Christianity*. New York: Oxford University Press, 2002.

Goeringer, Howard. *Haunts of Violence in the Church: A Look at the Answer That Overcomes Violence, A Biblical Interpretation of Peace and Violence*. West Conshohocken, PA: Infinity, 2005.

Goldstein, Joshua S. *Winning the War on War: The Decline of Armed Conflict Worldwide*. New York: Dutton, 2011.

Gordis, Robert. *Koheleth—the Man and His World: A Study of Ecclesiastes*. 3rd ed. New York: Schocken, 1968.

Gorman, Michael J. *Inhabiting the Crucified God: Kenosis, Justification, and Theosis in Paul's Narrative Soteriology*. Grand Rapids: Eerdmans, 2009.

————. "Justification and Justice in Paul, with Special Reference to the Corinthians." *JSPL* 1 (2011) 23–40.

————. *Reading Revelation Responsibly: Uncivil Worship and Witness: Following the Lamb into the New Creation*. Eugene, OR: Cascade, 2011.

Graham, M. Patrick. "Setting the Heart to Seek God: Worship in 2 Chronicles 30.1–31.1." In *Worship and the Hebrew Bible: Essays in Honour of John T. Willis*, edited by M. Patrick Graham et al., 124–41. JSOTSup 284. Sheffield: Sheffield Academic, 1999.

Greenberg, Moshe. *Ezekiel 1–20: A New Translation with Introduction and Commentary*. AB 22. Garden City, NY: Doubleday, 1983.

————. *Ezekiel 21–37: A New Translation with Introduction and Commentary*. AB 22A. New York: Doubleday, 1997.

Greenfield, Jonas C., Michael E. Stone, and Esther Eshel. *The Aramaic Levi Document: Edition, Translation, Commentary*. SVTP 19. Leiden: Brill, 2004.

Gressmann, Hugo. *Mose und seine Zeit: Ein Kommentar zu den Mose-Sagen*. FRLANT 18. Vandenhoeck & Ruprecht, 1913.

Griffith, Lee. *God Is Subversive: Talking Peace in a Time of Empire*. Grand Rapids: Eerdmans, 2011.

Grimsrud, Ted, and Mark Thiessen Nation. *Reasoning Together: A Conversation on Homosexuality*. Scottdale, PA: Herald, 2008.

Gummere, Richard M., translator. *Seneca. Epistles 1–65*. LCL 75. Cambridge, MA: Harvard University Press, 2002.

Gutmann, J. "The 'Second Commandment' and the Image in Judaism." *HUCA* 32 (1961) 161–74.

Haenchen, Ernst. *A Commentary on the Gospel of John*. Hermeneia. Translated and edited by Robert W. Funk. Edited by Ulrich Busse. Philadelphia: Fortress, 1984.

Halbertal, Moshe, and Avishai Margalit. *Idolatry*. Cambridge: Harvard University Press, 1992.

Hallo, William W., and K. Lawson Younger Jr., editors. *The Context of Scripture*. 3 vols. Leiden: Brill, 1997–2002.

Hamlin, E. John. *Inheriting the Land: A Commentary on the Book of Joshua.* ITC. Grand Rapids: Eerdmans, 1983.

Hamori, Esther J. *When Gods Were Men: The Embodied God in Biblical and Near Eastern Literature.* BZAW 384. Berlin: de Gruyter, 2008.

Handy, Lowell K. "Peaceful Kansas Mennonites and Joshua's Violent Jericho." *Proceedings of the Eastern Great Lakes and Midwest Biblical Societies* 29 (2009) 29–36.

Harder, Leland, editor. *The Sources of Swiss Anabaptism: The Grebel Letters and Related Documents.* CRR 4. Scottdale, PA: Herald, 1985.

Harink, Douglas. *Paul among the Postliberals: Pauline Theology beyond Christendom and Modernity.* Grand Rapids: Brazos, 2003.

Hart, David Bentley. *The Beauty of the Infinite: The Aesthetics of Christian Truth.* Grand Rapids: Eerdmans, 2003.

Hayden, Vaughan. "American Idolatry? Competition, Singing and Communicating Values." Center for Parent/Youth Understanding, 2007. Online: http://www.cpyu. org/Page.aspx?id=289010.

Hays, Richard B. "Faithful Witness, Alpha and Omega: The Identity of Jesus in the Apocalypse of John." In *Revelation and the Politics of Apocalyptic Interpretation,* edited by Richard B. Hays and Stefan Alkier, 69–84. Waco, TX: Baylor University Press, 2012.

———. *The Faith of Jesus Christ: An Investigation into the Narrative Substructure of Galatians 3:1—4:11.* 2nd ed. Grand Rapids: Eerdmans, 2002.

———. *The Moral Vision of the New Testament: A Contemporary Introduction to New Testament Ethics: Cross, Community, New Creation.* San Francisco: HarperCollins, 1996.

Hays, Richard B., and Stefan Alkier, editors. *Revelation and the Politics of Apocalyptic Interpretation.* Waco, TX: Baylor University Press, 2012.

Heard, R. Christopher. "Echoes of Genesis in 1 Chronicles 4:9–10: An Intertextual and Contextual Reading of Jabez's Prayer." *JHS* 4 (2002) n.p. Online: http://epe.lac-bac. gc.ca/100/201/300/journal_hebrew/pdf/2002/article_24.pdf.

Heil, John Paul. "Ezekiel 34 and the Narrative Strategy of the Shepherd and Sheep Metaphor in Matthew." *CBQ* 55 (1993) 698–708.

Heisey, Nancy R. "'Reading with' and Related Biblical Conversations: Ordinary Readers and Biblical Scholars around the World." *TIC Talk* 67 (2010) n.p. Online: http:// www.ubs-translations.org/tt/past_issues/tic_talk_67_2010/.

Hellerman, Joseph. *Reconstructing Honor in Roman Philippi: Carmen Christi as Cursus Pudorum.* SNTSMS 123. Cambridge: Cambridge University Press, 2005.

Henderson, Suzanne Watts. "'If Anyone Hungers . . .' An Integrated Reading of 1 Cor. 11:17–34." *NTS* 48 (2002) 195–208.

Hendrix, Holland Lee. "Archeology and Eschatology at Thessalonica." In *The Future of Early Christianity: Essays in Honor of Helmut Koester,* edited by B. Pearson, 107–18. Minneapolis: Fortress, 1991.

Hengel, Martin. "'Sit at My Right Hand!' The Enthronement of Christ at the Right Hand of God and Psalm 110:1." In *Studies in Early Christology,* 119–226. Edinburgh: T. & T. Clark, 1995.

Hershberger, Guy F. *Christian Relationships to the State and Community.* 2nd ed. Mennonites and Their Heritage 5. Akron, PA: MCC, 1942.

————. "Our Citizenship Is in Heaven." In *Kingdom, Cross and Community: Essays on Mennonite Themes in Honor of Guy F. Hershberger*, edited by J. R. Burkholder and C. Redekop, 273–85. Scottdale, PA: Herald, 1976.

————. *War, Peace, and Nonresistance.* 5th ed. Scottdale, PA: Herald, 2009.

————. *The Way of the Cross in Human Relations.* Scottdale, PA: Herald, 1958.

Hoffman, Joseph, editor. *The Just War and Jihad: Violence in Judaism, Christianity and Islam.* New York: Prometheus, 2006.

Holland, Glenn S. *The Tradition That You Received from Us: 2 Thessalonians in the Pauline Tradition.* Hermeneutische Untersuchungen zur Theologie 24. Tübingen: Mohr/Siebeck, 1988.

Hooker, Morna D. *Jesus and the Servant: The Influence of the Servant Concept of Deutero-Isaiah in the New Testament.* London; SPCK, 1959.

Horsley, Richard A. *1 Corinthians.* ANTC. Nashville: Abingdon 1998.

————. *Jesus and the Spiral of Violence: Popular Jewish Resistance in Roman Palestine.* San Francisco: Harper & Row, 1987.

————, editor. *Paul and Empire: Religion and Power in Roman Imperial Society.* Harrisburg, PA: Trinity, 1997.

————. *Paul and Politics: Ekklesia, Israel, Imperium, Interpretation.* Harrisburg, PA: Trinity, 2000.

————. *Paul and the Roman Imperial Order.* Harrisburg, PA: Trinity, 2004.

Hossfeld, Frank-Lothar, and Erich Zenger. *Psalms 2.* Translated by Linda M. Maloney. Hermeneia. Minneapolis: Fortress, 2005.

Houtman, Cornelis. *Exodus.* Vol. 2. Translated by Johan Rebel and Sierd Woudstra. Historical Commentary on the Old Testament. Kampen: Kok, 1996.

Huebner, Harry. "Christian Pacifism and the Character of God." In *The Church as Theological Community: Essays in Honour of David Schroeder*, edited by David Schroeder and Harry John Huebner, 247–72. Winnipeg: CMBC, 1990.

Jacobsen, Thorkild. "The Graven Image." In *Ancient Israelite Religion: Essays In Honor of Frank Moore Cross*, edited by Patrick D. Miller et al., 15–32. Philadelphia: Fortress, 1987.

Janzen, Anna. *Der Friede im lukanischen Doppelwerk vor dem Hintergrund der Pax Romana.* Frankfurt: Lang, 2002.

Janzen, Waldemar. "Christian Perspectives on War and Peace in the Old Testament." In *Still in the Image: Essays in Biblical Theology and Anthropology*, 193–211. Newton, KS: Faith & Life, 1982.

————. "The First Commandments of the Decalogue and the Battle against Idolatry in the Old Testament." *Vision* 12, no. 1 (2011) 15–24.

"Japanese Share Peace Message in Hiroshima and Nagasaki." *Courier* 1, no. 3 (1986) 16.

Japhet, Sara. *I & II Chronicles.* OTL. Louisville: Westminster John Knox, 1993.

————. *The Ideology of the Book of Chronicles and Its Place in Biblical Thought.* Translated by Anna Barber. BEATAJ 9. Frankfurt: Lang, 1989.

————. "The Supposed Common Authorship of Chronicles and Ezra–Nehemiah Investigated Anew." *VT* 18 (1968) 332–72.

Jassen, Alex P. "The Dead Sea Scrolls and Violence: Sectarian Formation and Eschatological Imagination." *BibInt* 17 (2009) 12–44.

Jewett, Robert. *Paul, the Apostle to America: Cultural Trends and Pauline Scholarship.* Louisville: Westminster John Knox, 1994.

Johns, Loren L. *The Lamb Christology of the Apocalypse of John: An Investigation into Its Origins and Rhetorical Force.* WUNT 2/167. Tübingen: Mohr/Siebeck, 2003.

Johns, Loren L., and James R. Kraybill, editors. *Even the Demons Submit: Continuing Jesus' Ministry of Deliverance.* Elkhart, IN: IMS, 2006.

Johnson, Luke Timothy. *The Gospel of Luke.* SP 3. Collegeville, MN: Liturgical, 1991.

Johnson, Raymond Eugene. "The Rhetorical Question as a Literary Device in Ecclesiastes." PhD diss., Southern Baptist Theological Seminary, 1986.

Joly, Robert. *Le vocabulaire chrétien de l'amour est-il original? Philein et agapan dans le grec antique.* Brussels: Presses University de Bruxelles, 1968.

Jones, L. Gregory. *Embodying Forgiveness: A Theological Analysis.* Grand Rapids: Eerdmans, 1996.

Josephus. *The Jewish War.* In *Josephus II.* Translated by H. St. J. Thackeray. LCL 141. Cambridge: Harvard University Press, 1956.

Joüon, Paul. *A Grammar of Biblical Hebrew.* Translated and revised by T. Muraoka. Subsidia biblica 27. Rome: Pontificio Istituto Biblico, 2006.

Joyce, Paul. *Ezekiel: A Commentary.* LBHOTS 482. New York: T. & T. Clark, 2009.

Judge, E. A. "Decrees of Caesar at Thessalonica (Acts 17:5–7)." *RTR* 30 (1971) 1–7.

Juergensmeyer, Mark. *Terror in the Mind of God: The Global Rise of Religious Violence.* 3rd ed. Berkeley: University of California Press, 2003.

Juergensmeyer, Mark, and Margo Kitts, editors. *Princeton Readings in Religion and Violence.* Princeton: Princeton University Press, 2011.

Kaiser, Otto. "Determination und Freiheit beim Kohelet/Prediger Salomo und in der Frühen Stoa." *NZSTh* 31 (1989) 251–70.

Kaiser, Walter C. *Ecclesiastes: Total Life.* Chicago: Moody, 1979.

Kalimi, Isaac. *The Reshaping of Ancient Israelite History in Chronicles.* Winona Lake, IN: Eisenbrauns, 2005.

Kampen, John. *Wisdom Literature.* ECDSS. Grand Rapids: Eerdmans, 2011.

Kaufmann, Yehezkel. *The Religion of Israel, from Its Beginnings to the Babylonian Exile.* London: Allen & Unwin, 1961.

Kearney, Richard. *Strangers, Gods and Monsters: Interpreting Otherness.* London: Routledge, 2003.

Keener, Craig S. *The Gospel of John: A Commentary.* 2 vols. Peabody, MA: Hendrickson, 2003.

Kelsey, David H. *Proving Doctrine: The Uses of Scripture in Modern Theology.* Harrisburg, PA: Trinity, 1999.

Kimball, Charles. *When Religion Becomes Lethal: The Explosive Mix of Politics and Religion in Judaism, Christianity, and Islam.* San Francisco: Jossey-Bass, 2011.

King, Martin Luther, Jr. *Strength to Love.* 1963. Reprint, Fortress Press Gift Edition. Minneapois: Fortress, 2010.

Kinzer, Mark S. *Post-Missionary Messianic Judaism: Redefining Christian Engagement with the Jewish People.* Grand Rapids: Brazos, 2005.

Kittredge, Cynthia Briggs. *Community and Authority: The Rhetoric of Obedience in the Pauline Tradition.* HTS. Harrisburg, PA: Trinity, 1998.

Klassen, William. "Coals of Fire: Symbol of Repentance or Revenge?" *NTS* 9 (1963) 337–50.

———. *Love of Enemies: The Way to Peace.* OBT 15. Philadelphia: Fortress, 1984.

———. "Peace." In *ABD* 5:207–12.

————. "Peace." In *Illustrated Dictionary and Concordance of the Bible*, edited by G. Wigoder, 767–69. New York: Macmillan, 1986.

————. "Peace." In *A Dictionary of Jewish-Christians Relations*, edited by Edward Kessler and Neil Wenborn, 338. Cambridge: Cambridge University Press, 1995.

————. "War (NT)." In *ABD* 6:867–75.

Knobel, Peter S. *The Targum of Qohelet*. Aramaic Bible 15. Collegeville, MN: Liturgical, 1991.

Knoppers, Gary N. *1 Chronicles 1–9*. AB 12. New York: Doubleday, 2004.

————. "Images of David in Early Judaism: David as Repentant Sinner in Chronicles." *Bib* 76 (1995) 449–70.

————. "Jerusalem at War in Chronicles." In *Zion, City of Our God,* edited by Richard S. Hess and Gordon J. Wenham, 57–76. Grand Rapids: Eerdmans, 1999.

Konstan, David. *Friendship in the Classical World*. Key Themes in Ancient History. Cambridge: Cambridge University Press, 1997.

Kraus, C. Norman. *The Jesus Factor in Justice and Peacemaking*. Vol. 1, *Theological Postings*. Telford, PA: Cascadia, 2011.

Krisetya, Mesach. "Living Together in Mission: The Call of the Church." *Courier* 12/1 (1997) 12–13.

————. "A Vision of Global Communion." *Courier* 16/1 (2001) 11.

Kristeva, Julia. *Powers of Horror: An Essay on Abjection*. Translated by Leon S. Roudiez. New York: Columbia University Press, 1982.

Krodel, Gerhard. "The 'Religious Power of Lawlessness' (*Katechon*) as Precursor of the 'Lawless One' (*Anomos*) 2 Thess. 2:6–7." *CurTM* 17 (1990) 440–46.

Krüger, Thomas. *Qoheleth*. Translated by O. C. Dean Jr. Hermeneia. Minneapolis: Fortress, 2004.

Kruger, H. A. J. "A Sword over His Head or in His Hand? Luke 22:35–38." In *The Scriptures in the Gospels*, edited by C. M. Tuckett, 597–604. Bibliotheca Ephemeridum theologicarum Lovaniensium 131. Leuven: Leuven University Press, 1997.

Kulungu, Pascal Tshisola. *Manuel de Formation de Formateurs sur la Résolution Pacifique, Médiation et Réconciliation de Conflits*. Kinshasa: CPLB, 2011.

Kutsko, John F. *Between Heaven and Earth: Divine Presence and Absence in the Book of Ezekiel*. Winona Lake, IN: Eisenbrauns, 2000.

Kwakkel, Gert. "Righteousness." In *Dictionary of the Old Testament: Wisdom, Poetry, and Writings,* edited by Tremper Longman III and Peter Enns, 3:663–68. Downers Grove, IL: InterVarsity, 2008.

Lane, William L. *The Gospel according to Mark*. NICNT. Grand Rapids: Eerdmans 1974.

Lapide, Pinchas. *The Sermon on the Mount: Utopia or Program for Action?* Translated by Arlene Swidler. Maryknoll, NY: Orbis, 1986.

Lechte, John. *Julia Kristeva*. London: Routledge, 1990.

Leiter, David. *Neglected Voices: Peace in the Old Testament*. Scottdale, PA: Herald, 2007.

Leonhardt-Balzer, Jutta. "Righteousness in Early Jewish Literature." In *NIDB* 4:807–13.

Levine, Amy-Jill. *The Misunderstood Jew: The Church and the Scandal of the Jewish Jesus*. New York: HarperSanFrancisco, 2006.

Levine, Étan, editor. *The Aramaic Version of Qohelet*. New York: Genesis, 1978.

Levitt Kohn, Risa. "'With a Mighty Hand and an Outstretched Arm': The Prophet and the Torah in Ezekiel 20." In *Ezekiel's Hierarchal World: Wrestling with a Tiered Reality*, edited by Stephen L. Cook and Corrine L. Patton, 159–68. SBL Symposium Series 31. Atlanta: SBL, 2004.

Liechty, Joseph. "The National Anthem Debate at Goshen College." *Journal of Religion, Conflict, and Peace* 3/1 (2010) n.p. Online: http://religionconflictpeace.org/editor/national-anthem-debate-goshen-college.

Linafelt, Tod, and F. W. Dobbs-Allsopp. "Poetic Line Structure in Qoheleth 3:1." *VT* 60 (2010) 249–59.

Lind, Millard C. *Yahweh Is a Warrior: The Theology of Warfare in Ancient Israel.* A Christian Peace Shelf Selection. Scottdale, PA: Herald, 1980.

Lindblom, Johannes. "Noch Einmal die Deutung des Jahwe-Namens in Ex 3, 14." *ASTI* 3 (1964) 4–15.

Lintott, Andrew. *Violence in Republican Rome.* 2nd ed. Oxford: Oxford University Press, 1999.

Loader, James A. *Ecclesiastes, a Practical Commentary.* Translated by John Vriend. Text and Interpretation. Grand Rapids: Eerdmans, 1986.

————. *Polar Structures in the Book of Qohelet.* BZAW 152. Berlin: de Gruyter, 1979.

————. "Qohelet 3,2–8: A 'Sonnet' in the Old Testament." *ZAW* 81 (1969) 240–42.

Loeb Dieter, Otto Alvin. "Stasis." In *Landmark Essays on Classical Greek Rhetoric,* edited by Edward Schiappa, 211–41. Davis, CA: Hermagoras, 1994.

Long, Michael G., editor. *Christian Peace and Nonviolence: A Documentary History.* Maryknoll, NY: Orbis, 2011.

Longman, Tremper, III. *The Book of Ecclesiastes.* NICOT. Grand Rapids: Eerdmans, 1998.

Longman, Tremper, III, and Daniel G. Reid. *God Is a Warrior.* Studies in Old Testament Biblical Theology. Grand Rapids: Zondervan, 1995.

Magistrale, Tony. *Abject Terrors: Surveying the Modern and the Postmodern Horror Film.* New York: Lang, 2005.

Malherbe, Abraham J. "Antisthenes and Odysseus, and Paul at War." *HTR* 76 (1983) 143–73.

————. *Moral Exhortation, a Greco-Roman Sourcebook.* LEC 4. Philadelphia: Westminster, 1986.

————. *Paul and the Thessalonians: The Philosophic Tradition of Pastoral Care.* Philadelphia: Fortress, 1987.

Marchal, Joseph A. "Boundaries, Binaries, and Belonging: Assessing and Engaging the Violent Rhetorics of Philippians." Paper presented at the 2006 SBL Annual Meeting, Washington, DC, November 18–21, 2006.

————. "Imperial Intersections and Initial Inquiries: Toward a Feminist, Postcolonial Analysis of Philippians." In *The Colonized Apostle: Paul through Postcolonial Eyes,* edited by C. Stanley, 146–60. Paul in Critical Contexts. Minneapolis: Fortress, 2011.

————. "Military Images in Philippians 1–2: A Feminist Rhetorical Analysis of Scholarship, Philippians, and Current Contexts." In *Her Master's Tools? Feminist and Postcolonial Engagement of Historical-Critical Discourse,* edited by C. Vander Stichele and Todd Penner, 265–86. Global Perspectives on Biblical Scholarship. Atlanta: SBL, 2005.

Markquart, Edward F. "Gospel Analysis: The Cleansing of the Temple." Sermons from Seattle, 2006. Online: http://www.sermonsfromseattle.com/series_b_the_cleansing_of_the_temple_GA.htm.

Marshall, Christopher D. *Beyond Retribution: A New Testament Vision for Justice, Crime, and Punishment.* SPS 5. Grand Rapids: Eerdmans, 2001.

————. "Gemeinsam auf dem Weg Jesu Christi." *Jahrbuch für Geschichte und Kultur der Mennoniten in Paraguay* 10 (2009) 19–26.

Marshall, Peter. *Enmity in Corinth: Social Conventions in Paul's Relations with the Corinthians.* WUNT 2/23. Tübingen: Mohr/Siebeck, 1987.

Martin, Dale B. *The Corinthian Body.* New Haven: Yale University Press, 1995.

Martyn, J. Louis. *Theological Issues in the Letters of Paul.* Nashville: Abingdon, 1997.

Marzouk, Safwat. "'Not a Lion but a Dragon': The Monstrification of Egypt in the Book of Ezekiel." PhD diss., Princeton Theological Seminary, 2012.

Mathews, Shelley, and E. Leigh Gibson, editors. *Violence in the New Testament.* New York: T. & T. Clark, 2005.

Matties, Gordon. *Joshua.* BCBC. Harrisonburg, VA: Herald, 2012.

Mauser, Ulrich. *The Gospel of Peace: A Scriptural Message for Today's World.* SPS 1. Louisville: Westminster John Knox, 1992.

May, Gerhard. *Creatio ex Nihilo: The Doctrine of "Creation out of Nothing" in Early Christian Thought.* Edinburgh: T. & T. Clark, 1994.

McAfee, Noëlle. *Julia Kristeva.* Routledge Critical Thinkers. New York: Routledge, 2004.

McDonald, Patricia M. *God and Violence: Resources for Living in a Small World.* Scottdale, PA: Herald, 2004.

McKenzie, Steven L. *The Chronicler's Use of the Deuteronomistic History.* HSM 33. Atlanta: Scholars, 1984.

————. *1–2 Chronicles.* AOTC. Nashville: Abingdon, 2004.

McNicol, Allan J. *The Conversion of the Nations in Revelation.* LNTS 438. London: T. & T. Clark, 2010.

"MCSFI Issues Statement on Nuclear Tests in India and Pakistan." *Courier* 14, no. 3 (1999) 3.

Meeks, Wayne A. *The First Urban Christians: The Social World of the Apostle Paul.* New Haven: Yale University Press, 1982.

————. "Social Functions of Apocalyptic Language in Pauline Christianity." In *Apocalypticism in the Mediterranean World and the Near East*, edited by David Hellholm, 687–705. Tübingen: Mohr/Siebeck, 1983.

Meeks, Wayne, editor. *The Writings of St. Paul.* Norton Critical Editions. New York: Norton, 1972.

Mendez, Leonor de. "Restore Us, O God! A Meditation Based on Psalm 85." *Courier* 15/4 (2000) 16.

"Mennonite World Conference Peace Commission Peace Audit: Summary and Commentary, June 2012." MWC, 2012. Online: http://www.mwc-cmm.org/sites/default/files/website_files/peace_audit_2012_en.pdf.

Michaels, J. Ramsey. *The Gospel of John.* NICNT. Grand Rapids: Eerdmans, 2010.

Middleton, J. Richard. "Created in the Image of a Violent God? The Ethical Problem of the Conquest of Chaos in Biblical Creation Texts." *Int* 58 (2004) 341–55.

Milbank, John. "The Soul of Reciprocity Part One: Reciprocity Refused." *Modern Theology* 17 (2001) 335–91.

————. "The Soul of Reciprocity Part Two: Reciprocity Granted." *Modern Theology* 17 (2001) 485–507.

Milik, J. T. *Ten Years of Discovery in the Wilderness of Judea.* Translated by J. Strugnell. Studies in Biblical Theology 1/26. London: SCM, 1959.

Miller, Douglas B. *Ecclesiastes.* BCBC. Scottdale, PA: Herald, 2010.

————. "Power in Wisdom: The Suffering Servant of Ecclesiastes 4." In *Peace and Justice Shall Embrace: Power and Theopolitics in the Bible*, edited by Ted Grimsrud and Loren L. Johns, 145–73. Telford, PA: Pandora, 1999.

————. *Symbol and Rhetoric in Ecclesiastes: The Place of* Hebel *in Qohelet's Work.* Atlanta: SBL, 2002.

————. "What the Preacher Forgot: The Rhetoric of Ecclesiastes." *CBQ* 62 (2000) 215–35.

Miller, John W. Review of *Yahweh Is a Warrior: The Theology of Warfare in Ancient Israel*, by Millard C. Lind. *MQR* 56 (1982) 392–94.

Miller, Marlin E., and Barbara Nelson Gingerich, editors. *The Church's Peace Witness.* Grand Rapids: Eerdmans, 1994.

Minear, Paul S. "A Note on Luke xxii 36." *NovT* 7 (1964) 128–34.

————. "The Peace of God." In *Celebrating Peace*, edited Leroy S. Rouner, 118–31. Boston University Studies in Philosophy and Religion. Notre Dame: University of Notre Dame Press, 1990.

Minj, Sudhir Kumar. *Egypt: The Lower Kingdom: An Exegetical Study of the Oracle of Judgment against Egypt in Ezekiel 29, 1–16.* European University Studies. Series XXIII, Theology 828. Frankfurt: Lang, 2006.

Mitchell, Alan C. "'Greet the Friends by Name': New Testament Evidence for the Greco-Roman *Topos* on Friendship." In *Greco-Roman Perspectives on Friendship*, edited by John T. Fitzgerald, 225–62. Resources for Biblical Studies 34. Atlanta: Scholars, 1997.

Moberly, R. W. L. *At the Mountain of God: Story and Theology in Exodus 32–34.* JSOTSup 22. Sheffield: Continuum, 1983.

————. "How May We Speak of God? A Reconsideration of the Nature of Biblical Theology." *TynBul* 53/2 (2002) 177–202.

————. *The Old Testament of the Old Testament: Patriarchal Narratives and Mosaic Yahwism.* OBT. Minneapolis: Fortress, 1992.

Molin, Georg. "Das Motiv vom Chaoskampf im alten Orient und in den Traditionen Jerusalems und Israels." In *Memoria Jerusalem,* edited by J. B. Bauer and J. Marböck, 13–28. Graz: Akademische Verlaganstalt, 1977.

Moloney, Francis J. *The Gospel of John.* SP 4. Collegeville, MN: Liturgical, 1998.

Moltmann, Jürgen. *Ethics of Hope.* Translated by Margaret Kohl. Minneapolis: Fortress, 2012.

————. *Theology of Hope.* London: SCM, 1967.

Moo, Douglas J. *The Old Testament in the Gospel Passion Narratives.* Sheffield: Almond, 1983.

Mudenda, P. C. "Churches Face Critical Task in Explosive Southern Africa." *Courier* 1/1 (1986) 16.

Muhenya Guwamba, Crispin. "Enseignement du Nouveau Testament face à la Guerre d'Agression en République Démocratique du Congo." Licence [bachelor's degree] thesis, Christian University of Kinshasa, 2001–2002.

Murphy, Andrew, editor. *The Blackwell Companion to Religion and Violence.* Blackwell Companions to Religion. Oxford: Wiley-Blackwell, 2011.

Murphy, Roland E. *Ecclesiastes.* WBC 23A. Dallas: Word Books, 1992.

Murray, Stuart. *Biblical Interpretation in the Anabaptist Tradition.* Studies in the Believers Church Tradition 3. Kitchener, ON: Pandora, 2000.

Nanos, Mark D. "Paul's Reversal of Jews Calling Gentiles 'Dogs' (Philippians 3:2): 1600 Years of an Ideological Tale Wagging an Exegetical Dog?" *BibInt* 17 (2009) 448–82.

Ndlovu, Danisa. "The Other Cheek, the Second Mile." *Courier* 23/3 (2008) 16.

Neville, David. J. *A Peaceable Hope: Contesting Violent Eschatology in New Testament Narratives*. SPS 11. Grand Rapids: Baker Academic, 2013.

Nevling Porter, Barbara. *What Is a God? Anthropomorphic and Non-Anthropomorphic Aspects of Deity in Ancient Mesopotamia*. Transactions of the Casco Bay Assyriological Institute 2. Winona Lake, IN: Eisenbrauns, 2009.

New Interpreter's Dictionary of the Bible. 5 vols. Edited by Katharine Doob Sakenfeld. Nashville: Abingdon, 2006–2009.

Newsom, Carol A. "Genesis 2–3 and 1 Enoch 6–16: Two Myths of Origin." In *Shaking Heaven and Earth: Essays in Honor of Walter Brueggemann and Charles B. Cousar*, edited by Christine Roy Yoder et al., 7–22. Louisville: Westminster John Knox, 2005.

———. *The Self as Symbolic Space: Constructing Identity and Community at Qumran*. STDJ 52. Leiden: Brill, 2004.

Nickelsburg, George W. E. "Eschatology (Early Jewish)." In *ABD* 2:579–94.

———. *1 Enoch 1*. Hermeneia. Minneapolis: Fortress, 2001.

———. *Resurrection, Immortality, and Eternal Life in Intertestamental Judaism and Early Christianity*. Expanded ed. HTS 56. Cambridge, MA: Harvard University Press, 2006.

Nickelsburg, George, and James VanderKam. *1 Enoch: The Hermeneia Translation*. Minneapolis: Fortress, 2012.

Niditch, Susan. *War in the Hebrew Bible: A Study in the Ethics of Violence*. Oxford: Oxford University Press, 1993.

Niebuhr, H. Richard. *The Responsible Self*. New York: Harper & Row, 1963.

Nolland, John. *Luke 18:35—24:53*. WBC 35C. Dallas: Word, 1993.

Noth, Martin. "Noah, Daniel und Hiob in Ezechiel 14:12–20." *VT* 1 (1951) 251–60.

Nygren, Anders. *Agape and Eros*. Translated by Philip S. Watson. London: SPCK, 1953.

Odell, Margaret S. *Ezekiel*. SHBC. Macon, GA: Smyth & Hellwys, 2005.

Oliver, Kelly. *Reading Kristeva: Unraveling the Double-Bind*. Bloomington: Indiana University Press, 1993.

Ollenburger, Ben. "Isaiah's Creation Theology." *ExAud* 3 (1988) 54–71.

———. *Zion, City of the Great King: A Theological Symbol of the Jerusalem Cult*. Sheffield: JSOT Press, 1987.

Pannenberg, Wolfhart. *Systematic Theology*. 3 vols. Translated by Geoffrey Bromiley. Grand Rapids: Eerdmans, 1991–1997.

Pardee, Dennis. "The 'Aqhatu Legend (1.103)." In *COS* , edited by William W. Hallo and K. Lawson Younger Jr., 1:343–56. Leiden: Brill, 1997.

Parker, Richard A., and Waldo Dubberstein. *Babylonian Chronology 626 B.C.–A.D. 75*. Brown University Studies 19. Providence, RI: Brown University Press, 1956.

Parker, Simon B, editor. *Ugaritic Narrative Poetry*. SBLWAW 9. Atlanta: SBL, 1997.

Patte, Daniel, editor. *Global Bible Commentary*. Nashville: Abingdon, 2004.

Pattemore, Stephen. *The People of God in the Apocalypse: Discourse, Structure, and Exegesis*. SNTSMS 128. Cambridge: Cambridge University Press, 2004.

Pawlikowski, John T., and Donald Senior. *Biblical and Theological Reflections on the Challenge of Peace*. Wilmington, DE: Glazier, 1984.

Peels, H. G. L. *The Vengeance of God: The Meaning of the Root NQM and the Function of the NQM-Texts in the Context of Divine Revelation in the Old Testament.* Oudtestamentische Studiën 31. Leiden: Brill, 1995.

Peters, Dorothy M. *Noah Traditions in the Dead Sea Scrolls: Conversations and Controversies of Antiquity.* SBLEJL 26. Atlanta: SBL, 2008.

Peters, Olutola K. *The Mandate of the Church in the Apocalypse of John.* Studies in Biblical Literature 77. New York: Lang, 2005.

Peters, Ted. "Eschatological Sanctions and Christian Ethics." *PSB* 15/3 (1994) S129–S152.

Philips, Dirk. *The Writings of Dirk Philips, 1504–1568.* Edited and translated by Cornelius J. Dyck, William E. Keeney, and Alvin J. Beachy. CRR 6. Scottdale, PA: Herald, 1992.

Pinker, Steven. *The Better Angels of Our Nature: Why Violence Has Declined.* New York: Viking, 2011.

Placher, William C. "Paul Ricoeur and Postliberal Theology: A Conflict of Interpretations?" *Modern Theology* 4 (1987) 35–52.

Polaski, Sandra Hack. *Paul and the Discourse of Power.* Gender, Culture, Theory 8. Sheffield: Sheffield Academic, 1999.

The Poverty and Justice Bible–CEV. New York: American Bible Society, 2008.

Pritchard, James B., editor. *Ancient Near Eastern Texts Relating to the Old Testament.* 3rd ed. Princeton: Princeton University Press, 1969.

Provan, Iain W. *Ecclesiastes/Song of Songs.* NIV Application Commentary. Grand Rapids: Zondervan, 2001.

Przybylski, Benno. *Righteousness in Matthew and His World of Thought.* SNTSMS 41. Cambridge: Cambridge University Press, 1980.

Rad, Gerhard von. *Holy War in Ancient Israel.* Translated by Marva J. Dawn. 1991. Reprint, Eugene, OR: Wipf & Stock, 2001.

———. *Wisdom in Israel.* Translated by James D. Martin. Nashville: Abingdon, 1972.

Reed, Annette Yoshiko. *Fallen Angels and the History of Judaism and Christianity: The Reception of the Enochic Literature.* Cambridge: Cambridge University Press, 2005.

Regev, Eyal. *Sectarianism in Qumran: A Cross-Cultural Perspective.* Berlin: de Gruyter, 2007.

Reimer, A. James. *Christians and War: A Brief History of the Church's Teachings and Practices.* Minneapolis: Fortress, 2010.

Rempel, John, editor. *Jörg Maler's Kunstbuch: Writings of the Pilgram Marpeck Circle.* CRR 12. Kitchener, ON: Pandora, 2010.

Rendtorff, Rolf. *Theologie des Alten Testaments: Ein kanonischer Entwurf.* Neukirchen-Vluyn: Neukirchener, 2001.

Rensberger, David. "Did Jesus *Always* Preach Nonviolence?" The Thoughtful Christian, 21 October 2009. Online: http://www.thethoughtfulchristian.com/Products/TC0359/did-jesus-ialwaysi-preach-nonviolence.aspx.

Reumann, John. "Righteousness (Early Judaism; Greco-Roman World; NT)." In *ABD* 5:736–73.

Riches, John K. *Conflicting Mythologies: Identity Formation in the Gospels of Mark and Matthew.* SNTW. Edinburgh: T. & T. Clark, 2000.

Rohr, Richard, and John Bookser Feister. *Hope against Darkness: The Transforming Vision of Saint Francis in an Age of Anxiety.* Cincinnati: St. Anthony Messenger, 2001.

Rosner, Brian S. "The Concept of Idolatry." *Themelios* 24/3 (1999) 21–30.

Ross, Jeffrey Ian, editor. *Religion and Violence: An Encyclopedia of Faith and Conflict from Antiquity to the Present.* 3 vols. Armonk, NY: Sharpe Reference, 2010.

Ross, W. D., translator. *Aristotle: Nichomachean Ethics.* 1908. Reprint, Stillwell, KS: Digiread, 2006.

Roth, Willard. "President Raul Garcia Opens His Heart." *Courier* 6/2 (1991) 2–3.

Rudman, Dominic. *Determinism in the Book of Ecclesiastes.* JSOTSup 316. Sheffield: Sheffield Academic, 2001.

Salyer, Gary D. *Vain Rhetoric: Private Insight and Public Debate in Ecclesiastes.* JSOTSup 327. Sheffield: Sheffield Academic, 2001.

Sanders, E. P. *Jesus and Judaism.* Philadelphia: Fortress, 1985.

———. *Paul and Palestinian Judaism: A Comparison of Patterns of Religion.* London: SCM, 1977.

Sanders, James A. *Canon and Community: A Guide to Canonical Criticism.* 1984. Reprint, Eugene, OR: Wipf & Stock, 2000.

Sasson, Jack M. "On the Use of Images in Israel and the Ancient Near East: A Response to Karel von der Toorn." In *Sacred Time, Sacred Place: Archaeology and the Religion of Israel,* edited by Barry M. Gittlen, 63–70. Winona Lake, IN: Eisenbrauns, 2002.

———. "Wordplay in the OT." In *Interpreter's Dictionary of the Bible: An Illustrated Encyclopedia,* 5:968–70. Nashville: Abingdon, 1976.

Scheper-Hughes, Nancy, and Philippe Bourgois, editors. *Violence in War and Peace: An Anthology.* Oxford: Blackwell, 2004.

Schild, E. "On Exodus III 14: 'I Am That I Am.'" *VT* 4 (1954) 296–302.

Schlabach, Theron F. "War, Peace, and Nonresistance." In *War, Peace and Social Conscience: Guy F. Hershberger and Mennonite Ethics,* 117–162. Scottdale, PA: Herald, 2009.

Schnackenburg, Rudolf. *The Gospel according to St John.* 3 vols. Translated by Kevin Smyth. New York: Crossroads, 1968–1982.

Schofield, Alison. *From Qumran to Yaḥad: A New Paradigm of Textual Development for The Community Rule.* STDJ 77. Leiden: Brill, 2009.

Schoors, Antoon. *The Preacher Sought to Find Pleasing Words: A Study of the Language of Qoheleth. Part II: Vocabulary.* Leuven: Peeters, 2004.

Schottroff, Luise. "'Give to Caesar What Belongs to Caesar and to God What Belongs to God': A Theological Response of the Early Christian Church to Its Social and Political Environment." In *The Love of Enemy and Nonretaliation in the New Testament,* edited by Willard M. Swartley, 223–57. SPS 3. Louisville: Westminster John Knox, 1992.

Schottroff, Luise, Silvia Schroer, and Marie-Theres Wacker. *Feminist Interpretation: The Bible in Women's Perspective.* Minneapolis: Fortress, 1998.

Schüssler Fiorenza, Elisabeth. "The Phenomenon of Early Christian Apocalyptic: Some Reflections on Method." In *Apocalypticism in the Mediterranean World and the Near East,* edited by David Hellholm, 295–316. Tübingen: Mohr/Siebeck, 1983.

———. *The Power of the Word: Scripture and the Rhetoric of Empire.* Minneapolis: Fortress, 2007.

Schultz, Brian. *Conquering the World: The War Scroll (1QM) Reconsidered.* STDJ 76. Leiden: Brill, 2009.

Schultz, Richard L. "A Sense of Timing: A Neglected Aspect of Qoheleth's Wisdom." In *Seeking Out the Wisdom of the Ancients: Essays Offered to Honor Michael V. Fox on* the Occasion of His Sixty-Fifth Birthday, edited by Ronald L. Troxel et al., 257–67. Winona Lake, IN: Eisenbrauns, 2005.

Schwartz, Baruch. "Ezekiel's Dim View of Israel's Restoration." In *The Book of Ezekiel: Theological and Anthropological Perspectives*, edited by Margaret S. Odell and John T. Strong, 43–68. SBL Symposium Series 9. Atlanta: SBL, 2000.

Schwarz-Bart, André. *The Last of the Just*. Translated by Stephen Becker. 1960. Reprint, New York: Overlook, 2000.

Schweitzer, Steven. *Reading Utopia in Chronicles*. LHBOTS 442. New York: T. & T. Clark, 2007.

Scullion, J. J. "Righteousness (OT)." In *ABD* 5:724–36.

Seitz, Christopher. "The Call of Moses and the 'Revelation' of the Divine Name: Source-Critical Logic and Its Legacy." In *Theological Exegesis: Essays in Honor of Brevard S. Childs*, edited by Christopher Seitz and Kathryn Greene-McCreight, 145–61. Grand Rapids: Eerdmans, 1999.

Seow, C. L . *Ecclesiastes*. AB 18C. New York: Doubleday, 1997.

Sharpe, Andrew Neville. *Foucault's Monsters and the Challenge of Law*. London: Routledge, 2010.

Sherwood, Yvonne, and Jonneke Bekkenkamp, editors. *Sanctified Aggression: Legacies of Biblical and Post-Biblical Vocabularies of Violence*. JSOTSup 400. London: T. & T. Clark, 2003.

Shillington, George. *2 Corinthians*. BCBC. Scottdale, PA: Herald, 1998.

Sim, David C. "Christian Judaism: A Reconstruction and Evaluation of the Original Christian Tradition." In *Themes in Jewish-Christian Relations*, edited by Edward Kessler and Melanie J. Wright, 39–58. Cambridge: Orchard Academic, 2005.

Simons, Menno. *The Complete Writings of Menno Simons*. Edited by J. C. Wenger. Translated by Leonard Verduin. Scottdale, PA: Herald, 1956.

Smith, Mark S. *The Early History of God: Yahweh and the Other Deities in Ancient Israel*. 2nd ed. Grand Rapids: Eerdmans, 2002.

———, et al. *Ugaritic Narrative Poetry*. Edited by Simon B. Parker. SBLWAW 9. Atlanta: Scholars, 1997.

Smith-Christopher, Daniel L. "Peace in the OT." In *NIDB* 4:423–25.

Snodgrass, Klyne R. "The Temple Incident." In *Key Events in the Life of the Historical Jesus: A Collaborative Exploration of Context and Coherence*, edited by Darrell L. Bock and Robert L. Webb, 429–80. WUNT I.247. 2009. Reprint, Grand Rapids: Eerdmans, 2010.

Snyder, C. Arnold, editor. *Sources of South German/Austrian Anabaptism*. Translated by Walter Klaasen, Frank Friesen, and Werner Packull. CRR 10. Scottdale, PA: Herald, 2001.

Snyder Belousek, Darrin W. *Atonement, Justice, and Peace: The Message of the Cross and the Mission of the Church*. SPS 10. Grand Rapids: Eerdmans, 2012.

———. "Nonviolent God: Critical Analysis of a Contemporary Argument." *CGR* 29 (2011) 49–70.

Soards, Marion. "Righteousness in the New Testament." In *NIDB* 4:813–18.

Song, Choan-Seng. "Ecclesiastes 3:1–8: An Asian Perspective." In *Return to Babel: Global Perspectives on the Bible*, edited by John R. Levison and Priscilla Pope-Levison, 87–92. Louisville: Westminster John Knox, 1999.

Soskice, Janet Martin. *Metaphor and Religious Language*. Oxford: Clarendon, 1985.

Stassen, Glen H., and David P. Gushee. *Kingdom Ethics: Following Jesus in Contemporary Context.* Downers Grove, IL: InterVarsity, 2003.

"Statement of AMBCE." *Courier* 9/4 (1994) 3.

Stendahl, Krister. "Hate, Non-retaliation, and Love: 1QS x, 17–20 and Rom. 12:19–21." *HTR* 55 (1962) 343–55.

———. *Meanings: The Bible as Document and as Guide.* Philadelphia, PA: Fortress, 1984.

Still, Todd D. "Organizational Structures and Relational Struggles among the Saints: The Establishment and Exercise of Authority within Pauline Assemblies." In *After the First Urban Christians: The Social-Scientific Study of Pauline Christianity Twenty-Five Years Later,* edited by Todd D. Still and David G. Horrell, 79–98. New York: T. & T. Clark, 2009.

Stoner, André Gingerich. "How Are We Doing as a Peace Church?" *The Mennonite* 15/7 (2012) 44–46.

Strauss, H. "Das Meerlied des Moses—Ein 'Siegeslied' Israels?" *ZAW* 97 (1985) 103–9.

Stutzman, Ervin R. *From Nonresistance to Justice: The Transformation of Mennonite Church Peace Rhetoric, 1908–2008.* Scottdale, PA: Herald, 2011.

Suderman, Derek. "Prayers Heard and Overheard: Shifting Address and Methodological Matrices in Psalms Scholarship." PhD diss., University of St. Michael's College, Toronto School of Theology, 2007.

Swaim, J. Carter. *War, Peace, and the Bible.* Maryknoll, NY: Orbis, 1982.

Swartley, Willard M. *Covenant of Peace: The Missing Peace in New Testament Theology and Ethics.* SPS 9. Grand Rapids: Eerdmans, 2006.

———. *John.* BCBC. Harrisonburg, VA: Herald, 2013.

———. "Peace." In *The Westminster Theological Wordbook of the Bible,* edited by Donald E. Gowan, 354–60. Louisville: Westminster John Knox, 2003.

———. "Peace." In *Dictionary of Scripture and Ethics,* edited by Joel B. Green et al., 583–86. Grand Rapids: Baker, 2011.

———. "Peace in the NT." In *NIDB* 4:422–23.

———. "Peace." In *The [Oxford] Encyclopedia of the Bible and Ethics,* edited by Robert Brawley. Oxford: Oxford University Press, forthcoming.

———. "Peace." In *The [Oxford] Encyclopedia of the Bible and Theology,* edited by Jerry Sumney. Oxford: Oxford University Press, forthcoming.

———. "Politics and Peace (Eirene) in Luke's Gospel." In *Political Issues in Luke-Acts,* edited by R. Cassidy and P. Scharper, 18–37. Maryknoll, NY: Orbis, 1983.

———. "The Relation of Justice/Righteousness to Shalom/Eirēnē." *ExAud* 22 (2006) 22, 29–53.

———. *Slavery, Sabbath, War, and Women: Case Issues in Biblical Interpretation.* Scottdale, PA: Herald, 1983.

———. "Sword" In *NIDB* 5:409–10.

———. "Sword." In *The Westminster Theological Wordbook of the Bible,* edited by Donald E. Gowan, 409–10. Louisville: Westminster John Knox, 2003.

———. "Violence, Violent." In *The Westminster Theological Wordbook of the Bible,* edited by Donald E. Gowan, 520–22. Louisville: Westminster John Knox, 2003.

———. "War and Peace in the New Testament." In *Aufstieg und Niedergang der Römischen Welt,* edited by W. Haase and H. Temporini, II.26/3:2298–2408. Berlin: de Gruyter, 1996.

———. "War." In *Encyclopedia of Early Christianity*, edited by Everett Ferguson, 1172–75. 2nd ed. New York: Garland, 1997.

———. "War." In *The Westminster Theological Wordbook of the Bible*, edited by Donald E. Gowan, 524–28. Louisville: Westminster John Knox, 2003.

Swartley, Willard M., editor. *The Love of Enemy and Nonretaliation in the New Testament*. SPS 3. Louisville: Westminster John Knox, 1992.

———. *Violence Renounced: René Girard, Biblical Studies, and Peacemaking*. SPS 4. Telford, PA: Pandora, 2000.

Tambasco, Anthony J., editor. *Blessed Are the Peacemakers: Biblical Perspectives on Peace and Its Social Foundation*. New York: Paulist, 1989.

Tamez, Elsa. *When the Horizons Close: Rereading Ecclesiastes*. Translated by Margaret Wilde. Maryknoll, NY: Orbis, 2000.

Tannehill, Robert C. *The Narrative Unity of Luke-Acts: A Literary Interpretation*. Vol. 1, *The Gospel according to Luke*. Vol. 2, *The Acts of the Apostles*. FF. Philadelphia: Fortress, 1986.

Tate, W. Randolph. *Biblical Interpretation: An Integrated Approach*. Rev. ed. Peabody, MA: Hendrickson, 1997.

Taylor, Joan E. "The Classical Sources on the Essenes and the Scrolls." In *The Oxford Handbook of the Dead Sea Scrolls*, edited by Timothy H. Lim and John J. Collins, 173–99. Oxford: Oxford University Press, 2010.

Teeham, John. *In the Name of God: The Evolutionary Origins of Religious Ethics and Violence*. 5th ed. Blackwell Public Philosophy Series 9. Oxford: Wiley-Blackwell, 2010.

Theological Dictionary of the New Testament. 10 vols. Edited by Gerhard Kittel and Gerhard Friedrich. Translated by Geoffrey W. Bromiley. Grand Rapids: Eerdmans, 1964–1976.

Thompson, Marianne Meye. "Reading What Is Written in the Book of Life." In *Revelation and the Politics of Apocalyptic Interpretation*, edited by Richard B. Hays and Stefan Alkier, 155–71. Waco, TX: Baylor University Press, 2012.

Tiede, David L. *Luke*. ACNT. Minneapolis: Augsburg, 1988.

Tite, Philip L. *Conceiving Peace and Violence: A New Testament Legacy*. Lanham, MD: University Press of America, 2004.

Toews, John E. "Righteousness in Romans: The Political Subtext of Paul's Letter." In *The Old Testament in the Life of God's People: Essays in Honor of Elmer A. Martens*, edited by Jon Isaak, 209–22. Winona Lake, IN: Eisenbrauns, 2009.

———. *Romans*. BCBC. Scottdale, PA: Herald, 2004.

Torijano, Pablo A. *Solomon the Esoteric King: From King to Magus, Development of a Tradition*. JSOTSup 73. Leiden: Brill, 2002.

Towner, W. Sibley. "Tribulation and Peace: The Fate of Shalom in Jewish Apocalyptic." *HBT* 6 (1984) 1–26.

Treier, Daniel J. *Proverbs and Ecclesiastes*. BTCB. Grand Rapids: Brazos, 2011.

Trocmé, André. *Jesus and the Nonviolent Revolution*. Translated by Michael H. Shank and Marlin E. Miller. Scottdale, PA: Herald, 1973.

Tsevat, Matitiahu. "The Biblical Narrative of the Foundation of Kingship in Israel." *Tarbiz* 36 (1966) 99–109.

———. "The Neo-Assyrian and Neo-Babylonian Vassal Oaths and the Prophet Ezekiel." *JBL* 78 (1959) 199–204.

Tsumura, David. *Creation and Destruction: A Reappraisal of the Chaoskampf Theory in the Old Testament.* Winona Lake, IN: Eisenbrauns, 2005.

Tuell, Steven. *Ezekiel.* NIBCOT. Peabody, MA: Hendrickson, 2009.

Van Wolde, Ellen. *Reframing Biblical Studies.* Winona Lake, IN: Eisenbrauns, 2009.

VanderKam, James C. *Enoch and the Growth of an Apocalyptic Tradition.* CBQMS 16. Washington, DC: Catholic Biblical Association of America, 1984.

VanderKam, James C., and Peter W. Flint. *The Meaning of the Dead Sea Scrolls: Their Significance for Understanding the Bible, Judaism, Jesus, and Christianity.* New York: HarperCollins, 2002.

VanGemeren, Willem. *New International Dictionary of Old Testament Theology and Exegesis.* Grand Rapids: Zondervan, 1997.

Vaux, Roland de. "The Revelation of the Divine Name YHWH." In *Proclamation and Presence: Old Testament Essays in Honour of Gwynne Henton Davies,* edited by John I. Durham and J. R. Porter, 48–75. London: SCM, 1970.

Villiers, Peter G. R., and Jan Willem van Henten, editors. *Coping with Violence in the New Testament.* STAR 16. Leiden: Brill, 2012.

Volf, Miroslav. *Exclusion and Embrace: A Theological Exploration of Identity, Otherness, and Reconciliation.* Nashville: Abingdon, 1996.

Wahl, Harald Martin. "Noah, Daniel und Hiob in Ezechiel XIV 12–20 (21–3): Anmerkungen zum Traditionsgeschichtlichen Hintergrund." *VT* 42 (1992) 542–53.

Wakeman, Mary K. *God's Battle with the Monster: A Study in Biblical Imagery.* Leiden: Brill, 1973.

Walton, John. *Genesis 1 as Ancient Cosmology.* Winona Lake, IN: Eisenbrauns, 2011.

Wanamaker, Charles. *The Epistles to the Thessalonians.* NIGTC. Grand Rapids Eerdmans, 1990.

Watts, Rikki E. *Isaiah's New Exodus and Mark.* WUNT 2/88. Tübingen: Mohr/Siebeck, 1997.

Weaver, J. Denny. *The Nonviolent Atonement.* Grand Rapids: Eerdmans, 2001.

———. "Violence in Christian Theology." *Cross Currents* 51 (2001) 150–76.

Wengst, Klaus K. *Pax Romana and the Peace of Jesus Christ.* Translated by John Bowden. Philadelphia: Fortress, 1987.

Whybray, R. N. "A Time to Be Born and a Time to Die: Some Observations on Ecclesiastes 3:2–8." In *Near Eastern Studies Dedicated to H.I.H. Prince Takahito Mikasa on the Occasion of His Seventy-Fifth Birthday,* edited by M. Mori et al., 469–83. Wiesbaden: Harrassowitz, 1991.

Wilch, John R. *Time and Event: An Exegetical Study of the Use of 'ēth in the Old Testament in Comparison to Other Temporal Expressions in Clarification of the Concept of Time.* Leiden: Brill, 1969.

Wilkinson, Richard H. *The Complete Gods and Goddesses of Ancient Egypt.* London: Thames & Hudson, 2003.

Williamson, H. G. M. "The Composition of Ezra i–vi." *JTS* 34 (1983) 1–30.

———. *Israel in the Books of Chronicles.* Cambridge: Cambridge University Press, 1977.

Wilson, Lindsay. "Artful Ambiguity in Ecclesiastes 1, 1–11: A Wisdom Technique?" In *Qohelet in the Context of Wisdom,* edited by Antoon Schoors, 357–65. Leuven: Leuven University Press, 1998.

Wink, Walter. *Engaging the Powers: Discernment and Resistance in a World of Domination.* Minneapolis: Fortress, 1992.

———. *Naming the Powers: The Language of Power in the New Testament.* Philadelphia: Fortress, 1984.

———. "Neither Passivity nor Violence: Jesus' Third Way (Matt. 5:38–42 par.)." In *The Love of Enemy and Nonretaliation in the New Testament,* edited by Willard M. Swartley, 102–25. SPS 3. Louisville: Westminster John Knox, 1992.

———. *Unmasking the Powers: The Invisible Forces that Determine Human Existence.* Philadelphia: Fortress, 1986.

Winn, Albert Curry. *Ain't Gonna Study War No More: Biblical Ambiguity and the Abolition of War.* Louisville: Westminster John Knox, 1993.

Winter, Bruce W. *After Paul Left Corinth: The Influence of Secular Ethics and Social Change.* Grand Rapids: Eerdmans, 2001.

Wise, Michael O., Martin G. Abegg, and Edward M. Cook. *The Dead Sea Scrolls: A New Translation.* San Francisco: HarperSanFransciso, 2005.

Wistrand, Magnus. *Entertainment and Violence in Ancient Rome: The Attitudes of Roman Writers of the First Century A.D.* GUPEA 56. Gothenburg: Acta University Gothoburgensis, 1992.

Wood, John A. *Perspectives on War in the Bible.* Macon, GA: Mercer University Press, 1998.

Wright, Addison G. "'For Everything There Is a Season': The Structure and Meaning of the Fourteen Opposites (Ecclesiastes 3,2–8)." In *De la Tôrah au Messie: Mélanges Henri Cazelles,* edited by Maurice Carrez, Joseph Doré, and Pierre Grelot, 321–28. Paris: Desclée, 1981.

Wright, Christopher J. H. "The Righteous Rich in the Old Testament." *ERT* 35 (2011) 255–64.

Wright, J. Robert, editor. *Proverbs, Ecclesiastes, Song of Solomon.* ACCS. Downers Grove, IL: InterVarsity, 2005.

Wright, John W. "The Fight for Peace: Narrative and History in the Battle Accounts in Chronicles." In *The Chronicler as Historian,* edited by M. P. Graham et al., 150–77. JSOTSup 238. Sheffield: Sheffield Academic, 1997.

Wright, N. T. *Jesus and the Victory of God.* Christian Origins and the Question of God 2. Minneapolis: Fortress, 1996.

———. *Paul for Everyone: 1 Corinthians.* Louisville: Westminster John Knox, 2004.

———. "Paul's Gospel and Caesar's Empire." In *Paul and Politics: Ekklesia, Israel, Imper-ium, Interpretation,* edited by Richard A. Horsley, 160–83. Harrisburg, PA: Trinity, 2000.

Yaguchi, Yorifumi. *Jesus.* Goshen, IN: Pinchpenny, 1987.

———. *The Wing-Beaten Air: My Life and Writing.* Intercourse, PA: Good, 2008.

Yanada, Hiroshi. "What Kind of Christianity Do Asian People Need Today?" *Courier* 1/4 (1986) 4–5.

Yinger, Kent. "Romans 12:14–21 and Nonretaliation in Second Temple Judaism: Addressing Persecution within the Community." *CBQ* 60 (1998) 74–96.

Yoder, John Howard. *The Christian Witness to the State.* IMS Series 3. Newton, KS: Faith & Life, 1964.

———. "The Church and Change: Violence versus Nonviolent Direct Action." In *The War of the Lamb: The Ethics of Nonviolence and Peacemaking,* edited by Glen Stassen, Mark Thiessen Nation, and Matt Hamsher, 151–63. Grand Rapids: Brazos, 2009.

———. *Discipleship as Political Responsibility.* Translated by Timothy J. Geddert. Harrisonburg, VA: Herald, 2003. Orignially published as *Nachfolge Christi als Gestalt politischer Verantwortung,* 2nd ed. Weisenheim am Berg: Agape, 2000.

———. *The Jewish-Christian Schism Revisited.* Edited by Michael G. Cartwright and Peter Ochs. Grand Rapids: Eerdmans, 2003.

———. *The Legacy of Michael Sattler.* CRR 1. Scottdale, PA: Herald, 1973.

———. *Peace without Eschatology?* Evanston, IL: Concern, 1959.

———. "A People in the World." In *A Royal Priesthood: Essays Ecclesiological and Ecumenical,* edited by Michael C. Cartwright, 65–101. Grand Rapids: Eerdmans, 1994.

———. *The Politics of Jesus: Vicit Agnus Noster.* 2nd ed. Grand Rapids: Eerdmans, 1994.

Yoder, Perry B. *Shalom: The Bible's Word for Salvation, Justice, and Peace.* IMS 7. Nappanee, IN: Evangel, 1987.

———. "Toward a Shalom Biblical Theology." *CGR* 1 (1983) 39–49.

Yoder, Perry B., and Willard M. Swartley, editors. *The Meaning of Peace: Biblical Studies.* 2nd ed. SPS 2. Elkhart, IN: IMS, 2001.

Yoder Neufeld, Thomas R. *Ephesians.* BCBC. Scottdale, PA: Herald, 2002.

———. *Killing Enmity: Violence and the New Testament.* Grand Rapids: Baker Academic, 2011.

———. "Power, Love, and Creation: The Mercy of the Divine Warrior in the Wisdom of Solomon." In *Peace and Justice Shall Embrace: Power and Theopolitics in the Bible; Essays in Honor of Millard Lind,* edited by Ted Grimsrud and Loren L. Johns, 174–91. Telford, PA: Pandora, 1999.

———. *"Put on the Armour of God": The Divine Warrior from Isaiah to Ephesians.* JSNTSup 140. Sheffield: Sheffield Academic, 1997.

———. *Recovering Jesus: the Witness of the New Testament.* London: SPCK, 2007.

Yokota, Paul. "Jesus the Messiah of Israel: A Study of Matthew's Narrative Christology with Reference to His Messianic Interpretation of Scripture." PhD diss., University of St. Andrews, 2004.

Zerbe, Gordon M. "Citizenship and Politics according to Philippians." *Direction* 38 (2009) 193–208.

———. *Non-Retaliation in Early Jewish and New Testament Texts: Ethical Themes in Social Contexts.* JSPSup 13. Sheffield: Sheffield Academic, 1993.

———. "On the Exigency of a Messianic Ecclesia: An Engagement with Philosophical Readers of Paul." In *Paul, Philosophy, and the Theopolitical,* edited by Doug Harink, 254–81. Eugene, OR: Cascade, 2010.

———. " 'Pacifism' and 'Passive Resistance' in Apocalyptic Writings: A Critical Evaluation." In *The Pseudepigrapha and Early Biblical Interpretation,* edited by James H. Charlesworth and Craig A. Evans, 65–95. JSPSup 14. Sheffield: JSOT Press, 1993.

———. "Paul's Ethic of Nonretaliation and Peace." In *The Love of Enemy and Nonretaliation in the New Testament,* edited by Willard M. Swartley, 177–222. SPS 3. Louisville: Westminster John Knox, 1992.

———. "Peace and Justice in the Bible." In *Peace and Justice: Essays from the Fourth Shi'i Muslim Mennonite Christian Dialogue,* edited by Harry J. Huebner and Hajj Muhammad Legenhausen, 124–43. Winnipeg: Canadian Mennonite University Press, 2011.

———. *Philippians.* BCBC. Harrisonburg, VA: Herald, forthcoming.

―――. "The Politics of Paul: His Supposed Social Conservatism and the Impact of Postcolonial Readings." In *The Colonized Apostle: Paul through Postcolonial Eyes*, edited by C. Stanley, 62–73. Minneapolis: Fortress, 2011.

―――. "The Relevance of Paul's Eschatological Ecclesiology for Ecumenical Relations." In *New Perspectives in Believers Church Ecclesiology*, edited by A. Dueck, H. Harder, and K. Koop, 30–47. Winnipeg: Canadian Mennonite University Press, 2010.

―――. "Soldiering and Battling: The Function of Military Imagery in Paul's Letters." In *Citizenship: Paul on Peace and Politics*, 123–40. Winnipeg: Canadian Mennonite University Press, 2012.

Zimmerli, Walther. *Ezekiel 1: A Commentary on the Book of the Prophet Ezekiel, Chapters 1–24*. Translated by Ronald E. Clements. Hermeneia. Philadelphia: Fortress, 1979.

―――. *Ezekiel 2: A Commentary on the Book of the Prophet Ezekiel Chapters 25–48*. Translated by James Martin. Hermeneia. Philadelphia: Fortress, 1983.

Zimmermann, Frank. *The Inner World of Qohelet (with Translation and Commentary)*. New York: KTAV, 1973.

Žižek, Slavoj. *Violence: Six Sideways Reflections*. Big Ideas/Small Books. New York: Picador, 2008.

Contributors

Wilma Ann Bailey is the Minnie Vautrin Professor of Christian Witness and professor of Hebrew and Aramaic Scripture at Christian Theological Seminary in Indianapolis, Indiana. She has been teaching Bible for more than twenty-two years, and Black and Urban Ministry prior to that. She is the author of *"You Shall Not Kill" or "You Shall Not Murder"? The Assault on a Biblical Text* (Liturgical Press, 2005). Wilma attends Shalom Mennonite Church in Indianapolis.

Jo-Ann A. Brant completed her doctoral work at McMaster University in Hamilton, Ontario, in 1991. From 1991 to 1993, she taught at Canadian Mennonite Bible College (now Canadian Mennonite University) in Winnipeg, Manitoba. She has taught at Goshen College (Goshen, IN) in the Bible, Religion, and Philosophy department since 1993. Her major publications include *Dialogue and Drama: Elements of Greek Tragedy in the Fourth Gospel* (Hendrickson, 2004) and *John* (Paideia; Baker Academic, 2011).

Laura L. Brenneman (PhD, Durham University, UK) is a visiting lecturer at the University of Illinois in Urbana-Champaign and New Testament editor of Studies in Peace and Scripture. Laura was a student of Perry Yoder and Willard Swartley at Associated Mennonite Biblical Seminary (AMBS; now Anabaptist Mennonite Biblical Seminary), Elkhart, IN (MA, 2001), and later served as associate professor at Bluffton University (Bluffton, OH). A graduate of the Eastern Mennonite University Center for Justice and Peacebuilding (Harrisonburg, VA), she works at the intersection of biblical studies and peace studies; her dissertation (Cascade, forthcoming) is about 1 Corinthians 5 and church discipline.

Jacob W. Elias is professor emeritus of New Testament at Anabaptist Mennonite Biblical Seminary (Elkhart, IN), and the author of *Remember the Future: The Pastoral Theology of Paul the Apostle* (Herald Press, 2006) and

1 and 2 Thessalonians (Believers Church Bible Commentary; Herald Press, 1995). He and his wife Lillian served as co-pastors of Parkview Mennonite Church in Kokomo, IN, 2001–2011. They have three married children and seven grandchildren.

Reta Halteman Finger taught Bible at Messiah College (Grantham, PA) from 1995 to 2009. She lives in Harrisonburg, VA, where she teaches part time at Eastern Mennonite Seminary and is engaged in a variety of writing and speaking projects. Reta edited the Christian feminist magazine *Daughters of Sarah* for fifteen years. She is the author of articles, essays, Sunday school materials, and the books *Of Widows and Meals: Communal Meals in the Book of Acts* (Eerdmans, 2007) and *Roman House Churches for Today* (Herald Press, 1993; Eerdmans, 2007). Reta has two sons and four grandchildren.

Michael J. Gorman holds the Raymond E. Brown Chair in Biblical Studies and Theology at St. Mary's Seminary and University in Baltimore, MD. He was formerly the dean of St. Mary's Ecumenical Institute of Theology, and he has been a visiting professor at Duke Divinity School. Michael is the author of numerous books in biblical studies and hermeneutics, including *Reading Revelation Responsibly: Uncivil Worship and Witness—Following the Lamb into the New Creation* (Cascade, 2011).

Nancy R. Heisey is professor of biblical studies and church history at Eastern Mennonite University (Harrisonburg, VA). Her work has been influenced by a childhood with missionary parents among the Navajo people. She also was shaped by her years serving with Mennonite Central Committee in the Democratic Republic of the Congo and serving as president of Mennonite World Conference from 2003 to 2009. In the past year Nancy has been learning many new things about care giving.

Paul Keim is professor of Bible, religion, and classical and modern languages at Goshen College in Goshen, IN. His primary areas of specialization and teaching are Hebrew Bible, biblical theology, and classical Hebrew language. His research and writing interests have included maledictions and other words of power, violence and nonviolence, forgiveness and revenge, and Christian higher education. Paul is married to Julie, and they have two adult daughters and a high school age son. They have led two international study terms in Germany and Morocco.

Christopher Marshall is head of the School of Art History, Classics and Religious Studies and teaches at Victoria University of Wellington, New

Zealand. His publications include *Faith as a Theme in Mark's Narrative* (Cambridge University Press, 1989), *Kingdom Come* (Impetus, 1994), *Beyond Retribution: A New Testament Vision for Justice, Crime, and Punishment* (Eerdmans, 2001), *Crowned with Glory and Honor: Human Rights in the Biblical Tradition* (Pandora, 2001), *The Little Book of Biblical Justice* (Good Books, 2004), and *Compassionate Justice: An Interdisciplinary Dialogue with Two Gospel Parables on Law, Crime, and Restorative Justice* (Cascade, 2012).

Safwat Marzouk is assistant professor of Old Testament at Anabaptist Mennonite Biblical Seminary (Elkhart, IN). Safwat graduated from Evangelical Theological Seminary in Cairo, Egypt (2001), Union Theological Seminary (New York) (2002), and received his PhD from Princeton Theological Seminary (2012). He is also an ordained minister with the Synod of the Nile, the governing body of the Presbyterian Church in Egypt.

Douglas B. Miller is professor of biblical and religious studies at Tabor College (Hillsboro, KS). He received his MDiv from Anabaptist Mennonite Biblical Seminary (Elkhart, IN) and his PhD from Princeton Theological Seminary. He serves as Old Testament editor of the BCBC series (Herald Press) and is author of *Symbol and Rhetoric in Ecclesiastes* (SBL; Brill, 2002), *An Akkadian Handbook* (with R. Mark Shipp, Eisenbrauns, 1996), and *Ecclesiastes* in the BCBC series (2010).

Ben C. Ollenburger is professor of biblical theology at Anabaptist Mennonite Biblical Seminary (Elkhart, IN), where Willard Swartley and Perry Yoder were his colleagues for many years. Ben graduated from California State University, Long Beach (BA), Mennonite Brethren Biblical Seminary (MA) [now Fresno Pacific University Biblical Seminary], and Princeton Theological Seminary (PhD). He was instructor in religious studies at Tabor College and assistant professor of Old Testament at Princeton Theological Seminary before coming to AMBS. Ben is the author of *Zion, the City of the Great King* (Sheffield Academic, 1987), *Old Testament Theology* (Eisenbrauns, 2004), and numerous articles and essays.

Dorothy M. Peters serves on the Religious Studies faculty at Trinity Western University in Langley, British Columbia. She holds masters degrees from Trinity Western University and the University of Oxford and a PhD from the University of Manchester (UK). Dorothy focuses on the interpretation of the Hebrew Bible in the Dead Sea Scrolls. She is the author of *Noah Traditions in the Dead Sea Scrolls: Conversations and Controversies of Antiquity* (SBL, 2008) and is currently working on a book-length manuscript on the "sword" in the Dead Sea Scrolls and sixteenth-century Anabaptism.

Dorothy, a mother of four and grandmother of four, lives with her husband, Greg, in Abbotsford and on Mayne Island (BC).

David Rensberger taught New Testament at the Interdenominational Theological Center in Atlanta for twenty-eight years, specializing in the Gospel of John. Now mostly retired from teaching, David concentrates on research, writing, and leading retreats. He is the author of *Johannine Faith and Liberating Community* (Westminster John Knox, 1988), two commentaries on the Epistles of John, and numerous articles on Christian spirituality.

Andrea Dalton Saner is assistant professor of Old Testament and Hebrew Language at Eastern Mennonite Seminary and Eastern Mennonite University in Harrisonburg, VA. She received a BA in Bible from Messiah College (Grantham, PA), an MA in theological studies from Anabaptist Mennonite Biblical Seminary (Elkhart, IN), and a PhD in Old Testament from Durham University (UK). Her research interests include theological interpretation, history of interpretation, and Pentateuch/Torah. Andrea enjoys cycling and knitting.

Brad D. Schantz Brad D. Schantz is a graduate of Associated Mennonite Biblical Seminary (2000) in Elkhart, IN, and also a former student of Perry Yoder and Willard Swartley. He is currently a dissertator in the Hebrew Bible program at the University of Wisconsin–Madison working on notions of soil in ancient Hebrew literature. He received a BA from Eastern Mennonite University (1992), Harrisonburg, VA; and an MA from the University of Wisconsin–Madison (2007). Brad taught for one year at Bluffton University (Bluffton, OH) before moving to Madison to pursue graduate studies.

Mary H. Schertz, professor of New Testament, received her PhD from Vanderbilt University School of Religion (1993). She became a colleague of Perry Yoder, Willard Swartley, and Ben Ollenburger at Anabaptist Mennonite Biblical Seminary (Elkhart, IN) in 1988. As director of Institute of Mennonite Studies (IMS), Mary helped launch *Vision: A Journal for Church and Theology*, jointly published with CMU. She co-wrote a book on biblical studies methodology with Perry Yoder, and she is currently working on the Luke commentary for Believers Church Bible Commentary. In the last few years, Mary has created opportunities to spend time with pastors studying the Bible.

Steven Schweitzer (PhD, Notre Dame) is academic dean and associate professor at Bethany Theological Seminary in Richmond, IN, where he teaches courses in Old Testament and in science fiction and theology. His publications include *Reading Utopia in Chronicles* (Bloomsbury, 2009) and articles and essays on various aspects of Chronicles, mythology in the LXX of Isaiah and in Proverbs, and Sexuality in the Bible. Steven previously taught at AMBS.

Willard M. Swartley is professor emeritus of New Testament at Anabaptist Mennonite Biblical Seminary (Elkhart, IN). Swartley began teaching at AMBS in 1978 and served as academic dean and director of IMS. A graduate of Eastern Mennonite University (Harrisonburg, VA) and Goshen Biblical Seminary (Goshen, IN), Willard earned his PhD in New Testament from Princeton Theological Seminary. He has edited more than thirty books and published eight books, including *Slavery, Sabbath, War, and Women: Case Issues in Biblical Interpretation* (Herald Press, 1983) and *Covenant of Peace: The Missing Peace in New Testament Theology and Ethics* (Eerdmans, 2006), honored with the 2008 Dale Brown Book-of-the-Year Award. Most recently released are *Health, Healing and the Church's Mission* (InterVarsity, 2012) and a commentary on John (Believers Church Bible Commentary; Herald Press, 2013).

Jackie Wyse-Rhodes is a PhD candidate at Emory University. Her dissertation examines ancient Jewish apocalyptic texts in which the natural world occupies four particular categories of significance: model, sign, testimony and judgment, and mystery. Her other research interests include biblical narrative, wisdom literature, theories of myth, feminist hermeneutics, ancient Near Eastern iconography, and the relevance of the work of Mikhail Bakhtin for biblical studies.

Joshua Yoder received his PhD in 2012 from the University of Notre Dame, in the area of Christianity and Judaism in antiquity. His dissertation examined the characterization of Roman governors in Luke-Acts. Prior to doctoral studies he worked as a pastor and as a member of Christian Peacemaker Teams. Joshua is currently teaching New Testament at the Evangelical Theological Seminary of Cairo (Egypt).

Perry B. Yoder has taught at Bluffton College (now Bluffton University), OH; Bethel College, KS; and Anabaptist Mennonite Biblical Seminary (Elkhart, IN) (where he taught for twenty years before retiring in 2005). In addition, Perry traveled for two years, along with his family, as an itinerant Bible teacher in Mennonite churches. While writing *Shalom: The Bible's Word for Salvation, Justice and Peace* (Faith and Life Press, 1987), he spent a semester in the Philippines. He is co-author, with Mary Schertz, of *Seeing* *the Text: Exegesis for Students of Greek and Hebrew* (Abingdon, 2001). Perry and his wife, Elizabeth, live in Ely, MN.

Thomas R. Yoder Neufeld is professor of religious studies (New Testament), teaching at Conrad Grebel University College at the University of Waterloo (ON) since 1983. Prior to that he served as a pastor and as a hospital and prison chaplain. Tom graduated with a BA (Hons.) in history from the University of Manitoba in 1970, an MDiv in 1973, and a Doctor of Theology in New Testament in 1989, both from Harvard Divinity School. He has published numerous articles and several books, among them *Ephesians* (BCBC; Herald Press, 2002), *Recovering Jesus: The Witness of the New Testament* (Brazos, 2007), and *Killing Enmity: Violence and the New Testament* (Baker Academic, 2011).

Paul Yokota is lecturer of New Testament studies at Kansai Bible College (Tarumi-ku, Hyogo, Japan). Paul graduated from Kyushu University (Fukuoka, Japan) with a BA and an MA in education. He also received an MA in biblical studies from Anabaptist Mennonite Biblical Seminary (Elkhart, IN) and a PhD from the University of St. Andrews in Scotland under the supervision of Richard Bauckham. He is a co-translator of Willard Swartley's book *Covenant of Peace* into Japanese (2006).

Gordon Zerbe is professor of New Testament at Canadian Mennonite University (CMU) in Winnipeg, MB. He received his PhD from Princeton Theological Seminary, and his published dissertation is titled *Non-Retaliation in Early Jewish and New Testament Contexts: Ethical Themes in Social Contexts* (Sheffield Academic, 1993). His most recent book is *Citizenship: Paul on Peace and Politics* (CMU Press, 2012). He has also contributed to *The Colonized Paul: Paul through Postcolonial Eyes* (Fortress, 2011) and *Peace and Justice: Essays from the Fourth Shi'i Muslim Mennonite Christian Dialogue* (CMU Press, 2011).

Ancient Document Index

Proverbs

Ecclesiastes

Jeremiah

Romans

1 Corinthians

2 Corinthians

Philippians

Colossians

DEAD SEA SCROLLS AND RELATED TEXTS

1Q28b

1Q20 (*Genesis Apocryphon*)

1QH^a *Hodayot*^a (*Thanksgiving Hymns*^a, *Thanksgiving Psalms*)

1QM (*War Scroll*)

1QpHab

1QS

4Q161

4Q169

4Q171

4Q174

4Q175

4Q212

Subject Index

war and, 92, 107–8, 297

peacemaking, 2, 148, 151, 155, 166–67, 180, 224–25, 230n8, 235, 256–67, 260–62, 265, 268, 270, 276, 281, 297, 303

persecution, 135, 152, 217–22, 227, 232, 272–73, 275–76; see also *suffering.*

Peter's denial, 192–93, 195–96, 203

politics, 144, 146, 150, 216–17, 219, 227, 268, 281
  of the gospel, 267
  of Israel, 37–39, 44, 72, 78
  structure of, 47, 68, 246

polytheism, 62, 64

power, 100, 102, 166, 198, 232, 249, 295
  of God, 258–60, 282
  of the gospel, 259
  in interpretation, 47, 53
  nonviolent, 203
  political, 76, 296

powers, 150, 254, 269–70, 275–76, 280

prayer, 83, 85, 111–12, 161, 165, 201
  at Olivet, 192–93, 195–96, 203

pride, 58, 64, 74, 111, 249

priesthood of believers, 109n26

providence, 15, 26–27, 35, 200–201

race, 220–21, 265

rape, 116n7, 249, 251

reciprocity, 205–7, 210–11, 214–15

reconciliation, 7–9, 22, 65, 144, 147, 205, 207–8, 212–14, 239, 255, 260, 262, 266, 280, 285, 291, 303
  cosmic, 264–65

redemption, 30, 269

relationships, 104, 109, 113, 133, 299

repentance, 46n48, 157–59, 211–12, 277, 289

restoration, 81, 87, 119, 171, 289

resurrection, 3, 160, 162, 174, 194, 215, 264, 275, 282, 291, 297
  bodily, 254
  life, 270
  post-resurrection appearance, 170

retaliation, 128, 270

retribution, 24

divine, 17, 19, 79, 81, 83–85, 86n31

revenge, 296

righteousness, 7, 79, 85, 102, 104, 117, 119–20, 143, 147, 155–67, 277, 280, 299
  of God, 16, 156, 158, 162, 166–67, 267, 270
  performed/practiced, 160–63
  "super," 8, 155, 161, 164, 166
  weapons of, 162, 164

ritual, 49, 57, 69, 90, 111, 127, 209, 273–74
  of circumcision, 49
  language, 51
  of shedding sandals, 49

rûaḥ, 33–34

salvation, 8, 31–32, 144, 147, 152, 156, 165, 173, 205, 212, 214–15, 223–24, 258–59, 262, 264, 268–69, 278, 280, 288
  cosmic, 268
  history of, 147
  individual, 267
  oracles, 77
  universal, 257n5

Satan, 35, 121n20, 143, 146n21, 170, 174, 200, 237, 271–74, 281, 284

ṣedeq, 16, 79; see also *tsedaqah.*

sex, 246, 249–50

sexuality, 92, 114, 118

shalom, xii, 2, 4, 7–9, 26, 103–9, 113, 142, 156, 180, 205–6, 214, 224–25, 279–80, 282–83, 286–90
  biblical theology of, xvi
  definition of, 280

slavery, 68, 71, 151, 162, 165–66, 209, 236, 250–51, 270

social justice, 155, 205, 229

social transformation, 268

Spirit, 34, 162, 187, 257–58, 260–66, 280, 282, 286, 288, 290, 298; see also *Holy Spirit.*

spiritual forces, 258, 298, 300, 303

suffering, 17, 24, 133, 136, 157, 164–65, 212, 217–18, 223, 227, 259, 268, 270, 276, 283, 285n19

Author Index